BLUE HIGHWAYS

A Journey into America

BLUE HIGHWAYS

WILLIAM LEAST HEAT-MOON

[William Trogdon]

Photographs by the Author

A Peter Davison Book

Houghton Mifflin Company / Boston

Published by arrangement with Little, Brown and Company, Inc.

Library of Congress Cataloging-in-Publication Data
Heat-Moon, William Least.
Blue highways : a journey into America / William Least Heat-Moon
(William Trogdon) : photographs by the author. — 2nd paperback ed.
p.   cm.
"A Peter Davison book."
Includes index.
ISBN 0-395-92502-9 (pbk.)
1. United States — Description and travel — 1960–1980.   2. Heat-
Moon, William Least — Journeys — United States.   I. Title.
E169.02.H385   1991   91-16091
917.3'04927 — dc20   CIP

Printed in the United States of America

QUM 10 9 8 7 6 5 4 3 2 1

Portions of this book appeared in *The Atlantic Monthly*.

"Daniel Boone" by Stephen Vincent Benét
From: *A Book of Americans* by Rosemary & Stephen Vincent Benét
Copyright, 1933, by Rosemary & Stephen Vincent Benét
Copyright renewed ©, 1961 by Rosemary Carr Benét
Reprinted by permission of Brandt & Brandt Literary Agents, Inc.

Houghton Mifflin Company paperback 1991

Second paperback edition

*This book is
for the wife of the Chief
and for the Chieftain too.
In love.*

CONTENTS

BLUE HIGHWAYS

On the old highway maps of America, the main routes were red and the back roads blue. Now even the colors are changing. But in those brevities just before dawn and a little after dusk — times neither day nor night — the old roads return to the sky some of its color. Then, in truth, they carry a mysterious cast of blue, and it's that time when the pull of the blue highway is strongest, when the open road is a beckoning, a strangeness, a place where a man can lose himself.

One

EASTWARD

BEWARE thoughts that come in the night. They aren't turned properly; they come in askew, free of sense and restriction, deriving from the most remote of sources. Take the idea of February 17, a day of canceled expectations, the day I learned my job teaching English was finished because of declining enrollment at the college, the day I called my wife from whom I'd been separated for nine months to give her the news, the day she let slip about her "friend" — Rick or Dick or Chick. Something like that.

That morning, before all the news started hitting the fan, Eddie Short Leaf, who worked a bottomland section of the Missouri River and plowed snow off campus sidewalks, told me if the deep cold didn't break soon the trees would freeze straight through and explode. Indeed.

That night, as I lay wondering whether I would get sleep or explosion, I got the idea instead. A man who couldn't make things go right could at least go. He could quit trying to get out of the way of life. Chuck routine. Live the real jeopardy of circumstance. It was a question of dignity.

The result: on March 19, the last night of winter, I again lay awake in the tangled bed, this time doubting the madness of just walking out on things, doubting the whole plan that would begin at daybreak — to set out on a long (equivalent to half the circumference of the earth), circular trip over the back roads of the United States. Following a circle would give a purpose — to come around again — where taking a straight line would not. And I was going to do it by living out of the back end of a truck. But how to begin a beginning?

A strange sound interrupted my tossing. I went to the window, the cold air against my eyes. At first I saw only starlight. Then they were there. Up in the March blackness, two entwined skeins of snow and blue geese honking north, an undulating W-shaped configuration across the deep sky, white bellies glowing eerily with the reflected light from town, necks stretched northward. Then another flock pulled by who knows what out of the south to breed and remake itself. A new season. Answer: begin by following spring as they did — darkly, with neck stuck out.

THE vernal equinox came on gray and quiet, a curiously still morning not winter and not spring, as if the cycle paused. Because things go their own way, my daybreak departure turned to a morning departure, then to an afternoon departure. Finally, I climbed into the van, rolled down the window, looked a last time at the rented apartment. From a dead elm sparrow hawks used each year came a high *whee* as the nestlings squealed for more grub. I started the engine. When I returned a season from now — if I did return — those squabs would be gone from the nest.

Accompanied only by a small, gray spider crawling the dashboard (kill a spider and it will rain), I drove into the street, around the corner, through the intersection, over the bridge, onto the highway. I was heading toward those little towns that get on the map — if they get on at all — only because some cartographer has a blank space to fill: Remote, Oregon; Simplicity, Virginia; New Freedom, Pennsylvania; New Hope, Tennessee; Why, Arizona; Whynot, Mississippi. Igo, California (just down the road from Ono), here I come.

A PLEDGE: I give this chapter to myself. When done with it, I will shut up about *that* topic.

Call me Least Heat-Moon. My father calls himself Heat-Moon, my elder brother Little Heat-Moon. I, coming last, am therefore Least. It has been a long lesson of a name to learn.

To the Siouan peoples, the Moon of Heat is the seventh month, a time also known as the Blood Moon — I think because of its dusky midsummer color.

I have other names: Buck, once a slur — never mind the predominant Anglo features. Also Bill Trogdon. The Christian names come from a grandfather eight generations back, one William Trogdon, an immigrant Lancashireman living in North Carolina, who was killed by the Tories for providing food to rebel patriots and thereby got his name in volume four of *Makers of America*. Yet to the red way of thinking, a man who makes peace with the new by destroying the old is not to be honored. So I hear.

One summer when Heat-Moon and I were walking the ancestral grounds of the Osage near the river of that name in western Missouri, we talked about bloodlines. He said, "Each of the people from anywhere, when you see in them far enough, you find red blood and a red heart. There's a hope."

Nevertheless, a mixed-blood — let his heart be where it may — is a contaminated man who will be trusted by neither red nor white. The attitude goes back to a long history of "perfidious" half-breeds, men who, by their nature, had to choose against one of their bloodlines. As for me, I will choose for heart, for spirit, but never will I choose for blood.

One last word about bloodlines. My wife, a woman of striking mixed-blood features, came from the Cherokee. Our battles, my Cherokee and I, we called the "Indian wars."

For these reasons I named my truck Ghost Dancing, a heavy-handed symbol alluding to ceremonies of the 1890s in which the Plains Indians, wearing cloth shirts they believed rendered them indestructible, danced for the return of warriors, bison, and the fervor of the old life that would sweep away the new. Ghost dances, desperate resurrection rituals, were the dying rattles of a people whose last defense was delusion — about all that remained to them in their futility.

A final detail: on the morning of my departure, I had seen thirty-eight Blood Moons, an age that carries its own madness and futility. With a nearly desperate sense of isolation and a growing suspicion that I lived in an alien land, I took to the open road in search of places where change did not mean ruin and where time and men and deeds connected.

4

THE first highway: Interstate 70 eastbound out of Columbia, Missouri. The road here follows, more or less, the Booneslick Trail, the initial leg of the Oregon Trail; it also parallels both the southern latitude of the last great glacier in central Missouri as well as the northern boundary of the Osage Nation. The Cherokee and I had skirmished its length in Missouri and Illinois for ten years, and memory made for hard driving that first day of spring. But it was the fastest route east out of the homeland. When memory is too much, turn to the eye. So I watched particularities.

Item: a green and grainy and corrupted ice over the ponds.

Item: blackbirds, passing like storm-borne leaves, sweeping just above the treetops, moving as if invisibly tethered to one will.

Item: barn roofs painted VISIT ROCK CITY — SEE SEVEN STATES. Seven at one fell swoop. People loved it.

Item: uprooted fencerows of Osage orange (so-called hedge apples although they are in the mulberry family). The Osage made bows and war clubs from the limbs; the trunks, with a natural fungicide, carried the first telegraph lines; and roots furnished dye to make doughboy uniforms olive drab. Now the Osage orange were going so bigger tractors could work longer rows.

At High Hill, two boys were flying gaudy butterfly kites that pulled hard against their leashes. No strings, no flight. A town of surprising flatness on a single main street of turn-of-the-century buildings paralleling the inter- state, High Hill sat golden in a piece of sunlight that broke through. No one moved along the street, and things held so still and old, the town looked like a museum diorama.

Eighty miles out, rain started popping the windshield, and the road became blobby headlights and green interstate signs for this exit, that exit. LAST EXIT TO ELSEWHERE. I crossed the Missouri River not far upstream from where Lewis and Clark on another wet spring afternoon set out for Mr. Jefferson's "terra incognita." Then, to the southeast under a glowing skull-cap of fouled sky, lay St. Louis. I crossed the Mississippi as it carried its forty hourly tons of topsoil to the Louisiana delta.

The tumult of St. Louis behind, the Illinois superwide quiet but for the rain, I turned south onto state 4, a shortcut to I-64. After that, the 42,500 miles of straight and wide could lead to hell for all I cared; I was going to stay on the three million miles of bent and narrow rural American two-lane, the roads to Podunk and Toonerville. Into the sticks, the boondocks, the burgs, backwaters, jerkwaters, the wide-spots-in-the-road, the don't-blink-or-you'll-miss-it towns. Into those places where you say, "My god! What if you lived here!" The Middle of Nowhere.

The early darkness came on. My headlamps cut only a forty-foot trail through the rain, and the dashboard lights cast a spectral glowing. Sheet lightning behind the horizon of trees made the sky look like a great faded orange cloth being blown about; then darkness soaked up the light, and, for a moment, I was blinder than before.

In the approaching car beams, raindrops spattering the road became little beacons. I bent over the wheel to steer along the divider stripes. A frog, long-leggedy and green, belly-flopped across the road to the side where the puddles would be better. The land, still cold and wintery, was alive with creatures that trusted in the coming of spring.

On through Lebanon, a brick-street village where Charles Dickens spent a night in the Mermaid Inn; on down the Illinois roads — roads that leave you ill and annoyed, the joke went — all the way dodging chuckholes that *Time* magazine said Americans would spend 626 million dollars in extra fuel swerving around. Then onto I-64, a new interstate that cuts across southern Illinois and Indiana without going through a single town. If a world lay out there, it was far from me. On and on. Behind, only a red wash of taillights.

At Grayville, Illinois, on the Wabash River, I pulled up for the night on North Street and parked in front of the old picture show. The marquee said TRAVELOGUE TODAY, or it would have if the O's had been there. I should have gone to a cafe and struck up a conversation; instead I stumbled to the bunk in the back of my rig, undressed, zipped into the sleeping bag, and watched things go dark. I fought desolation and wrestled memories of the Indian wars.

First night on the road. I've read that fawns have no scent so that predators cannot track them down. For me, I heard the past snuffling about somewhere close.

5

THE rain came again in the night and moved on east to leave a morning of cool overcast. In Well's Restaurant I said to a man whose cap told me what fertilizer he used, "You've got a clean little town here."

"Grayville's bigger than a whale, but the oil riggers get us a mite dirty around the ears," he said. "I've got no oil myself, not that I haven't drilled up a sieve." He jerked his thumb heavenward. "Gave me beans, but if I'da got my rightful druthers, I'da took oil." He adjusted his cap. "So what's your line?"

"Don't have one."

"How's that work?"

"It doesn't and isn't."

He grunted and went back to his coffee. The man took me for a bindlestiff. Next time I'd say I sold ventilated aluminum awnings or repaired long-rinse cycles on Whirlpools. Now my presence disturbed him. After the third tilt of his empty cup, he tried to make sense of me by asking where I was from and why I was so far from home. I hadn't traveled even three hundred miles yet. I told him I planned to drive around the country on the smallest roads I could find.

"Goddamn," he said, "if screwball things don't happen every day even in this town. The country's all alike now." On that second day of the new season, I guess I was his screwball thing.

Along the road: old snow hidden from the sun lay in sooty heaps, but the interstate ran clear of cinders and salt deposits, the culverts gushed with splash and slosh, and the streams, covering the low cornfields, filled the old soil with richness gathered in their meanderings.

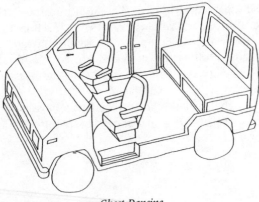

Ghost Dancing

Driving through the washed land in my small self-propelled box — a "wheel estate," a mechanic had called it — I felt clean and almost disentangled. I had what I needed for now, much of it stowed under the wooden bunk:

1   sleeping bag and blanket;
1   Coleman cooler (empty but for a can of chopped liver a friend had given me so there would *always* be something to eat);
1   Rubbermaid basin and a plastic gallon jug (the sink);
1   Sears, Roebuck portable toilet;
1   Optimus 8R white gas cook stove (hardly bigger than a can of beans);
1   knapsack of utensils, a pot, a skillet;
1   U.S. Navy seabag of clothes;
1   tool kit;
1   satchel of notebooks, pens, road atlas, and a microcassette recorder;
2   Nikon F2 35mm cameras and five lenses;
2   vade mecums: Whitman's *Leaves of Grass* and Neihardt's *Black Elk Speaks.*

In my billfold were four gasoline credit cards and twenty-six dollars. Hidden under the dash were the remnants of my savings account: $428.

Ghost Dancing, a 1975 half-ton Econoline (the smallest van Ford then made), rode self-contained but not self-containing. So I hoped. It had two worn rear tires and an ominous knocking in the waterpump. I had converted the van from a clangy tin box into a place at once a six-by-ten bedroom, kitchen, bathroom, parlor. Everything simple and lightweight — no crushed velvet upholstery, no wine racks, no built-in television. It came equipped with power nothing and drove like what it was: a truck. Your basic plumber's model.

The Wabash divides southern Illinois from Indiana. East of the fluvial flood plain, a sense of the unknown, the addiction of the traveler, began seeping in. Abruptly, Pokeberry Creek came and went before I could see it. The interstate afforded easy passage over the Hoosierland, so easy it gave no sense of the up and down of the country; worse, it hid away the people. Life doesn't happen along interstates. It's against the law.

At the Huntingburg exit, I turned off and headed for the Ohio River. Indiana 66, a road so crooked it could run for the legislature, took me into the hilly fields of CHEW MAIL POUCH barns, past Christ-of-the-Ohio Catholic Church, through the Swiss town of Tell City with its statue of William and his crossbow and nervous son. On past the old stone riverfront houses in Cannelton, on up along the Ohio, the muddy banks sometimes not ten feet from the road. The brown water rolled and roiled. Under wooded bluffs I stopped to stretch among the periwinkle. At the edge of a field, Sulphur Spring bubbled up beneath a cover of dead leaves. Shawnees once believed in the curative power of the water, and settlers even bottled it. I cleared the small spring for a taste. Bad enough to cure something.

I crossed into the Eastern Time Zone and then over the Blue River, which was a brown creek. Blue, Green, Red: yes — yet who ever heard of a Brown River? For some reason, the farther west the river and the scarcer the water, the more honest the names become: Stinking Water Branch, Dead Horse Fork, Cutthroat Gulch, Damnation Creek. Perhaps the old trailmen and prospectors figured settlers would be slower to build along a river named Calamity.

On through what was left of White Cloud, through the old statehouse town of Corydon, I drove to get the miles between me and home. Daniel Boone moved on at the sight of smoke from a new neighbor's chimney; I was moving from the sight of my own. Although the past may not repeat itself, it does rhyme, Mark Twain said. As soon as my worries became only the old immediate worries of the road — When's the rain going to stop? Who can you trust to fix a waterpump around here? Where's the best pie in town? — then I would slow down.

I took the nearest Ohio River bridge at Louisville and whipped around the city and went into Pewee Valley and on to La Grange, where seven daily Louisville & Nashville freight trains ran right down Main Street. Then southeast.

Curling, dropping, trying to follow a stream, Kentucky 53 looked as if it needed someone to take the slack out of it. On that gray late afternoon, the creek ran full and clear under the rock ledges that dripped out the last meltwater. In spite of snow packs here and about, a woman bent to the planting of a switch of a tree, one man tilled mulch into his garden, another cleaned a birdhouse.

At Shelbyville I stopped for supper and the night. Just outside of town and surrounded by cattle and pastures was Claudia Sanders Dinner House, a low building attached to an old brick farmhouse with red roof. I didn't make the connection in names until I was inside and saw a mantel full of coffee mugs of a smiling Colonel Harlan Sanders. Claudia was his wife, and the Colonel once worked out of the farmhouse before the great buckets-in-the-sky poured down their golden bounty of extra crispy. The Dinner House specialized in Kentucky ham and country-style vegetables.

I waited for a table. A man, in a suit of sharp creases, and his wife, her jacket lying as straight as an accountant's left margin, suggested I join them. "You can't be as dismal as you look," she said. "Just hunger, we decided."

"Hunger's the word," I said.

We talked and I sat waiting for the question. It got there before the olives and celery. "What do you do?" the husband asked.

I told my lie, turned it to a joke, and then gave an answer too long. As I talked, the man put a pair of forks, a spoon, and knife into a lever system that changed directions twice before lifting his salad plate.

He said, "I notice that you use *work* and *job* interchangeably. Oughten to do that. A job's what you force yourself to pay attention to for money. With work, you don't have to force yourself. There are a lot of jobs in this country, and that's good because they keep people occupied. That's why they're called 'occupations.' "

The woman said, "Cal works at General Electric in Louisville. He's a metallurgical engineer."

"I don't *work* there, I'm employed there," he said to her. Then to me, "I'm supposed to spend my time 'imagineering,' but the job isn't so much a matter of getting something new made. It's a matter of making it *look like* we're getting something made. You know what my work is? You know what I pay attention to? Covering my tracks. Pretending, covering my tracks, and getting through another day. That's my work. Imagineering's my job."

"It isn't that bad, darling."

"It isn't that bad on a stick. What I do doesn't matter. There's no damn future whatsoever in what I do, and I don't mean built-in obsolescence. What I do begins and stops each day. There's no convergence between what I know and what I do. And even less with what I *want* to know."

Now he was hoisting his wife's salad plate, rolling her cherry tomato around. "You've learned lots," she said. "Just lots."

"I've learned this, Twinkie: when America outgrows engineering, we'll begin to have something."

6

IN the morning, an incident of blackbirds happened. Swarm following swarm wheeled above Ghost Dancing and dropped into the tall oaks to watch the dawn. They seemed to be conducting some sort of ancient bird worship of the spring sun. New arrivals fluttered helter-skelter into the branches but immediately turned toward the warm light with the others. Like sunflowers, every head faced east. The birds chattered among the fat buds, their throaty squeakings like thousands of unoiled wheels. Heat Moon says it's the planting season when the blackbirds return; yet not long after sunrise, the warm and golden light disappeared as if the blackness in the trees had absorbed it, and it was days before I saw sun again.

To walk Main Street in Shelbyville, Kentucky, is to go down three centuries of American architecture: rough-hewn timber, postbellum brick, Victorian fretwork, 1950s plate glass. Founded in 1792, it's an old town for this part of the country.

At the west end of Main, a man stripping siding from a small, two-story house had exposed a log cabin. I stopped to watch him straighten the doorway. To get a better perspective, he came to the sidewalk, eyed the lintel, then looked at me. "It's tilting, isn't it?" he said.

"There's a little list to it, but you could live with that."

"I want it right." He went to the door, set up a jack, measured, then leaned into it. The timbers creaked and squared up. He shoved a couple of two-by-fours behind the lintel to hold it true then cranked down the jack. "Come in for a look," he said. "After a hundred and fifty years, she's not likely to fall down today."

1. *Bob Andriot, Tony Hardin, Kirk Littlefield in Shelbyville, Kentucky*

"That's before people started jacking around with it."

The interior, bare of plaster and lath, leaked a deep smell of old timbers. Bigger than railway ties, the logs lay locked in dovetails, all careful work done only with ax, adz, froe, and wedge. The man, Bob Andriot, asked what I thought. "It's a beauty. How long have you been at it?"

"Ten days. We want to move in the first of April."

"You're going to live here?"

"My wife and I have a picture-framing and interior design shop. We're moving it out of our house. We just bought this place."

"Did you know the log cabin was underneath the siding?"

"We thought it possible. Shape of the house and the low windows looked right. We knew some were along Main." He went to the door. "That little house across the street. Could be one under the siding. A lot of cabins still buried under asphalt shingles, and nobody knows it. I've heard Kentucky's got more log houses than any other state."

A squarely solid man stepped through a back window. Andriot said, "Tony here got himself one last year in Spencer County."

"But I knew what I was gettin'," Tony said. "It wasn't sided over. Some fellas clearin' a field were discussin' whether to burn the cabin or push it in the holler. We were lookin' for a house, so we bought it and moved it. Only three inches off square, and I know factually it'd been there since eighteen oh seven. Good for another couple hundred years now."

"Tony's logs are chestnut and a lot more termite-resistant than these poplar logs here," Andriot said. "Somebody let a gutter leak for a long time on the back corner, and termites came up in the wet wood. Now that end's like a rotted tooth, except we can't pull it. So we'll reinforce."

He took me around to the east wall. "Look at this." He pointed to a worn Roman numeral I cut between adz marks into the bottom log. The eighth tier had a VIII scratched in it. "They're numbered, and we don't know why. I don't think it was ever moved. Maybe precut to a plan."

"A prefab nineteenth-century log house?"

"Don't think this was a house originally. Records show it was a coach stop on the old road to Louisville in eighteen twenty-nine, but it's probably older. Main Street's always been the highway."

"What about the gaps between the logs?"

Andriot stuck a crowbar between two timbers and pried out a rock caked with mud as hard as the stone. "They chinked with rocks and mud, but we aren't going to be that authentic. We'll leave the rocks but chink with concrete." He locked the crowbar onto a wooden peg, its color much lighter than the logs, and pulled it free. "Hand-whittled oak. Sniff it." The peg smelled of freshly cut wood. "You're sniffing a tree from seventeen seventy-six." Andriot touched his nose. "Gives you a real sense of history. Take it with you."

He asked where I was from. Tony listened and asked whether I had ever read *Walking Through Missouri on a Mule*.

"Never heard of it, but I like that title."

"It's about an old boy that tramped across the state a hundred years ago. Boy that walked it wrote the book. Now, that's good reading."

A head popped in the window. "Hey, Kirk," Andriot said. "Coke time."

"I went yesterday."

"And today," Andriot said.

Kirk crossed the street to the Exxon station and came back with three Cokes and a Kickapoo Joy Juice. "Ran flat out of Coke," he said.

There was a discussion over who had to drink the "Injun piss." "I've never had it," I said. "Let me try it."

"Man won't never come back to Kentucky now," Kirk said.

We sat on the plank floor and talked. "You know," Andriot said, "this old place makes a difference here. To us, of course, but to the town too before long. I feel it more than I can explain it. I don't know, I guess rescuing this building makes me feel I've done something to last. And people here need to see this old lady. To be reminded."

"Old lady? That's not what you were calling her yesterday."

"That was yesterday. She gets better as she gets older."

The men got up to work again, and we shook hands around. When I got to the sidewalk, Kirk called to me, "What about the Injun piss?"

I thought before I spoke. "The red man's revenge."

I drove on east. I thought how Bob Andriot was rebuilding a past he could see and smell, one he could shape with his hands. He was using it to build something new. I envied him that.

7

U.S. 60, running from Norfolk, Virginia, to Los Angeles, used to be a major east-west route. But Interstate 64 now has taken up the heavy traffic and left 60 to farm pickups and kids on horses. For the blue highway traveler, freeing roads like this one is the purpose of the interstates. Comprising only one percent of American highways, the interstate system has opened a lot of roadway to the dawdler. And a lot of space: the billboards have followed the traffic. The Department of Transportation expects the interstates to carry a quarter of all traffic by the early eighties; that statistic, more than any billboard legislation, has cleared the back roads of the United States.

I came to a ramshackle place called Smitty's Trading Post. Smitty was a merchant of relics. He could sell you a Frankfort, Kentucky, city bus that made its last run down Shively Street, or an ice cream wagon made from a golf cart, or a used bulldozer, or a bent horseshoe. I stopped to look. Lying flat as the ground, a piebald mongrel too tired to lift its head gave a one-eyed stare. I pulled on the locked door, peered through windows grimed like coalminers' goggles, but I couldn't find Smitty. A pickup rattled in. A man with a wen above his eye said, "Smitty ain't here."

"Where is he?" I was just making talk.

"You the feller wantin' the harness?"

"Already got one."

"What'd you come for then?"

"I don't know. Have to talk to Smitty to find out."

"That's one I ain't heard," he said.

8

FRANKFORT is a tale of two cities. Once the citizens called it Frank's Ford after Stephen Frank, a pioneer killed by Indians in 1780 near a shallow crossing in the Kentucky River. As the town grew, people found the name too rustic. Not wanting to chuck their history entirely, they changed it to Frankfort, although there were probably more Bolivians in town than Germans. If it made cosmetic sense, it didn't make historical sense, and the people cut something between them and their beginnings.

A traveler coming from the west sees no hint of the town because the highway abruptly angles down a bluff into a deep, encircled river valley that conceals even the high dome of the capitol. If you're ever looking for the most hidden statehouse in America, look no farther than Frankfort.

The river loops from the east bluffs to the west bluffs and back again, a serpentine among old buildings that almost makes the town a little Venice. Had it not been for the last thirty years, Frankfort would be an architecturally distinguished capital city with streets of forcefully simple, aesthetically honest houses and shops. But the impulse to "modernize" nineteenth-century commercial buildings, an impulse that has blasted the business districts of almost every town in the country, defaced Frankfort. The harmonious, proportioned, historic lines of the buildings now wore veneers of ceramic tile, cedar siding, imitation marble, extruded aluminum, textured stucco, precast concrete; and the street level had become a jumble of meretricious, tawdry fronts. But at the second- and third-story levels, graceful designs in brick and stone remained; disregarding the plywood over the upper-story windows, you had unrenovated history. Frankfort or Frank's Ford, take your pick.

Old Frankfort did nothing to prepare me for the new Frankfort that spread over the eastern bluffs, where the highway ran the length of one of those carnival midway strips of plastic-roof franchises. It was past noon, and I could have had lunch from any of two dozen frylines without knowing I was seven hundred miles from home. Maybe America should make the national bird a Kentucky Fried Leghorn and put Ronald McDonald on the dollar bill. After all, the year before, franchisers did nearly three hundred billion dollars of business. And there's nothing wrong with that except the franchise system has almost obliterated the local cafes and grills and catfish parlors serving distinctly regional food, much of it made from truly secret recipes. In another time, to eat in Frankfort was to know you were eating in Kentucky. You couldn't find the same thing in Lompoc or Weehawken. A professor at the University of Kentucky, Thomas D. Clark, tells of an old geologist who could distinguish local cooking by the area it came from and whether it was cooked on the east or west side of the Kentucky River.

But franchisers don't sell many of their thirty-three billion hamburgers per year in blue highway towns where chophouses must draw customers through continuing quality rather than national advertising. I had nothing to lose but the chains, and I hoped to find down the county roads Ma in her beanery and Pap over his barbecue pit, both still serving slow food from the same place they did thirty years ago. Where-you-from-buddy restaurants.

9

NOT out of any plan, but just because it lay in front of me, I headed for the Bluegrass region. I took an old road, a "pike," the Kentuckians say, since their first highways were toll roads with entrances barred by revolving poles called "turn pikes." I followed the old pike, today route 421, not out of any plan either, but because it looked pleasant — a road of white fences around Thoroughbred farms. Many of the fence planks now, however, were creosoted and likely to remain the color of charred stumps until someone invents a machine to paint them.

Along the Leestown Road, near an old whitewashed springhouse made useless by a water-district pipeline, I stopped to eat lunch. Downstream from the spring where butter once got cooled, under peeling sycamores, the clear rill washed around clumps of new watercress. I pulled makings for a sandwich from my haversack: Muenster cheese, a collop of hard salami, sourdough bread, horseradish. I cut a sprig of watercress and laid it on, then ate slowly, letting the gurgle in the water and the guttural trilling of red-winged blackbirds do the talking. A noisy, whizzing gnat that couldn't decide whether to eat on my sandwich or ear joined me.

Had I gone looking for some particular place rather than any place, I'd never have found this spring under the sycamores. Since leaving home, I felt for the first time at rest. Sitting full in the moment, I practiced on the god-awful difficulty of just paying attention. It's a contention of Heat Moon's — believing as he does any traveler who misses the journey misses about all he's going to get — that a man becomes his attentions. His observations and curiosity, they make and remake him.

Etymology: *curious*, related to *cure*, once meant "carefully observant." Maybe a tonic of curiosity would counter my numbing sense that life inevitably creeps toward the absurd. *Absurd*, by the way, derives from a Latin word meaning "deaf, dulled." Maybe the road could provide a therapy through observation of the ordinary and obvious, a means whereby the outer eye opens an inner one. STOP, LOOK, LISTEN, the old railroad crossing signs warned. Whitman calls it "the profound lesson of reception."

New ways of seeing can disclose new things: the radio telescope revealed quasars and pulsars, and the scanning electron microscope showed the whiskers of the dust mite. But turn the question around: Do new *things* make for new ways of seeing?

10

It's an old debate here: Is bluegrass indigenous to Kentucky or did it come accidentally to America as padding to protect pottery shipped from England? As for the rock under the bluegrass, there's no debate. Water percolating through the soft limestone leaches out the calcium and phosphorus that make for strong yet light-framed stake winners whose spine and leg bones have the close grain of ivory rather than the more porous grain of horses pastured in other areas.

And it's also limestone percolation that engenders good handmade bourbon; after all, hundred proof is half water. To make bourbon with purified water, as today the distilleries must to maintain consistent quality, is to take the Kentucky out of the whiskey. And that raises another old debate in the Bluegrass about who made the first straight bourbon. One group holds — with evidence as good as anyone's — that it was a Baptist preacher.

In Lexington, I passed row after row of tobacco warehouses and auction barns on my way into the thousand square miles of bluegrass wold once called "God's footstool," a fertile land where pumpkin vines grow so fast they wear out the melons dragging them along. So they say.

Ghost Dancing leaned in and out of the easy curves — running east, west, south — and I steered a course over the swells of land. The captain before his binnacle. Past creosoted tobacco barns with silvery galvanized roofs, past white farmhouses, down along black lines of plank fences that met at right angles and linked the countryside into a crossword puzzle pattern.

It was late afternoon, and mares and foals were coming to drink at small quarry pits cut into limestone outcroppings. These old exposures of rock had furnished the material for the miles of mortarless fieldstone fences that slaves built in a distinctively regional style more than a century ago. Held together only by the cut of one stone conforming to another, the walls consisted of horizontal slabs laid on each other to a height of about three feet, then capped by smaller pieces set on edge to form a jagged top. New Englanders, proud of their piled dry walls, have nothing to match these of the Bluegrass for precision. But where runaway cars had knocked down the fences, the rocks had been heaped haphazardly back. Like the slaves, the skill and time necessary to build a good stone fence were gone.

Among catalpa and black cherry trees, a billboard pictured beams radiating from a carmine sun surmounted by a cross; below was THINK ABOUT IT. So I did and found the Gospel According to Acme Outdoor Advertising an abomination. But then, it's such mixtures that give the Kentucky flavor of born-again religion, bourbon whiskey, bluegrass farms, burley tobacco, and blooded horses.

The highway, without warning, rolled off the plateau of green pastures and entered a wooded and rocky gorge; down, down, precipitously down to the Kentucky River. Along the north slope, man-high columns of ice clung to the limestone. The road dropped deeper until it crossed the river at Brooklyn Bridge. The gorge, hidden in the tableland and wholly unexpected, was the Palisades. At the bottom lay only enough ground for the river and a narrow strip of willow-rimmed floodplain.

Houses on stilts and a few doublewides rose from the damp flats like toadstools. Next to one mobile home was a partly built steel boat longer than the trailer. I turned back and stopped at the Palisades Filling Station, a building with a chimney of round river stones, to ask the way to the boat. Inside you could buy sorghum and honey in hand-labeled quarts, peacock feathers, or framed Renoir reproductions. On the walls, counters, doors, high and low, were signs: DONT LEAN ON GLASS, NO CREDIT, NO CHECKS, NO PETS INSIDE, KEEP OUT. By a row of windows opening to the water, a woman dipped river perch in cornmeal batter and dropped them, crackling, into a skillet. I forgot why I'd stopped and asked to buy a fish dinner.

"That's our supper you're wantin'. But I can heat you up one of them sandwiches in the microwave radio oven."

The dry sandwiches, wrapped in plastic, had started to warp like old lumber. "Actually," I said, "I just wanted to ask a couple of questions."

"Questions?" For some reason, she looked behind herself.

"How do I get to that steel boat being built up the river?"

"Past the pumps and down the dirt road. You said questions."

"What goes on in the cave across the highway — the one fenced off and posted with U.S. Government signs?"

"Some time ago they tested a gun in there soldiers used in Veet-Nam. I heard so. But years before it was a gas station and diner. Even had slot machines in the back. That cave's seen it all."

I followed the road to the boat. The big hull, a smooth skin of steel plates fused like a surgeon's sutures, sat on concrete blocks in drydock fashion. The door of the trailer opened and a man stepped out. He seemed made of cut and welded steel too. I said, "I'm looking for the shipwright."

"You're looking at him."

11

BILL Hammond's first boat was an ice cake on the Wabash River near Peru, Indiana, where he grew up. In the thirties, he was fascinated with the shanty boats of the mussel hunters, those people who poled their boats up and down the Wabash and lived and gave birth and died, too, on the water, while they dug mussels to sell to button makers. Although landless and among the poorest in northern Indiana, they owned their houseboats and took them wherever they went. Hammond never forgot that community of free and mobile people.

"Saw your boat from the highway," I said. "I didn't much like my Navy time, but I loved the ships. Do you mind?"

His expression relaxed. "You'll walk off before I get tired of talking boats. This one's *Bluebill.* She's sixty-four feet and six inches. Almost as long as the *Santa Maria.*"

"Have you built all of her yourself?"

"Hull, deck, superstructure, and now I'm starting on the innards. We bought the engines, prop, and some special fittings. Rosemary, my wife, helps with everything. I'm finishing the water and holding tanks now. If you want an insider's view, I'll put you in the fresh water tank and let you lay the concrete coating on."

"Concrete?"

"Only thing that doesn't give drinking water a bad flavor. Tar tastes, plastic tastes, steel tastes rusty. Stainless is too expensive."

"Are you a boat builder? I mean, do you build for a living?"

"Rosy says I live to build boats. I'm an architect's representative. I make sure the structure's put up according to the blueprints. But I was a Navy shipfitter during the war. That's where I learned to cut steel."

"You're an acetylene wizard. The hull looks like one piece."

"It is." He winked. "Now. Ten feet longer than our trailer and twice the square footage. Built better in every detail. She's a *real* mobile home."

A woman waved from the trailer. "Time for supper," he said. "Come in and put your feet under our table."

Rosemary Hammond, a jolly woman, used to be a schoolteacher, but she was now the librarian in Danville. Hammond called her "the brains." She set out baked chicken, spinach, mashed potatoes, radishes, pickles, hot tea. Above the table was a sign I read aloud: "A boat is a hole in the water surrounded by wood into which one pours money."

"And your life," Mrs. Hammond added.

"We started building six years ago," Hammond said, "and I reckoned on finishing in two years. Three times longer than I figured with a couple more to go. Shot for a star, but I think I hit the moon."

"He's worked weekends, vacations, and evenings. Whenever we do get away for a while, it's to look for boat fittings. In Louisiana, we found exactly the right prop with the right pitch. Bent, but cheap for a propeller. Sometimes, though, I wonder if *Bluebill* will ever be finished." She looked out at the darkening sky. "But some April when the redbuds are in bloom, we'll sell this old trailer and sail *Bluebill* right out of the valley."

"We almost sailed out in April of 'seventy-two before I'd even started the boat," Hammond said. "The Kentucky came up higher and higher, slipped under the trailer — this trailer — and raised it off the blocks. We stood up on the highway and watched it float away. I already had the idea of building *Bluebill*, but if I hadn't, I'd have got the notion from the trailer's cruise."

"We'd just sold a beautiful home up on Herrington Lake to move to

2. *Rosemary and Bill Hammond in Brooklyn Bridge, Kentucky*

this riverbank to be close to a boat still only in Bill's mind. I watched our
trailer float off, and I wondered what we'd done."

"How do you get started on a boat that big?"

"By slipping into things, not knowing quite where you're going. We
built a sixteen-foot runabout several years ago from a kit. Before that, we
rebuilt a Grumman laminated canoe in the fifties. And once I started a
sailboat but quit when I ran out of money for two pieces of marine plywood,
although I think the real reason was I lost interest."

"How have you kept interest in *Bluebill* over six years?"

"Ask how he's kept interest in his salaried job over six years. He lives
and sleeps that boat. Cuts steel in his dreams and wakes up exhausted."

"A seventy-seven-thousand-pound dream?"

"A seventy-seven-thousand-pound way of life," she corrected. "Sailing,
ports of call, sitting on deck with fishing poles — that's the dream still to
come."

Hammond said, "It's flat beautiful here in the spring." He was thinking
of what was to come. "Our first trip's going to be three miles upriver to

Lock Seven. Later, a one-hundred-thirteen-mile shakedown to the Ohio. From the Ohio we can go to the Gulf, the Great Lakes, the Atlantic, the Rockies. We might even load her on a freighter and ship her to the Mediterranean."

"Old sailors never die," Mrs. Hammond said, "they just weigh anchor."

"What about the name *Bluebill?* Work turning Bill blue in the face?"

"More like black and blue," she said. "No, we named her after a dry-docked sailing yacht we saw in Rhode Island during World War Two when we were young marrieds. It gave us a dream."

"Ought to name her *Red Rosy,*" Hammond said. "Rosy gets one pair of red feet whenever we weld. About once a month, I get a curve or angle I can't clamp properly for welding. So Rosy stands on the plate or pushes it up into position with her feet. That steel gets warm underfoot."

"We run through a lot of sneakers — sneakers and liniment."

"How do you know your forty-ton hole in the water's going to float?"

"*Bluebill* was designed by C. A. Coleman, a Lexington architect, and Joseph Kobel, a well-known New York builder, looked over the plans and provided specifications."

"So the answer is faith," Mrs. Hammond said.

"*Was* faith. We hired a crane to turn her over. I built the hull upside down. Not long after she was top-side up, highwater took her off the blocks. She floated even better than our trailer."

"She was just a hull and deck then, but she was so beautiful on that muddy water," Mrs. Hammond said. "I knew then why we'd built a life out of building a boat."

Hammond and I went out in the darkness to go aboard *Bluebill.* Charley, the orange tomcat, shot up the ladder to show his trim for the nautical life. The Franklin stove was in place, and the cabins, wheelhouse, and galley were divided off; otherwise, I had to imagine a finished *Bluebill.*

Through scattered clouds, moonlight wobbled on the silent river currents, and shadows lay against the high palisades on the opposite bank. Thunder rumbled low in the west, and from the far trees a dog moaned and shook in its chain. I asked whether the river would be big enough for *Bluebill.*

"Years ago, before the railroads took over, packet boats, eighty-five feet and longer, hauled tobacco, hemp, whiskey, corn. And slaves and tourists. The Shakers that lived up on the hill loved river boats. This Kentucky was the main highway." He looked again at the river. "There's enough water out there for the boat all right. But for me, maybe not enough space."

"Dreams take up a lot of space?"

"All you'll give them."

As best I could determine, it was coincidental that the next morning, Good Friday, I was on my way to eat breakfast in the Trustees' Hall of the United Society of Believers in Christ's Second Appearing, a colony of charitable people known somewhat whimsically as "Shakers." Before the utopian dreams of Charles Fourier, Robert Owen, Brook Farm, and the Oneida community, the Shakers (inventors of the wooden clothespin) worked toward their millennium and became America's most successful utopians. They lived apart yet not separate and earned a name (said William Dean Howells, who visited them at Shirley, Massachusetts, in 1875) not just for ecstatic worship but also for brisk commerce in applesauce, flatbrooms, and punctually sprouting seeds.

The last of these celibate Kentuckians died in 1923, but a nonprofit group restored the Society's 1805 village at Pleasant Hill and served singular meals of traditional Kentucky cuisine. Travelers, whom the Society called "the world's people," had stopped here to eat and sleep for nearly a century and a half.

On a typically Shaker single street stood the three-story brick Trustees' Hall, an 1839 building of spare and harmonious design the Believers used as a countinghouse and inn. Rich guests paid moderately and the poor not at all. One Shaker even spoke of tramps who looked as if "the Pit had vomited [them] up" coming to stay — especially in cold weather; because of their interpretation of scripture, the Society said to all, "We make you kindly welcome."

I took a sideboard breakfast of scrambled eggs, thick-cut bacon, sausage, grits, peaches, figs, grapefruit, tomato juice, milk, and pumpkin muffins. An inappropriate place for gluttony, but I lost my restraint. From my table I looked through long windows onto a tomato patch from the year before; a meadowlark let loose a piece of plaintive song in the mist, and a recognition moved in my memory as if I'd been here before.

After breakfast, I walked the scrupulous simplicity of the old halls. At the front door, a broad twin stairway with a sinuous walnut handrail coiled up to the third story. Generations of hands had polished the wood to the texture of plumskin. Inside one of the white-walled rooms, a woman, forlorn in the quiet economy of things, sat staring numbly through the miasma of her cigarette into the March grayness. On a chair lay a *Successful Marketing* magazine. Her flesh looked as if it had been dumped into her stripy dress the way grain gets dumped into a feed sack. She jarred the lean Shaker lines. I imagined her in the company of Mrs. Butterworth and Betty Crocker and Mr. Coffee, only now to find herself alone.

From a window on the third floor, where grim watchers had assured Shaker celibacy, I saw far to the east a yellow smear from a power generating plant smokestack. Some historians attribute the decline of the United Believers to their unnatural views on procreation and cite the Shaker song:

> Come life, Shaker life,
> Come life eternal;
> Shake, shake out of me
> All that is carnal.

But, since the Kentucky Shakers disappeared at the time of widespread electrification, maybe the lure of a 110/220 way of life kept new blood away from Pleasant Hill. After all, even the inventive people themselves (circular saw and washing machine) had to check a love of ingeniously useful mechanical gadgets and to guard against (as Howells said) "the impulse of the age toward a scientific, a sensuous, an aesthetic life." The yellowed sky gave me the sense the Shakers were right and that I was standing in the future in that hundred-thirty-nine-year-old building. Because they cared more about adapting to the cosmos than to a society bereft of restraint, the Shakers — like the red man — could love craft and yet never become materialists.

13

THE highway took me through Danville, where I saw a pillared antebellum mansion with a trailer court on the front lawn. Route 127 ran down a long valley of pastures and fields edged by low, rocky bluffs and split by a stream the color of muskmelon. In the distance rose the foothills of the Appalachians, old mountains that once separated the Atlantic from the shallow inland sea now the middle of America. The licks came out of the hills, the fields got smaller, and there were little sawmills cutting hardwoods into pallets, crates, fenceposts. The houses shrank, and their colors changed from white to pastels to iridescents to no paint at all. The lawns went from Vertagreen bluegrass to thin fescue to hard-packed dirt glinting with fragments of glass, and the lawn ornaments changed from birdbaths to plastic flamingoes and donkeys to broken-down automobiles with raised hoods like tombstones. On the porches stood long-legged wringer washers and ruined sofas, and, by the front doors, washtubs hung like coats of arms.

A cold drizzle fell as I wound around into the slopes of the Cumberland Mountains. Clouds like smudged charcoal turned the afternoon to dusk, and the only relief from the gloom came from a fiddler on the radio who ripped out "Turkey Bone Buzzer."

At Ida, a sign in front of a church announced the Easter sermon: "Welcome All God's Children: Thieves, Liars, Gossips, Bigots, Adulterers, Children." I felt welcome. Also in Ida was one of those hitching posts in the form of a crouching livery boy reaching up to take the master's reins; but the face of this iron Negro had been painted white and his eyes Nordic blue. Ida, on the southern edge of Appalachia, a place (they said) where change comes slowly or not at all, had a church welcoming everyone and a family displaying integrated lawn decorations.

I lost the light at Bug, Kentucky, and, two miles later, at a fork in the road with three rickety taverns in the crotch, I crossed into Tennessee. Since I had left Lexington, the Kentucky counties had been dry, kept that way, I was told, by an unwritten covenant between Bible Belt fundamentalists and moonshiners. Yet, in two dry counties, half the routine police reports in newspapers listed cases of public drunkenness. A man I spoke with did not hold moonshiners responsible; rather, he believed the problem lay with bootleggers who brought in factory whiskey. Insobriety wasn't the worst of it; people have to know where to buy bootleg, and that requires cooperation from public officials. The solution, he said, was state liquor stores that would kill bootlegging and put an end to the corruption while doing little harm to the long tradition of the moonshiners — reasonably industrious men who pursue a business older than the Federal Revenue Department. "Shine's paid for a lot of college education in these hills," he said, "but don't try to tell me that about bootleg."

Tennessee 42 mostly kept to the crests of the steep ridges, the road twisting like tendrils of a wild grapevine. Some of the curves were so sharp I had to look out the side window to steer through them. At last the mountains opened, and I came into Livingston, Tennessee, a homely town. Things were closed but for a highway grocery where I walked the fluorescent aisles more for entertainment than need. Had I come for lard, I'd have been in the right place: seven brands in five sizes, including one thirty-eight-pound drum.

I drove back to the square and pulled up for the night in front of the Overton County Courthouse. Adolescents cruised in half-mufflered heaps; a man adjusted a television in the appliance store window; a cat rubbed against my leg; windows went dark one by one. I think someone even unplugged the red blinker light after I went to bed. And that's how I spent my evening in Livingston, Tennessee.

14

HAD it not been raining hard that morning on the Livingston square, I never would have learned of Nameless, Tennessee. Waiting for the rain to ease, I lay on my bunk and read the atlas to pass time rather than to see where I might go. In Kentucky were towns with fine names like Boreing, Bear Wallow, Decoy, Subtle, Mud Lick, Mummie, Neon; Belcher was just down the road from Mouthcard, and Minnie only ten miles from Mousie.

I looked at Tennessee. Turtletown eight miles from Ducktown. And also: Peavine, Wheel, Milky Way, Love Joy, Dull, Weakly, Fly, Spot, Miser Station, Only, McBurg, Peeled Chestnut, Clouds, Topsy, Isoline. And the best of all, Nameless. The logic! I was heading east, and Nameless lay forty-five miles west. I decided to go anyway.

The rain stopped, but things looked saturated, even bricks. In Gaines-boro, a hill town with a square of businesses around the Jackson County Courthouse, I stopped for directions and breakfast. There is one almost infallible way to find honest food at just prices in blue-highway America: count the wall calendars in a cafe.

No calendar: Same as an interstate pit stop.
One calendar: Preprocessed food assembled in New Jersey.
Two calendars: Only if fish trophies present.
Three calendars: Can't miss on the farm-boy breakfasts.
Four calendars: Try the ho-made pie too.
Five calendars: Keep it under your hat, or they'll franchise.

One time I found a six-calendar cafe in the Ozarks, which served fried chicken, peach pie, and chocolate malts, that left me searching for another ever since. I've never seen a seven-calendar place. But old-time travelers — road men in a day when cars had running boards and lunchroom windows said AIR COOLED in blue letters with icicles dripping from the tops — those travelers have told me the golden legends of seven-calendar cafes.

To the rider of back roads, nothing shows the tone, the voice of a small town more quickly than the breakfast grill or the five-thirty tavern. Much of what the people do and believe and share is evident then. The City Cafe in Gainesboro had three calendars that I could see from the walk. Inside were no interstate refugees with full bladders and empty tanks, no wild-eyed children just released from the glassy cell of a stationwagon backseat, no longhaul truckers talking in CB numbers. There were only townspeople wearing overalls, or catalog-order suits with five-and-dime ties, or uniforms. That is, here were farmers and mill hands, bank clerks, the dry goods merchant, a policeman, and chiropractor's receptionist. Because it was Saturday, there were also mothers and children.

I ordered my standard on-the-road breakfast: two eggs up, hashbrowns, tomato juice. The waitress, whose pale, almost translucent skin shifted hue in the gray light like a thin slice of mother of pearl, brought the food. Next to the eggs was a biscuit with a little yellow Smiley button stuck in it. She said, "You from the North?"

"I guess I am." A Missourian gets used to Southerners thinking him a Yankee, a Northerner considering him a cracker, a Westerner sneering at his effete Easternness, and the Easterner taking him for a cowhand.

"So whata you doin' in the mountains?"

"Talking to people. Taking some pictures. Looking mostly."

"Lookin' for what?"

"A three-calendar cafe that serves Smiley buttons on the biscuits."

"You needed a smile. Tell me really."

"I don't know. Actually, I'm looking for some jam to put on this biscuit now that you've brought one."

She came back with grape jelly. In a land of quince jelly, apple butter, apricot jam, blueberry preserves, pear conserves, and lemon marmalade, you always get grape jelly.

"Whata you lookin' for?"

Like anyone else, I'm embarrassed to eat in front of a watcher, particularly if I'm getting interviewed. "Why don't you have a cup of coffee?"

"Cain't right now. You gonna tell me?"

"I don't know how to describe it to you. Call it harmony."

She waited for something more. "Is that it?" Someone called her to the kitchen. I had managed almost to finish by the time she came back. She sat on the edge of the booth. "I started out in life not likin' anything, but then it grew on me. Maybe that'll happen to you." She watched me spread the jelly. "Saw your van." She watched me eat the biscuit. "You sleep in there?" I told her I did. "I'd love to do that, but I'd be scared spitless."

"I don't mind being scared spitless. Sometimes."

"I'd love to take off cross country. I like to look at different license plates. But I'd take a dog. You carry a dog?"

"No dogs, no cats, no budgie birds. It's a one-man campaign to show Americans a person can travel alone without a pet."

"Cain't travel without a dog!"

"I like to do things the hard way."

"Shoot! I'd take me a dog to talk to. And for protection."

"It isn't traveling to cross the country and talk to your pug instead of people along the way. Besides, being alone on the road makes you ready to meet someone when you stop. You get sociable traveling alone."

She looked out toward the van again. "Time I get the nerve to take a trip, gas'll cost five dollars a gallon."

"Could be. My rig might go the way of the steamboat." I remembered why I'd come to Gainesboro. "You know the way to Nameless?"

"Nameless? I've heard of Nameless. Better ask the amlance driver in the corner booth." She pinned the Smiley on my jacket. "Maybe I'll see you on the road somewhere. His name's Bob, by the way."

"The ambulance driver?"

"The Smiley. I always name my Smileys — otherwise they all look alike. I'd talk to him before you go."

"The Smiley?"

"The amlance driver."

And so I went looking for Nameless, Tennessee, with a Smiley button named Bob.

15

"I DON'T know if I got directions for where you're goin'," the ambulance driver said. "I *think* there's a Nameless down the Shepardsville Road."

"When I get to Shepardsville, will I have gone too far?"

"Ain't no Shepardsville."

"How will I know when I'm there?"

"Cain't say for certain."

"What's Nameless look like?"

"Don't recollect."

"Is the road paved?"

"It's possible."

Those were the directions. I was looking for an unnumbered road named after a nonexistent town that would take me to a place called Nameless that nobody was sure existed.

Clumps of wild garlic lined the county highway that I hoped was the Shepardsville Road. It scrimmaged with the mountain as it tried to stay on top of the ridges; the hillsides were so steep and thick with oak, I felt as if I were following a trail through the misty treetops. Chickens, doing more work with their necks than legs, ran across the road, and, with a battering of wings, half leapt and half flew into the lower branches of oaks. A vicious pair of mixed-breed German shepherds raced along trying to eat the tires. After miles, I decided I'd missed the town — assuming there truly *was* a Nameless, Tennessee. It wouldn't be the first time I'd qualified for the Ponce de Leon Believe Anything Award.

I stopped beside a big man loading tools in a pickup. "I may be lost."

"Where'd you lose the right road?"

"I don't know. Somewhere around nineteen sixty-five."

"Highway fifty-six, you mean?"

"I came down fifty-six. I think I should've turned at the last junction."

"Only thing down that road's stumps and huckleberries, and the berries ain't there in March. Where you tryin' to get to?"

"Nameless. If there is such a place."

"You might not know Thurmond Watts, but he's got him a store down the road. That's Nameless at his store. Still there all right, but I might not vouch you that tomorrow." He came up to the van. "In my Army days, I wrote Nameless, Tennessee, for my place of birth on all the papers, even though I lived on this end of the ridge. All these ridges and hollers got names of their own. That's Steam Mill Holler over yonder. Named after the steam engine in the gristmill. Miller had him just one arm but done a good business."

"What business you in?"

"I've always farmed, but I work in Cookeville now in a heatin' element factory. Bad back made me go to town to work." He pointed to a wooden building not much bigger than his truck. By the slanting porch, a faded Double Cola sign said J M WHEELER STORE. "That used to be my business. That's me — Madison Wheeler. Feller came by one day. From Detroit. He wanted to buy the sign because he carried my name too. But I didn't sell. Want to keep my name up." He gave a cigarette a good slow smoking. "Had a decent business for five years, but too much of it was in credit. Then them supermarkets down in Cookeville opened, and I was buyin' higher than they was sellin'. With these hard roads now, everybody gets out of the hollers to shop or work. Don't stay up in here anymore. This tar road under my shoes done my business in, and it's likely to do Nameless in."

"Do you wish it was still the old way?"

3. Madison Wheeler outside Nameless, Tennessee

"I got no debts now. I got two boys raised, and they never been in trouble. I got a brick house and some corn and tobacco and a few Hampshire hogs and Herefords. A good bull. Bull's pumpin' better blood than I do. Real generous man in town let me put my cow in with his stud. I couldna paid the fee on that specimen otherwise." He took another long, meditative pull on his filtertip. "If you're satisfied, that's all they are to it. I'll tell you, people from all over the nation — Florida, Mississippi — are comin' in here to retire because it's good country. But our young ones don't stay on. Not much way to make a livin' in here anymore. Take me. I been beatin' on these stumps all my life, tryin' to farm these hills. They don't give much up to you. Fightin' rocks and briars all the time. One of the first things I recollect is swingin' a briar blade — filed out of an old saw it was. Now they come in with them crawlers and push out a pasture in a day. Still, it's a grudgin' land — like the gourd. Got to hard cuss gourd seed, they say, to get it up out of the ground."

The whole time, my rig sat in the middle of the right lane while we stood talking next to it and wiped at the mist. No one else came or went. Wheeler said, "Factory work's easier on the back, and I don't mind it, understand, but a man becomes what he does. Got to watch that. That's why I keep at farmin', although the crops haven't ever throve. It's the doin' that's important." He looked up suddenly. "My apologies. I didn't ask what you do that gets you into these hollers."

I told him. I'd been gone only six days, but my account of the trip already had taken on some polish.

He nodded. "Satisfaction is doin' what's important to yourself. A man ought to honor other people, but he's got to honor what he believes in too."

As I started the engine, Wheeler said, "If you get back this way, stop in and see me. Always got beans and taters and a little piece of meat."

Down along the ridge, I wondered why it's always those who live on little who are the ones to ask you to dinner.

16

NAMELESS, Tennessee, was a town of maybe ninety people if you pushed it, a dozen houses along the road, a couple of barns, same number of churches, a general merchandise store selling Fire Chief gasoline, and a community center with a lighted volleyball court. Behind the center was an open-roof, rusting metal privy with PAINT ME on the door; in the hollow of a nearby oak lay a full pint of Jack Daniel's Black Label. From the houses, the odor of coal smoke.

Next to a red tobacco barn stood the general merchandise with a poster of Senator Albert Gore, Jr., smiling from the window. I knocked. The door opened partway. A tall, thin man said, "Closed up. For good," and started to shut the door.

"Don't want to buy anything. Just a question for Mr. Thurmond Watts."

The man peered through the slight opening. He looked me over. "What question would that be?"

"If this is Nameless, Tennessee, could he tell me how it got that name?"

The man turned back into the store and called out, "Miss Ginny! Somebody here wants to know how Nameless come to be Nameless."

Miss Ginny edged to the door and looked me and my truck over. Clearly, she didn't approve. She said, "You know as well as I do, Thurmond. Don't keep him on the stoop in the damp to tell him." Miss Ginny, I found out, was Mrs. Virginia Watts, Thurmond's wife.

I stepped in and they both began telling the story, adding a detail here, the other correcting a fact there, both smiling at the foolishness of it all. It seems the hilltop settlement went for years without a name. Then one day the Post Office Department told the people if they wanted mail up on the mountain they would have to give the place a name you could properly address a letter to. The community met; there were only a handful, but they commenced debating. Some wanted patriotic names, some names from nature, one man recommended in all seriousness his own name. They couldn't agree, and they ran out of names to argue about. Finally, a fellow tired of the talk; he didn't like the mail he received anyway. "Forget the durn Post Office," he said. "This here's a nameless place if I ever seen one, so leave it be." And that's just what they did.

Watts pointed out the window. "We used to have signs on the road, but the Halloween boys keep tearin' them down."

"You think Nameless is a funny name," Miss Ginny said. "I see it plain in your eyes. Well, you take yourself up north a piece to Difficult or Defeated or Shake Rag. Now them are silly names."

The old store, lighted only by three fifty-watt bulbs, smelled of coal oil and baking bread. In the middle of the rectangular room, where the oak floor sagged a little, stood an iron stove. To the right was a wooden table with an unfinished game of checkers and a stool made from an apple-tree stump. On shelves around the walls sat earthen jugs with corncob stoppers, a few canned goods, and some of the two thousand old clocks and clock-works Thurmond Watts owned. Only one was ticking; the others he just looked at. I asked how long he'd been in the store.

"Thirty-five years, but we closed the first day of the year. We're hopin' to sell it to a churchly couple. Upright people. No athians."

"Did you build this store?"

"I built this one, but it's the third general store on the ground. I fear it'll be the last. I take no pleasure in that. Once you could come in here for a gallon of paint, a pickle, a pair of shoes, and a can of corn."

"Or horehound candy," Miss Ginny said. "Or corsets and salves. We had cough syrups and all that for the body. In season, we'd buy and sell blackberries and walnuts and chestnuts, before the blight got them. And outside, Thurmond milled corn and sharpened plows. Even shoed a horse sometimes."

"We could fix up a horse or a man or a baby," Watts said.

"Thurmond, tell him we had a doctor on the ridge in them days."

"We had a doctor on the ridge in them days. As good as any doctor alivin'. He'd cut a crooked toenail or deliver a woman. Dead these last years."

"I got some bad ham meat one day," Miss Ginny said, "and took to vomitin'. All day, all night. Hangin' on the drop edge of yonder. I said to Thurmond, 'Thurmond, unless you want shut of me, call the doctor.' "

"I studied on it," Watts said.

"You never did. You got him right now. He come over and put three drops of iodeen in half a glass of well water. I drank it down and the vomitin' stopped with the last swallow. Would you think iodeen could do that?"

"He put Miss Ginny on one teaspoon of spirits of ammonia in well water for her nerves. Ain't nothin' works better for her to this day."

"Calms me like the hand of the Lord."

Hilda, the Wattses' daughter, came out of the backroom. "I remember him," she said. "I was just a baby. Y'all were talkin' to him, and he lifted me up on the counter and gave me a stick of Juicy Fruit and a piece of cheese."

"Knew the old medicines," Watts said. "Only drugstore he needed was a good kitchen cabinet. None of them antee-beeotics that hit you worsen your ailment. Forgotten lore now, the old medicines, because they ain't profit in iodeen."

Miss Ginny started back to the side room where she and her sister Marilyn were taking apart a duck-down mattress to make bolsters. She stopped at the window for another look at Ghost Dancing. "How do you sleep in that thing? Ain't you all cramped and cold?"

"How does the clam sleep in his shell?" Watts said in my defense.

"Thurmond, get the boy a piece of buttermilk pie afore he goes on."

"Hilda, get him some buttermilk pie." He looked at me. "You like good music?" I said I did. He cranked up an old Edison phonograph, the kind with the big morning-glory blossom for a speaker, and put on a wax cylinder. "This will be 'My Mother's Prayer,' " he said.

While I ate buttermilk pie, Watts served as disc jockey of Nameless, Tennessee. "Here's 'Mountain Rose.' " It was one of those moments that you know at the time will stay with you to the grave: the sweet pie, the gaunt man playing the old music, the coals in the stove glowing orange, the scent of kerosene and hot bread. "Here's 'Evening Rhapsody.' " The music was so heavily romantic we both laughed. I thought: It is for this I have come.

Feathered over and giggling, Miss Ginny stepped from the side room. She knew she was a sight. "Thurmond, give him some lunch. Still looks hungry."

4. *The Wattses: Marilyn, Thurmond, Virginia, and Hilda in Nameless, Tennessee*

Hilda pulled food off the woodstove in the backroom: home-butchered and canned whole-hog sausage, home-canned June apples, turnip greens, cole slaw, potatoes, stuffing, hot cornbread. All delicious.

Watts and Hilda sat and talked while I ate. "Wish you would join me."

"We've ate," Watts said. "Cain't beat a woodstove for flavorful cookin'."

He told me he was raised in a one-hundred-fifty-year-old cabin still standing in one of the hollows. "How many's left," he said, "that grew up in a log cabin? I ain't the last surely, but I must be climbin' on the list."

Hilda cleared the table. "You Watts ladies know how to cook."

"She's in nursin' school at Tennessee Tech. I went over for one of them football games last year there at Coevul." To say *Cookeville*, you let the word collapse in upon itself so that it comes out "Coevul."

"Do you like football?" I asked.

"Don't know. I was so high up in that stadium, I never opened my eyes."

Watts went to the back and returned with a fat spiral notebook that he set on the table. His expression had changed. "Miss Ginny's *Deathbook*." The thing startled me. Was it something I was supposed to sign? He opened it but said nothing. There were scads of names written in a tidy hand over pages incised to crinkliness by a ballpoint. Chronologically, the names had piled up: wives, grandparents, a stillborn infant, relatives, friends close and distant. Names, names. After each, the date of *the* unknown finally known and transcribed. The last entry bore yesterday's date.

"She's wrote out twenty years' worth. Ever day she listens to the hospital report on the radio and puts the names in. Folks come by to check a date. Or they just turn through the books. Read them like a scrapbook."

Hilda said, "Like Saint Peter at the gates inscribin' the names."

Watts took my arm. "Come along." He led me to the fruit cellar under the store. As we went down, he said, "Always take a newborn baby upstairs afore you take him downstairs, otherwise you'll incline him downwards."

The cellar was dry and full of cobwebs and jar after jar of home-canned food, the bottles organized as a shopkeeper would: sausage, pumpkin, sweet pickles, tomatoes, corn relish, blackberries, peppers, squash, jellies. He held a hand out toward the dusty bottles. "Our tomorrows."

Upstairs again, he said, "Hope to sell the store to the right folk. I see now, though, it'll be somebody offen the ridge. I've studied on it, and maybe it's the end of our place." He stirred the coals. "This store could give a comfortable livin', but not likely get you rich. But just gettin' by is dice rollin' to people nowadays. I never did see my day guaranteed."

When it was time to go, Watts said, "If you find anyone along your way wants a good store — on the road to Cordell Hull Lake — tell them about us."

I said I would. Miss Ginny and Hilda and Marilyn came out to say goodbye. It was cold and drizzling again. "Weather to give a man the weary dismals," Watts grumbled. "Where you headed from here?"

"I don't know."

"Cain't get lost then."

Miss Ginny looked again at my rig. It had worried her from the first as it had my mother. "I hope you don't get yourself kilt in that durn thing gallivantin' around the country."

"Come back when the hills dry off," Watts said. "We'll go lookin' for some of them round rocks all sparkly inside."

I thought a moment. "Geodes?"

"Them's the ones. The county's properly full of them."

COOKEVILLE: Easter morning and cold as the bottom of Dante's Hell. Winter had returned from somewhere, whistling thin, bluish snowflakes along the ground, bowing the jonquils. I couldn't warm up. The night had been full of dreams moving through my sleep like schools of ocean fish that dart this way, turn suddenly another way, never resting. I hung in the old depths, the currents bending and enfolding me as the sea does fronds of eelgrass.

Route 62 went across the Cumberland Plateau strip-mining country and up into the mountains again. In the absence of billboards were small, ineptly lettered signs: USED FURNITURE, HOT SANDWITCHES, TURKEY SHOOT SATERDAY (NO DRINKING ALOUD). It was like reading over someone's shoulder.

Wartburg, on the edge of the dark Cumberlands, dripped in a cold mist blowing down off the knobs. Cafes closed, I had no choice but to go back into the wet mountain gloom. Under massive walls of black shale hanging above the road like threats, the highway turned ugly past Frozen Head State Park; at each trash dumpster pullout, soggy sofas or chairs lay encircled by dismal, acrid smoke from smoldering junk. Golden Styrofoam from Big Mac containers blew about as if Zeus had just raped Danae. Shoot the Hamburglar on sight.

The mountains opened, and Oak Ridge, a town the federal government hid away in the southern Appalachians during the Second World War for the purpose of carving a future out of pitchblende, lay below. Here, scientists working on the Manhattan Project had made plutonium. In the bookstore of the Museum of Atomic Energy were *The Complete Book of Heating With Wood* and *Build Your Own Low Cost Log Home*.

Again to the mountains and more spinning the steering wheel back and forth, more first gear, more mist that made everything wet and washed nothing clean. Narrow, shoulderless highway 61 looked as if a tar pot had overturned at the summit and trickled a crooked course down. A genuine white-knuckle road.

I should have stopped at Tazewell before the light went entirely, but no. It was as if the mountains had me. Across the Clinch River and into the Clinch Mountains; a YOUR HIGHWAY TAXES AT WORK sign loomed up and then one in heart-sinking, detour orange: CONSTRUCTION AHEAD. It should have said, ABANDON ALL HOPE YE WHO ENTER HERE. Figuring I was past the point of return, I pressed on. The pavement ended and the road became a crater-shot slough of gravel-impacted mud that shook the Ghost so terribly at ten miles an hour my foot repeatedly slipped off the accelerator. Other crossers, trying to find the roadbed, veered toward each other only to peel apart at the last minute in a blinding spray of red grit. Jaws tight, hands locked to wheei. Clench Mountain. Higher up, headlights pointed at me although we both were crossing west to east. At each bent-back curve, my lights shone off into clouds, which turned the route into a hellacious celestial highway. It was as if I'd died — one of those movies where somebody breathes his last but still thinks he's alive.

The crossing became a grim misadventure, and I wasn't prepared for it. I tried to think of other things. Helen Keller, who never drove the Clinch Mountains, said life is a daring adventure or it is nothing. Adventure — an advent. But no coming without a going. Death and rebirth. Antithetical notions lying next to each other, as on a globe the three-hundred-sixtieth degree does to the first. Past and future.

The road reached the summit, started dropping fast, then a blessed END CONSTRUCTION, the pavement reappeared, and the mist turned to rain that at last washed the windshield clean. Goodbye, mountain.

I came to a long sprawling of businesses in metal buildings: auto upholstery recovered, brakes relined, transmissions rebuilt, radiators reconditioned, mufflers replaced. Nothing for renewing a man. Across the Holston River, wide and black as the Styx, and into the besooted factory city of Morristown, where, they say, the smoke runs up to the sky. Sorely beset by the blue devils, I wandered looking a long time for a quiet corner to spend the night. Finally, I gave up and pulled in a bank parking lot. "They can run me out or in. To hell with it." With the curse, I went to bed.

18

I MIGHT as well admit that the next morning in smoky Morristown I was asking myself what in damnation I thought *he* was doing. One week on the road — a week of clouds, rain, cold. And now it was snowing. Thirty-four degrees inside the Ghost, ice covering the windshield, my left shoulder aching from the knot I'd slept in. "It is waking that kills us," Sir Thomas Browne said three centuries ago. Without desire, acting only on will, I emerged from the chrysalis of my sleeping bag and poured a basin of cold water. I thought to wash myself to life.

Outside, the spiritless people were clenched like cold fists. A pall of snow lay on the city, and black starlings huddled around the ashy chimney tops.

Clearing the windows, I wondered why I had ever come away to this place and began thinking about turning back. Could I?

I cranked the sluggish engine. Four lanes of easy interstate from Morristown to Missouri. One day. The engine fired, sputtered, and caught. I listened as I did every morning. Smooth but for the knocking waterpump. I moved out. A red light at U.S. 11 East. Home was a left turn, right was who knows. "A man becomes what he does," Madison Wheeler had said. I took who knows.

Snow plastered the highway markers, so I watched the compass and guessed. The road to Jonesboro via Whitesburg and Chuckey wound about hillocks of snowy trees and houses puffing chimney smoke. It was like riding through a Currier and Ives monochrome. Meadowlarks, fluffing full, crouching on fenceposts, held their song for the sun. A crooked sign: ICE COLD WATERMELON.

The highway once was a stage route of inns, but the buildings that had withstood the Civil War weren't surviving the economics of this century. East of Bulls Gap, surveyors' pennants snapped in the wind. Another blue road about to join the times. Taverns and creaky Gen. Mdse. stores (two gas pumps and a mongrel on the porch) were going for frontage-road minisupers. The rill running back and forth under the highway, of course, would have to be straightened to conform to the angles and gradients of the engineers.

Highway as analog: social engineers draw blueprints to straighten treacherous and inefficient switchbacks of men with old, curvy notions; taboo engineers lay out federally approved culverts to drain the overflow of passions; mind engineers bulldoze ups and downs to make men level-headed. Whitman: "O public road, you express me better than I can express myself."

19

THE fourteenth state in the Union, the first formed after the original thirteen, was Franklin and its capital Jonesboro. The state had a governor, legislature, courts, and militia. In 1784, after North Carolina ceded to the federal government its land in the west, thereby leaving the area without an administrative body, citizens held a constitutional convention to form a sovereign state. But history is a fickle thing, and now Jonesboro, two centuries old, is only the seat of Washington County, which also was once something else — the entire state of Tennessee. It's all for the best. Chattanooga, Franklin, just doesn't come off the tongue right.

Main Street in Jonesboro, solid with step-gabled antebellum buildings, ran into a dell to parallel a stream; houses and steeples rose from encircling hills. After breakfast, I walked snowy Main to the Chester Inn, a wooden building with an arched double gallery, where Andrew Jackson almost got tarred and feathered, for what I don't know. Charles Dickens spent the night here as did Andrew Johnson, James Polk, and Martin Van Buren (whose autobiography never mentions his wife).

At the inn, now the library, I read about ears in Jonesboro's history. A sheriff once branded a horsethief's cheeks with H and T before nailing him by the ears to a post; later, to set him free, he cut them off. Then there was pioneer Russell Bean, who returned from a two-year business trip to find his wife nursing an infant; to make known the identity of his true sons, he bit off the baby's ears.

On the way out of town, I saw a billboard advertising a bank: WHEN YOU'RE BETTER YOU GET BIGGER. Pleasant little Jonesboro, a size Martin Van Buren would recognize, gave the lie to that. Snow still fell, but the flakes seemed to be dropping one at a time. Route 321 was closed for construction; a fifty-mile detour followed the Little Doe River, a stream of clear water cascades, up through fields of hand-piled haycocks. Then the highway rose to cross Iron Mountain and brought me down in North Carolina. The hazy Blue Ridge Mountains lay at my back, the snow stopped, and I drove among gentle hills. A thousand miles into the journey.

Two

EAST BY SOUTHEAST

WHAT happened next came about because of an obese child eating a Hi-Ho cracker in the back of an overloaded stationwagon. She gave me a baleful stare. As I passed, the driver, an obese woman eating a Hi-Ho, gave me a baleful stare, Ah, genetics! Oh, blood!

Blood. It came to me that I had been generally retracing the migration of my white-blooded clan from North Carolina to Missouri, the clan of a Lancashireman who settled in the Piedmont in the eighteenth century. As a boy, again and again, I had looked at a blurred, sepia photograph of a leaning tombstone deep in the Carolina hills. I had vowed to find the old immigrant miller's grave one day.

Highway 421 became I-85 and whipped me around Winston-Salem and Greensboro. For a few miles I suffered the tyranny of the freeway and watched rear bumpers and truck mudflaps. As soon as I could, I took state 54 to Chapel Hill, a town of trees, where I hoped to come up with a lead on the miller in the university library. All I knew was this: William Trogdon (1715–1783) supplied sundry items to the Carolina militia for several years during the Revolutionary War; finally, Tories led by David Fanning found him watering his horse on Sandy Creek not far from his gristmill and shot him. His sons buried him where he fell. Fanning terrorized the Piedmont through a standard method of shooting any man, white or red, who aided the patriots; and he was known to burn a rebel's home, even with a wife and children inside. Faster than King George, Colonel Fanning turned Carolinians to the cause.

After I'd given up in the library, by pure chance as if an omen, in a bookshop I came across an 1856 map showing a settlement named Sandy Creek east of Asheboro. That night I calculated the odds of finding in the woods a grave nearly two hundred years old. They were lousy.

The next morning I headed back toward Asheboro, past the roads to Snow Camp and Silk Hope, over the Haw River, into pine and deciduous hills of red soil, into Randolph County, past crumbling stone milldams, through fields of winter wheat. Ramseur, a nineteenth-century cotton-mill village secluded in the valley of the Deep River, was the first town in the county I came to. I had to begin somewhere. Hoping for a second clue, I stopped at the library to ask about Sandy Creek. Another long shot. "Of course," the librarian said. "Sandy Creek's at Franklinville. Couple miles west. Flows into Deep River by the spinning mill. Town's just sort of hanging on now. You should talk to Madge in the dry goods across the street. She knows county history better than a turtle knows his shell."

Madge Kivett was out of town, but a clerk took me back across the street to the Water Commissioner, Kermit Pell, who owned the grocery and knew something of local history. In Pell's store you still weighed vegetable seed on a brass counterbalance with little knobbed weights; the butcher's block was so worn in the center you could pour a bucket of water over it and only a pint would run off.

Pell, a graying, abdominous man with Groucho Marx eyebrows, chewed gum and continually took off and put on his spectacles. Sitting in a dugout of ledgers and receipt books, he couldn't reach the phone so I had to hand it to him the six times it rang. Between rings, it took an hour to get this: the miller's isolated grave had been covered by a new hundred-twenty-seven-acre raw water reservoir (the town bought the grave twice when two men claimed ownership — buying was cheaper than court). The old tombstone, broken up by vandals digging in the grave to look for relics, had been moved to the museum; the commissioners transferred a few token spades of dirt and put up a bronze and concrete marker a few feet from the original gravesite. The Asheboro *Courier-Tribune*, in an article dated two years earlier to the day, told of the imperiled grave setting off a hurried archaeological survey to turn up both colonial history and artifacts from a thousand years of Indian camps. The site, the clipping said, "although known to historians, is deep in the wilds of the creek."

"I've got to see it," I said.

"It's a hell of a walk in. You better know what you're doing before you go into that woods. I mean, it's way back in there."

"Can you give me directions?"

"Only one person I know of could show you — if he would. Noel Jones over in Franklinville might lead you in. Lived along the creek all his life. He's getting on now, but you can ask for him at the mill."

2

THICK muddy water in the ancient millrace of Randolph Mills at Franklinville curled in slow menace like a fat water moccasin waiting for something to come to it. The mill ran on electricity now, and the race was a dead end — what went in didn't come out. Inside, spoked flywheels tall as men spun, rumbling the wavy wooden floors and plankways, but no one was around. It seemed a ghost mill turned by Deep River. I knocked on the crooked pine doors; I tapped on a clouded window and pressed close to see in. On the other side, an old misshapen face looked back and made me jump.

"Looking for Noel Jones!" I shouted.

The face vanished and reappeared at a doorway. It said, "Gone home. First street over," and disappeared again. I took the street, asked at a house, and found Jones at the end of the block.

"I know the place you're alookin' for," he said, "but I'm not up to goin' back in there just now. Got a molar agivin' me a deal of misery."

"I understand, but maybe you could describe the way."

He took off his cap and ran his hand over his head. "It's possible to walk in. Not so far you cain't. But directions gonna be hard. Sorry I cain't take you." He put his cap back on. "Tell you what. Get in my truck and I'll show you where to start. It'll keep my mind off this molar. One thing though, you got some work in front of you, son. And not aknowin' the way, well, that's a worry of its own."

In the warm afternoon, we followed a dirt road until it turned into a grassy trail so narrow the brush screeched against the windows. At a small clearing, he stopped. "This is my old family property," he said. "Just down the hill you can see Sandy Crick. The old mill of yours musta been right along there. Let me show you somethin' else."

We walked over to a cabin with only the back wall of logs still standing. Hanging to it was a warped kitchen cabinet lined with layers of newspaper. "July of 'thirty-six on this paper," Jones said. "Used to stick it up to keep wind out of the cracks. Pitiful. But look at the price of shoes."

He pulled a broken coffee cup from the cabinet, scowled, and put it back. "When I was a boy, an old fieldhand lived in this house. He was adyin' of pneumonia one night my daddy took me by, and I watched through the window. Man was out of his mind with fever, and he thrashed in bed. He thought he was aplowin' with his mule, John. 'Come on over, John! Pick it up there, John!' Whole night he and that mule plowed, we heard. Dead by mornin'. My daddy said he worked himself to death that night. Said if he coulda put the plow down, he mighta rested enough to live. Those days, it was hard livin' and no easier dyin'. Took thirteen months a year to grow 'bacca."

We went on through a hump of woods into another clearing where

5. Noel Jones near Franklinville, North Carolina

stood several small tobacco sheds with roofs falling in and an old smoke-house.

"These the old curin' barns where they dried the 'bacca. Haven't been used in years, but you can still smell the 'bacca inside." We walked over to one. "Look here. That hearth cover's a Model T hood the blacksmith's touched up with his hammer. Nobody ever heard of junk then. Junk's a modrun invention." We went in the low doorway. Poles that women once strung tobacco on were still in place under the roof.

Jones explained the curing: to "fix the color," leaves hung from cross poles for three days and nights as heat from the fire cured the burley. Skill in getting a good color could mean the difference between loss and profit. In his boyhood he had stayed up all night with the men tending the hearths. "They told stories the night long. Mostly true stories and mostly how troubles come in a thousand shapes."

We walked down the wooded hillside to Sandy Creek Reservoir. "Here musta been your granddaddy's mill. Before the dam, you could walk the length of the crick and hardly see the sun, trees grew so heavy. Animals too. Bobcats, foxes, weasels, deer, wood ducks. Good soil along the crick bottom. That's why Indians took to it. Had all they needed — water, meat, berries, protection."

"It's a big reservoir for such a little town."

"Got dry a few summers back — a real drouth — and the old town reservoir below where the dam is now almost run dry. Some people got scared. But I heard said too — couldn't tell you the truth of it — that there's some awantin' new industry in here. Mills don't produce like they did. Randolph Mills used to spin raw cotton into cloth. All we do today is finish cloth. Bleach, nap, and print patterns on cotton flannel mostly. We're printers now."

He sat on a rock and stared out over the flat, silent water to a bulldozed hill. "I'm not atakin' sides, I'm just atellin' you, but there's people who say there was plenty of water in that old reservoir. They say, 'Who needs a bigger reservoir?' "

"New industry means more people to buy clothes and open savings accounts."

"I mind my own business." He looked toward the dam. "Already a crack in the spillway. Cain't seem to get it fixed. I wouldn't say how long this crick'll stay drowned." He got up. "Good fishin' along Sandy. Wasn't lunkers in it, but it was cool in here and the water moved. Now you cain't put as much as a fishin' line from the bank in that lake legally. No swimmin', no nothin'. It's a watchin' lake because that's about all you can do with it."

We walked back up the slope into the woods. Halfway, Jones stopped and edged his shoe into a small depression. "Dried up now, but this used to be a spring where women came to boil their wash clothes in iron pots. One time a woman was here, they say, abeatin' a rug clean with a stick. Had her daughter along. The little girl disappeared, but the woman just figured she was aplayin' hide and seek. The mother was athumpin' her rug when it commenced aturnin' red. She got vexed with the child for hidin' raspberries in the rug. She opened it to wash away the stain and her little girl rolled out. Child was hid in the rug. Woman run off through the woods acryin', 'I bludgeoned my baby! I beat my baby dead!' Next night she come out here to a big oak and hung herself with a bedsheet. That sheet, they say, blowed in the trees until it rotted away. Terrified many a man acomin' through at night."

On the road back, Jones pointed out the trail to start with. "Grave's yonder, dead ahead, but the hills and water is in the way. Woods gets terrible heavy over that first rise, and if you follow the reservoir around, you'll be in water or mud most the way. The grave sits out on a little tip of land about seven feet above the water line."

"I'll try through the woods. Get that molar fixed."

"Gonna have to see a tooth dentist. Stop by tomorrow if you make it. Best you wait 'til mornin', or you'll be wipin' shadows all the way."

3

BUT I didn't wait until morning. The smell in the pines was sweet, the spring peepers sang, and the trail over the first hill was easy. Whippoorwills ceaselessly cut sharp calls against the early dark, and a screech owl shivered the night. Then the trail disappeared in wiry brush. I began imagining flared nostrils and eyed, coiled things. Trying to step over whatever lay waiting, I took longer strides. Suddenly the woods went silent as if something had muffled it. I kept thinking about turning back, but the sense that the grave was just over the next hill drew me in deeper. Springs trickled to the lake and turned bosky coves to mud and filled the air with a rank, pungent odor. I had to walk around the water, then around the mud — three hundred yards to cross a twenty-foot inlet. Something heavy and running from me mashed off through the brush.

When I was a boy, my mother would try to show the reality of danger by making up newspaper headlines that described the outcome of foolhardy activity. I could hear her: REMAINS OF LONE HIKER FOUND. She would give details from the story: ". . . only the canteen was not eaten."

Common sense said to turn back, but the old sense in the blood was stronger. I compromised: one more cove. It wasn't there. On the ridge above the last cove I went sprawling over something hard. Concrete. Had the grave been open, I'd have fallen into it.

A brass plate indicated that the original grave lay just beyond the shoreline. "Who knows the fate of his bones?" Sir Thomas Browne asked. Whatever was left of the old miller, whatever the red soil and grave robbers and town commissioners had missed, was now under ten feet of Sandy Creek. Even this far back in the fastness, the twentieth century had found him out. Now, the citizens drank from his grave.

I sat so long, the sky cleared and showed all of the moonrise. I tried to imagine the incident here, tried to see the seditious old miller as he lay bleeding to death on the white Piedmont flint, and I wondered whether he knew he was dying for something greater than himself.

The smooth, dark water reflected stars as brilliant points of light — a mirror couldn't have shown a crisper image. I went down to it and washed away the thicket and sweaty dust. In my splashing, I broke the starlight. And then I too drank from the grave.

4

I saw better under the moonlight, and the passage back seemed as long but not so hard. Big grunts from bullfrogs directed me along the shore until I came out of the dark trees to Ghost Dancing. I drove to a clearing by the dam. Ten-thirty. I hadn't eaten, and now I was too tired to do anything but crawl into the sleeping bag.

At the moment of sleep, I heard something, something moving in the near woods, then into the clearing toward the truck. A slow stepping. I couldn't remember whether I'd locked all the doors. But it wasn't the steps that bothered me; it was the slowness of them, the deliberate coming. It came on. Then it started to lurk.

I lay perfectly still, wondering whether I'd set the emergency brake and hoping Ford Motor Company hadn't skimped on a millimeter of steel wall. I had the sense that something was crouching outside, near my head. A soft brushing along the truck — a hand, a body — then an impacted silence. It moved again, and I tried to tell how many legs were stepping away.

There was a rational explanation for whatever it was, but I didn't have the nerve to find it. Instead, I started thinking about a hanged woman with a sheet around her neck who goes looking for her dead baby. I imagined a bleeding miller hunting the men who put a musket ball in him or the ones who drowned his grave.

There are two kinds of adventurers: those who go truly hoping to find adventure and those who go secretly hoping they won't. Midnight. I forced myself out of the ball I'd curled into, afraid as I did my toes would touch something that didn't belong inside. The bullfrogs, squatting in the cold water, went at it again. It sounded as though they were talking about the good old days of the swift, shallow creek. They said, "How deep?" "Knee deep." "How deep?" Again and again.

At three o'clock I sat bolt upright. I had no idea where I was, but I had just heard a yelp, and the walls of the Ghost pulsed blood red. I looked out the back window into a pair of ruby, oscillating eyes. Someone yelled. I clambered out barefoot, wearing only skivvies, and hobbled gingerly to the squadcar. "What's wrong?"

In a Carolina cadence, the deputy said, "Ain't no sleepin' up here."

"That's what I'm finding out."

A fleck of yellow paint from a pencil stub stuck to his lip and bobbed up and down as he talked. "We close the dam area at sundown."

"I'll be gone in the morning." He stared at me. "I guess I could get dressed and leave now." He said nothing. "Just drove in from Missouri, though, and this bad leg I got in the U.S. Navy starts acting up if I don't rest it. Hurt it fighting Communism."

"What's your name?"

I started to say Standing Bull. Some Indians believe that to give your name is to put yourself in a stranger's power. But because he already might have run a license check, I told the truth. He pronounced the first name as "Wim."

"Wim, I've logged your machine in. Maybe you're innocent, but just bein' near the dam makes you suspect if anything happens tonight."

"Happens? What do you mean happens?"

"Been trouble around the dam. Things rollin' into the reservoir, gas drums knocked over. Always happens after dark."

"I heard something about midnight — don't know what."

He looked a moment as if to assess. "Garrantee one thing, Wim. This boy wouldn't sleep up here mongst the whangdoodles withouten his peace of mind."

"Peace of mind?"

"Peace of mind." He tapped a thumb on the butt of his pistol. "Go ahead on and stay tonight. I'd sure secure those doors though."

Before I fell asleep again, I remembered the red men who walked backwards and brushed out their tracks so no dead soul could follow.

WHEN I opened the side door of my rig, it was there, all over the place —
in the trees, on the ground, over the water. Sunlight. In Chapel Hill I'd
seen a bumper sticker: IF GOD ISN'T A TARHEEL, WHY IS THE SKY CAROLINA
BLUE? From a tall elm, a mockingbird knocked out a manic of quodlibets.
I took towel and soap and went down to Sandy Creek below the dam and
knelt on a flat rock slanting into the water and washed. You never feel
better than when you start feeling good after you've been feeling bad. In
the truck I laid out a breakfast of bread, cheese, raisins, and tomato juice.

Then to the road. I bought supplies at Siler City, where the grocery sold
twenty-two kinds of chewing tobacco: Blood Hound, Brown's Mule, Red
Coon, Red Horse, Red Fox, Red Juice, Black Maria, Big Man, Cannonball,
Bull's Eye ("Hits the Spot"); also fifteen brands of snuff in three sizes, the
largest big enough to give the whole county a snort.

Highway 421 dropped out of the Piedmont hills onto the broad coastal
plain where the pines were taller, the soil tan rather than orange, and
black men rode tractors around and around square fields of tobacco and
cotton as they plowed wavelets into the earth. At the center of many fields
were small, fenced cemeteries under a big pine. All day farmers circled the
acres, the white tombstones an axis for their planters, while tree roots
reached into eye sockets and ribcages in the old boxes below.

Near Dunn, North Carolina, I pulled up at a cemetery to eat lunch in
the warm air. Last names on the markers were Smith and Barefoot and
Bumpass. All around, the buds, no more than tiny fists, were beginning
to break the tight bindings and unclench. A woman of age and size, her
white legs blue-veined like Italian marble columns, stooped to trowel a
circle of sprouts growing in the hollow center of a large oak dead from
heart rot.

I thought about "whangdoodles" in the night, about how they too were
gifts of the road in their rupture of order, their break of throttling security;
they were a challenge to step out and shake one's own skeleton at the
world.

Highway 13 took me across fields lying flat as a flounder, broken only
by broad squares of pine. Unpainted sharecropper cabins were slipping off
their blocks, and, although brick veneer bungalows had replaced some, to
the side of even the new houses collard patches remained. Tar-papered
and asphalt-shingled curing barns, each with a propane tank to give heat
for drying tobacco, were all about the fields, and bleached signs on barns
near the road advertised flour or fertilizer or a long-dead cotton buyer.

Acre after acre. Only the pines kept bright-leaf tobacco fields from sweeping like waves all the way to the coast.

Along the highway, generations of feet had worn narrow depressions in the shoulders. Walking the paths were women and children, everyone carrying something: a woman a child, a child a bag of sugar. An old black man in suitcoat and overalls, his spine straight, pedaled a rattle of a bicycle, a bunch of bananas in the handlebar basket. The walkers paused to talk with men who bent like wickets to the hacking of briars out of the culverts. I heard voices and laughter, and sometimes people waved. Whitman saw it:

> *You paths worn in the irregular hollows by the roadsides!*
> *I believe you are latent with unseen existences . . .*
> *From the living and dead you have peopled your impassive surfaces,*
> *and the spirits thereof would be evident and amicable with me.*

At Greenville, I stopped for the night on the campus of East Carolina University. Out of the west, with suddenness, a nimbo-stratus cloudbank like a precipice obscured the sun, and a ferocious wind pulled the fine sandy soil into a corrosive blast. Then the wind ceased, raindrops pelted the sand back into place, the temperature dropped from eighty degrees to sixty-five, the clouds blew on toward the sea, and the low sun shone again. The whole demonstration lasted twenty minutes.

That evening I bought a hot shower in a dormitory. It cost a dollar contribution and a thirty-minute I FOUND IT bumper-sticker talk intended to drive the infidel from my red heart and bring me safely unto the Great White Bosom. Take the land, take the old ways, Christian soldiers, but please, goddamnit, leave me my soul.

6

I SLEPT deeply until a terrible clanking against the back of the truck. I woke witless as stone. The Ghost filled with hot, yellow light that seemed to spin my head. Another clank and a violent jolting and shaking. I raised the rear curtain. A shrunken, sallow face just inches away stared at the rattling chains of a tow truck. I jumped out — again — shoeless and pantless, the Carolina sand cool between my toes. "Don't tow it!"

Behind me, a man in corporal's stripes said, "You sleepin' in there?"

I felt as if I'd been caught in the women's dorm. The simple truth seemed inadequate. "Just resting some."

"Didn't know you were inside. I'll get the citation off the windshield."

"What about my rig? Could you see your way to putting it down?"

"If you'll get a visitor's permit tomorrow. Unhitch him, Ronnie."

"Hooked up," the shrunken face said. .

"I see he's hooked up. Unhook him. You can hook the Chevalet."

Ronnie cursed Ghost Dancing back onto the sand. The corporal said, "Sorry we wokened you up. We're about through bumper bangin'."

"Thanks." I hope he makes general. Again in bed, I wondered whether police would beset me across America. Give me the quiet lurk of whang-doodles any night.

7

OUT of Greenville, on route 32 just northeast of the road to Pinetown, gulls dropped in behind the Farmalls and poked over the upturned soil for bugs, and the east wind carried in the smell of the sea. People here call the dark earth "the blacklands." Scraping, scalping, bulldozers were clearing fields for tobacco and pushing the pines into big tumuli; as the trees burned, the seawind blew smoke from the balefires down along the highway like groundfog. Trees burned so tobacco could grow so tobacco could burn. But where great conifers still stood, they cast three-hundred-foot shadows through the morning, and the cool air smelled of balsam.

In Plymouth I saw a sign at a gas station: DIESEL FUEL AND OYSTERS IN SEASON. A man, his eyes a camouflage of green and brown speckles, white hair to the wind, filled the tank and said, "How's this weather for ye?"

"Fine today. But it's been rough."

"Hard weather makes good timber. How's that Missouri weather?"

"Hard."

"Yessir," one word, "that's why your Harry Truman was good timber. Toughern oak. No trees out your way is there?"

"Lots of trees. Especially oaks. Red, white, bur, blackjack."

"Flat though, ain't it?"

"Lots of hills. *This* is flat land."

"Whistle me Dixie! This county don't get up in the air no higher than a boy can throw a mud turtle. But it's God's Country. And a good town. Woulda been a better town but the Yankees shot it all to hell. Union gunboats got it, sir. Hard to believe now gunboats out in the Roanoke. Fierce river fightin'. They had to make coffins out of pews from Grace Church. Buried men in their own pew. That's no joke to us."

As he wrote up the credit slip, I said, "Looks like they're taking out timberlands for tobacco fields."

"Govnor comes out and shoots you personally if you say against tobacco in this state. I smoked thirty-odd years. Did my duty and got a right to talk. Truth is you cain't buy a real, true cigarette anymores. That's why they name them that way — tryin' to convince you what ain't there. Real. True. Nothin' to it. They cut them long, they cut them skinny, they paint them red and green and stuff them with menthol and camphor and eucalyptus. What the hell, they's makin' toys. I'll lay you one of them bright-leaf boys up in Winston-Salem is drawin' up a cigarette you gotta plug in the wall. Nosir, your timber's comin' down to make toys."

"You don't smoke now?"

"Why smoke what's no taste to it? Same as them light beers and whiskies: no flavor. Americans have just got afraid to taste anything. You ask me, sir, it started with oleo. Or maybe the popalation got scared by them mouse spearmints wheres they give a mouse a needle-shot of a substance ever day until he dies a cancer. Nosir, my advice is to live your life."

"That's solid advice."

"And harder to do than you think. Take me. I retired and ended up settin' and worryin' about myself, about my health. Then I bought this station to get away from myself. My own worst enemy. Don't need the money comes in — it's the people comin' in I need. But I been remarkin' recently, people don't listen liken they used to."

"I've noticed that." I was down the road when I realized his tumble of notions had distracted me from the oysters. There would be more.

The face of the tidewater peninsula lying between Albemarle Sound and the Pamlico River showed clear now: cypress trees cooling their giant butts in clean swamp water black from the tannin in their roots, the road running straight and level and bounded on each side by watery "borrow ditches" that furnished soil to build the roadway. Ditches, road, trees — all at right angles. The swamp growth was too thick to paddle a greased canoe through, and, although leafless, the dense limbs left the swamp without sun.

Then, precipitately, the vegetable walls stopped, and the wide Alligator River estuary opened to sky and wind. Whitecaps broke out of the strange burgundy water. As I drove the long bridge over the inlet, a herring gull, a glare of feathers, put a wingtip a few feet to the left of Ghost Dancing, and, wings steady, accompanied me across.

Dare County, named after the first white child (says tradition) born in America, is a curious county with four times as much water as land and only two highways and four towns — a pair on the mainland and a pair on Roanoke Island. Most of mainland Dare is a spongy place, a bog that until recently discouraged developers. But now, about the county, men with caliper hands and parallelogram brains were taking the measure of the salt marsh and trying to "reclaim" it — a misleading word since this tidewater has always belonged to the sea.

A second long bridge crossed Croatan Sound to Roanoke Island, a low rise a little larger than Manhattan and lying just inside one of the most unusual geographic features in the country: the Outer Banks. A skinny chain of sand, the Banks stretch for nearly two hundred miles along the North Carolina coast. On Roanoke Island, there is no enduring symbol for the first "permanent" English settlement in America like the rock at Plymouth, Massachusetts. In place of a symbol, Roanoke has mystery. Here Virginia Dare was born only to vanish from history without a trace nine days later. The woods, a thick mat of shrubs and trees, looked in places as it must have when the Dares, members of Raleigh's third Roanoke expedition, came ashore. It may be that the absence of such a ready symbol as Plymouth Rock has helped keep Roanoke from the destruction of this time.

The highway wound into the dark trees again as it traversed the very place where the English colonies disappeared, the last group leaving behind America's most famous mystery word — *Croatoan* — carved in a stockade timber. Roanoke Island gave a shadowy sense of an older time that Plymouth Rock, surrounded, dwarfed, and protected in stone and steel, has lost. A man told me, "Out on Roanoke, you can *feel* the beginning."

8

At the bottom of Queen Elizabeth Avenue, the main street of Manteo, North Carolina, where it comes down to the sound, stood a Brobdingnagian statue, ten feet of a single cypress trunk cut into a sixteenth-century English courtier. A woodpecker, with uncanny accuracy, had drilled a hole in Sir Walter Raleigh's pantalooned posterior, and now there were predictable jokes in Manteo about the hole and Sir Walter's woodpecker.

Manteo is the seat of Dare County and one of the few courthouse towns, as the Carolinians call them, on an island in the Atlantic Ocean. Not so remote as Key West, or so big as Newport, Rhode Island, or so famous as Nantucket, or so elitist as Edgartown on Martha's Vineyard, Manteo was a pleasant place: smaller, humbler, quieter. The docks once lining the harbor had dwindled to three, and the seashell-paved streets were now macadam like everywhere else. The red-brick, turn-of-the-century courthouse opened to the waterfront where formerly a fleet of mail, freight, passenger, and fishing boats tied up. Now the sport-fishing craft in red, blue, and yellow, each sprouting long whip antennas that gave them the look of water bugs, rocked in the little marina. Even still, Manteo looked as if it belonged with its face in the Atlantic winds.

At Raleigh's immense wooden boots, a man worked quickly in the bright, cold wind as he brushed preservative over the base of the statue. He was one of the town commissioners working to refurbish the old wharfside of Manteo. Between two big oil tanks abandoned by the owners, the town had built a park reaching into the basin off Roanoke Sound.

He spoke with the old London accent of the Banks that some people believe to be the speech of the Elizabethans. "We may be able to use one of the tanks in our new sewage system," he said. "If not, down they'll come. This statue is the focal point for rehabilitating Queen Elizabeth Street. New bridges did in most of the work boats, but it's the bridges that bring out tourists now. We've got six million dollars of federal funds coming here over the next two years. When we finish, you won't recognize Manteo."

Across the sound at Nag's Head, a new highrise broke the flat horizon of the Banks where once only small, low buildings stood. "I hope you're not going to put highrises here too," I said.

"That's a Ramada Inn."

"Overwhelms everything out there — no harmony at all between it and the land. Architecture without regard for place or history. They've been Jersey Shored, if you ask me."

"The sea never forgets where it's been, and it's been over that land many times. We haven't had a major hurricane in nearly twenty years, whereas we used to have a hard blow every few years. New people don't know that. They come in and see open beach and figure they've found open land. But the Banks aren't ordinary islands, and that's why they've been left alone. People didn't used to build much they couldn't afford to see washed away, because sooner or later most things out there get washed away. I know — I've lived there. It's always been a rough place. Land pirates, sea pirates. Blackbeard was killed down at Ocracoke where my family comes from. One of my ancestors was on the Arabian ship that wrecked and spilled the Banks ponies that used to run wild."

"They don't now?"

"Fenced in by the Park Service. They overpopulated and started cropping beach grass so close as to kill it. Pawed holes in the sand to get fresh water and caused erosion — the number-one problem on the Banks. People get up in arms about the fencing, but the ponies aren't natural to the island. Of course, grass isn't either. Or men. Indians used to hunt the Banks, but I don't think they lived there. They're barrier islands. Some of that land's moving south as much as twenty feet a year. It's a natural process, the way the sea washes sand over the islands from the coast side and drops it on the sound side. But the Corps of Engineers and Park Service have built jetties and grassed dunes so sand doesn't get washed over now. They've tried to stop a natural process, and so you get erosion on the east and no build-up on the west."

"That's the Corps: redesigning and stabilizing nature."

"Today we've got bridges over land and roads ending up in the water. Been millions of dollars spent trying to pin down the Banks. You talk about the Ramada. A motel at Wrightsville Beach is built where an inlet used to be. They have to pump sand back in to keep the building standing. An architect has to understand our natural balance of the change that keeps things — in the long run — almost unchanged. It's not stability, it's balance. Living on the Banks, you learn the difference real quick."

"Sounds like somebody wants to keep something not his to keep."

"Ninety percent of the U.S. coast is privately owned. It isn't easy to give up your land — even to the ocean."

9

BUCK's (Open 24 Hours) Fish House in Manteo sat on pilings, its backside in the water. It smelled right: like fish. On mounds of ice lay crab slough oysters (fresh-shucked or in the shell), jimmy crabs, littleneck clams, chowder clams, croaker, mullet, flounder, bluefish.

I got hungry and went to the Duchess of Dare restaurant on Budleigh Street, a street trying to look like sixteenth-century London. The town commissioner had said the place served a good plate of seafood. The Duch-

ess was a tired, motherly woman in mid-life who had been in her Olde
English Swiss chalet cooking, washing, cleaning, and figuring the books
since five-thirty that morning. The ocean wind rattled the windows, and
beside me at the counter the Duchess sat drinking coffee from a heavy
mug.

"They call me Duchess now, but thirty years ago I was Doris Walker of
Walker's thirteen-stool diner. Made out of a surplus Navy bus. Thirteen's
my lucky number. Later, I added a wing and seated forty-five. Then remodeled again to get eighty-five in. It's successful because I worked all the
time."

Against one paneled wall, a preternaturally blue swordfish leapt over a
Formica table. The Duchess had tried to get rid of the diner image in the
successive remodelings and through decorator touches like the Mexican
wrought-iron chandeliers. But the lunchwagon still showed in places: above
the wine rack little boxes of Special K and All-Bran, near the oil paintings
of Moorish Spain the booster club gumball machine.

"The diner," I said, "the real diner of olden times, is dying out, you
know. Thirteen-seat surplus Navy bus diners are rare."

"They're rare because you can't make a living wage off one today." She
nodded toward the big circular table under the front window. "See
that?"

Around the ledge above the table were men's caps: an orange hard hat,
navy-blue watch cap, soiled yachting cap, a Forest Service hat. Like an
all-night poker game, the composition of the table changed one at a
time.

"Those are friends and customers. I need them and they need my place,
but it's hard to make a living off coffee. When I first opened, I was happy
to sell a dozen cups a day. That won't make it now. Manteo lost most of
the work boats. Today, tourists and county government keeps us alive.
Tourists don't want a Navy bus — they want your 'olden' days with all
the conveniences. Me, I need volume in season to survive. If you want
the real yesterday, go to Wanchese. They haven't seen neon light down
there yet."

The Duchess went back to the kitchen, and the waitress set out my
platter of fried fresh fish, grilled potatoes, and slaw. Basic food, tasty without expertise, prepared by the Duchess and her daughter personally.

Maybe she was right that tourists want half-timbered facades and stained-
plastic windows; maybe they want an Elizabethan town even when the
real Manteo had been clapboard and shingles. Progress, retrogression —
the Duchess knew best. But for me, I headed toward the town that hadn't
seen neon light.

In 1584, Philip Amadas and Arthur Barlowe, the leaders of Raleigh's first colonial exploratory expedition, returned to London from Roanoke with tobacco, potatoes, and a pair of "lustie" Indians to be trained as interpreters. Their names were Manteo and Wanchese. The Virgin Queen and the courtiers in their lace ruffs were fascinated by the red men. Months later when the Indians returned to the sound, Manteo, the first man baptized by the British in America, was on his way to becoming a proper English gentleman. But Wanchese, after seeing London, came back an enemy of "civilized" society. Four hundred years later, the towns carrying their names, sitting at almost opposite ends of the island, still show that separation.

Wanchese, smelling of fish and the sea wind, was on the lower tip of Roanoke. For generations the trawlers had passed through Oregon Inlet of the Banks to tie up at the little stilt piers of Wanchese. They still did, although the fleet worked out of here only in winter. The boats, maybe a hundred and fifty strong, came from the north — Massachusetts and Rhode Island, New York and New Jersey — to work the milder waters, where they trawled for flounder and dragged the mud for hibernating hardshell crabs. In spring, they followed the fish north, and the summer party-boats and a few yachts motored in.

The town had a craft shop now, but mostly it was splintered pilings and warped gangways and fish barrels. The small houses, built by seamen used to working in limited quarters, were made even smaller by the expanse of marsh weed and scrub loblolly stretching away to the sound. Rusting boilers and winches and broken hulls bobbed up like buoys from the waving grass; on lawns, under the crimson violence of camellias, fishermen had set admiralty anchors rusted to fragility or props painted red, white, and blue. From any home the boatmen could look to the wharf and see the white wheelhouses trimmed only in black, and the booms with lines and nets dripping like kelp.

The sun was just gone, the time Carolinians call "day down." I walked the wharf and read names of the trawlers: *Country Cousin, Brother's Pride, Blue Chip.* I came to a wooden shed with two windows gleaming like cat eyes in the night. A sign above the door: JAMES GRIGGS WHOLESALE. As I passed, a low, dusky whisper slipped from the side of the building, and a shadowy arm hooked me. "Hey, sport. You be here to help load?" It was a small, compact black man without age. He fixed me with his left eye while the milky right one shone like a moonstone.

Then a rasp from the shed: "Bring him in, Balford, and let's git the hell movin'." Balford motioned for me to follow inside. He stood behind me in the doorway and said, "Here, Griggs."

The room, a glowing of yellow bug lights and redolent with fish and diesel fuel, was stacked with crates of hardshell crabs. The crabs clacked their bony claws and reached through the slats at my eyes. Griggs, a white man, took a good pull on a can of beer. "Our third man ain't comin'. Kin you work? For money." Why not, I thought. I told him I could. "You a strong boy?"

"Lift my own weight with two men helping."

"How much you weigh, topper?"

"About one-thirty-five."

"Fancy that. These here crates weighs one thirty-five. Some's a tot heavier."

So we started. The truth was they all were a tot heavier. Balford and I slid crates to the scales, I weighed them, Balford in a slow and uncertain hand wrote down the number, and we hoisted them to Griggs on the truck.

There were more crabs than crates, and the critters kept hopping out of the overfilled boxes like popcorn in a hot skillet. The floor crawled with their oblique scuttles for the nearest dark underside. They scrabbled and clacked, and we crunched them into an agony of yellow ooze as we heaved on the crates. I started shuffling to avoid stepping on them. Balford got mad. "Pull on that drawhook, sport. They's crabs, not custard pies." A jimmy reached up and clamped onto my pant leg and slid back and forth across the floor with me until we finished. I had to break its claw to free my cuff.

The pickup, loaded beyond the legal maximum, listed to port. I asked Griggs how far he had to take them. "Over to Belhaven, couple hours away." He gave Balford and me a beer, relieved himself against the shed, and fished up his wallet. His fingers fumbled among the bills and drew out a five. He said, "There you be."

From the darkness, a man with legs like masts and arms like spars and great blue-ebony lips walked up. Griggs called him Big Man. Never had I heard speech like his. "We bean oat since yahstudy. Got mebbee leven hunred pounds o' blues."

He had missed his regular truck and wanted Griggs to take his crabs. Griggs pointed to the crates stacked high on the pickup. "Be money for me could I haul them, but surely I cain't."

Big Man said he would have to take his blues out in the sound and dump them. "It gone hurt me someten good."

Griggs was sorry. "See if the fish house can put them on ice." He gave Big Man a beer. The diesel engines of Big Man's trawler mumbled at the wharf, and Griggs' crabs clacked and chattered in the crates, and the men looked for a solution. Then Big Man went off to the fish house, Griggs and Balford to Belhaven, and I walked to my truck.

Later that night, just before I fell asleep, I heard Big Man's boat pull out, and I knew he was heading for open water to dump a half ton of blue crabs. He had said, "Most, day nebba make it to da bottom what da big fish eatem." For me, it had been one fine day.

11

I ENCOUNTERED Thomas Harriot, who died in 1621, the next morning because I had on the red suspenders I wear on the road. I was finishing breakfast at the edge of Wanchese harbor, my legs dangling over the pier as I watched the fishermen, rubbing sleep from their eyes and squinting into the sun, move about the docks.

A man sat down beside me, nodded, and unfolded a pair of glasses; on the temple was an embossed plastic label: NEAR. He removed the pair he wore, FAR, and put on NEAR. A person shows himself in the way he opens an orange. Some tear jaggedly with fingers, some slice with a thumbnail, some spiral latitudinally, while others go at the longitude. That man pulled out a pocketknife and precisely quartered the skin stem to navel so the fruit came out in sections. When he finished cutting, the peel, still attached at the base, lay on the pier like an open blossom.

He was not a young man. "I used to wear braces," he said. "We all did. I'm afraid I can't remember why I put them away. And that's odd because old men traditionally wear them. They are of surprising comfort. Would that be your reason for wearing them?"

"Part of it. When I'm traveling, I wear clothes in layers to be ready for a range of temperatures. Jacket, khaki shirt, turtleneck, and T-shirt. I have to buy pants a size bigger to get everything tucked in."

"So you peel like our friend the onion?"

"Or put on. Comfortable from about ninety degrees to thirty."

"And every ounce is cotton?"

"One hundred percent."

"You might guess that North Carolinians, with our heritage, are not fond of plastic fiber clothing. We believe pure cotton is the most civilized of fabrics. We and the ancient Egyptians. At least we used to before we made tobacco the crop of our hands. Now, what about the military shirt?"

"Army issue. It's a heavy twill. Doesn't wrinkle much."

He opened to a smile. "Would you say this garb suits you?"

I laughed with him. He said, "I read not long ago — I mention this because of the license on your panel truck — that there's a Missouri bank named after Jesse James. Now, is there any truth in that?"

"It's near where James lived."

"Well, then, may I say it might be the only honestly named bank in the country?" We laughed again. "I'm not apologetic about my lack of respect for bankers — and I'm not speaking of those out there." He pointed toward Bodie Island Light on the Outer Banks. "You wouldn't recall the tenant farmer system that developed after the War Between the States, but it was bankers — and I speak of men, not institutions — that worked hand in glove with landowners — sometimes they were one and the same — to keep so many Carolinians propertyless. Living in rural America without land is to be without strength." He paused for a slice of orange. "May I suggest how it was that Jimmy Carter rose from what some have called 'nowhere' to the Presidency?"

"You may."

"Because he showed us he came from the land. To an American, land is solidity, goodness, and hope. American history is about land."

I kept my silence, and he finished the orange and with precision wiped his fingers with a tissue. "Now I remember the sharecropper families. My father was a county agent. The sharecropper system descended from the plantation system but left behind the protective responsibility of the head of house for his workers. Farmers — black and white — became economic helots. The tenant system is indeed gone, but corporate farming comes on apace and systems and machinery will dispossess men one step further. The hired hand will never see the boss's face — unless he goes to Hartford and reads the corporate bylaws."

He put the orange peel in his pocket. "Must hurry. When you get as slow as I have, you spend a lot of time hurrying. I'm late for breakfast, and my daughter expects me. She doesn't like me down on the water alone. I have no worry. Dried-out old men float like sticks. I consent to a partial cooperation for her. These are the days when parents accommodate children."

He switched to FAR and rose carefully. "At times, I find I miss my nimbleness." He straightened his coat. "Two things — remember the land and visit Fort Raleigh. Thomas Harriot is the greatest unknown Elizabethan."

FORT Raleigh — the second group of settlers optimistically named it "the Cittie of Ralegh" — is both more and less than it once was. The sixteenth-century thatched huts, outbuildings, and palisades are gone, but an amphitheater, adminstration building, museum, parking lot, and "Elizabethan garden" have come. And more trees surround the fort than four centuries ago. Win some, lose some. At the beginning of this century, the raised earthworks of the bastioned fort had washed back into the moat, leaving only humpy ground covered with live oak and yaupon holly. Restoration work began in 1950, and now the outline of the fort is clear.

Because of its setting in deep woods, its age, its Croatoan mystery, and because it is the lone remnant of the first English attempt at settlement in America, Fort Raleigh is fascinating. But it is also a monument to the disease of an old world, gone tired and corrupt, trying to exploit a newer land. The whole ugly European process is here in capsule history: England, wanting to emulate Spain's financial success in pillaging the New World (but learning nothing from Spanish mistakes in dealing with Indians) and at the same time trying to circumscribe the expansion of colonial Spain out of Florida, sent a group of men, most nothing more than gentlemen pirates called "privateers," to establish a colony and enrich England with marketable commodities.

Many of the adventurers came infected with the European attitude toward America, expressed by a man no less than John Donne, who referred to Virginia, which then included North Carolina, as "a spleen to drain ill humours of the body." The privateers did not come to build a new society, for Raleigh was no utopian like Thomas More or Roger Williams; rather he was merely an intelligent man who envisioned a continuation of Elizabethan mercantile society. They came as Raleigh, the leading sponsor of the Roanoke expeditions, himself said, "to seek new worlds for gold, for praise, for glory." And John Smith, who built on Raleigh's failures, wrote in his *General History of Virginia,* that there was "no talk, no hope, nor work, but dig gold, wash gold, refine gold." There was, of course, no gold anywhere about.

Although Edmund Spenser called Sir Walter the "Shepherd of the Ocean," much of Raleigh's motivation for colonizing Roanoke Island came from the basest of motives, and the Cittie deserved its fate. The second expedition, the one of 1585 that returned Wanchese and Manteo, was led by Raleigh's cousin, Sir Richard Grenville. Surely there were Englishmen less suited to found a colony than Grenville, but it's hard to name them. As a seaman, he was hell on the high sea; as a colonist, he was a pirate. He manifested an outlook toward the Indians, a people whose help the new colony desperately needed, that the New World hasn't yet gone entirely beyond. Never mind that Arthur Barlowe earlier reported to Raleigh that the Indians were a "very handsome and goodly people, and in their behaviour as mannerly and civil as any of Europe." Never mind that Granganimeo, brother of Chief Wingina, greeted the English by making "signs of joy and welcome, striking his head and his breast and afterwards on ours to show we were all one, smiling, and making show the best he could of all love and familiarity." Never mind that the natives greeted whites "with all love and kindness and with as much bounty, after their manner, they could possibly devise." Columbus, too, had carried back reports about Indian gentleness — it helped him take sixteen hundred Indian slaves to Spain on the second voyage.

In spite of the propitious Anglo-Indian relations of Raleigh's first expedition, Grenville still saw Indians as savages and ignored their kindnesses. The Manitowocs planted crops and made fish traps for the colonists and Indian women washed English stockings; but when a native stole a silver cup, Grenville's men burned a village and "spoiled" the Indians' corn — corn the free-booting white men would need that winter. Unwilling to tend fields or catch their own fish, they began stealing from the natives. During the skirmishes that ensued for the next months, Grenville's men were not satisfied with shooting the red people — they beheaded in the old European manner. Commander Ralph Lane even launched one attack with the watchword, "Christ Our Victory!" On and on. Whitman says:

While how little the New after all, how much the Old, Old World!

For these reasons, Thomas Harriot, who accompanied Grenville, is all the more remarkable. Harriot, the expedition scientist, wrote an absorbing botanical, zoological, and anthropological account of the Pamlico-Albemarle region called *A Brief and True Report of the New Found Land of Virginia.* His book, containing the striking watercolors of his shipmate and Virginia Dare's grandfather, John White, is the most important historical record of precolonial, coastal America.

Ahead of his time, Harriot saw the Manitowocs as admirable people who lacked advanced civilization but not intelligence or decency. They were to him cheerful human beings "void of all covetousness . . . a people free from all care of heaping up riches for their posterity, content with their state." Of the Manitowocs, who had no interest or need to discover a new world, he wrote:

... considering the want of such means as we have, they seem very ingenious; for although they have no such tools, nor any such crafts, sciences
and arts as we, yet in those things they do, they show an excellency of
wit. ... Whereby it may be hoped if means of good government be used,
they may in short time be brought to civility, and the embracing of true
religion.

His idea was to enter into an exchange: Indian knowledge of the new land
and its produce for European technology and "true" religion.

Harriot's work would help the Jamestown colony succeed a generation
later. Nonetheless, the failure of the new people to give comparable respect
to the Indians — not just on Roanoke, but over the whole continent for
four centuries — would, more than any other cause, open a gulf between
red men and white, a division not yet closed.

13

BECAUSE of Pamlico Sound, the largest island-enclosed salt sea on the
Atlantic coast, North Carolina has more water surface than all but two
other contiguous states. Sizes are deceptive here: from Cape Hatteras in
the Atlantic west to Hot House, North Carolina, in the Appalachians is five
hundred miles.

Along highway 264, skirting the sound, grew stands of loblolly and slash
pine, as well as water oaks, bayberry, and laurel. Away from the open
waters, the day was warm, and in pocosins drained by small canals and
natural sloughs, mud turtles, their black shells the color of the water,
crawled up to the warmth on half-submerged logs.

The road passed through the fishing town of Engelhard, then down
along Lake Mattamuskeet (drained in the thirties for farming but once
again full of water and wildlife), to Swanquarter, around Hell Swamp to
Bath. It was in Bath, the oldest town in North Carolina, that Edna Ferber
went on board the James Adams Floating Palace Theater in 1925 to see a
showboat performance — the only one she ever saw.

I didn't want to drive the route I'd come the day before, so I headed
toward the free ferry across the Pamlico River above where it enters the
sound. Two hours later, the ferry, with a loud reversing of props, banged
into the slip; three of us drove aboard, and we left in an uproar of engines,
water, diesel exhaust, and birds. Laughing gulls materialized from the air

to hang above the prop wash and shriek their maniacal laugh (Whitman thought it nearly human) as they dropped like stones from twenty feet into the cold salt scuds; some entered beak first, some with wings akilter, but all followed the first to see an edible morsel, real or imagined. A boy wearing an Atlanta Braves ballcap askew on his head got so excited by this excellent show, he almost tumbled in. I had to pull him back twice.

The other side of the river was warmer, the land high and flattened field after field. New Bern, on the Neuse River, was well-preserved antebellum Georgian houses. The military devastation — the repeated exchange of a town by Union and Confederate troops as the course of the war shifted — that did in so many other Southern cities did not happen to New Bern. Federal forces occupied the town early in the war and held it until the surrender. Later, as railroads developed in North Carolina, New Bern lost its importance as a port city, and "progress" came slower, the old ways remained longer. Most of all, the people retained an interest in the continuity of their past, and they made the new blend with the old. As a result, New Bern is an architecturally interesting city where the Old South still shows on the streets rather than in a museum.

It was afternoon. Maybe I should have stayed in New Bern, but I violated a rule of the road and drove south just because I felt I should move on. The map showed more towns: Comfort, Beulaville, Chinquapin. Either I failed to find the towns or they were clusters of shut-up buildings. I drove on through rising fields, many given to strawberries. No longer was I in the coastal South but coming now into the so-called Deep South. The sun, glaring, began to set, and I couldn't find a place to suit me.

Finally, at Wallace, I gave up. I had two towns to choose from: a long, bright stretch of hurry-up food and one-stop convenience stores on U.S. 117, or the old town of brick and stone buildings closed for the night. I parked along the railroad tracks, across from the vacant depot. I'd been looking forward to a conversation in a cafe or tavern, but the cafes weren't open and there were no taverns. It was the first of several Southern evenings when I couldn't quench a thirst with anything but a sugar drink or sit for conversation at any place other than the softserve stand.

In a parking lot, six boys squatted about a Harley-Davidson and talked as they passed a can of beer. But for the outward trappings, they might have been Bedouins around the evening campfire. I asked one wearing a BORN TO RAISE HELL T-shirt what there was to do on Friday night. "Here?" Everybody laughed. "You got yourself a choice. You can watch the electric buglight at DQ. That's one. Or you can hustle up a sixpack and cruise the strip. That's two. And three is your left hand, a boy's best friend."

"Maybe there's a tent revival or something like that."

"Hey! How do you revive the dead?"

I went back to my little bus, washed the strawberry fields off me, ate a sandwich of something, opened a can of beer I'd brought from the last wet county, and looked through the windshield. Cars and trucks drove by. Some were noisy. Some were not. Sometimes a beercan flew out a car window. Once somebody shouted from a pickup. A dog peed on a mailbox.

I wished for a corner tavern with neon and a wooden bar, but I would have settled for a concrete block beerjoint. I grumbled at a hypocrisy that encouraged people to drink in the back ends of pickups. I wanted to go into the churches and hard cuss the congregations as if they were gourd seeds.

14

HAD Stephen Foster not changed his mind, the Pee Dee River would be much better known today than it is. The first version of his famous song about Southern homesickness began, "Way down upon the Pee Dee River, far, far away." In a morning of wrong moves, I crossed the Pee Dee and almost missed seeing it.

Since daylight I'd been hunting a good three- or four-calendar cafe. Nothing in Tomahawk or White Lake. Elizabethtown, no. I crossed the Cape Fear River, looked in Lumberton, and found nothing right. Then I overshot a turn and got pulled onto I-95. Truck diesel spouts blowing black, the throttle-guts slammed past me as if I were powered by caged gerbils; campers hauling speedboats rushed into Saturday, and so did stationwagons with windows piled full of beachballs, cardboard boxes, and babies.

I escaped the damnation at the Dillon exit and found South Carolina 34, a smooth road built up high out of the low wetlands. The country lay quiet again except for the wind slipping over the roof and mixing with birdsong. The people of the Pee Dee valley waved from their aluminum chairs in the back ends of pickups, and I smelled cattle rather than carbon monoxide. Driving once more instead of being driven. But I was still hungry.

Then Darlington, a town of portico and pediment, iron fences, big trees, and an old courthouse square that looked as though renovated by a German buzz bomb. But on the west side of the square stood the Deluxe Cafe. The times had left it be. The front window said AIR CONDITIONED in icy letters, above the door was neon, and inside hung an insurance agency calendar and another for an auto parts store. Also on the walls were the Gettysburg Address, Declaration of Independence, Pledge of Allegiance, a picture of a winged Jesus ushering along two kids who belonged in a Little Rascals film, and the obligatory waterfall lithograph. The clincher: small, white, hexagonal floor tiles. Two old men, carrying their arms folded behind, stopped to greet each other with a light, feminine touching of fingertips, a gesture showing the duration of their friendship. I went in happy.

I expected a grandmother, wiping her hands on a gingham apron, to come from the kitchen. Instead I got Brenda. Young, sullen, pink uniform, bottlecaps for eyes, handling her pad the way a cop does his citation book. The menu said all breakfasts came with grits, toast, and preserves. I ordered a breakfast of two eggs over easy. "Is that all you want?"

"Doesn't it come with grits and so forth?"

"Does if you ast fort."

"I want the complete, whole thing. Top to bottom."

She snapped the pad closed. I waited. I read the rest of the menu, the Gettysburg Address, made a quick run over the Pledge of Allegiance, read about famous American women on four sugar packets, read a matchbook and the imprints on the flatware. I was counting grains of rice in the saltshaker (this *was* the South), when Brenda pushed a breakfast at me, the check slick with margarine and propped between slices of toast. The food was good and the sense of the place fine, but Brenda was destined for an interstate run-em-thru. Early in life she had developed the ability to make a customer wish he'd thrown up on himself rather than disturb her.

Highway 34 out of Darlington ran past a rummage of steel and concrete where the Rebel 500 stockcar race would be held in a week. I stopped and asked a man leaning on a rake if I could look at the track. He told me how to get in. To be honest, I had little interest in an arena where men with a single talent — driving a car fast — performed. I was just looking into things. The immense asphalt oval lay baking in the quiet heat, and I walked around. Hmmm. When I came back out the man at the rake said, "That your honeywagon?"

"That's my truck."

"I spect you can stack the ladies in there like cut cordwood." He became animated, and his eyes opened and closed alternately like an old-time two-bulb blinker stoplight. He was a homely man and the blinking didn't help.

"Haven't done any stacking," I said. "Been moving along."

"Travelin' alone! Ever ascared alone?" I shrugged. "Me, I ain't never ascared," he said. "Looky here." From his left breast pocket, he took a worn bullet: a .22 long rifle. "I carried a live forty-five round in the war and never got shot by friend or foe. Always carry me a round over my heart, and ain't never ascared because I know when I die it's agonna be from this. And quick. Lord'll see to that — when it's my time."

"You mean you'll put it in a gun and shoot yourself?"

"It's a sin to do that, ain't it now?" He waited for an answer.

"I've heard that's the case."

"Nope, this here little lady will go off by herself some way or t'other. When it's my time. Won't know it neither."

"What if it goes off by accident before it's your time?"

"You ain't alistenin'. Ain't no accidents in the Lord's Plan. When she pops off, my ticket's agettin' punched. Oughter get yourself one. They make a man right peaceful."

The sun was like slaps on the neck. Maybe I should have talked longer to that fatalist who made sure he remained a fatalist, but I yielded to the heat. On the road again, I wondered whether there were times when he didn't put the bullet in his pocket, days he didn't feel up to the extra risk. Sooner or later, a man carries the seeds of his destruction with him, but I'd never seen a seed like that one.

Dusty little clouds went puffing over powdery tobacco fields in the hot wind, the pine needles looked dry and bleached, and the buds in the deciduous trees afforded no shade. A horse stood up to its belly in a pond of rust-colored water. For me, there was nothing to do but go on into the sun. I'd forgotten to refill the water jugs and had only a few swallows of warm, stale water left from yesterday. I hoped for a soda fountain or rootbeer stand, but the road was dry fields and sunglare, and it went on and on.

Then, like a mirage, a sign: ARTESIAN WELL. I turned around. In a cool grove of loblolly, from an upright L-shaped pipe the diameter of a saucer flowed a silvery bash of water among ferns and moss. It gushed into my jugs, filling them instantly, almost knocking one from my grip. I drank off most of the first, gulping, spilling, drinking the coldness so long I came up gasping. I put my head under the cataract, and the force bent me over. I shook the water off.

Someone was laughing. Behind me, a black man with white balls of hair at his temples said, "Had a tickhound used to do that." From the backseat of his Ford Galaxie, he and his wife unloaded forty-six empty plastic milk containers. He filled each gallon, capped it, and set it on the seat his wife had covered with oilcloth; then he opened the trunk and took out six five-gallon lard buckets and filled those. He finished in ten minutes.

"Do you use the water in gardening?"

"We uses it in us." They lived three miles away, had no running water, and came to the well Saturday mornings for seventy-six gallons of "sweetwater."

"What makes it sweet?" I said.

"Nothin' in that water but water. Be comin' up from four hundred feet, gettin' cleaned all the way down and all the way back up. Natural wells used to be all over here, but them new, drilled wells dried up the othern. But this one, he be too deep." The man closed the trunk and helped his wife into the car. "Govment man come round and say he'd drill a well by the house. I tole him all we'd do with it was flush a water toilet, and we got no water toilet. I says, 'How that water gone get up to me?' He say with a lectric pump. I says, 'We drinks water what come up of his own mind.' "

When I went back for more, the water pressure shifted, answering some change in the aquifer deep below. I wondered how old the water was, how long it had taken to get down and back up. I've never drunk glacier water from snows that fell a thousand years ago, but I couldn't imagine it being any better than the South Carolina water what come up of his own mind.

Out of the pines it was fifteen degrees hotter. A car passed, the driver slumped under the steering wheel, his left shoeless and sockless foot stuck out the window. Southern comfort. Four words describe the history here of the last three centuries: indigo, rice, cotton, tobacco. One crop yielded to another as economics, society, science, and the land changed. In the last generation alone, erosion control, crop rotation, fertilizer, and pesticide have changed the face of the South, and the people's lives showed it. Along the highway stood remnants of a Reconstructed South: sharecropper cabins. Many, like the ones in North Carolina, had been deserted for a subdivision green prefab next door, but not all. On one slanting porch, a woman worked at her wringer washer and on another a man sat at the ready with a flyswatter. The Old South disappears. Yet, the cabins, once an emblem of a land and a way of life, were something you couldn't see in Provo or Fort Wayne. Only on humanitarian grounds can a traveler approve the nationally standardized boxes replacing them.

I crossed the Wateree River, which meets up with the Congaree to the south and forms the Santee. South Carolinians like their rivers with paired Indian vowels: the two Pee Dees (Big and Little), the Combahee, Keowee, Tugaloo, Ashepoo. In Kershaw County, the land began rising once more as the road went into the eastern foothills of the Appalachians. I'd come again to the Piedmont Plateau. The people call it the Up Country and the coastal plain the Low Country. Oak and pine covered the slopes except where sections had been logged out or a pasture opened. In the sunny flats, kudzu from last year had climbed to wrap trees and telephone poles in dry, brown leaves. Whole buildings looked as if they had been bagged. Introduced from Japan in the thirties to help control erosion that had damaged eighty-five percent of the tillable land, kudzu has consumed entire fields, and no one has found a good way to stop it. Kudzu and water hyacinth, another Japanese import, have run through Dixie showing less restraint than Sherman.

The heat held until sundown in Newberry. There, wearied from the eighty-five degrees, the glare, the racket of wind, I stopped. Newberry was a town of last-century buildings, old trees, columned houses with cast-iron fences, and gardens behind low brick walls. A lacy town. Old people moved along old sidewalks or pulled at greenery in old flowerbeds; they sat on old porches and shook the evening paper into obedience, or they rocked steady as old pendulums and looked into the old street as if reading something there. Living out the end of an era.

15

I DIDN'T know until ten o'clock the next morning that Captain George Chicken, the Indian fighter, killed a buffalo in 1716 at Ninety Six, South Carolina. Not at new — 1855 — Ninety Six up on highway 34, a living town along the railroad tracks, but at old Ninety Six — 1769 — two miles south on route 248, a road from the eighteenth century.

I drove up next to a pickup under the trees. Bent over a fender, half buried in the engine well, a man tinkered and cursed. I called to him, "Is this old Ninety Six?"

He pulled himself out. He wore a National Park Service uniform. "This truck runs about as well as the government. Got a Crescent wrench?" I went to my tool kit for the wrench. "Would you hop in and crank it?" The engine turned hard, then started, and I goosed it pretty good to clear it. He closed the hood. "Now, what was it you asked?"

"Is this old Ninety Six?"

"Almost. Actually, it's back in the woods. This is where Cambridge was. Old Ninety Six was the courthouse town, but they moved it out here after the Revolutionary War and renamed it. Even had a college. Then the courthouse was moved two miles north where the railroad passed through, and they had an epidemic down here. All that killed off Cambridge, but it saved old Ninety Six from being built over. It's alive today because it died a hundred and some years ago. But nothing's left of Cambridge as you see."

"What about the log cabin?"

"We hauled that in for a temporary visitor center. Old Ninety Six is the newest historical site in the Park Service. Just added last year, and things are still backward. Want to see it? Haven't given a tour today."

His name was something like Rocky Durham. He'd worked at old Ninety Six for two years, starting when Greenwood County still held title to the site. It was time for the morning rounds, so we went off in the government-green pickup on a jolting, crashing ride through pines and brambles. I rolled up the window to keep from lacerating my eyeballs.

"Eighteen months ago the county turned the land over to the Park Service," he said. "Since then, the government's put in a parking lot, graveled the trails, and started archaeological research on the Star Fort and the old stockade town where Ninety Six was."

"I don't know what I'm seeing. Just came down because I liked the name."

"The name refers to what traders figured the mileage was from Keowee — the old Indian village — to here by way of the Cherokee Path. Keowee was sort of the Cherokee's Rome. All mileages were measured from it. Traders named places along the trail to mark distances: Six Mile Branch, Twelve Mile Creek. If you like names, just up north is Gluck and Due West and Thicketty."

Durham braked, opened the door, and swept in an empty beercan in one motion. "People still think it's county land. They come here at night and hunt, drink, make out. Even throw a party inside the Star Fort the way they've done for who knows how long. All illegal now, of course."

"What's the Star Fort?"

Durham gave the history. Indians for hundreds of years used a long trail that ran from the Appalachian foothills to the sea at Charleston. Hernando de Soto very likely came up the path as well as everyone else going to or leaving the Up Country: traders, soldiers, settlers. Incensed by the Declaration of Independence, Loyalists wrote a Declaration of Dependence, and clashes between patriots and Tories broke out along the trail.

Just north of the stockade settlement of Ninety Six that sat astride — literally — the Cherokee Path, patriots built a fort shaped like an eight-pointed star to control the communication of goods and messages. By 1780, the British and Tories had seized it. In the spring of 1781, General Nathanael Greene, with a thousand infantrymen, moved in to recapture the outpost. But Greene had trouble because he lacked heavy artillery for a bombardment; fortunately for him, so did the enemy. He tried other means to crack open the fort and stockade. First he diverted the stream furnishing water; the British countered by digging a well inside the fort, but it proved dry, and they began sending out at night blacks of deepest hue to carry water from a nearby stream. Next, Greene tried tunneling toward the redoubt in an attempt to plant explosives under it. The Polish engineer and soldier, Thaddeus Kosciuszko, directed the excavations, but he started the twin tunnels too close to the fort. The defenders countered with an ingenious warning device, which consisted of a leather thong stretched from a lance stuck in the ground outside the redoubt to a drum that amplified vibrations in the earth. Listening to the drum skin, Loyalists knew when to send snipers up to pin diggers in the tunnels like woodchucks. While the soldiers sniped, Loyalist women inside the stockade fortified walls with sandbags made from their undergarments.

For twenty-eight days, the longest siege by the Continental Army, Greene's troops tried to drive out the enemy. Two hundred and some men died — more from heat than guns — in the futile exchange. One minor casualty was Kosciuszko, who, a contemporary wrote, got shot in the "seat of honor."

In June, two thousand British regulars moved toward Ninety Six, and Greene withdrew. The fort never did fall, but Greene's continual pressure in the Up Country forced the English to weaken their position at Charleston, and soon after the siege, they evacuated the Carolina Loyalists and abandoned both fort and stockaded town. Although the conflict at this last British outpost in the interior was a battle both sides won and lost, four months later the Redcoats relinquished everything at Yorktown.

"We had some folks in from Nova Scotia," Durham said. "Their ancestors lived here before the British moved them to Canada. Most who come in, come for specific reasons. They aren't just sightseeing. But once the government develops the area, it'll be another story. We'll get vacationers who go from national park to park and see scenery and other tourists."

We came to a small lake. A man sat in the brush with a cane pole. "Fishing's illegal now," Durham said, "but he's probably been working the pond since it was built in the forties. I couldn't tell the poor guy to clear out. A carp may be all he eats today. Old boys still slip around at night to string trotlines. It'll always be open county land to them."

No one had come in when we returned to the cabin. "I'll show you the Star Fort." An odd-looking dog named Hector led the way into the woods. "He's been here longer than any of us, and he'll be here after we get transferred. If his nose was a brain, he'd be the expert on Ninety Six."

The pines had dropped a sulphurous pollen over everything, and our boots exploded little yellow puffs. We crossed the Cherokee Path. Eroded several feet into the earth, about twelve feet wide, the trail, in spite of trees and brush, was unmistakable.

"That's it," he said. "Probably a thousand years old. The Cherokee chiefs, Old Hop and Hanging Maw, walked here. De Soto. General George Chicken. Millions of feet. The Park Service has plans for a visitor center and roads and more restoration. They've already brought in cannon replicas. If I managed the site, though, I'd leave it pretty much overgrown like it's been for two hundred years. Maybe clear the Cherokee Path for hiking, and that would be it. I love the place too much to change it. But one day we'll have pavement so high-heeled ladies and overweight men can tiptoe a few steps to the Star Fort, see something they don't understand, take a snapshot of themselves, and hurry on. Without trees and isolation, you lose the mystery."

Beyond lay the redoubt. Under the oaks was a moat-like depression surmounted by an eight-pointed mound. Trees grew from the rise and inside the earthworks; one even grew out of a concavity that had been the well the British had dug. Just north of the fort were angled banks and trenches: the freshly reconstructed patriot siege works. The original mounds, piled up hastily, had soon fallen back into the ditches. Yet, after all the years, the spirit of the place — its numen — was strong.

"Everything's so compressed," I said. "Firing at each other point-blank like this, how could Greene dig trenches and tunnels?"

"He built a rifle platform of logs so sharpshooters could keep the enemy ducking. But you're right about distance — they could have fought with mudballs and slingshots. There's a novel by Kenneth Roberts called *Oliver Wiswell* that describes the siege. Fascinating especially because it takes the Loyalist view."

A man limped out of the woods. He once lived nearby and had returned for a look. He asked Durham what had happened to the tunnels. "We filled in the entrances for safety, but they're still here. You're standing over one."

"We used to fool in them tunnels when we was kids," the man said. "I'll tell you, this land seen some times — cockfights, even a duel inside the fort." He gave a broken smile. "I'll tell you boys somethin' else. They was some girls who got their panties took off in them tunnels."

Durham said quietly to me, "History speaking."

A woman joined the man and asked whether he'd found what he was looking for. He nodded. As they strolled off, he said, "They was mischief out here, honey." He looked excited.

"I'm glad Kosciuszko's tunneling didn't go for naught."

"That's our kind of visitor — ones who remember Ninety Six from before or history buffs who come out to mentally reconstruct the battle. They give a better tour than I do. We get a thousand folks a year now, but when the site's developed, they estimate we'll have fifty thousand. Twenty years ago all the national parks took in seventy million people. Now it's about three hundred million. Ninety Six will have to be standardized. Won't be allowed off the walks."

"Tell them to leave it alone."

"Not possible, not now that it's in federal hands. Some of the work the government's done here is good though. Archaeologists have excavated and found the locations of the jail and courthouse inside the stockade. They've found several bivouac areas with magnetometers that detect acid in the soil from old latrines. Infrared aerial surveys have revealed a lot. We know more about Ninety Six than we did two years ago, and they've uncovered so many relics, we'll never be able to display them all at once."

The heat was up when we hiked back, and it was bringing out copperheads. Watching the trail, I saw something on the ground. A nugget of melted glass.

"Probably an old bottle," Durham said. "One guy's found a uniform button from every regiment that served here — just by scuffling his feet. Now it's illegal to take anything off the site."

Durham told about a man in the eighteenth century who lived nearby and wrote an account of the local Indians to prove they descended from a lost tribe of Israel. A crazy book, but his descriptions of their life saved crucial details of history from disappearing.

"What about Ninety Six? Will it disappear now that it's being opened?"

"For a couple hundred years," he said, "it's been cared for by people of the county through a sort of benign neglect. They used it, but they knew what had happened here and didn't disturb it much except to pick up souvenirs when they came across one. The houses are full of tomahawks and powder horns. Somebody even found a cannon in the woods years ago. But they loved the place. A guy wrote a letter in eighteen fifty and said people here considered the trees and bushes of the battleground too sacred to be 'molested' — that's his word, *molested*. But who knows about the Service? The boss says, and he's been with the Interior Department twenty years, that if the feds ever need NPS land for another purpose — timber, mining — you can bet it will go."

"Maybe it's gone already then."

"Could be, but to a historian, it's been going since the beginning."

16

In the land of "Coke-Cola" it was hot and dry. The artesian water was finished. Along route 72, an hour west of Ninety Six, I tried not to look for a spring; I knew I wouldn't find one, but I kept looking. The Savannah River, dammed to an unnatural wideness, lay below, wet and cool. I'd come into Georgia. The sun seemed to press on the roadway, and inside the truck, hot light bounced off chrome, flickering like a torch. Then I saw what I was trying not to look for: in a coppice, a long-handled pump.

I stopped and took my bottles to the well. A small sign: WATER UNSAFE FOR DRINKING. I drooped like warm tallow. What fungicide, herbicide, nematicide, fumigant, or growth regulant — potions that rebuilt Southern agriculture — had seeped into the ground water? In the old movie Westerns there is commonly a scene where a dehydrated man, crossing the barren waste, at last comes to a water hole; he lies flat to drink the tepid stuff. Just as lips touch water, he sees on the other side a steer skull. I drove off thirsty but feeling a part of mythic history.

The thirst subsided when hunger took over. I hadn't eaten since morning. Sunset arrived west of Oglesby, and the air cooled. Then a roadsign:

SWAMP GUINEA'S FISH LODGE
ALL YOU CAN EAT!

An arrow pointed down a county highway. I would gorge myself. A record would be set. They'd ask me to leave. An embarrassment to all.

The road through the orange earth of north Georgia passed an old, three-story house with a thin black child hanging out of every window like an illustration for "The Old Woman Who Lived in a Shoe"; on into hills and finally to Swamp Guinea's, a conglomerate of plywood and two-by-fours laid over with the smell of damp pine woods.

Inside, wherever an oddity or natural phenomenon could hang, one hung: stuffed rump of a deer, snowshoe, flintlock, hornet's nest. The place looked as if a Boy Scout troop had decorated it. Thirty or so people, black and white, sat around tables almost foundering under piled platters of food. I took a seat by the reproduction of a seventeenth-century woodcut depicting some Rabelaisian banquet at the groaning board.

The diners were mostly Oglethorpe County red-dirt farmers. In Georgia tones they talked about their husbandry in terms of rain and nitrogen and hope. An immense woman with a glossy picture of a hooked bass leaping the front of her shirt said, "I'm gonna be sick from how much I've ate."

I was watching everyone else and didn't see the waitress standing quietly by. Her voice was deep and soft like water moving in a cavern. I ordered the $4.50 special. In a few minutes she wheeled up a cart and began off-loading dinner: ham and eggs, fried catfish, fried perch fingerlings, fried shrimp, chunks of barbecued beef, fried chicken, French fries, hush puppies, a broad bowl of cole slaw, another of lemon, a quart of ice tea, a quart of ice, and an entire loaf of factory-wrapped white bread. The table was covered.

"Call me if y'all want any more." She wasn't joking. I quenched the thirst and then — slowly — went to the eating. I had to stand to reach plates across the table, but I intended to do the supper in. It was all Southern fried and good, except the Southern-style sweetened ice tea; still I took care of a quart of it. As I ate, making up for meals lost, the Old-Woman-in-the-Shoe house flashed before me, lightning in darkness. I had no moral right to eat so much. But I did. Headline: STOMACH PUMP FAILS TO REVIVE TRAVELER.

The loaf of bread lay unopened when I finally abandoned the meal. At the register, I paid a man who looked as if he'd been chipped out of Georgia chert. The Swamp Guinea. I asked about the name. He spoke of himself in the third person like the Wizard of Oz. "The Swamp Guinea only tells regulars."

"I'd be one, Mr. Guinea, if I didn't live in Missouri."

"Y'all from the North? Here, I got somethin' for you." He went to the office and returned with a 45 rpm record. "It's my daughter singin'. A little promotion we did. Take it along." Later, I heard a husky north Georgia voice let go a down-home lyric rendering of Swamp Guinea's menu:

> That's all you can eat
> For a dollar fifty,
> Hey! The barbecue's nifty!

And so on through the fried chicken and potatoes.

As I left, the Swamp Guinea, a former antique dealer whose name was Rudell Burroughs, said, "The nickname don't mean anything. Just made it up. Tried to figure a good one so we can franchise someday."

The frogs, high and low, shrilled and bellowed from the trees and ponds. It was cool going into Athens, a city suffering from a nasty case of the sprawls. On the University of Georgia campus, I tried to walk down Swamp Guinea's supper. Everywhere couples entwined like moonflower vines, each waiting for the blossom that opens only once.

17

THE Baptists have a way with church names in the South. The road out of Athens went past Baby Farms Church, and in the last several days I'd seen Baptist churches called Sinking Creek, Little Doe, Sweet Home. Along the blue highways, I saw few churches that could have been banks (First Church of Whatever, United Church of So-and-so) or athletic stadiums (Memorial Park Church of the Etcetera).

That morning, down on route 20 near Conyers, Georgia, while I ate breakfast in the Smyrna Presbyterian Church cemetery, I read the Scotch-Irish names on tombstones and listened to the radio. A stained-glass voice beating repentence into the ungraced at 95.6 megahertz a second may have influenced what happened next.

Again on the road, I noticed an old-style water tower — the kind on stilts with a conical lid — topped by a cross. Even in the Bible Belt, *that* was out of place. Then I saw the tank stood on the grounds of the Monastery of the Holy Spirit. I turned up the drive of magnolias.

Built into a high wall, off the arched gateway, was a small bookshop. And there *were* books inside, but also jams and jellies, bread, sand castings, window hangings, religious pictures, rosaries, and plaques saying "Have you not seen Him in the things He has made?"

A monk, about sixty, in the white tunic and black scapular of the Trappist, watched me open *The Seven Storey Mountain*, the autobiography of the Trappist father, Thomas Merton. Years ago I had started it only to put it down. "That's one you should read," he said in a voice like a truck in low gear.

"Did you ever meet Merton?"

"*Meet* Merton?" The tone was both raw and humorous, rough and inviting. "I *knew* Merton. I started out at the monastery in Gethsemani, Kentucky, where Merton wrote that book. I came from there in nineteen forty-seven to help build this place out of pasture and woods. We put up everything you see except the old barn. That was here. We built as we could. Did the work ourselves with only a little help in architecture and circuitry."

"Were you a carpenter or tradesman of some kind?"

"Tradesman. That's it. I traded stock on Wall Street for twenty years."

That meant he had to be nearly eighty. He seemed a character out of *Lost Horizon*. "Why did you give up Wall Street to become a monk?"

He cleared his throat and shifted down. "Look — talking about the spiritual life is a lot of crap. You just live it."

Idling tourists must have pestered him with that question for thirty years. I felt simple and abashed.

"Why don't you go inside to the Retreat House and tell the Guestmaster to invite you to lunch? You can ask your question in there."

"Lunch?" I had thought the gates demarked a forbidden ground where the secret and medieval life went on.

"Go tell him. He's Father Francis. Through the gate, follow the walk."

"Lunch?"

"What's your name, lad?" I almost said Lunch, but I got it right. He said, "My name used to be Bill." Used to be. It sounded strange, as if he'd said, "I used to be a Bill too." Later, I learned that was just what he did mean. All the monks used to be someone else. "I'm Brother Pius now."

So I went through to the other side of the stone walls. Pius! What was wrong with Brother Bill? I felt guilty. I was here out of curiosity, a spiritual voyeur, an ecclesiastical window peeper. What's more, such cloistered spirituality made me suspicious. Dubious about men who sought change-lessness to release them from uncertainty and turmoil, I questioned a faith that has to be protected by illusory immutability. Intimidated by ignorance of Trappist beliefs, I was uneasy about what I imagined went on in a monastery. I mean, I've read Chaucer. Monasteries, I knew, were remnants from the Dark Ages — dying vestiges of medievalism — and monks were religious atavisms. Why would a sane man sequester himself? Renounce the world? How could he serve a religion that makes so much of love among peoples and then keep to himself? Still, I wanted to see the strange rites that must occur inside. But why would they let *me* in?

I found the Retreat Lodge. A man, small and gray, moving up and down the halls, disappeared in one door, hurried out another, popped up here, then vanished again like Alice's Wonderland rabbit. Somehow he came up behind me. He spoke the way he moved: dartingly. "Are you here for lunch?"

"I'd like to be."

"Yes, yes. Fine. That's fine. Yes."

He scurried away a few steps then scurried back. "There's a reading room. Make yourself comfortable. I've got to tell the cook you'll be with us. That's fine." He was through the door, down the hall.

On a desk I saw a flyer that said "Come aside for a while." Aside. In the reading room there was only a single shelf of worn books, but I found the Merton and took it to a balcony overlooking a small, enclosed garden. Quiet and cool. No voices, no steps, nothing but a towhee in the bush whistling a one-note monotony. Aside.

I sat and stared into the trees, the book open across my legs. The monks had spoken as if they had met me long ago, as if I'd said years back, "I'll be there someday. Don't wait up." I began reading *The Seven Storey Mountain*. Here is Merton's response to his first visit to a Trappist monastery:

> The logic of the Cistercian life was, then, the complete opposite to the logic of the world, in which men put themselves forward, so that the most excellent is the one who stands out, the one who is eminent above the rest, who attracts attention.
>
> But what was the answer to this paradox? Simply that the monk in hiding himself from the world becomes not less than himself, not less of a person, but more of a person, more truly and perfectly himself: for this personality and individuality are perfected in their true order, and the spiritual, interior order, of union with God, the principle of all perfection.

The passage brought something back, something from long ago: three times I had seen Heat Moon disappear when he sought the deepest union. Here was no Whitman celebrating himself, finding no sweeter fat than what sticks to his own bones.

An hour later, Brother Francis called me to lunch. The meal was a strange combination of monastic spareness and a Little League picnic: on a plain white plate, boiled cabbage, a boiled potato, figs, rye bread, and hotdog; raspberry Kool-Aid to drink. No second helpings. Swamp Guinea's was a world away.

I was the only non-Catholic at the table of four other guests and three monks. While the conversation rambled over papal encyclicals and the chances of the Atlanta Braves, I watched the monks closely, knowing they might talk a good ballgame, but, sooner or later, they would betray their medievalism by lapsing into Latin or intoning a prayer. All I had to do was watch. They would try to root the heresy out of me or sell an indulgence. But they ate their hotdogs with ketchup or mustard and their lips turned Kool-Aid blue just like mine. Then, as if to a tolling only they heard, they rose and disappeared, the other guests with them. Alone again.

On the balcony I read more Merton until Father Anthony Delisi, a man with a dark, Latin face, asked if I'd like to see the monastery. As we walked, he answered novice questions about the order. Cistercians, trying to return to a basic simplicity, separated from the Benedictine order in 1098. In 1664, the Trappists, wishing to move even closer to pure necessity and unadorned worship, formed a suborder within the Cistercians.

The monastery grounds and buildings showed the Trappist desire for directness in the clarity of line, the openness, in the unclutter. It reminded me of the Shaker village. The buildings were concrete with touches of brick, stone, and unfinished wood, everything free of decoration except the geometry of stained glass in the chapel.

"Some find our place austere," Father Anthony said.

"Then I'll take austerity."

"The purpose is freedom — for body and mind. Simplicity is flexible. It endures well. Without so many things around, we have more time."

He showed the subsistence industries: raising Black Angus, growing hay and vegetables and houseplants and bonsai, baking bread. Recently the brothers had started fabricating stained-glass windows for churches and synagogues after monks learned the craft while constructing windows for their own sanctuary.

"The brothers do all the work without any help from outside?"

"Almost. The majority practice a trade as part of the daily routine. Of course, the spiritual life is our real work. But we have to have bakers and plumbers and haycutters. We get up at three-forty-five and go to bed at eight-thirty. In between, we attend services, eat, and spend four hours a day at manual labor, and still take time for the hardest work — reflection."

"I thought Trappist life was exceedingly strict. Severe, you might say."

"You can see we're not disco priests on the streets. But some restrictions have eased. When I first came, we lived under the rule of silence and spoke only through sign language."

"Which one? I know some signs of the Plains Indians."

"I've forgotten most of it now. Words I remember are pictorial signs. Here, what am I saying?" His right fingers wiggled over his left palm.

"Run up the hill and get a pail of water."

"No, no. 'The dog chased the cat into the church.'"

"I think you misspelled *dog*. It has four thumb wiggles, not two. Any complexity of thought, I take it, had to occur between man and God rather than between monks."

"Maybe. But you just don't talk as much if you have to use fingers. We don't waste words today. In the refectory, for instance, we still observe to a degree a monastic silence. But now, as we eat, a brother will read to us."

"Scripture and Biblical commentary? Things like the Holy Fathers?"

"We just finished *Nicholas and Alexandra*. We began *Understanding Media* not long ago but voted it out. We vote on books to be read, then vote again one-third and two-thirds of the way through to see if we're interested in continuing. Had trouble understanding McLuhan."

As we walked the grounds, Father Anthony introduced the monks. They were friendly in a plain and open manner, unsanctimonious, and not outwardly pious. They did not, as Whitman says, "make me sick discussing their duty to God"; neither were they, to use Merton's word, "disinfected" men. Yet the older ones appeared a decade or more younger than men of their ages I was accustomed to seeing. Twisted or hanging faces were few. And, I must say, there was a life, a spirit, in the old who moved slowly. I realized I was trying to catch in their faces something I wouldn't see outside the walls — something hidden, transcendental, even mystical. But I noticed only a quietude, and I felt that more than saw it.

I asked to see a dormitory. He didn't answer immediately. Instead he picked up a leaf and twirled it. "Nothing's secret about the rooms, but some brothers don't want disturbance. The opportunity for uninterrupted devotion and reflection is the reason many come here. *Monastic* means 'living alone.' " He was almost apologetic. "The brothers you've met are ones whose duties put them before visitors. But others prefer solitude. One lives alone in the woods. It's his choice. A few still keep the rule of silence. You must understand the importance of quiet to us."

"A noisy man doesn't hear God?"

"I wouldn't presume to answer that."

"There is something else then — something I'd like if it's permitted."

"We don't copy manuscripts by hand."

"I know — you've got a brother who repairs Xerox machines. No, that's not it. I'd like to talk with a brother about why he became a monk. You must get tired of the question, but still, I'd like to ask again."

"Are you staying the night?"

"Never crossed my mind."

"After dinner, I'll try to send someone around. Won't be easy."

The evening meal was vegetable soup, peas, rice, bread, vanilla pudding. Again, just enough. At the table, talk turned toward a Savannah visitor recuperating from a coronary bypass who had come to see his novitiate son. Although the conversation was alternately serious and jocular, the man's quiet presence, the impending farewell between father and son, touched us all. Once more the silent tolling. This time I rose with them.

Father Anthony asked me to join him at vespers. On the way to the chapel, we didn't talk. I think he was preparing. I remembered my denim and suspenders. "My clothes," I said.

He didn't break stride or turn his head. "How could that matter? But singing on key does. Can you?"

"Never could."

"Don't sing loud then. God doesn't mind. I do."

The monks filed noiselessly into the great, open sanctum and sat facing each other from both sides of the choir. At a signal I didn't perceive, they all stood to begin the antiphonal chanting of plainsong. Only younger ones and I looked at the hymnals. The sixty-five monks filled the church with a fine and deep tone of the cantus planus, and the setting sun warmed the stained glass. It could have been the year 1278.

I looked at the faces. Quietude. What burned in those men that didn't burn in me? A difference of focus or something outside me? A lack or too much of something? To my right a monk sat transfixed, eyes unblinking, and his lips, the tiniest I'd ever seen on a man, never moved. I thought if I could know where he was, then I would know this place.

There was nothing but song and silences. No sermon, no promise of salvation, no threat of damnation, no exhortation to better conduct. I'm not an authority, God knows, but if there is a way to talk into the Great Primal Ears — if Ears there be — music and silence must be the best way.

Afterwards, I returned to the balcony. Empty but for the sounds of dusk coming on: tree frogs, whippoorwills, crickets. I've read that Hindus count three hundred thirty million gods. Their point isn't the accuracy of the count but rather the multiplicity of the godhead. That night, if you listened, it seemed everywhere. I sat staring and felt "strong upon me," as Whitman has it, "the life that does not exhibit itself." Someone behind, someone tall, said my name.

18

HE used to be Patrolman Patrick Duffy. Now he was usually just Brother Patrick. A name didn't count for much anyway. Angular, sinewy, red beard, shaved head, white tunic. Distinctly medieval in spite of the waffle-soled hiking boots. About him was an unacademic, unpietistic energy — the kind that the men who made Christianity must have possessed. Quite capable of driving snakes out of Ireland, or anywhere else for that matter.

"I hear you have questions," he said. None of the usual feeling out before a conversation on a sensitive topic begins. A frontal assault man.

I picked it up. "Tell me why a man becomes a Trappist monk. Answers I heard today sounded like catechism recited a thousand times."

"It isn't an easy question — or at least the answer isn't easy."

"Tell me how it happened to you. How you got here."

"I've been here five years. I was a policeman in Brooklyn — Bedford-Stuyvesant. On my way to becoming a ghetto cop. Did it for seven years. Before that, I was an Army medic. Attended St. Francis College part-time and worked in the Brooklyn Public Library. And education has come in other ways too. I hitched around the country in nineteen fifty-seven and again in 'fifty-eight. Went to Central America on the second trip and spent time in Honduras."

"Jack Kerouac? *On the Road?*"

"Something like that. I came back to New York and worked as a sandhog digging subway tunnels in Manhattan. Then I got seaman's papers to go into the merchant marine — listen, papers are hard to come by. I had to scramble to get them, then I never used them."

"Why not?"

"Got interested in police work, but I was still unsettled and afraid of getting stuck on a ship. Afraid of drudgery. I like changes."

"Changes? In here? Of all you could find here, I'd think change would be the least likely."

"I mean growth and a change of pace. I work four hours as an electrician's assistant. Watch out, this is going to be philosophical, but you could make some kind of analogy between being an electrician and a monk — the flow of energy from a greater source to smaller outlets. Still, the electrical work is different from the spiritual work, even if I try to merge them."

"Two things don't seem like much change."

"I'm also what you might describe as the monastery forest ranger. They call me Smokey the Monk. I oversee the wooded part of the grounds. Try to keep the forest healthy. Just for fun, I've been cataloging all the wildflowers here. We've identified about two hundred species, not counting the blue unknowns and pink mysteries. Working on shrubs now. And I've taken to bird-watching since I came. I spend a lot of time in the woods reading, thinking. That's when real changes can happen."

"What do you read?"

"In the woods, some natural history, some Thoreau. Always scripture and theology. Reading about the charismatic movement now." He was silent a moment. "Does any of this explain why I'm here?"

"It all must be part of an answer."

"For years I've been fascinated by intense spiritual experiences of one kind and another. When I was seventeen — I'm forty-two now — I thought about becoming a monk. I'm not sure why, other than to say I felt an incompleteness in myself. But after a while, the desire seemed to disappear. That's when I started traveling. I learned to travel, then traveled to learn. Later, when I was riding a radio car in Brooklyn, I began to want a life — and morality — based not so much on constraint but on aspiration toward a deeper spiritual life. Damn, that was unsettling. I thought about seeing a psychiatrist, but after a couple of months, I just stopped worrying whether I was crazy."

"What happened?"

"I'm not sure. Maybe I got cured when I started working part-time with the Franciscans in New York. They do a lot of community work at the street level, and that gave me a chance to look into this 'monkey business,' as a friend calls it. I joined the Franciscans Third Order for two years, to test whether I really wanted to enter a monastery, although their work is secular rather than monastic. Then I worked with the Little Brothers of the Gospel. They live communally, in stark simplicity, in the Bowery. That helped make up my mind. I liked what I could see of a religious life. I began to see my problem was not trusting myself — being afraid of what I really wanted."

He pulled up his tunic and scratched his leg. "Understand, there was nothing wrong with riding a radio car, although I got tired of the bleeding and the shot and cut people I was bandaging up. Seemed I was a medic again. And delivering babies in police car backseats. Thirteen of those. The poor tend to wait to the last minute, then they call the police." He stopped. "Forgot what I was talking about."

"Trusting yourself."

"Better to say a lack of self-trust. As a kid, I was always searching for something beyond myself, something to bring harmony and make sense of things. Whatever my understanding of that something is, I think it began in the cop work and even more when I was assisting the friars in New York. I was moving away from things and myself, toward concerns bigger than me and my problems, but I didn't really find a harmony until I came here. I don't mean to imply I have total and everlasting harmony; I'm just saying I feel it more here than in other places."

He was quiet for some time. "Tonight I can give you ten reasons why I'm a monk. Tomorrow I might see ten new ones. I don't have a single unchanging answer. Hope that doesn't disappoint you."

"Try it in terms of what you like about the life here."

"I've always been attracted to hermitic living — I didn't say 'hermetic living' — but only for short periods. I go off in the woods alone, but I come back. Here, nobody asks, 'What happened to you? You off the beam again?' Living behind that front wall — it doesn't surround us, by the way — living here doesn't mean getting sealed off. This is no vacuum. We had a new kid come in. He left before he took his vows because he couldn't find so-called stability — stability meaning 'no change.' I told him this place was alive. People grow here. The brothers are likely to start sprouting leaves and blossoms. This is no place to escape from what you are because you're still yourself. In fact, personal problems are prone to get bigger here. Our close community and reflective life tend to magnify them."

6. *Brother Patrick Duffy at the monastery near Conyers, Georgia*

"How did you finally make the decision to 'come aside'?"

"A friend's father told me, 'If you don't do what you want when you're young, you'll never do it.' So I quit waiting for certainty to come."

"A five-year experiment. Was it the right thing?"

"Right? It's *one* of the right things. The *best* right thing. I believe in it enough I'm taking my permanent vows in October."

"You don't have second thoughts?"

"Second, third, fourth. I go with as much as I can understand. And I've gotten little signs. Like listening to Beethoven. I loved Beethoven. Been here two years, and one day I just went over and turned the stereo off. Beethoven was too complex, I guess, for me. My tastes have developed toward simpler things. Merton calls it 'the grace of simplicity.' Haven't broken myself of Vivaldi though."

I wanted to ask a question, but it seemed out of bounds. I decided to anyway. "I'd like to know something, partly out of curiosity and partly out of trying to imagine myself a monk." He didn't laugh but I did. "My question, let's see, I guess I want to know how you endure without women."

"I don't 'endure' it. I choose it." He was silent again. "Sometimes, when I'm doing my Smokey duties, I come across a couple picnicking, fooling around. Whenever that happens, when I'm reminded where I've been, I sink a little. I feel an emptiness. Not for a woman so much as for a child — I would like to have had a son. That's the emptiness."

"What do you do?"

His answers were coming slowly. "I try to take desires and memories of companionship — destructive ones — and let them run their course. Wait it out. Don't panic. That's when the emptiness is intense."

"And that's it?"

"That's the beginning. Then I turn the pain of absence into an offering to God. Sometimes that's all I have to offer."

"You mean what you've given up?"

"Does it seem like I'm giving nothing?"

"It seems like a gift of giving up a gift. For he so loved God he gave up his only unbegotten son."

Brother Patrick smiled. "Just say I try to turn the potential for destructiveness into a useful force. In that way, the attraction of the outside reinforces. It's another way to come closer to God."

"Someone else today used that phrase about coming closer to God. It sounds like the Hindus who renounce the world and move away from things, including their own desires, so they can get closer to their god."

"Simplicity reveals the universals we all live under. Material goods can blunt your perception of greater things. Here, the effort is to free yourself from blindness, arrogance, selfishness."

The bells rang for compline. It was so dark I heard Duffy more than I saw him. He said, "I begin with this broken truth that I am. I start from the entire broken man — entire but not whole. Then I work to become empty. And whole. In looking for ways to God, I find parts of myself coming together. In that union, I find a regeneration."

"Sounds like spiritual biology."

"Why not?" After a pause he said, "Coming here is following a call to be quiet. When I go quiet I stop hearing myself and start hearing the world outside me. Then I hear something very great."

Three

SOUTH BY SOUTHEAST

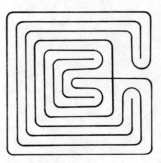

AMIDST a clangor of bells in the middle of the night, the brothers began their day. I heard shuffling along the walks as they went to morning prayers. Admiring men who can give thanks for a day still two hours from first light, I again burrowed down into the bed in deep sloth.

After breakfast, I put my duffel together, left a contribution, and shook hands with a surprising number of people before going back through the big gate. When I stepped into my rig, I thought for a moment I was in the wrong truck. It seemed small and enclosed like a cell — not a monk's cell, but a prisoner's. Even simple and necessary gear looked foreign. Dross.

On Georgia 155, I crossed Troublesome Creek, then went through groves of pecan trees aligned one with the next like fenceposts. The pastures grew a green almost blue, and syrupy water the color of a dusty sunset filled the ponds. Around the farmhouses, from wires strung high above the ground, swayed gourds hollowed out for purple martins.

The land rose again on the other side of the Chattahoochee River, and highway 34 went to the ridgetops where long views over the hills opened in all directions. Here was the tail of the Appalachian backbone, its gradual descent to the Gulf. Near the Alabama stateline stood a couple of LAST CHANCE! bars — those desperate places that run at a higher pitch than taverns part of the whole fabric of a town; there's an unnaturalness in them, isolated as they usually are from the ordinary circuits of people. On into Talapoosa County and Alexander City (just north of Our Town), where I found a place for the night by the tennis courts of the community college. That evening was to change the direction of the journey.

THE woman was an authority. Whatever there was, she knew it. Her face, pallid like a partly boiled potato, looked as if carved out with a paring knife. She was a matron of note in Alexander City. Two other women, dark in eighteen-hole tans, sat with her on a bench alongside the tennis courts, while their daughters took lessons under the lights. The discussion on the bench was Tupperware. The potato had just said, "For a shower gift, you can't do better than a Pak-N-Stor." Another explained how her eldest had received an upright freezer full of nesting food containers from the Walkers.

"That reminds me," said the third woman, "how is Mildred?"

"How good can you be, taking cobalt?" the authority answered.

A daughter in pearl-mint lipgloss jogged up to a handsome man standing by the courts. On his shirt, a famous little crocodile was laughing at something. Her damp halter top and tennis shorts clung to her like tattoos. She didn't mind my staring. "Buy me a cola drink, Daddy."

A sunburned man at the end of the bench said, "Doesn't she get her share of the attention! Goes to school in the North. Nobody here can touch her."

"North, South," I said, "makes no difference."

He said nothing. The girls returned to their lessons, the father went back to courtside, and the women talked about aboveground swimming pools. The sunburned fellow muttered, "That your green van?" I nodded and told him I was looking around the South. He asked, "You go through Atlanta?"

"Trying to stay out of cities."

"Not seeing the South then. Better go back." He moved down the bench. I smelled booze. "I went to Emory University for five years. Drove a city bus in Atlanta to pay for my schooling." As he rambled, I watched the players chase tennis balls. He said something about a "martyr bus."

"What's a martyr bus?"

"M-A-R-T-A. Metropolitan Atlanta Rapid Transit Authority, otherwise known as Moving Africans Rapidly Through Atlanta."

"I don't get it."

"The blacks — you know, the domestics living in Buttermilk Bottom, the goddamn ghetto — they take buses to the suburbs to clean houses."

"I see."

"No, you don't. You're goggling the coeds in their cute tans. Listen, church in Atlanta, down on West Peachtree, had a signboard. Big letters. WHERE THE FOLKS ARE FRIENDLY. Same church that wouldn't let a black preacher speak at a worldwide Methodist conference."

"Nothing particularly Southern about that."

He wasn't listening. He was convincing me. "I can tell you about a boutique in Underground Atlanta that sold little plastic ax handles signed by a former governor. Even being a Yankee, you might've heard of Lester Maddox taking his stand in front of his Pick-Rick restaurant with a goddamn ax handle in his goddamn hands. I mean, he got elected governor because he got photographed with a goddamn ax handle. I wasn't with MARTA then, but if I'da been, I'da driven my bus right into Lester's fucking cream pies."

The blue crocodile man turned to us. He said, "Easy, Marlin. Ladies about. We've heard all that stuff by now. Times have changed for ideas like that."

"Changed?" He looked at the tall man. "I'll tell you change." He turned to me, his sunburn reddening. "Here's change: a monument to the boll weevil in Enterprise, Alabama, because it broke King Cotton's back so beans and corn could take over. Here's change: Atlanta Klan rally, Klan as in KufuckingKlux, year or two ago. Little ad in the *Constitution* advertising the rally. At the bottom it says, 'Bring your own robe.' Organization changed from furnishing the stinking bedsheets."

Looking at me, the handsome man put his hand on Marlin's shoulder. "You're the one needs changing, Marlin. Next thing, you'll be spouting again about your great-grandaddy up in the quarry at Sylacauga cutting marble for the Supreme Court building. Hear yourself: it's all old talk now."

To me, Marlin said, "I drove a bus, and he drives a real estate office. You figure it out, Yankee." He got up, knocked the man's hand from his shoulder, and put his face close to mine. In a mocking, *Gone-with-the-Wind* accent, he said, "Why don't y'all git youah fuckin' eyes off the darlin' belles' butts and go ovah to Selma? See what Uncle Remus got to say since he done give up the cake walk."

He went off up the hill. That was it.

3

By midmorning I was following route 22, as I had from the Alabama line, on my way to Selma. The truck license plates said HEART OF DIXIE, and I was going into the middle of the heart. West of the bouldery Coosa River, I saw an old man plowing an old field with an old horse, and once more I wasn't sure whether I was seeing the end or beginning. Then an outbreak of waving happened — first at Maplesville, again in Stanton, again in Plantersville; from galleries and sidewalks people waved. Where folks are friendly.

It was late afternoon in Selma, and big trees along Broad Street, a clean and orderly avenue, shaded the way; citizens swept porches and talked over hedges. At the bottom of Broad, the Edmund Pettus Bridge arched high above the Alabama River. The span, named after a Confederate private who mustered out as a brigadier general, was the point where mounted troopers forced a halt to Martin Luther King's first attempt to march to Montgomery. But the afternoon I saw the bridge, it looked silvery and quiet, more ordinary than historic.

Water Avenue intersected Broad Street and ran parallel to the river on the high, north side. West on the avenue was a boarded-up building of Doric columns and an inscription chiseled in stone: HARMONY CLUB. East stood two- and three-story brick buildings with ornamental ironwork supporting galleries that gave the street an aspect of the Vieux Carré in New Orleans. What little remained of Selma's old commercial architecture — buildings Walker Evans photographed during the Depression — was here.

I looked along Broad Street for a beer to chase the heat and furnish opportunity for conversation; two places appeared to be bars, but signs outside gave no indication. Water Avenue, down where Confederate ship-fitters had built ironclads to fight Farragut at Mobile Bay, was quiet but for an old cotton warehouse with a buzzing electric sign: MICKEY'S PLACE. A second sign above showed a champagne glass, a plus symbol, and a human figure either dancing or falling over dead.

Mickey's was, in fact, a tavern and the sign a Bible Belt hieroglyphic to say that. I was the only customer. The barmaid, in her early twenties, wore a see-through blouse that surrendered transparency at the last possible point of decency; at the center she had pinned a Made-in-Taiwan red plastic rose, which matched another stuck into a pair of black lace underpants nailed to the wall. She stood looking forlorn, I thought, twisting a highball glass on stacks of joke napkins, turning them into little ziggurats.

In the dimness, the bar mirror, only a few feet away, returned no reflection, and I checked to see if I had on sunglasses. I didn't, but she wore hers. Perfume stuck to the wet bottle of beer she set down. "What's with the sign outside?" I said. "Wasn't sure this was a bar."

"Cain't advertise bars or liquor in the city. About the most you can get away with is 'cold beverages of all kinds.'"

Four new, antiqued Pabst Blue Ribbon wall lamps behind the bar were mounted upside down with the name smeared over. "What's with the lights?"

"That's advertisin'."

"I can read 'Pabst' on the bottle in my hand but not on the wall?"

"You catch on fast. Where you from? Chicago?"

I told her. She took off her sunglasses to get or give a better look, then put them on again when a man came in for a bottle of beer to go. She rolled it carefully in a paper sack, but the outline was unmistakable. It looked like a little mummy.

"Where are *you* from?"

"Right here," she said. "Selma, everlovin' Alagoddamnbama, Heart of D-I-X-I-E." I smiled. "Don't laugh, Chicago. Here's the only place I ever been ceptin' Montgomery. And Biloxi once as a baby. But I'm headin' for New Orleans soon. This little number is on the move. Look away, Dixieland!" She removed her sunglasses. "So, what's Mr. Chicago doin' in Selma?"

"Mr. Chicago was encouraged to come to see what the march changed."

"What march?"

"King's march."

She lowered her voice. "Touchy shit, Chicago. You're two blocks from Brown's Chapel. That's where it all started."

"Still touchy? How long's it been?"

"Don't know. I was just a little kid."

"Do blacks come in here now?"

"*Here?* They got their clubs, we got ours."

"Doesn't sound like much has changed."

She turned to a sharp-edged man who had just sat down. He loudly said, "Can I get me a Tom and Collins or is lollygaggin' all that gets done in here?" She mixed his drink and talked with him. Every so often he turned on me his small, round eyes. She walked back up the bar.

"Thirteen years ago Ray says the march was. Want another?"

"Sure, if you mean a beer."

"Why don't you talk to Ray? He saw it both times."

"Ray doesn't look like the chummy sort."

"He's all right, usually. I cain't tell you anything." She looked down the bar. "Hey, Ray. I was tellin' Chicago about that night those dudes came in here and saw there wasn't any of their kind and left."

"So?"

"So, like he wanted to know if things changed."

Ray, a jagged man, sat down beside me and looked hard at the woman. He said, "How's it his concern?" Still talking to her, he turned to me and in my face opened a smile like a jackknife. "All these Northern boys wanna know is 'How's your nigger problem?' Don't they think we get sick of that? Won't they let us rest? Ain't they got nothin' new to say?"

"I got accused last night of ignoring it."

"Okay, sonny-jim. I'll tell you about change." It came out like a threat. "Change ruined this town. Bar I just came from, three of them sittin' in there big as sin. Fifteen years ago you couldna hired a nigger to go in there. You talk about change, and I say to you, 'Go to hell.' "

I let it pass. Headline: YANKEE HALF-BREED KNIFED.

He waited, then said, "I'll tell you this too. Problems we got ain't so much from niggers. They're more likely from Northern jacks comin' down here messin' where it ain't their concern. Tellin' us how to live. That's what's got everbody riled includin' niggers. You a reporter?"

"Just traveling through. Wanted to see what's changed in Selma."

"Way we do bidness what's changed. For the worse. But the thinkin' ain't. We live ever man like he wants. Take Bernita here. She wants to get on the bar and strip and show off her bidness, ain't no man gonna stop her."

"Would anybody stop a black man if he wanted a drink in here?"

"I'll be go to hell. Shit. I been all through this. I'm sick of it." He turned away and talked to Bernita. She left to serve a table, and he looked at me again. "Cain't figure what you're gettin' at."

"Just want to see how things are. All I know is from books or TV."

"There it is. That whole march was a TV stunt. Niggers knew what would happen here. That's why they came. Hardly none of them lived here. They knew the sheriff had himself a reputation. They picked him, not the town. Well, they got what they were lookin' for. I'm sick of goin' over and over it." He went to the toilet. When he came back, he had another drink. "Cain't figure what you're drivin' at."

I didn't answer. He kept turning to the topic as if I were pushing him into it. He wanted to talk it through, and he blamed me for that.

"Those marchers rolled their own dice, and we got flammed. Course it ain't hard to flam George Wallace."

"What are you saying?"

"I'm tellin' you sickin' dogs and poundin' the niggers was a lack of ignorance. We shoulda paid no mind. Then the cameras woulda stayed in the bags. That's what ruined us — photographers and reporters. Like with the Klan. Some Grand Genie comes crawlin' outa his rotten stump, and there go the cameras and the tongue-cluckin' over the poor South." He stared into the dark mirror. "Used to be everbody stayed in their place. That's what's got all mixed round. I'm sick of talkin' about it."

"Don't get the wrong idea," Bernita said. "Selma's a nice town. We got Coloreds in city hall and places. Only thing I don't like is people are two-faced — friendly at first, then you see the truth."

Ray said, "Don't know what he's tryin' to get at. Hell, I got niggers workin' for me over at the dealership. I hire them, but they up and quit."

"What kind of work?"

"Washin' cars."

"They ever get to sell a car?"

"You know anything? I'd lose ever one of my customers."

"Looks like you've got each other by the balls. Somebody needs to let go."

He leaned back on the stool. "Well, well, well. Got a lot of advice, don't you now? You don't know a damn thing. Come in for a day and got the answers. No use explainin' to you. Tell me, you talk with any niggers?"

"Not here."

"Not here. You got a picture in your brain all made up like a bed. Know all about it. We never burned our cities."

"Who said it was a Southern problem? It's a world problem."

"You finally come up with somethin'."

As we talked, he said *nigger* less, as if he'd drained the poison for a while. He didn't soften; he just expressed himself in other terms, although at no time did he try to hide where he stood. But he held more sorrow and regret than hatred. He was more empty than malicious.

4

MARTIN Luther King, Jr., Drive used to be Sylvan Street. Some whites in Selma still called it Sylvan Street. It's the main route through the so-called project — a typical federally sponsored housing district — and the street the Southern Christian Leadership Conference assembled the marchers on, using the block under the high steeple of Brown's Chapel as the starting point. The first marchers walked down Sylvan (as it was then), up Water Avenue, turned left, and started across Pettus Bridge. About half a mile. At the other end of the bridge, deputies and troopers, shouting to the people they had no permit to march, forced them back to Water Street. But for once, chants and signs and feet were better weapons than anything the state could summon. Whitman, the egalitarian, said it a century before:

> I will make a song for the ears of the President, full of weapons
>   with menacing points,
> And behind the weapons countless dissatisfied faces.

When King assembled the marchers again two weeks later, he had not only a permit, he had also the protection — albeit spotty — of federal troops called out by President Johnson, the man with the big ears. People gathered at Brown's Chapel and walked fifty miles to Montgomery. The two marches roused Washington as none of the other SCLC confrontations had, and a few months later the Congress passed the Federal Voting Rights Act.

It was dark and moonless when I started looking for Brown's Chapel. I planned just to drive by, but I stopped near a big brick church that fit the description to ask a black man if it was the chapel. "That's it," he said. "What difference does it make?"

Without knowing it, he had asked me the question I'd come to Selma to answer. "Isn't this where King started the march?"

"What they say. So who cares?"

I stood on the step of the van. "I'm trying to find out if things have changed since the march."

"Tell you in three words. *Ain't nothin' changed.*"

"Let me ask another question. Could you get a drink in Mickey's tonight?"

"Go ask me if I *want* in there, because I'll tell you they don't gotta keep this man out because he don't want in."

"I hear you, but *could* you?"

"Minute I do it's membership time."

"I just went in and nobody said anything about membership."

"Your membership's got a way of standin' out — just like mine."

Several teenagers gathered around. I was the wrong color on the wrong street, but no one said anything. The man talking to me was James Walker, born and raised in the Selma project and just discharged from four years in the Air Force. "Been almost ten years to the day since King got shot," he said, "and the movement's been dead that long. Things slippin'. Black man's losin' ground again. My momma's afraid to talk to a white, and my grandmomma don't care. She just worries about the kids."

"Didn't the march do anything you can see?"

"Say what? Last week I went to get my driver's license. Twelve-thirty. Lunchtime. Sign on the door says they open again at one. I wanted to wait inside, so I pulled on the door. Trooper comes out and says, 'What's wrong, fool? Cain't read? Get off that door less you want me next time comin' out shootin'.' There's your change."

"Where?"

"Ten years ago he woulda come out shootin' the first time."

"What happened?"

"Nothin', dude. This man's not stupid. I know when to shut up and I know when to talk. This man knows when he's got a chance."

A police car cruised by. A teenager said, "That's twice." A Buick pulled up and Walker got in. He said, "You're makin' people nervous comin' in down here. You ain't the right color, you know. Better watch your ass tonight." The car jumped forward then backed up. "If you ain't jivin' about the church, come round the basketball court in the mornin'."

I drove out to George Corley Wallace Community College, one of three new schools by that name in the state. Sometime after midnight, the Ghost shook a little and I woke up. It shook again. I crept to the front curtain. A man standing on the bumper played a light over the seats. Just as I opened the door, he got into a squadcar. "What's wrong?" I called out.

"Only checking, neighbor." He drove off quickly.

I closed up again and went back to bed. Checking? What the hell for?

5

At ten the next morning, I was back on King Drive, a block south of where it crosses Jefferson Davis Avenue. On the basketball court, Walker was alone, juking and shooting. "Hey! You showed up." For the first time I saw him smile. "Just workin' on my game till school starts. Didn't get out of the Air Force in time to make spring term."

"What school?"

"Alabama Lutheran here in Selma. All-black, which is what I want. I'm tired of hasslin' with whites. Got enough in the Force."

"You don't want to go North or West?"

"And be a minority? That ain't my land."

"What'll you do here?"

"Study guidance counselin'. I'm stayin' where I can do some good. Fifty-five percent of Selma's black. We got potential. First, though, brothers gotta see what's on the other side of Pettus Bridge, see where to go from here."

"What do you mean?"

"I mean figurin' a new course. King said turn the other cheek. Malcolm X said fight fire with fire. I don't want that. But we gotta show the brothers they can do more than just hang cool like meat in a locker."

"Maybe things haven't changed because of apathy in the project."

"I ain't lettin' nobody off that easy. A man shouldn't gotta care so much about gettin' a fair game. *You* gotta worry every day about a fair game?"

"Not usually."

"So why should this man? Sure, the brothers could do more, and they would if they didn't spend so much time gettin' and keepin' a job. Wearies a man out. It never quits. If a brother gets hired and then gets active — there goes the job he worked his ass off to get."

"Can't legally let a man go if he's not talking around on company time."

"They don't fire him — ain't that clean. They hassle him. Get him thinkin' new ideas ain't worth it. Stay on him till he quits. A mover gets to stay only if boss-man's under quota. Otherwise, carry your hat in your hand."

A friend of Walker's came up. "Saw you down here last night," he said. "We doan get many calls from your people." His name was Charles Davis. He worked the middle shift at a battery factory. "I'll tell you about jobs. If I quit mine and go over to the job office, they'll hand me a shovel or send me to Florida to pick oranges. I can do more than dig a hole or cut a weed."

"Lotta people in the project feel like they cain't be nobody," Walker said. "Me? I feel I can be President of the United States."

"Sheeeit, man!" Davis said. "Force musta did your brain-housing group in."

"I know things ain't changed, but things gonna change."

"Young, and mad, and believe so much," Davis said.

"I'm twenty-four and he's thirty-one. So I *am* from nowhere. I'm talkin' future. Anyway, this man wants to know about the march."

"Think I was fifteen," Davis said. "Made both marches. People be sayin' we wasted our time, but things are better. Least a little bit."

"Ain't nothin' changed didn't have to change," Walker said.

"Some of those things be important, though. But lotta times it's like always. Take yesterday. I put a quarter in a sodapop machine at the gas station. Money keeps comin' down. Two honkies sit watchin'. I ask if the machine was broke, and one honker says it takes thirty cents now. Machine says twenty-five on it. Then he says, 'Wondered how long fore you figured it out.' He couldn't tell me they changed it. I said, 'Don't take long to figure you,' and walked off. Other honker says, 'Want me to whup the nigger?' Five years ago I'da fought him. Now I try to ignore it. But hey, I used to follow Malcolm X."

"I'll tell you one," Walker said. "Alabama state motto is 'Defendin' Our Rights.' And that's all we're doin'. All the time."

"Motto doan have you in mind, James."

"Better start."

"Hey, we finally got a black Santa Claus at the mall. Only thing, he scared hell out of the little black kids. They be dreamin' of a white Christmas."

"That's just education," I said.

"Yeah, but you see how far it goes. Littlest thing's work and worry.

Gotta always have your back in the air, and that wears you down, just like they want. Here's another one. Six people killed in the project last year, and nobody's gone uptown for murder yet. If a white dude gets it, somebody goes uptown inside three weeks. Maybe the wrong man, but somebody's goan. Law don't care what we do to ourself. Black on black's outside their law."

"No black police?"

"They be worsen a honky pig. Those black motherheads'll manhandle you. Nothin' but Oreos — black out, white in."

"All honky law wants is get a man in jail so's they know where he's at."

"But whiteys that run things here don't mind a little black poontang now and then. That's their contribution to equality — hump a nigger."

"Yeah, but let a black dude even walk down the street next to a white woman, and in six months they goan frame you. Goan plant some dope in your ride or your house. Put a white bitch on you and pay her to yell rape. They come up with somethin'. They want our best women, but they take you uptown if you say 'hey' to a honky woman none of them would touch with a fence rail."

We walked around to a small, windowless, brick sweetshop run by a blindman named Louie. Davis bought three cigarettes, lit one, and put two under his hat. A white candy vendor came in. Louie asked how many of each item he was leaving. They conducted the transaction on trust.

Davis said, "Saw whitey rip you, Louie."

"Naw, you didn't. Candyman ain't rippin' off old Louie."

Walker and I drank grape Nehi. He said, "Louie, tell the man here what it was like when we all did the march."

"Louie done a business like he never seen."

"Just business to you, ain't that right, Louie?"

"Business be business."

Outside the shop, Davis said, "I'll tell you a funny one. Last week watchin' at the ballgame. A couple of us sittin' on the fender of some Pontiac. Little bitty white dude comes up draggin' a baseball bat. He's just learnin' to talk. He says, 'You niggers get off my daddy's car!' Couldn't hardly pronounce *nigger*. We laughed. Then Daddy comes up and moves the car and never says nothin'. We never blamed the kid. We know where it's comin' from."

A uniformed man drove by in a Bell Telephone truck. Walker nudged Davis. "That's four today. Two last night."

"What's going on?" I said.

"Sheriff's deputy. That's their undercover truck."

7. *James Walker and Charles Davis in Selma, Alabama*

"Great undercover to wear a uniform," I said. "Why are they watching you?"

"They ain't watchin' us, my man — they be watchin' you."

"Me? Why me? They think I'm agitating?"

Walker and Davis laughed derisively. "They doan give a shit about that. They think you the dope man."

"A dealer? How do they come up with that?"

"Eyeballs, man. White dude in the project at night, drivin' a van, Northern license. Yeah, man, you be dealin' all right."

"If you ain't, they gonna put some stuff on you if you look like trouble."

"A cop checked the truck over last night."

"Pickin' information. Figurin' how to handle you. When they pull you in, you goan be surprised they know the size of your jockstrap."

"You got any stuff, hide it good or dump it. Don't try to sell now."

"I've got beer and some bourbon. Clean as a whistle."

"Until they stop you and look your ride over."

"Stay long enough, and they goan get you — two miles over the speed limit, forgettin' to signal, somethin'."

"To them, you be worsen a nigger now."

Davis had to go to work, and Walker had someone to see. I headed up Broad Street — clean, orderly Broad Street. I'd gone into the project for a few hours, and already I felt marked. I was suspicious. Just paranoia, of course.

On the way out of town, I passed three police cars stationed at intersections. They must have been only waiting for traffic to clear because no one followed me. But I drove under the speed limit, came to absolute stops at every light and sign, signaled turns a block ahead. And I hardly took my eyes off the rearview mirror. What a way to go.

6

UNIONTOWN, Demopolis. The Tombigbee River and blue highway 28. I missed the turnoff to Sucarnochee, Mississippi, and had to enter the state by way of Scooba on route 16, a road of trees and farmhouses. The farmhouses weren't the kind with large, encircling porches and steeply pitched roofs and long windows you used to see, but rather new houses indistinguishable from wet-bar, walk-out basement, Turfbuilder-Plus surburban models.

Then Philadelphia, Mississippi. Here, too, the old, sad history. The town, like others in the area, was built over the site of a Choctaw village. The Choctaw, whose land once covered most of Mississippi, earned a name from their skill in horticulture and diplomacy; they were a sensible people whose chieftains attained position through merit. In the early nineteenth century, they learned from white men and began building schools and adding livestock to their farms. Later, whites would refer to them as one of the "five civilized tribes." Nevertheless, as pressure from white settlement increased, the Choctaw had to cede to the government one piece of land (in million-acre increments) after another. Federal agents pressured tribes to sign treaties through mixed-bloods bribed with whiskey and trinkets; they promised Indians annuities, land grants, and reparations, almost none of which the Congress ever paid. To President Andrew Jackson, it made no difference that Choctaw officers like Ofahoma had fought with him against rebellious Creeks; Jackson pushed on with land-gobbling compacts. With the Treaty of Dancing Rabbit Creek, held in the woods northeast of Philadelphia, the Choctaw gave up the last of their land and reluctantly agreed to leave Mississippi forever. They walked to the arid Indian Territory where they set up their own republic modeled after the government that had just dispossessed them.

It's a sad history not because of the influx of settlers — after all, Indians had encroached upon each other for thousands of years. It's a sad history because of the shabby way the new people dealt with tribal Americans: not just the lies, but the utter unwillingness to share an enormous land.

Yet, a thousand or so Choctaw secretly stayed in Mississippi to claim land promised, although few ever saw a single acre returned. That afternoon their descendants were shopping along the square in Philadelphia, eating a hotdog at the Pow Wow drive-in, taking a few hours away from the reservation west of town. Holding to the token parcel now theirs, they could watch towns white men had built wither: Improve, Enterprise, Increase, Energy, Progress. As for what the land around the towns produced, they could watch that too.

Highway 16 passed through green fields, blue ponds, clumps of pine; it crossed the earthy Yokahockana River, a name that stands with other rivers of strong name in Mississippi: the Yazoo, Yalobusha, Little Flower, Noxubee, Homochitto, Bogue Chitto, Chickasawhay, Skuna, the Singing River.

At Ofahoma, I drove onto the Natchez Trace Parkway, a two-lane running from Natchez to near Nashville, which follows a five-hundred-mile trail first opened by buffalo and Indians. Chickasaws called it the "Path of Peace." In 1810, the Trace was the main return route for Ohio Valley traders who, rather than fight the Mississippi currents, sold their flatboats for scrap in Natchez and walked home on the Trace. The poor sometimes traveled by a method called "ride and tie": two men would buy a mule; one would ride until noon, then tie the animal to a tree and walk until his partner behind caught up on the jack that evening. By mid-century, steamboats made the arduous and dangerous trek unnecessary, and the Trace disappeared in the trees.

Now new road, opening the woods again, went in among redbuds and white blossoms of dogwood, curving about under a cool evergreen cover. For miles no powerlines or billboards. Just tree, rock, water, bush, and road. The new Trace, like a river, followed natural contours and gave focus to the land; it so brought out the beauty that every road commissioner in the nation should drive the Trace to see that highway does not have to outrage landscape.

Northeast of Tougaloo, I stopped to hike a trail into a black-water swamp of tupelo and bald cypress. The sun couldn't cut through the canopy of buds and branches, and the slow water moved darkly. In the muck pollywogs were starting to squirm. It was spring here, and juices were getting up in the stalks; leaves, terribly folded in husks, had begun to let loose and open to the light; stuff was stirring in the rot, water bubbled with the froth of sperm and ova, and the whole bog lay rank and eggy, vaporous and thick with the scent of procreation. Things once squeezed close, pinched shut, things waiting to become something else, something greater, were about ready.

I had a powerful sense of life going about the business of getting on with itself. Pointed phallic sprouts pressed up out of the ooze, green vegetable heads came up from the mire to sniff for vegetation of kin. Staminate and pistillate, they rose to the thrall of the oldest rhythms. Things were growing so fast I could almost feel the heat from their generation: the slow friction of leaf against bud case, petal against petal. For some time I stood among the high mysteries of being as they consumed the decay of old life.

Then I went back to the Trace and followed dusk around the spread of Jackson highways that had broken open like aneurisms and leaked out strawberry-syrup pancakes, magic-finger motel beds, and double-cheese pizzas. Across the Pearl River and into Clinton, a hamlet that Sherman pillaged but decided not to burn. The place was shut down. Near the campus of old Mississippi College, I parked for the night and ate a tin of tuna and three soft carrots. Rejected the chopped liver. I ate only because I didn't know what else to do. I'd got uppity about multilane America and was paying the price. Secretly, I hungered for a texturized patty of genetically engineered cow.

7

A CENTURY and a half ago, the founders of Mississippi College hoped the school would become the state university. But that didn't work out, so they gave it to the Presbyterians; that didn't work out either, and the Presbyterians gave it back. The Baptists had a go at it, and the college got on in its own quiet way, eventually turning out three governors. Actually, all the changing around may have made little difference. A student told me that everyone in town was a Baptist anyway, even the Presbyterians.

I was eating breakfast in the cafeteria. A crewcut student wearing mesh step-in casuals sat down to a tall stack of pancakes. He was a methodical fellow. After a prayer running almost a minute, he pulled from his briefcase a Bible, reading stand, clips to hold the book open, a green felt-tip, a pink, and yellow; next came a squeeze-bottle of liquid margarine, a bottle of Log Cabin syrup wrapped in plastic, a linen napkin, and one of those little lemony wet-wipes. The whole business looked like the old circus act where twelve men get out of a car the size of a trashcan.

A woman with a butter-almond smile sat down across from me. Her hair, fresh from the curling wand, dropped in loose coils the color of polished pecan, and her breasts, casting shadows to her waist, pressed full against a glossy dress that looked wet. A golden cross swung gently between, and high on her long throat was a small PISCES amulet. Her dark, musky scent brought to mind the swamp. We nodded and she said in soft Mississippian, "You were very interested in Jerry's pancakes."

"It was the briefcase. I thought he was going to pull out a Water-Pik and the Ark of the Covenant next."

"He's a nice boy. His parameters just aren't yours." She couldn't have surprised me more had she said floccinaucinihilipilification. "The bottom line is always parameters no matter what the input."

"Let me make a crazy guess. You're in computer programming."

"I'm in business, but my brother is a computer programmer in Jackson. He's got me interested in it. He plays with the computer after hours. Made up his Christmas cards on an IBM three-sixty-one-fifty-eight last year and did his own wedding invitations two years ago. But we're channelized different. I want to use the computer to enrich spiritual life. Maybe put prayers on a computer like that company in California that programs them. For two dollars, they run your prayer through twice a day for a week. They send up ten thousand a month."

"What if God doesn't know Fortran?"

"Come on, you! People are critical, but they don't ridicule prayer wheels or rosaries and those are just prayer machines."

"Does God get a printout?"

"Quit it! You get the printout. Suitable for framing. Quit smiling!"

"Sorry, but you said they send the prayers 'up,' and I just wondered what kind of hard copy we're dealing with here."

"You're a fuddydud! It's all just modalities. The prayer still has to come from a heart. Japanese write prayers on slips of paper and tie them to branches so the wind sort of distributes them. Same thing — people just trying to maximize the prayer function."

"You're a Pisces?"

"Would a Sagittarius wear a Pisces necklace?"

"How can you believe in astrology and wear a cross?"

"What a fuddydud! Who made the stars? Astrology's just another modality too." She took a computer card from her notebook. "I've got to get to class, but here's one more modality. In India, people pray when they eat — like each chew is a prayer. Try it sometime. Even grumpy fuddyduds like it."

She handed me the card and hurried off. Here it is, word for word:

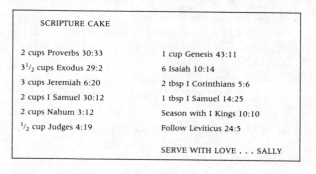

SCRIPTURE CAKE

2 cups Proverbs 30:33	1 cup Genesis 43:11
3 ½ cups Exodus 29:2	6 Isaiah 10:14
3 cups Jeremiah 6:20	2 tbsp I Corinthians 5:6
2 cups I Samuel 30:12	1 tbsp I Samuel 14:25
2 cups Nahum 3:12	Season with I Kings 10:10
½ cup Judges 4:19	Follow Leviticus 24:5

SERVE WITH LOVE . . . SALLY

8

I WENT to the Trace again, following it through pastures and pecan groves and tilled fields; wildflowers and clover pressed in close, and from trees, long purple drupes of wisteria hung like grape clusters; in one pond a colony of muskrats. I turned off near Learned and drove northwest to cross the Mississippi at Vicksburg. South of town, I ate a sandwich where Civil War earthworks stuck out on a bluff high above the river. From these aeries, cannoneers had lobbed shells onto Union gunboats running the river. Anything — a rock, a stick — falling from that height must have hit with a terrible impact.

The western side of the river was Louisiana, and the hills of Mississippi gave way to low and level cotton fields where humid heat waves boiled up, turning dusty tractors into shimmering distortions. The temperature climbed to eighty-six. Once, a big oak or gum grew in the middle of each of these fields, and under them, the farmer ate dinner, cooled the team, took an afternoon nap. Now, because they interfered with air-conditioned powerhouse tractors plowing the acres, few of the tall trees remained.

The traffic on U.S. 80 had gone to I-20, and the two-lane carried only farm trucks and tractors pulling big cannisters of liquid fertility. The federal highway, like most I'd driven, was much rougher than state or county highways, so we all went slowly, just trundling along in the heat.

A traveler who leaves the journey open to the road finds unforeseen things come to shape it. "The fecundity of the unexpected," Proudhon called it. The Cajun Fried Chicken stand in Monroe (accent the first syllable), where I'd stopped for gas, determined the direction of the next several days. I wasn't interested in franchise chicken, but the word *Cajun* brought up the scent of gumbo, hot boudin, and dirty rice. Monroe is a long way from Cajunland, but while the tank filled, I decided to head south for some genuine Cajun cooking.

On the other side of the pump, a man with arms the size of my thighs waited for the nozzle. He said, "You driving through or what?"

"On my way south."

"You want some meat?" It sounded aggressive, like, "Want a knuckle sandwich?"

"Pardon me?"

"You want meat? I'm flying out of Shreveport this afternoon. Can't carry the steaks with me. Just got called to Memphis. If you're cooking out, might as well take them. It's you or the garbage can."

He had a way with words.

"Get him the steaks, Roger." A boy, about ten, came around and handed me four nice flank cuts still frozen. I thanked the man.

"What'd you pay for your Ford?" the boy said.

"Three thousand in round numbers."

"How much to build the insides?"

"Couple hundred dollars."

"How about that homemade bed? Could I try it?" I opened the door, he jumped on the bunk, stretched out, and made a loud snoring noise. Dreaming of far places. His eyes popped open. "Inflation's added about twelve percent. These models run higher now too. How's the gas mileage?"

"Around twenty-five to the gallon."

"Can't be."

"Can be and is. Straight shift, no factory options except highback seats, lightweight, and I drive around fifty." That short man of a boy depressed me. Ten years old and figuring the rate of interest and depreciation instead of the cost of adventure. His father handed me a loaf of bread.

"Thanks very kindly," I said, "but I'm not much for white bread."

"Just have to leave it along the interstate for possums and niggers."

He did it again.

With the steaks and white bread (would go well with chopped liver) I drove south toward the flat, wet triangle of gulf-central Louisiana that is Cajunland. The highway clattered Ghost Dancing and shook me so that my head bounced like one of those plastic dogs in car rear windows. The heat made me groggy, and I couldn't shake it, and I didn't want to stop. After a while, the road seemed a continuum of yellow-lined concrete, a Möbius strip where I moved, going neither in nor out, but around and up and down to all points of the compass, yet always rolling along on the same plane.

My eyes were nearly closed. Then a dark face staring in. My head snapped back, and I pulled the truck out of the left lane. A hitchhiker. I stopped. His skin shone like wet delta mud, and his smile glittered like a handful of new dimes. He was heading home to Coushatta after spending two days thumbing along I-20 from Birmingham, where he'd looked for work as a machinist. He'd found nothing. Usually he got long rides on freeways if he could manage one, but it was easier for a black man to get a lift on the small roads where there were more Negro drivers. Sometimes the ride included a meal and bed, but last night he'd slept in a concrete culvert. I asked where he learned his trade. "In the Army. I was a Spec Four."

"Were the jobs filled in Birmingham?"

"They said they were. I don't know."

"Was it a racial question, do you think?"

He moved warily in his seat. "Can't always tell. It's easy to say that."

"What will you do now?"

"Go home and wait for something to open up." We rode quietly, the even land green and still. He was a shy man and appeared uncertain about what to say. I filled some silence, and then he said, "Seems things I wait for don't come along, and the ones I want to see pass on by, stop and settle in."

"I'm between jobs myself. Waiting for something to open up too."

"I hope I'm just between jobs. I went in the Army to learn a trade. Figured I'd found a good one for civvy life. Now I'm looking like my uncle. He only had one good job in his life. Good for his time anyway. Ran an elevator at the Roosevelt Hotel in New Orleans. Then they put in push-button elevators. He said he drove his old elevator a hundred thousand miles. He came back to Coushatta and did a little field work, then went hunting a better job in Dallas and got shot dead. I used to think he musta been a bum. Don't see it like that now."

The rest of the way was mostly quiet. "I'll get out here," he said at last.

"A man gave me some steaks. My cooler won't keep them in this heat.

Why don't you take a couple?" I pulled out a steak and handed him the rest. "Gave me this bread too. Take it if you like."

He put the steaks in his plaid suitcase but had to carry the bread in his hand. "Can I ask you a question? Why did you give me a ride?"

"I was dozing off. Owed you for waking me up."

He shook his head. "Maybe. It'll be a good night at home. Mama loves steak."

Up the road he went, thumb out, smiling into the tinted windshields. Home is the hunter, home from the hill; home the sailor, home from the sea. And what about the Specialist Four home from Birmingham?

9

ALL the way to Opelousas, I thought of the machinist whose name I never learned. He had gone out and come back only to find a single change: he was older. Sometimes a man's experience is like the sweep second hand on a clock, touching each point in its circuit but always the arcs of movement repeating.

Near Ville Platte a scene of three colors: beside a Black Angus, in a green pasture, a white cattle egret waited for grubbings the cow stirred up. The improbable pair seemed to know each other well, standing close yet looking opposite directions. I don't know what the egret did before it flew into the New World; I suppose it took its long, reedy legs to shallow water and picked in the bottoms for a couple of million years, each bird repeating until the new way of life came to it.

I switched on the radio and turned the dial. Somewhere between a shill for a drive-up savings and loan and one for salvation, I found a raucous music, part bluegrass fiddle, part Texas guitar, part Highland concertina. Cajun voices sang an old, flattened French, part English, part undecipherable.

Looking for live Cajun music, I stopped in Opelousas at the Plantation Lounge. Somebody sat on every barstool; but a small man, seeing a stranger, jumped down, shook my hand, and insisted I take his seat. In the fast roll of Cajun English, he said it was the guest stool and by right belonged to me. The barmaid, a woman with coiled eyes, brought a Jax. "Is there Cajun music here tonight?" I asked.

"Jukebox is our music tonight," she snapped.

A man called Walt, with dark hair oiled and slicked back in the style of an older time, squeezed in beside me. "If you're lookin' for French music, you need to get yourself to laugh yet."

"What's that mean?"

"Means haul your butt to laugh yet. Biggest Coonass city in the world."

"Lafayette?" I made it three syllables.

"You got it, junior, but we don't say Lah-fay-et."

"Where should I go in Laughyet?"

He drew a map so detailed I could almost see chuckholes in the streets. "Called Eric's. That's one place. In Laughyet they got whatever you want: music, hooch, girls, fights, everything." He passed the bar peanuts. "By the way, junior," he asked casually, "ever had yourself a Cajun woman?" His question silenced the bar. "Don't think I have."

"Got some advice for you then — if you find you ever need it."

It was the quietest bar I'd ever been in. I answered so softly no sound came out, and I had to repeat. "What advice?"

"Take off your belt before you climb on so you can strap your Yankee ass down because you'll get taken for a ride. Up the walls and around."

Now the whole bar was staring, I guess to surmise whether my Yankee ass was worth strapping down. One rusty geezer said, "Junior ain't got no belt."

Walt looked at my suspenders and pulled one, letting it snap back. "My man," he said, "tie on with these and you'll get zanged out the window like in a slingshot."

The men pounded the bar and choked on their Dixie beer. One began coughing and had to be slapped on the back. Two repeated the joke.

Walt shouted to the barmaid, "Let's get junior another Jax." To me he said, "Don't never take no offense at a Coonass. We're all fools in God's garden. Except for bettin'. Now that's serious. These boys'll bet on anything that moves or scores points and even some things that don't do neither. Charles, here, for example, will bet he can guess to within four how many spots on any Dalmatian dog. I bet on movement because I don't know dogs and not too many things score points. But everything moves — sooner or later. Even hills. Old Chicksaw taught me that."

10

If you've read Longfellow, you can't miss Cajunland once you get to the heart of it: Evangeline Downs (horses), Evangeline Speedway (autos),

Evangeline Thruway (trucks), Evangeline Drive-in, and, someone had just said, the Sweet Evangeline Whorehouse.

I found my way among the Evangelines into an industrial area of La-fayette, a supply depot for bayou and offshore drilling operations. Along the streets were oil-rig outfitters where everything was sections of steel: pipes, frames, ladders, derricks, piles, cables, buoys, tanks. Crude oil opened Acadian Louisiana as nothing in the past three centuries had, and it seemed as if little could be left unfound in Cajun hamlets once quite literally backwaters.

Eric's, on the edge of the outfitters' district, was a windowless concrete-block box with steel door and broken neon and a parking lot full of pickups, Cadillacs, and El Caminos ("cowboy Cadillacs"). But no French music.

I drank a Dixie and ate bar peanuts and asked the bartender where I could hear "chanky-chank," as Cajuns call their music. She, too, drew a map, but her knowledge gave out before she got to the destination. "It's called Tee's. It's down one of these roads, but they all look alike to me out there."

"Out there?"

"It's in the country. Follow my map and you'll be within a couple miles."

When I left she said good luck. The traveler should stand warned when he gets wished luck. I followed her map until the lights of Lafayette were just a glowing sky and the land was black. I wound about, crossing three identical bridges or crossing one bridge three times. I gave up and tried to find my way back to town and couldn't do that either.

Then a red glow like a campfire. A beer sign. Hearty music rolled out the open door of a small tavern, and a scent of simmering hot peppers steamed from the stovepipe chimney. I'd found Tee's. Inside, under dim halos of yellow bug lights, an accordion (the heart of a Cajun band), a fiddle, guitar, and ting-a-ling (triangle) cranked out chanky-chank. The accordionist introduced the numbers as songs of *amour* or *joie* and the patrons cheered; but when he announced "*un chanson de marriage,*" they booed him. Many times he cried out the Cajun motto, "*Laissez les bons temps rouler!*"

While the good times rolled, I sat at the bar next to a man dying to talk. My Yankee ass and his were the only ones in the place. His name was Joe Seipel and his speech Great Lakes. I asked, "You from Wisconsin?"

"Minnesota. But I been here seven years working for P.H.I."

"What's P.H.I.?"

He put down his bottle and gave me an exaggerated, wide-eyed, open-mouthed look to indicate my shocking ignorance. "You gotta be kidding!"

"About what?"

"Petroleum Helicopters Incorporated!" He shook his head. "Jees!"

"Oh, that's right. What kind of helicoptering do you do?" I tried to talk between numbers, but he talked through it all.

"I don't fly. I'm a mechanic. But Stoney here flies out to the offshore rigs. Delivers materials, crews. You know."

The pilot, in his fifties, wore cowboy boots and a jaunty avocado jumpsuit. He was applying a practiced *Bridges-at-Toko-Ri* machismo to a hugely mammaried woman who had painted on a pair of arched, red lips the likes of which the true face of womankind has never known.

Seipel said, "I was just like you when I came here — dumb as hell. But I've read about Louisiana. Learned about Coonasses from that yellow book."

"What yellow book is that?"

"That one comes out every month."

"National Geographic?"

"That's it. They had a story on Coonasses."

"Did they explain the name 'Coonass'?"

"I think they missed that."

A small, slue-footed Gallic man wearing a silky shirt with a pelican on it dragged an upturned metal washtub next to the band and climbed on. I think he'd taken out his dentures. A mop handle with baling twine tied to it projected from the tub, and he thrust the stick about in rhythm with the music, plucking out the sound of a double bass.

"That's DeePaul on the gut bucket," Seipel said. "He's not with the band."

After a couple of numbers on the tub, the small man hopped down and waltzed around the floor, quite alone, snapping his wrists, making sharp rapid clacks with four things that looked like big ivory dominoes.

"Those are the bones," Seipel said. "Sort of Cajun castanets."

When the band folded for the night, the little fellow sashayed to the lighted jukebox, drawn to it like a moth, and clacked the bones in fine syncopation, his red tongue flicking out the better to help him syncopate, his cropped orb of a head glowing darkly. Seipel hollered him over.

He showed how to hold the bones one on each side of the middle fingers, then flung out his wrist as if throwing off water and let loose a report like the crack of a bullwhip. "Try dem in you hands."

The bones were smooth like old jade. I laboriously inserted the four-inch counters between my fingers and snapped my wrist. *Cluk-cluk.* "Lousy," Seipel said. I tried again. *Cluk-cluk.* Wet sponges had more resonance. Seipel shook his head, so I handed them to him. He got them mounted, lashed out an arm, and a bone sailed across the room.

"You boys don't got it," DeePaul said, his words looping in the old Cajun way. DeePaul's name was in fact Paul Duhon. He had cut the clappers from a certain leg bone in a steer and carved them down to proper shape and a precise thickness. "You got to have da right bone, or da sound she muffle. And da steer got to be big for da good ringin' bones."

I tried again. *Cluk-cluk.* "I work at dis forty years," Duhon said, "and just now do I start gettin' it right. Look at me, gettin' ole and just now gettin' good. Dat's why only ole, ole men play da good bones."

"Where'd you learn to make them?"

"Ole color man, he work on da rayroad. He got nuttin' but he love music so he play da bones. He play dem in da ole minstrel shows. He da one day call 'Mister Bones,' and it Mister Bones hisself he show me carvin'. Now people say, 'Come play us da bones in Shrevepoat.' But da bones just for fun."

"DeePaul flies kites," Seipel said. "Wants in the *Guinness Book.*"

"My kites day fly for time in da air, not how high. Someday I want people to be rememberin' Duhon. I want 'Duhon' wrote down."

"I can play the musical saw," Seipel said and called to the barmaid, "Got a saw here?" She pushed him a saltshaker. "What's this?"

"That's the salt you're yellin' for." Seipel and I laughed, holding on to the bar. Duhon went home. Everybody went home. The barmaid watched us wearily. "Okay," she said, "come on back for some hot stuff."

"Is this where we find out why they call themselves 'Coonasses'?" I said, and we laughed again, holding on to each other.

"All right, boys. Settle down." She led us not to a bedroom but to a large concrete-floor kitchen with an old picnic table under a yellow fluorescent tube. We sat and a young Cajun named Michael passed a long loaf of French bread. The woman put two bowls on the oil cloth and ladled up gumbo. Now, I've eaten my share of gumbo, but never had I tasted anything like that gumbo: the oysters were fresh and fat, the shrimp succulent, the spiced sausage meaty, okra sweet, rice soft, and the roux — the essence — the roux was right. We could almost stand our spoons on end in it.

The roots of Cajun cookery come from Brittany and bear no resemblance to Parisian cuisine and not even much to the Creole cooking of New Orleans. Those are *haute cuisines* of the city, and Cajun food belongs to the country where things got mixed up over the generations. No one even knows the source of the word *gumbo.* Some say it derives from an African word for okra, *chinggombo,* while others believe it a corruption of a Choctaw word for sassafras, *kombo,* the key seasoning.

The woman disappeared, so we ate gumbo and dipped bread and no one talked. A gray cat hopped on the bench between Seipel and me to watch each bite of both bowls we ate. Across the room, a fat, buffy mouse moved over the stove top and browsed for drippings from the big pot. The cat eyed it every so often but made no move away from our bowls. Seipel said, "I've enjoyed the hell out of tonight," and he laid out a small shrimp for the cat. Nothing more got spoken. We all went at the gumbo, each of us, Minnesotan, Cajun, cat, mouse, Missourian.

1 1

SOMETIME in the darkness of morning, the rain started. It pecked, then pelted, then fell in a steady, soft patter on the steel roof of Ghost Dancing, and my sleep was without shadows.

At six-thirty the sky was still dark, the rain falling steadily. An hour later: rain. Two hours later: no change. I got up, washed, ate some fruit and cheese. I draped across the bunk and read, occasionally looking into the gray obscuring rain, listening to thunder (puts the sugar in the cane), watching Spanish moss (a relative of the pineapple) hang still in the trees like shredded, dingy bedsheets. At ten-thirty the rain dropped straight down as if from a faucet; I was able to leave the front windows half open. I didn't know then, but in April in coastal Louisiana you don't wait for the rain to stop unless you have all day and night. Which I did.

Reading my notes of the trip — images, bits of conversations, ideas — I hunted a structure in the events, but randomness was the rule. Outside, sheltered by a live oak, a spider spun a web. Can an orb weaver perceive the design in its work, the pattern of concentric circles lying atop radiating lines? When the mystical young Black Elk went to the summit of Harney Peak to see the shape of things, he looked down on the great unifying hoop of peoples. I looked down and saw fragments. But later that afternoon, a tactic returned to me from night maneuver training in the Navy: to see in deep darkness you don't look directly at an object — you look to the left; you look at something else to see what you really want to see. Skewed vision.

At five-thirty the rain stopped; it didn't ease, it just stopped. I walked through the west side of Lafayette where I'd parked for the night — and day as it turned out. The wetness deepened the tones of things as if the rain had been droplets of color. Azaleas dripped blood-red blossoms, camellias oozed carmine. The puddly ground squelched under me. The overcast moved east like a gray woolen blanket being pulled back, and the sun came in low beneath a wrinkling of clouds. Then a sunset happened, a gaudy polychrome sky — mauve, cerise, puce — so garish I couldn't take my eyes away.

On a front porch threatened with a turbulence of blooming vegetation, a man stood before his barbecue grill, the ghostly blue smoke rising like incense. His belly a drooping bag, his face slack, he watched the coals burn to a glow. He'd built many briquette fires. The man's numb stasis disturbed me.

Got to get moving, I thought, and hurried to my rig and drove to Breaux Bridge, "the crawfish capital of the world." I was looking for a crawdad supper. Breaux Bridge, on the Bayou Teche, stirred slowly with an awakened sense of Acadianism. Codofil, an organization working to preserve Cajun traditions and language, had placed signs in the dusty shop windows, things like SOYONS FIERS DE PARLER FRANÇAIS or PARLEZ FRANÇAIS — C'EST DE L'ARGENT EN POCHE. I asked a man locking his store where to eat crawfish. He sent me east across the bayou, through banks of willow and hanging moss, past little fencepost signs advertising Evangeline Maid bread, past front-yard shrines to the Virgin, past lots piled with fishing gear. At Henderson I found a wooden building hanging over Bayou Peyronnet just below the massive west levee of the Atchafalaya River basin; the heavy air of increase smelled of marine creatures and mud and hot peppers. On the roof of Pat's restaurant sat a six-foot, red plastic model of the Cajun totem: a boiled crawdad.

The menu claimed the catfish were fresh because they had slept the night before in the Atchafalaya. All well and good, but it was little crustaceans I was after. As journalist Calvin Trillin once said, the Atchafalaya swamp is to crawfish as the Serengeti to lions. The waitress wore threads of wrinkles woven like Chantilly lace over her forehead and spoke her English in quick, rounded Cajun measures. She brought a metal beer tray piled with boiled, whole crawfish glowing the color of Louisiana hot sauce. I worked my way down through the stack. The meat was soft and piquant, sweeter than shrimp, but I had no stomach for the buttery, yellow fat the Cajuns were sucking from the shells.

The waitress said, "Did they eat lovely like mortal sin?" and winked a lacy eyelid. "You know, the Cajun, he sometime call them 'mudbugs.' But I never tell a customer that until he all full inside. But the crawfish, he live smilin' in the mud, he do."

"They're just miniature lobsters. Are you Cajun?"

"Don't you know that now, *cher*?"

"Do you use your French?"

"Time to time, but not like my old aunt. She don't speak English except death's at the door, and then it sound like her French. People you age understand but don't speak it much, no. And the kids? They don't tell French from Eskimo. Schools, they hire a hundred teachers to give little ones French. But teachers they teach Paris people's French. Hell, we speak Cajun, us. The teachers, they look down at their noses on Cajun, so we don't care. I'm afraid for Cajun. Us, we're the last. But when I was a girl on the schoolyard, when they open the day with raisin' Old Glory, we sing the Marseillaise — we thought it was America's song."

In the warm night that came on to relieve the colors of the day, I went down through the rockless, liquid land, down along the Bayou Teche to St. Martinville, a crumbling hamlet where the past was the future.

12

TALK about your three-persons-in-one controversies. In St. Martinville a bronze statue of a seated young woman in wooden shoes, hands folded peacefully, head turned toward the Bayou Teche, commemorates — at one and the same time — Emmeline Labiche, Evangeline Bellefontaine, and Dolores Del Rio. The monument sits in the Poste de Attakapas Cemetery behind the great Catholic church of Saint Martin de Tours. After the bayou, the cemetery and church are the oldest things in town. The cruciform building, full of flickering candles, bloodied crucifixes, anguished representations of the Stations of the Cross, and plaster saints with maces and drawn swords, contains in one wing a twelve-foot high replica of the Grotto of Lourdes. Although mass is now celebrated in English, the place, with its ancient torments, remains quite French in the old manner.

The bronze woman sits, literally, above the eighteenth-century grave of Emmeline Labiche, who, Cajuns say, wandered primitive America in search of her lover, Louis Arcenaux, whom she was separated from during the forced Acadian exodus (Le Grand Dérangement) out of British Nova Scotia. At the army outpost on the Teche, she finally found Louis — engaged to another. Emmeline, exhausted from her wanderings, went mad from the shock of his faithlessness and died shortly later. They buried her behind the church. That's history.

But the name on the statue above Emmeline's tombstone is Evangeline. Cajuns believe Longfellow patterned his wandering heroine on Emmeline, and probably he did, although the poet never visited Louisiana, relying instead on information furnished by Nathaniel Hawthorne and a St. Martinville lawyer once Longfellow's student at Harvard. To visualize the land, he went to Banvard's "Moving Diorama" of the Mississippi — a three-mile-long canvas painting of a boat-level view. Longfellow said the river came to him. He filled in with details from Darby's *Geographical Description of Louisiana* and his own imagination, changing the outcome so that in old age Evangeline at last finds her love on his deathbed in a Philadelphia almshouse. That's the poetry.

Then there's Hollywood. The face on the statue, smooth and beautiful and untouched by madness or years of wandering the wilderness, is that of Dolores Del Rio, the Mexican-born actress who completed the trinity by playing Evangeline in the 1929 movie filmed nearby at Lake Catahoula. To thank the townspeople, the cast presented a statue of Evangeline-Emmeline that Miss Del Rio posed for. The actress, cynics said, saw a chance to have her beauty immortalized in something more durable than celluloid. If many citizens no longer know the name, they all know the face.

St. Martinville was pure Cajun bayou, distinctive and memorable in a tattered way. Wood and iron galleries were rickety, brick buildings eroded, corrugated metal roofs rusting. The church stood on the square, the courthouse down Main Street. On the upper side of the square that morning, Maurice Oubre's bakery turned out the last of the day's pastry, and on the west side at Thibodeaux's Cafe & Barbershop, Mr. Thibodeaux had been cutting hair since five A.M. Across the street, taverns got swept out, and the smell of last night's beer mixed with Thibodeaux's thick *café noir*, Oubre's croissants, and the damp air off the Teche.

In the *Petit Paris de l'Amerique* Museum gift shop next to the church, a powdery old lady asked the priest to bless a souvenir candle she'd just bought; he waved his hand over it and said, "May God bless this candle and all who use it, in the name of the Father, Son, and Holy Spirit." Above his head, on the Coke machine, a sign: SHOPLIFTING IS A CRIME AND SIN. GOD SEES ALL AND REMEMBERS!!! Sin was underlined three times.

13

BECAUSE of a broken sealed-beam headlight and Zatarain's Creole Mustard, an excellent native mustard, I met Barbara Pierre. I had just come out of Dugas' grocery with four jars of Zatarain's, and we almost collided on the sidewalk. She said, "You're not from St. Martinville, are you? You can't be."

"I'm from Missouri."

"What in the world are you doing here? Got a little Huck Finn in you?"

"Just followed the bayou. Now I'm looking for the Ford agency."

"Coincidences. I work there. I'll show you the way."

She was a secretary at the agency and took classes at the University of Southwestern Louisiana in Lafayette when she could. I asked about St. Martinville, but she had to start working before we could say much.

"Here's an idea," she said. "Come by at noon and we can have lunch at my place. I live in the project on the other side of the bayou."

I picked her up at twelve. She asked about the trip, especially about Selma and how things were as I saw them. "A white man griped about changes, and a black said there weren't enough changes to gripe about."

"That's us too. What we want is slow coming — if it's coming at all. Older blacks here are scared of whites and won't do much for change if it means risk. Others don't care as long as everything gets smothered over with politeness by whites. Young blacks see the hypocrisy — even when it's not there. But too many of them are juked on drugs, and that's where some of this town wants us."

"Don't any whites here try to help?"

"A few, but if a white starts helping too much, they get cut off or shut down by the others and end up paying almost the price we do. Sure, we got good whites — when they're not scared out of showing sympathy."

On Margaret Street, she pointed to her apartment in a small one-story brick building. Standard federal housing. As we went to the door, a shadowy face watched from behind a chintz curtain in another apartment.

"See that? Could be the start of bad news," she said.

"Maybe I should leave. I don't want to cause trouble for you."

"Too late. Besides, I live my own life here. I won't be pushed. But it'll come back in some little way. Smart remark, snub. One old white lady kicks me at the library. Swings her feet under the table because she doesn't want my kind in there. I could break her in two, she's so frail. She'll be kicking like a heifer if she gets wind of this."

Barbara Pierre's apartment was a tidy place but for books on the sofa. "You can see I still use the library even with the nuisances. The kicking bitch hides books I return so I get overdue notices and have to go prove I turned the book in. I explain what's going on, but nothing changes. Simplest thing is trouble."

"That's what I heard in Selma."

"I'm not alone, but sometimes it seems like a conspiracy. Especially in little towns. Gossip and bigotry — that's the blood and guts."

"Was that person who just looked out the window white?"

"Are you crazy? Nobody on this end of Margaret Street is white. That's what I mean about us blacks not working together. Half this town is black, and we've only got one elected black official. Excuse my language, but for all the good he does this side of the bayou, he's one useless black mofo."

"Why don't you do something? I mean you personally."

"I do. And when I do, I get both sides coming down on me. Including my own family. Everywhere I go, sooner or later, I'm in the courtroom. Duplicity! That's my burning pot. I've torn up more than one court of law."

We sat down at her small table. A copy of *Catch-22* lay open.

"Something that happened a few years ago keeps coming back on me. When I was living in Norristown, outside Philadelphia, I gained a lot of weight and went to a doctor. She gave me some diet pills but never explained they were basically speed, and I developed a minor drug problem. I went to the hospital and the nuns said if I didn't sign certain papers they couldn't admit me. So I signed and they put me in a psychiatric ward. Took two hellish weeks to prove I didn't belong there. God, it's easy to get somebody adjudicated crazy."

"Adjudicated?"

"You don't know the word, or you didn't think I knew it?"

"It's the right word. Go on."

"So now, because I tried to lose thirty pounds, people do a job on my personality. But if I shut up long enough, things quiet down. Still, it's the old pattern: any nigger you can't control is crazy."

As we ate our sandwiches and drank Barq's rootbeer, she asked whether I had been through Natchitoches. I said I hadn't.

"They used to have a statue up there on the main street. Called the 'Good Darkie Statue.' It was an old black man, slouched shoulders, big possum-eating smile. Tipping his hat. Few years ago, blacks made them take it down. Whites couldn't understand. Couldn't see the duplicity in that statue — duplicity on *both* sides. God almighty! I'll promise them one thing: ain't gonna be no more gentle darkies croonin' down on the levee."

I smiled at her mammy imitation, but she shook her head. "In the sixties I wanted that statue blown to bits. It's stored in Baton Rouge now at LSU, but they put it in the wrong building. Ought to be in the capitol reminding people. Preserve it so nobody forgets. Forgives, okay — but not forgets."

"Were things bad when you were a child?"

"Strange thing. I was born here in 'forty-one and grew up here, but I

8. *Barbara Pierre in St. Martinville, Louisiana*

don't remember prejudice. My childhood was warm and happy — especially when I was reading. Maybe I was too young to see. I don't know. I go on about the town, but I love it. I've put my time in the cities — New Orleans, Philly. Your worst Southern cracker is better than a Northern liberal, when it comes to duplicity anyway, because you know right off where the cracker crumbles. With a Northerner, you don't know until it counts, and that's when you get a job done on yourself."

"I'd rather see a person shut up about his prejudices."

"You haven't been deceived. Take my job. I was pleased to get it. Thought it was a breakthrough for me and other blacks here. Been there three weeks, and next Wednesday is my last day."

"What happened?"

"Duplicity's what happened. White man in the shop developed a bad back, so they moved him inside. His seniority gets my job. I see the plot — somebody in the company got pressured to get rid of me."

"Are you going to leave town?"

"I'm staying. That's my point. I'll take St. Martinville over what I've seen of other places. I'm staying here to build a life for myself and my son. I'll get married again. Put things together." She got up and went to the window. "I don't know, maybe I'm too hard on the town. In an underhanded way, things work here — mostly because old blacks know how to get along with whites. So they're good darkies? They own their own homes. They don't live in a rat-ass ghetto. There's contentment. Roots versus disorder." She stopped abruptly and smiled. "Even German soldiers they put in the POW camp here to work the cane fields wanted to stay on."

We cleared the table and went to the front room. A wall plaque:

OH LORD, HELP ME THIS DAY
TO KEEP MY BIG MOUTH SHUT.

On a bookshelf by the window was the two-volume microprint edition of the *Oxford English Dictionary,* the one sold with a magnifying glass.

"I love it," she said. "Book-of-the-Month Club special. Seventeen-fifty. Haven't finished paying for it though."

"Is it the only one in town?"

"Doubt it. We got brains here. After the aristocracy left Paris during the French Revolution, a lot of them settled in St. Martinville, and we got known as *Le Petit Paris.* Can you believe this little place was a cultural center only second to New Orleans? Town started slipping when the railroad put the bayou steamers out of business, but the church is proof of what we had."

"When you finish the college courses, what then?"

"I'd like to teach elementary school. If I can't teach, I want to be a teacher's aide. But — here's a big 'but' — if I can make a living, I'll write books for children. We need black women writing, and my courses are in journalism and French. Whatever happens, I hope they don't waste my intelligence."

She went to wash up. I pulled out one of her books: *El Señor Presidente* by Guatemalan novelist Miguel Asturias. At page eighty-five she had underlined two sentences: "The chief thing is to gain time. We must be patient."

On the way back to the agency, she said, "I'll tell you something that took me a long time to figure out — but I know how to end race problems."

"Is this a joke?"

"Might as well be. Find a way to make people get bored with hating instead of helping. Simple." She laughed. "That's what it boils down to."

14

THE Corps of Engineers calls it the Atchafalaya Basin Floodway System. Some Acadians call it a boondoggle in the boondocks. The Atchafalaya River, only one hundred thirty-five miles long, has an average discharge more than twice as great as that of the Missouri River although the area it drains is less than a fifth of the Missouri's and the Big Muddy is nearly twenty times as long. Yet, the Atchafalaya forms the biggest river basin swamp in North America, and before it became an overflow drain, its swamp was at least as biologically rich and varied as the Everglades. Maybe it still is, despite claims by older Cajuns that wildlife isn't what it was a generation ago. Nevertheless, some ornithologists believe the swamp might hold the last ivory-billed woodpecker.

After the great flood of 1927, the Corps built hundreds of miles of "protection levees" around the upper Atchafalaya and down the length of the basin to create an "emergency discharge" route for the Mississippi and Red rivers. The Corps said had it done nothing to the Atchafalaya, the Mississippi — always trying to change course — would eventually open a new channel about sixty miles north of St. Martinville and leave New Orleans on a backwater oxbow.

The problem is that engineers built so injudiciously, the swamp is filling with some of the one million tons of silt the big rivers carry in daily; and those Cajuns who traditionally make a living from the wetlands by fishing, frogging, mudbugging, trapping, and mosspicking are having to leave their fastness and take work in industry. The Corps altered not just the Atchafalaya and a great swamp but also one of the distinctive ethnic peoples in America.

Maybe the swamp is doomed anyway, what with bayous being dredged and channels dug so oil and gas drilling equipment can get in, what with pipelines being laid, and wipe-out logging of cypress and tupelo. To be sure, dry-land farmers — a minority — are happy. At the north end of the basin, they have cleared sixty thousand acres of swamp hardwoods for pasturage and soybeans.

Now, to rectify their errors, the Corps wants permanent control of the basin, and, of all things, many environmentalists support the plan. Everyone believes what the dredge and bulldozer can do, they can also undo; but a Cajun named Cassie Hebert told me he had yet to see a bush-hog make a mink.

Some Cajuns believe in only one thing — the Mississippi. Hebert said: "The Atchafalaya's a shorter way to the Guff than the Missippi take. Big river gonna find us down here, Corps be damned. One day rain gonna start and keep on like it do sometimes. When the rainin' stop, the Missippi gonna be ninety miles west of N'Orleans and St. Martinville gonna be a seaport. And it won't be the firstest time the river go runnin' from Lady N'Orleans."

Indian legend tells of a serpent of fabulous dimension living in the Atchafalaya basin; when Chitimacha braves slew it, its writhing throes gouged out Bayou Teche. *Teche* may be an Indian word for "snake," and Cajuns say the big river will one day avenge the serpent. We have only to wait.

The Teche, at the western edge of the basin and paralleling the Atchafalaya, has been spared the salvation wreaked on the river, even though, before roads came, the little Teche — not the Atchafalaya — was the highway from the Gulf into the heart of Louisiana. Half of the eighteenth-century settlements in the state lay along or very near the Teche: St. Martinville, Lafayette, Opelousas, New Iberia. The Teche was navigable for more than a hundred miles. Indians put dugouts on it; Spanish adventurers and French explorers floated it in cypress-trunk pirogues (some displacing fifty tons); settlers rode it in keelboats pulled by mules or slaves; merchandise arrived by paddlewheelers; and during the Civil War, Union gunboats came up the Teche to commandeer the fertile cane fields along its banks. All of this on a waterway no wider than the length of a war canoe, no deeper than a man, no swifter than mud turtles that swim it.

Blue road 31, from near Opelousas, follows the Teche through sugarcane, under cypress and live oak, into New Iberia. St. Martinville had dozed on the bayou for two hundred years. Not so New Iberia. A long strip of highway businesses had cropped up to the west, and the town center by the little drawbridge was clean and bright. No dozing here.

Bayouside New Iberia gave a sense of both the new made old and the old made new: contemporary architecture interpreting earlier designs rather than imitating them; a restored Classic Revival mansion, Shadows on the Teche; a society whose members are hundred-year-old live oaks; and the only second-century, seven-foot marble statue of the Emperor Hadrian in a savings and loan. New Iberia suggested Cajun history, but St. Martinville lived it.

I took Louisiana 14: roadsides of pink thistle, cemeteries jammed with aboveground tombs, cane fields under high smokestacks of sugar factories, then salt-dome country, then shrimp trawlers at Delcambre. My last chance at Cajun food was Abbeville, a town with two squares: one for the church, one for the courthouse. On the walk at Black's Oyster Bar a chalked sign: FRESH TOPLESS SALTY OYSTERS. Inside, next to a stuffed baby alligator, hung an autographed photo of Paul Newman, who had brought the cast of *The Drowning Pool* to Black's while filming near Lafayette. Considering that a recommendation, I ordered a dozen topless ("on the halfshell") and a fried oyster loaf (oysters and hot pepper garnish heaped between slices of French bread). Good enough to require a shrimp loaf for the road.

On the highway, I wished the British had exiled more Acadians to America if only for their cooking. Somewhere lives a bad Cajun cook, just as somewhere must live one last ivory-billed woodpecker. For me, I don't expect ever to encounter either one.

The rice fields began near Kaplan, where the land is less than twenty feet above the sea only thirty miles south, and kept going all the way to Texas. The Lake Arthur bridge made a long, curvilinear glide into space as it rose above the water; passage was like driving the chromium contours of Louisianan Jose de Rivera's famous "Construction 8." At Lake Charles, another sinuous parabola of bridgeway, an aerial thing curving about so I could see its underside as I went up.

The city stretched below in a swelter of petrochemical plants and wharves. I got through only with effort and pressed north to state 27. When I had left home, I announced a stop, sooner or later, at a cousin's in Shreveport. I hoped for mail. U.S. 171 was traffic, fumes, heat, grim faces. I became a grim face and drove. Rosepine, Anacoco, Hornbeck, and Zwolle — alphabetically, the last town in the Rand-McNally *Road Atlas* (Abbeville, just south, is the first).

A yellow simmer of glaring haze sat on Shreveport like a pot lid. I pulled in at a honky-tonk called Charlie's to telephone my cousin. No one home. I took a seat at the bar. Charlie's was built-in-spare-time-after-bowling-league construction, the ceilings so low I could almost touch them flat-footed. After ten minutes I regained my vision in the cool darkness. Near the bar hung one of those pictures of dogs playing poker and cheating in a multitude of cleverly canine ways. The west fire exit unexpectedly opened and sunlight poured in; like Draculas before the cross, we cried out and covered our eyes.

Next to me, a lady nearing her seventh decade kept between us a white purse big enough for a mugger to hide in. She wore a black wig. Her devil-may-care red lipstick had come unhitched and slipped a notch; her layers of nail polish were chipped like paint on an old dory; and her hands lay in two piles on the bar, the slack skin taken up by plumpness. As for the Jungle Gardenia perfume, it was only a question of time before tsetse flies hit.

She reached over and lifted my can of Jax as if to test the weight. Then she turned, saw me, and jumped. "Oh! Gracious! You've scared me! I'm sorry! I thought you went off and left your beer. Gracious!"

"May I buy you one?"

"Oh! Gracious, no! Beer does things to me. I just look after the girls."

"Are you related?"

"Goodness, no! Only a friend. I worry about them with these cowboys."

The "girls" were the bartender and a pool player, both of whom looked quite capable of handling any of the spinstool cowboys (Shreveport is more Dallas than New Orleans). The bartender was, in the lingo, one tough broad. A snake fits its skin no tighter than she fit her bluejeans. The pool player, a woman of sleek legs, wore a tank top and cut-offs that had seen the absolute maximum of strategic cutting. The game she played was, nominally, eight ball, but the real purpose was to make spectacular shots — never mind if the cue ball ended up in someone's Schlitz.

After each shot, she groaned and took a long, hard stretch out of her hustler's crouch and said, "Ah cain't shoot worth a damn today." Who had noticed her shooting, watching as we were her form? She kept a beercan on a stack of damp dollar bills. As lousy as she played, she managed to beat the Louisiana cowboys who laughed with beer commercial heartiness. They knew a good entertainment value when they saw it.

The overripe lushness of Jungle Gardenia enveloped me again. "Who's your favorite picture-show actor?" she said.

"I don't know. Alan Bates. Jimmy Stewart. Chief Dan George."

"Mine's Franchot Tone."

There followed a long recital of movie titles, bits of plot, pieces of dialogue. As she talked, she laid a soft curl of fingers over my wrist; it wasn't a gesture of friendship so much as an ascertaining of my presence, a holding of her audience. Once she had heard that Mr. Tone wore a stomach corset in his later years, but she knew that couldn't have been true. The lady must have known more about Franchot Tone than anyone else in the world. Whatever empty spaces had opened in her life she filled with dreams of a flickering vision. As Jesus or Mozart or Crazy Horse fill hollows in others, so Franchot Tone had come to his lady moist in her Jungle Gardenia.

I called my cousin again, got directions, and drove to her house. The sun was gone when the family sat down to dinner. A pair of heavy moths bumped the screen, and we took barbecued chicken from the platter. It had been a long time since I'd eaten among faces I'd seen before, and I knew it would be hard leaving.

Four

SOUTH BY SOUTHWEST

FROM the Cherokee there had been no letter. Now, under a low gray sky, highway 79 stretched out like a dead snake. I watched the empty road and hated the solitude. The wanderer's danger is to find comfort. A weekend in Shreveport around friends, and security had started to pull me into a warm thrall, to enfold me, to make the wish for the road a craziness. So it was only memory of times in strange places where the scent of the unknown is sharp that drew me on to the highway again.

William Carlos Williams: "Memory is a kind of accomplishment." Maybe. And maybe too, in the end, it's the only thing one can call truly his own. Memory is each man's own last measure, and for some, the only achievement.

I crossed into Texas. I've heard Americans debate where the West begins: Texans say the Brazos River; in St. Louis it's the Mississippi, and they built a very expensive "Gateway Arch" to prove it; Philadelphians say the Alleghenies; in Brooklyn it's the Hudson; and on Beacon Hill the backside of the Common. But, of course, the true West begins with the western state lines of Louisiana, Arkansas, Missouri, Iowa, and Minnesota. It's a line, as close to straight as you could hope to find, that runs from the Gulf of Mexico to Canada; fewer than a hundred miles from the geographical east-west division of the continental states, it lies close to the hundredth meridian, the twenty-inch rainfall line, and the two-thousand-foot contour line — all of which various geographers recognize as demarcations between East and West. When you stand east of those states you're in the East; cross over and you're in the West. It's simple and clear.

I'm an authority because my family lives two hundred feet from where this line passes through Kansas City. I've hit numerous backyard homeruns from the East into the West. Kansas City, Missouri, is the last Eastern city, and Kansas City, Kansas — the two divided only by hedges, a street, a piece of river — is the first Western one.

The land west of this line used to be known as the Great American

Desert, but only geographers use that term now as far as I can tell. By "desert" they mean a high land (two thousand feet and up), commonly arid (less than twenty inches rainfall), with mountains, evergreen forests, prairie grasses, and even some sand. They don't mean trackless Saharan dunes and palmy oases.

The true West differs from the East in one great, pervasive, influential, and awesome way: space. The vast openness changes the roads, towns, houses, farms, crops, machinery, politics, economics, and, naturally, ways of thinking. How could it do otherwise? Space west of the line is perceptible and often palpable, especially when it appears empty, and it's that apparent emptiness which makes matter look alone, exiled, and unconnected. Those spaces diminish man and reduce his blindness to the immensity of the universe; they push him toward a greater reliance on himself, and, at the same time, to a greater awareness of others and what they do. But, as the space diminishes man and his constructions in a material fashion, it also — paradoxically — makes them more noticeable. *Things show up out here.* No one, not even the sojourner, escapes the expanses. You can't get away from them by rolling up the safety-glass and speeding through, because the terrible distances eat up speed. Even dawn takes nearly an hour just to cross Texas. Still, drivers race along; but when you get down to it, they are people uneasy about space.

On the west side of the Sabine River, the land became hilly and green with deciduous trees and open in a way Louisiana was not. The long horizon gave a sense of flatness, but in truth, it was only a compression through distance of broad-topped hills.

The towns: Carthage, Mount Enterprise, old Nacogdoches (not to be confused with old Natchitoches, Louisiana; Nacogdoches sounds as it looks, but Natchitoches comes out NACK-uh-tesh). Alto, on Texas 21 and about an hour west of the great line, was a pure Western town: streets broad and at right angles, canopies over sidewalks, false-front stores, the commercial section a single long street rather than a cluster around a confluence of streets. And the businesses tended in one manner or another toward ranching and lumbering.

To drive blue highway 21 is to follow Texas history. Older than the mind of man, it started as a bison trail (buffalo walk in surprisingly straight lines); then Indians came up it to hunt the buffalo. In 1691, Spain established a thousand-mile *camino real*, a royal road, that would link San Antonio with Mexico, French Louisiana, and Spanish Florida; the Spaniards figured the Indians knew best and marked their course over the old track (often the *camino* was only a direction). Up it came adventurers, padres, traders, smugglers, armies, settlers. And so it was that wandering bison, in a time even before red men came to east Texas, laid down a route that a nation whose explorers steer tangents past the planetary arcs still follow. And all travelers coming in season see the orange and red nobs of Indian paintbrush blow in the spring winds.

Signboards: NEW BOGGY BAPTIST CHURCH. NEW ENERGY BAPTIST CHURCH. YARD EGGS. I stopped for that one. A disfigured dog, ancestral bloodlines so crossed it looked like the first dog on earth, took up a crouch at the van door and gave a long, low, ugly snarl. A woman, shrunken into odd angles, her fingers wrung into arthritic claws, came from the house; with a swing of her cane, she sent the son-of-a-bitch howling. She pushed her old head up to the window. Had her face been cut from cloth, it would have been in tatters. "You the tellyvision repair feller?" Like a curtain opening, the tatters drew back in a smile.

"I'd like to buy some eggs."

"Oh." The tatters dropped. "You see, my layers fell sick over winter, and I got no extries for sale." The dog had crept back into growling range. "Sure you ain't the tellyvision feller? This looks like one of them repair trucks. Don't let the mutt cur scare your bones." I assured her it didn't and never took my eyes off the mongrel as it growled me back to the road. But my loneliness fell away after seeing hers.

The sky turned the color of chimney soot. A massive, squared mound, quite unlike the surrounding hills, rose from a level valley; it had been the central element in a Caddoan Indian village a thousand years ago. I took a sandwich and climbed to the top to eat in the low overgrowth of wild blackberry bushes. There I was — a resident from the age of lunch meat, no-lead, and Ziploc bags — sitting on a thousand-year-old civic center.

The aura of time the mound gave off seemed to mock any comprehension of its change and process — how it had grown from baskets of shoveled soil to the high center of Caddoan affairs to a hilly patch of blackberries. My rambling metaphysics was getting caught in the trap of reducing experience to coherence and meaning, letting the perplexity of things disrupt the joy in their mystery. To insist that diligent thought would bring an understanding of change was to limit life to the comprehensible.

A raw scorch of lightning — fire from the thunderbird's eye — struck at the black clouds. A long peal. Before the rumble stopped, raindrops bashed the blackberry blossoms, and I ran for Ghost Dancing. Warm and dry, I watched the storm batter the old mound as it worked to wash the hill level again. The wind turned leaves white side up and bent small trees into bows and snapped them like buggy whips, and thunder sounded like shivered timbers. It was a fine, loud, fulminating, cracking storm.

When it passed, I went back up to see what I'd missed. Later, on the way down, I saw in the bushes a great white rump. A woman crapping. Along the road, a black girl sat beside a window van, hands between her knees, a cigarette between her lips. I asked how she liked the Indian mound. She lifted her hands, both of them, to pull the cigarette away. She was handcuffed. "What mound?"

The woman in the bushes returned. "Get in, Karen."

"I gotta go too."

"How you gonna wipe in cuffs?"

The black girl looked at me. "Hit the dike on the head and take me witchoo."

"Don't mess, Charley, or you'll be sorry."

They drove off. I left and went through North Zulch on the way to College Station. I had witnessed an hour in the history of the Caddoan mound. Black Elk, looking down on the whole hoop of the world from Harney Peak, understood more than he saw. For me it was the other way.

2

DIME BOX, Texas, is not the funniest town name in America. Traditionally, that honor belongs to Intercourse, Pennsylvania. I prefer Scratch Ankle, Alabama, Gnawbone, Indiana, or even Humptulips, Washington. Nevertheless, Dime Box, as a name, caught my ear, so that's where I headed the next morning out of College Station.

In the humid night, the inside windows had dripped like cavern walls. Along state 21, I opened up and let warm air blow out the damp. West of the Brazos, the land unfolded even farther to the blue sky. Now the horizon wasn't ten or fifteen miles away, it was thirty or forty. On telephone wires sat scissor-tailed flycatchers, their oddly long tails hanging under them like stilts. Roadside wildflowers — bluebonnets, purple winecups, evening primroses, and more — were abundant as crops, and where wide reaches of bluebonnets (once called buffalo clover, wolf flower, and, by the Spanish, "the rabbit") covered the slopes, their scent filled the highway. To all the land was an intense clarity as if the little things gave off light.

Across the Yegua River a sign pointed south to Dime Box. Over broad hills, over the green expansion spreading under cedars and live oaks, on into a valley where I found Dime Box, essentially a three-street town. Vegetable gardens and flowerbeds lay to the side, behind, and in front of the houses. Perpendicular to the highway, two streets ran east and west:

one of worn brick buildings facing the Southern Pacific tracks, the other a double row of false-front stores and wooden sidewalks. Disregarding a jarring new bank, Dime Box could have been an M-G-M backlot set for a Western.

You can't walk down a board sidewalk without clomping, so I clomped down to Ovcarik's Cafe and through the screendoor, which banged shut as they always do. An aroma of ham and beans. Four calendars. From long cords three naked bulbs burned, and still the place was dim. Everything was wood except a heating stove and the Coca-Cola cooler. Near the door, a sign tacked above the flyswatter and next to the machete explained the ten-year prison term for carrying a weapon onto premises where liquor is served.

At the counter I drank a Royal Crown; the waitress dropped my quarter into the cash register, a King Edward cigarbox. Forks and knives clinked on plates behind a partition at the rear. It was too much. I ordered a dinner.

She set down a long plate of ham, beans, beets, and brown gravy. I seasoned everything with hot peppers in vinegar. From the partition came a *thump-thump* like an empty beer bottle rapping on a table. The waitress pulled two Lone Stars from the faded cooler, foam trickling over her fingers as she carried them back. In all the time I was there, I heard a voice from the rear only once: "I'm tellin' you, he can flat out thow that ball."

A man came from the kitchen, sat beside me, and began dropping toothpicks through the small openings of Tabasco sauce bottles used as dispensers. Down the counter, a fellow with tarnished eyes said, "Is it Tuesday?" The waitress nodded, and everything fell quiet again but for the clinking of forks. After a while, a single *thump,* and she carried back a single Lone Star. The screendoor opened; a woman, old and tall, stepped into the dimness cane first, thwacking it to and fro. Loudly she croaked, "Cain't see, damn it!"

A middle-aged woman said, "Straight on, Mother. It isn't that dark." She helped the crone sit at one of the tables. They ordered the meal.

"Ain't no use," the waitress said. "Just sold the last plate to him."

Him was me. They turned and looked. "Let's go, Mother." The tall woman rose, breaking wind as she did. "Easy, Mother."

"You don't feed me proper!" she croaked and thwacked out the door.

The man with the Tabasco bottles said to no one in particular, "Don't believe the old gal needed any beans."

Again a long quiet. Then the one who had ascertained the day said to the waitress, "Saw a cat runned over on the highway. Was it yourn?"

She shifted the toothpick with her tongue. "What color?" He couldn't remember. "Lost me an orange cat. Ain't seen Peewee in a week."

"I got me too many cats," he said. "I'll pay anybody a quarter each to kill my spares."

That stirred a conversation on methods of putting away kittens, and that led to methods of killing fire ants. The man beside me put down a toothpick bottle. It had taken some time to fill. He said, "I've got the best way to kill far ants, and it ain't by diggin' or poison." No one paid attention. Finally he muttered, "Pour gasoline into the hive." No one said anything.

"Do you light it?" I asked.

"Light what?"

"The gasoline."

"Hell no, you don't light it." He held out a big, gullied palm and pointed to a tiny lump. "Got nipped there last year by a far ant. If you don't pick the poison out, it leaves a knot for two or three years."

The other man talked of an uncle who once kept sugar ants in his pantry and fed them molasses. "When they fattened up, he put them on a butter sandwich. Butter kept them from runnin' off the bread." The place was so quiet you could almost hear the heat on the tin roof. If anyone was listening to him, I couldn't tell. "Claimed molasses gave them ants real flavor," he said.

Thump-thump. The woman turned from the small window, her eyes vacant, and went to the cooler for two more bottles of Lone Star.

I walked to the post office for stamps. The postmistress explained the town name. A century ago the custom was to drop a letter and ten cents for postage into the pickup box. That was in Old Dime Box up on the San Antonio road, now Texas 21. "What happened to Old Dime Box?"

"A couple houses there yet," she said, "but the railroad came through in nineteen thirteen, three miles south, so they moved the town to the tracks — to here. Now the train's about gone. Some freights, but that's it."

"I see Czech names on stores."

"We're between Giddings and Caldwell. Giddings is mostly German and Caldwell's mostly Czech. We're close to fifty-fifty. Whites, that is. A third of Dime Box is black people."

"How do the different groups get along?"

"Pretty well. We had a to-do in the sixties over integration, but it was mostly between white groups arguing about who had the right to run the schools. Some parents bussed kids away for a spell, but that was just anger."

"Bussing in Dime Box?"

"City people don't think anything important happens in a place like Dime Box. And usually it doesn't, unless you call conflict important. Or love or babies or dying."

3

THE big bass had a pair of horns, and beneath it, the barber of Dime Box dozed in his chair. He woke when I stopped in front of the long, open windows to look at the trophy on his wall. "Texas bull bass," he said. "More bull than bass." It was so craftily assembled I couldn't see how he'd done it. "I caught the fish and mounted it to the steer horns. Kids come in to stare. Spooks them. Don't know why nature never put horns on a fish."

"Or fins on a longhorn?" I needed a trim. "Just nip the ends."

"One of them no-ears cuts. Took an ear off a week back — didn't see it."

I trusted that was a joke. I hadn't paid $1.50 for a haircut in a decade. The old clock in Claud Tyler's barbershop had stopped at two-ten, and in the center of the room stood an iron woodstove, now assisted by a small gas one. Above the sink were bottles of Lucky Tiger hair tonic. I'd forgotten about tonics.

"Where you hail from, bub?" he said.

"Same place your Lucky Tiger's made."

He stepped away from the chair to look me over closely. "Ever know a feller named Wendell Thompson from up in Missouri? Called him 'Hop'?"

I said I didn't. Several other times he asked if I knew So-and-so from up my way, each time giving the moniker: Beep, Cherry, Pard, Tinbutt.

"Hop lived in the county awhile. I and him was in the Fox and Wolf Hunters Association. Now that was a bunch of fellers. I had a history of the Association. Plumb interesting. The mother-in-law burned it up."

He took from the wall a framed panoramic photograph of a group of men in hunting garb and laid it across my lap. The picture was a good three feet long, and there must have been a hundred men standing or kneeling in a field, with a beagle here and about. "Can you find me?"

I tried four or five times. I think it disheartened him that I couldn't recognize a younger Tyler. "Have I changed that much?" He pointed himself out and then brought a worn copy of a Texas hunting magazine with several photographs of men around campfires. I looked carefully and took a chance.

"Hell, that's Raymond Mueller. Called him 'Dipper.' This one's me."

"I see it now. How could I miss it? Got a bad eye."

"Hooey. That's before I started fading away. I had an aneurism removed, and I just ain't the man I was. I can abide that, but take you, you're a stranger, and all you see is a seventy-six-year-old man. I wasn't always

/ 137

9. Claud Tyler in Dime Box, Texas

like this. That's what hurts — people forget what you been." He stepped away from the chair again. "Listen to me. I used to cut hair and press suits all day then go out and hunt half the night. Now I just talk a big stick. Only thing that don't run down is your mouth."

"What's that about pressing suits?"

"Come here." I followed him to a small backroom, the striped chaircloth still around my neck, hair half cut. He pointed to an old steam press.

"Sold the dry-cleaning machine, but there's where I put a million creases in pants. Started in nineteen twenty-five. Feller would come in for a shave, haircut, and suit pressing. All for thirty-five cents. This was as good a shop as any in Texas. And I did a business. Listened to a million stories cutting those old squirrels' heads. Barber's the third most lied-to person, you know."

"Who's first?"

"Man's wife is first anywhere in the world. Priest is second."

We went back to the chair, and he took more snips. "Used to barber across the street. West of Sonny's. Oughta go see the rattlesnake skins in there." He motioned south, and for a moment I thought I would have to cross the street with a half-cut head to look at Sonny's rattlesnakes. "Been in this shop since the forties. Built it myself. How many barbers left that built their own shops?"

"Saw some figures on it. I think it was three — not counting you."

Tyler smiled. "Come here." I followed him to the side window where a big cottonwood grew from under the edge of the wooden building. It had started to lift the floor. "Tree's old as the shop. Cut it down once a year for six years. Finally gave up. I'll be gone before it turns the place over. Filled in that west side with river sand when I built the shop. Musta took in a seed." We went back to the chair. "Gotten old watching that tree grow. It's so cussed fixed on making its way, I've thought about pulling the shop down to give it room. Kind of living memorial to shade-tree barbering. Ain't much need of a barbershop in Dime Box now. People get out to the bigger towns anymore."

"A lot of small towns are coming back."

"Could happen to us. They located a big pool of oil here — deep oil. Way down. Feller picked up some land for back taxes, turned around and discovered oil. Now people believe oil's gonna bring things back like they used to be. I say hoping's swell, but better be ready for it to go as fast as it comes. Who listens? People thought the railroad wouldn't ever play out neither. That's why they moved the town here. We used to say there'd always be the railroad. You could count on it because it don't depend on weather and weevils don't eat steel. Well, bub, how'd you like our depot?"

"I haven't seen it."

"Tore down, that's why. But Model T's used to line up all along the road to the depot. Cars, trains, girls in big hats. Dime Box made noise then."

"Freights still come through, don't they?"

"Can't live off a toot and a whistle unless you can eat steam. Hell, it ain't even steam anymore. We get on now with ranching, farming, people stopping off on the way to the artificial lake."

"Artificial?" I imagined a giant plastic pond, the height of Disney World fool-the-eye stuff.

"Lake Somerville. One of those dam lakes." He whisked away the hair with his little white brush. "Before the cattle business got big in here, we used to grow cotton — even had a gin. All gone. When I was a whippersnapper, I used to look at the cotton fields and wonder which boll would end up in my shirt. Now shirts are this polyester made from oil. But I reckon when we go to pumping oil, Dime Box will be back in the shirt business, and they'll call that progress."

He started to dress me down with Lucky Tiger. "Leave it dry if you would."

"You young fellers take all the fun out of barbering. I'da got run out of town thirty years ago for a haircut like that."

To me, it was the best haircut I ever got in Dime Box, Texas.

4

THE wooden floor creaked, the bar warped in the middle; the rattlesnake skins nailed to the wall, and the stuffed bobcat, and deer trophy heads, all looked parched. Even the ceiling supports, peeled cedar trunks with lopped branches, had split in the dry Texas air. In Sonny's Place was a dusty upright piano, dusty because the entertainment at Sonny's wasn't music. It was dominoes. Of the six domino tables, each with a complement of worn tiles, only the one nearest the bar had a game that afternoon. A man in a yellow cap that said CAT twice announced he was playing his last round; he said it before the first last game and again before the second last game.

A large old fellow walked in, greeted everyone, sat at the bar, ordered a glass of Pearl, drank it off in two tilts, licked the foam from his upper lip, looked at me, gave a smile that pinned his great jowls to his ears, and said, "Good!" I nodded. He watched me, and I could tell he was getting ready to ask in his own manner for my version of the human saga. As if playing in an old Western, he actually said, "What brings you to Dime Box?"

I told him I was on a long motor tour, but he was a little hard of hearing, and I had to repeat twice to get the right volume. The whole tavern turned to ears; perhaps the old gentleman pretended hearing problems in order to share stories with everyone — after all, a new story was a thing of value in Sonny's. I felt like a radio, but I got used to the little audience at the domino table.

The man's name was, as I understood it, Mr. Valca, and he'd been born in Dime Box in the last century. Some voices I'd heard in town carried slight old-world accents, but his was pronounced. All *w*'s came out as *v*'s, and his lips had never known the sound of *th*. His parents had emigrated from Czechoslovakia, and he learned English only after beginning school. He reminisced about his Slavic past.

"In see Great Var against see Germans, you remember vee Americans fight vis see Poles and Roossians against see evil," he said. "Here vas me, a poor boy from Dime Box, Texas, talking vis see foreign soldiers in sair langvage. See city boys — Chicago and Cleveland — even say vas amazed. Vee Slavs all understand each ozzer. Ohh! Vee haff some good times, me and soze Slavs! Vee play cards, not see dominoes, and vee trink see slivovitz. Sat vas a var!"

Once he had been a clothing merchant. "But I might haff done ozzer sings too." He drank a second beer, this one more slowly. "Are you pheelosopher?"

"Too dangerous. That's a hardhat area."

"Never mind sat. I giff you a simple problem. On see floor, I put down sree sings — rifle, hoe, fishing rod and reel. Take vun and liff only by it for vun year. Alone. Vitch do you take?"

While I thought, a man wearing a Coors T-shirt came in. Everyone said, in turn, "Hello, Father." He was the priest of Dime Box. Straddling a chair, resting his arms on the back, drinking an orange sodapop, he watched the domino game. The man CAT said it was his last round. The wife would wonder.

"You take so long to answer, you must be pheelosopher. I tell you sis — you von't choose see rifle."

"How do you know?"

"Hunters make decisions fast, like a bullet. Bang!"

"Okay, I'll take the rod and reel."

"Now vy is sat?"

"You didn't say anything about ammunition, and I'd die before crops came up. I can make hooks and line and eat immediately."

"Ahh. A man's answer shows him."

"Which would you take?" It was the question he was waiting for.

"Me! I take see rifle!"

A domino player said, "All you ever shot was the breeze."

"No? No, you say? Vell, I sink about it for eighty years. And you don't know about see var. I shot see Germans left and right. Mow sem down like hay."

Everyone in the bar, some with slight German accents, laughed.

To me, he said, "Say sink I only can sell pants." To the room he said, "I tell you, see muzzle vas hot like a poker. Except on veekends because sen vee trink see slivovitz."

They all laughed again. When I left Sonny's, the game, like a potato cell, had subdivided into two identical ones, and the little tiles fell softly on the old tables, and the man CAT was playing his last game. After all, the wife would wonder.

5

AT Austin, on a hill west of the Colorado River — not *the* Colorado River, but the one flowing from near the New Mexico line to the Gulf — the desert began. Desert as in dry, rocky, vast. There was nothing gradual about the change — it was sudden and clear. Within a mile or so, the bluebonnets vanished as if evaporated, the soil turned tan and granular, and squatty trees got squattier with each mile as if reluctant to reach too far from their deep, wet taproots. Highway 290, running from rimrock to rimrock of the Edwards Plateau, climbed, dropped a little, climbed again until I was twelve hundred feet higher than Dime Box. From the tops of the tableland, I could watch empty roadway reaching for miles to the scimitar of a horizon visible at every compass point. It was fine to see the curving edge of the old blue ball of a world.

Johnson City was truly a plain town. The "Lyndon B. Johnson Boyhood Home," pleasantly plain, is here; and commercial buildings on the square were plain and homely. The best piece, the refurbished Johnson City Bank of rough-cut fieldstone, was perhaps the only bank in the country to be restored rather than bulldozed for a French provincial Tudor hacienda time-and-temperature building.

The road went directly into a sunset that could have been a J. M. W. Turner painting. Colors, texture, the horizontal composition were his. I'd never thought Turner a realist. The land, now cattle and peach country, wasn't so rocky and dry as the great ridges I'd just crossed. West of Stonewall, I saw the last of dusk, and under a big desert night, I drove in the small coziness of my headlamps until Sonny's beer made me stop. While I stood, an uncommon amount of noise came invisibly through the brush. Whatever it was, I felt vulnerable and tried to hurry. The moonlight wasn't much, but what I could make out looked like a tiptoeing army helmet. I was moving backwards when I realized it was an armadillo. I stopped, it waddled on, sniffed me out at the last moment, and shifted direction without hurry.

The conquistadors named the armadillo ("little armored one"), but Texans call them "diggers" because of the animal's penchant for scratching up larvae and worms, especially from soft soil of new graves. In spite of both the belief that armadillos feed on corpses and the animal's susceptibility to leprosy, poor whites ate them with greens and cornbread during the Depression and called them "Hoover hogs" or "Texas turkeys" (on the Christmas table); even now, poor blacks, calling them just "dillas," barbecue the soft meat. Ancient Mayas refused to eat them because they believed the carrion vulture did not die but rather shed wings and metamorphosed into an armadillo. But now, for a creature hardly changed from its Cenozoic ancestors, things are a little better. Texas law protects it from commercial exploitation, and that means it's harder today to buy a lamp or purse made from an armadillo carapace.

When I got back to my rig, the critter was nosing along the highway, looking for bugs popped by cars — that's why in the warm season so many armadillos get pressed like fossils into the soft asphalt. I honked it back to cover and drove into Fredericksburg, where I parked for the night behind the old Gillespie County Courthouse and went looking for calendars on cafe walls. The only eatery open was a big laminated place called the Hofhaus or Meisterhof or Braumeister — something like that. Having to order by number, I knew I was in for it. I chose number whatever, which proved to be three gray sausage corpses in a nest of sauerkraut that squeaked like rubber bands as I chewed and Bavarian potato salad dissolved into a post-factory slurry. I would have been better off with barbecued Hoover hog.

6

HISTORY has a way of taking the merely curious and turning it into significance. Consider the old Nimitz Hotel in Fredericksburg, for example. Not the rebuilt Nimitz Hotel I saw, but the 1852 version.

A German immigrant, Charles H. Nimitz, knowing the value of distinctive architecture, in 1880 built on his hotel, which had long afforded some protection from the Comanches, an addition shaped like a steamboat with a prow thrusting into the bounty of Main Street. The place, with hurricane deck, pilot house, and crow's nest, was unique, and the food toothsome. Nimitz had a good trade, once including Robert E. Lee, who slept in a spool bed here. Charles Nimitz was the grandfather of the Commander-in-Chief of the United States Pacific Fleet in the Second World War, Chester

W. Nimitz. The only thing resembling a ship young Nimitz saw on the Texas plains was the steamboat hotel, and all he knew of the sea (not counting the marine fossils in the native limestone) were his grandfather's stories about the German merchant fleet. No wonder Chester, in his first command at sea, ran his destroyer aground and got court-martialed; that was natural for a boy who grew up steering a hotel across the prairie. Nevertheless, this son of the Great American Desert later directed the victory in the largest naval war ever fought. I didn't hear anyone in town offer a theory on the role that old Charlie Nimitz's ship hotel played in determining the outcome of World War II, but somebody will think of it sooner or later.

For all I know, Main Street in Fredericksburg is the widest in the nation. It was so broad, I had to make a point of remembering why I was crossing to keep from forgetting by the time I reached the other side. And it was broad not for a few blocks but for two miles. Settlers from the compacted villages of the Rhine Valley laid Main out to enable ox carts to turn around in it. A shopkeeper explained: "We don't say somebody's dumb as an ox anymore because we've forgotten how dumb that is. We say a guy's a 'dumbass,' although I doubt we know how dumb that is either. Be that as it may, you can't teach an ox to back up. You can teach a horse to back up, but forget an ox. Main Street's wide because an ox is stupid."

People who think the past lives on in Sturbridge Village or Mystic Seaport haven't seen Fredericksburg. Things live on here in the only way the past ever lives — by not dying. It wasn't a town brought back from the edge of history; rather, it was just slow getting there. And most of the old ways were still comparatively unselfconscious.

Item: Otto Kolmeier & Co., a hardware store with an oiled wooden floor and shelves requiring a trolley ladder, where you could buy a cast-iron skillet, or graniteware pots to outfit a chuckwagon, or horseshoes in a half dozen sizes, a coal bucket, a coyote trap, or a brass cuspidor; the tinsmith (no sheetmetal worker this man), whistling off-key, could take his mallet and hammer out a galvanized tin trough or well cover.

Item: a flagstone sidewalk shuffled to the slickness of a marble monument.

Items: nineteenth-century buildings of scabbled and dressed limestone, sunburned to a soft yellow, erected by German settlers as soon as the Comanches left them alone long enough. The rock in building after building was so sharply cut it seemed the chink of hammer and stone chisel still vibrated in the street.

Item: a century plant, its steely spines ceaselessly dragged against a rock foundation by the wind, leaving deep incisions like a bear claw.

Item: a fieldstone building, as simple and direct as the Texas tableland, with a relief carving in white stone of an elephant above the door. Albino elephants were once symbols of hospitality, but it had been years since you could buy a drink at the White Elephant; the tavern was even long gone when the place sold Hudsons and Essexes. Now it was a German import boutique peddling Muenchen beersteins, Bavarian cuckoo clocks, and Teutonic trifles. And so the future came on in Fredericksburg, a little here, a little there.

A popular piece of sociology holds that Americans are losing confidence in the future because they are losing sight of the past. No wonder, when the good places that show the past seem so hard to find. Yet, in Fredericksburg, Texas, a few Americans were beginning to acknowledge the civilizing influence of historical continuity. They had turned the old courthouse into a library and community hall; next to its pioneer grace, the newer courthouse looked like a memorial gymnasium.

7

OUTSIDE of Fredericksburg, a small brown man, unable to bend his right knee, a paper sack under his arm, limped along the road to Hedwig's Hill. He looked directly at me, smiled, and oddly waved an upright thumb. As I passed, he waved goodbye. That's when I realized he was hitching. I stopped.

"*Gracias,*" he said in a soft voice accented in a peculiar way. "I like to go in trucks."

I didn't understand everything he said over the next couple of hours, but I did make out he had left Corpus Christi that morning on his way to visit a sick brother in Big Spring. He had traveled about two hundred and fifty miles on only two rides — one with a trucker, the other with a Texas Ranger, and neither noted for picking up hitchers.

"I have these thirty-five cents," he said and showed the coins to prove it. "That's all. The cop buy me a doughnut and coffee, and so I eat. I walk one mile before another ride. When I wait, I kill a big rotlah."

"A big what?"

"Rotlah." He trilled his tongue and moved his hand in a serpentine.

"A rattlesnake?"

He nodded and said yes in a high, trailing voice. "Very big rotlah." He rolled his hands into a circle to show its thickness. "Big."

With a rock the size of a cantaloupe, he had crushed the snake. The kill pleased him, and he talked about it for some time. It was good to destroy rattlers that came to live near men. He said cowboys used to pull the fangs from rattlesnakes and wear them around their necks to ward off fever.

"My father was a *vaquero*. Real cowboy. His hands made many things. He like best horsehair for things. Weave tail horsehair to make things. My mother she was Apache. I'm a redskin." He smiled at that.

"What's your name?" I thought he said "Perfidio," but no one would name a child that. "Perfidio?" I asked, and he nodded, and I repeated and spelled it. He nodded and I shook my head. He took out his billfold, a fat thing full of slips of paper folded small, and held up his Social Security card: Porfirio Sanchez.

"Oh, Porfirio. Not Perfidio."

"Yes." He fished among the bits of paper for a school photograph of a girl. "Grandbaby. I have seven boys and nine girls from five wives. Now grandkids. But for marriage, I say good to be out."

At Grit, we turned west onto route 29, a road that struck a bold, narrow course straight into the heart of the Texas desert. "Pretty good country here," he said. Over the miles, he repeated that several times, and the way he said it — softly — sounded as if he knew, as if he'd seen many kinds of country.

The land was fenceposts and scrubby plants and not many of those. Mostly the acres were for the goats that produced the big crop here: mohair. It was the country of the San Saba River, a route of deserted stone cavalry forts built six generations ago to control the "Indian trouble." In 1861, the post at Mason was under the direction of a lieutenant-colonel suddenly called to Washington by President Lincoln and offered field command of forces being readied for a civil war. The officer declined, and Fort Mason became his last U.S. Army duty. Robert E. Lee never forgot the isolated place.

To Sanchez I said, "Are you a cowboy?"

"I work ranches. Work many jobs. Drive trucks in Dallas. Dump trucks. But now I'm sixty-seven and don't have no employment. I have a government check each month, but I give most money to my babies, to my grandkids." He suddenly thrust an arm toward the desert. "Ears!" Just above the bush, a pair of long, erect ears, pinkly translucent in the afternoon light, gave away the position of a jackrabbit. "If you hunt big rabbits, look for big ears," he said. "Mr. Rabbit hide everything but ears. Those he can't hide unless he go deaf."

10. *Porfirio Sanchez near Eldorado, Texas*

"The jackrabbit gets its name from the jackass because of the ears."

"Yes." Sanchez tapped my knee. I had wandered into the left lane. It didn't matter — we hadn't seen a car in twenty minutes or passed a ranch gate for miles.

"Not many people out here," I said.

"Not many people, but pretty good country."

"Would you like to live here?"

"No country for a poor man. It take much land to live. Animals need hundred acres to eat. I like Dallas. Do you like to live here?"

"Yes." It struck me odd. Here was a man some of whose ancestors earned a name as the most intractable and savage of Southwestern Indians, a people who had lived in the hard land for ten thousand years; he wanted the city. And here was another man some of whose forebears built cities, who wanted the desert.

"Maybe you tell me different when you live here," Sanchez said.

Perhaps, but the names on the ranchgates were Wilson and Martin and Howard.

"I'm having a beer," I said. "How about you?" He opened the bottles and we drank, talking little. When the silence got noticeably long, he said, "Pretty good country." The land rose and brush was higher. Then a few trees, some with mistletoe in them. I pointed them out, but he didn't know what I meant.

The entire time he had kept his right leg straight. I asked about it, and he pulled up a pantleg to show several vicious surgical scars on his knee. First I understood him to say he had hurt it in the war, but later I thought he said he'd hurt it working. "Did you hurt the leg in the war or at work?"

"Yes."

"Were you in World War Two?"

"The Navy." He pointed to a scar on his hand and another running from his ear down the cheek. "Scars don't kill you." He smiled. "Men should have scars. Women should have wounds but no infection." He laughed. It was an obscenity. Suddenly he shouted out, *"Paisano!"* and pointed ahead to a long-legged bird, feathers akimbo, doing a clownish, stiff-knee number down the roadside.

"A roadrunner."

As we came up to the bird, he yelled out the window, *"Andale, paisano! Aquí viene el coyote!"* The roadrunner wheeled into the chapparal and disappeared. Sanchez laughed. "Pretty good country here."

And it was good country, made even better by having along a man who was at the age when others take to crossword puzzles and shopping-center cafeterias, a man who couldn't bend one leg and was hitching five hundred miles across the Texas desert and carrying his clothes in a grocery bag. He was the only Apache, mestizo or otherwise, I'd ever talked to. Forgive my romanticism, but I thought the old blood still showed.

He got out at Eldorado on the Del Rio–San Angelo highway. The last I saw of him, he was in his funny little stiff walk, waving his odd gesture at cars rushing past. A year earlier, had I been where he was, I would have believed I'd accomplished nothing. Now, I didn't see it that way. Not at all.

8

Straight as a chief's countenance, the road lay ahead, curves so long and gradual as to be imperceptible except on the map. For nearly a hundred miles due west of Eldorado, not a single town. It was the Texas some people see as barren waste when they cross it, the part they later describe at the motel bar as "nothing." They say, "There's nothing out there."

Driving through the miles of nothing, I decided to test the hypothesis and stopped somewhere in western Crockett County on the top of a broad mesa, just off Texas 29. At a distance, the land looked so rocky and dry, a religious man could believe that the First Hand never got around to the creation in here. Still, somebody had decided to string barbed wire around it.

No plant grew higher than my head. For a while, I heard only miles of wind against the Ghost; but after the ringing in my ears stopped, I heard myself breathing, then a bird note, an answering call, another kind of birdsong, and another: mockingbird, mourning dove, an enigma. I heard the high *zizz* of flies the color of gray flannel and the deep buzz of a blue bumblebee. I made a list of nothing in particular:

1. mockingbird
2. mourning dove
3. enigma bird (heard not saw)
4. gray flies
5. blue bumblebee
6. two circling buzzards (not yet, boys)
7. orange ants
8. black ants
9. orange-black ants (what's been going on?)
10. three species of spiders
11. opossum skull
12. jackrabbit (chewed on cactus)
13. deer (left scat)
14. coyote (left tracks)
15. small rodent (den full of seed hulls under rock)
16. snake (skin hooked on cactus spine)
17. prickly pear cactus (yellow blossoms)
18. hedgehog cactus (orange blossoms)
19. barrel cactus (red blossoms)
20. devil's pincushion (no blossoms)
21. catclaw (no better name)
22. two species of grass (neither green, both alive)
23. yellow flowers (blossoms smaller than peppercorns)
24. sage (indicates alkali-free soil)
25. mesquite (three-foot plants with eighty-foot roots to reach water that fell as rain two thousand years ago)
26. greasewood (oh, yes)

27. joint fir (steeped stems make Brigham Young tea)
28. earth
29. sky
30. wind (always)

That was all the nothing I could identify then, but had I waited until dark when the desert really comes to life, I could have done better. To say nothing is out here is incorrect; to say the desert is stingy with everything except space and light, stone and earth is closer to the truth.

I drove on. The low sun turned the mesa rimrock to silhouettes, angular and weird and unearthly; had someone said the far side of Saturn looked just like this, I would have believed him. The road dropped to the Pecos River, now dammed to such docility I couldn't imagine it formerly demarking the western edge of a rudimentary white civilization. Even the old wagonmen felt the unease of isolation when they crossed the Pecos, a small but once serious river that has had many names: Rio de las Vacas (River of Cows — perhaps a reference to bison), Rio Salado (Salty River), Rio Puerco (Dirty River).

West of the Pecos, a strangely truncated cone rose from the valley. In the oblique evening light, its silhouette looked like a Mayan temple, so perfect was its symmetry. I stopped again, started climbing, stirring a panic of lizards on the way up. From the top, the rubbled land below — veined with the highway and arroyos, topographical relief absorbed in the dusk — looked like a roadmap.

The desert, more than any other terrain, shows its age, shows time because so little vegetation covers the ancient erosions of wind and storm. What appears is tawny grit once stone and stone crumbling to grit. Everywhere rock, earth's oldest thing. Even desert creatures come from a time older than the woodland animals, and they, in answer to the arduousness, have retained prehistoric coverings of chitin and lapped scale and primitive defenses of spine and stinger, fang and poison, shell and claw.

The night, taking up the shadows and details, wiped the face of the desert into a simple, uncluttered blackness until there were only three things: land, wind, stars. I was there too, but my presence I felt more than saw. It was as if I had been reduced to mind, to an edge of consciousness. Men, ascetics, in all eras have gone into deserts to lose themselves — Jesus, Saint Anthony, Saint Basil, and numberless medicine men — maybe because such a losing happens almost as a matter of course here if you avail yourself. The Sioux once chanted, "All over the sky a sacred voice is calling."

Back to the highway, on with the headlamps, down Six Shooter Draw.

In the darkness, deer, just shadows in the lights, began moving toward the desert willows in the wet bottoms. Stephen Vincent Benét:

> When Daniel Boone goes by, at night,
> The phantom deer arise
> And all lost, wild America
> Is burning in their eyes.

From the top of another high mesa: twelve miles west in the flat valley floor, the lights of Fort Stockton blinked white, blue, red, and yellow in the heat like a mirage. How is it that desert towns look so fine and big at night? It must be that little is hidden. The glistering ahead could have been a golden city of Cibola. But the reality of Fort Stockton was plywood and concrete block and the plastic signs of Holiday Inn and Mobil Oil.

The desert had given me an appetite that would have made carrion crow stuffed with saltbush taste good. I found a Mexican cafe of adobe, with a whitewashed log ceiling, creekstone fireplace, and jukebox pumping out mariachi music. It was like a bunkhouse. I ate burritos, chile rellenos, and pinto beans, all ladled over with a fine, incendiary sauce the color of sludge from an old steel drum. At the next table sat three big, round men: an Indian wearing a silver headband, a Chicano in a droopy Pancho Villa mustache, and a Negro in faded overalls. I thought what a litany of grievances that table could recite. But the more I looked, the more I believed they were someone's vision of the West, maybe someone making ads for Levy's bread, the ads that used to begin "You don't have to be Jewish."

9

WAY out here they have a name for wind, the wind they call Maria. They could, more sensibly, call it a son-of-a-bitch. The desert windflaws eased with darkness, only to settle into a steady blowing, rocking my rig all night, carrying in the sounds of men and the yip and whoop of the desert, then blowing them out into the expanse, always coming and going, sliding around and over and off things, picking up anything not held down: tumbleweed, grit, the moist exhalation of life.

With dawn, the wind came strong again from the north, blasting the dusty mesa tops into the irrigated valley, pushing my little coach from shoulder to centerline until my arms tired from holding a course against it. Far to the south, long purple stretches of the Glass Mountains slowed the rush of wind into the Chihuahua desert, but nothing was big enough to shut it down altogether. The radio warned gusts would hit fifty miles an hour by afternoon.

The land rose steadily, then at Balmorhea the highland mesas became the eastern ridges of the Rocky Mountains. Interstate 10, the only way west, differed here from a two-lane simply by extra strips of concrete — there were almost no towns to bypass. And so, like the locomotive, Ghost Dancing lapped the miles across the Apache Mountains and Devil Ridge and onward. Bugs popping the windshield left only clear fluid instead of a yellow and green pollen-laden goo of woodland insects; it was as if they extracted their colorless essence from the desert wind itself.

Somewhere near Eagle Flat, before a rider-against-the-sky horizon, I stopped to rest from the buck of sidewinds. Annual rainfall here averaged less than seven inches, and the Rio Grande to the south often ran dry before it crossed the desert. Spindly ocotillo stalks, some twenty-five feet high and just coming into orange blossom, bent under the north wind. Creosote bushes had cleared dead zones by secreting a toxic substance from their roots to insure whatever moisture fell they would get. As for creosote leaves, only one animal was known to eat them: a camel. Texans had learned that during unsuccessful experiments by the cavalry at Fort Bliss to use the beasts for desert patrols in the Civil War.

Between the creosote and stony knobs streamlined by gritty winds grew grasses in self-contained clumps and cactuses compacted like fists. Everything as spare and lean as a coyote's leg. Under that sprawl of sky and space, the minimal land somehow reduced whatever came into it, laying itself austerely open as if barren of everything except simplicity. But it was a simplicity of form — not content.

The Ghost ran the easy road in a way old wagoners must have dreamed of. To the south lay the slender green strip of the Middle Valley of the Rio Grande, a place of seventeenth-century Spanish missions; near one, Ysleta, men had cultivated the same plot every year since 1681. Across the river was Mexico, full of the sharp apexes of the Sierra Madres. The mountains opened at El Paso, where the sun had failed to shine only thirty days in the last fifteen years, and let the Rio Grande and highways through. On the Mexican side rose steep, gravelly hills covered with adobe houses, small squalid things painted pink and aquamarine. On the other side, the American equivalents: pink and aquamarine house trailers.

The Rio Grande lay safely bedded in concrete and bound with a chainlink fence called the "Tortilla Curtain." Mexicans know the Rio Grande as the

Rio Bravo, the "wild river," but it didn't look either *bravo* or *grande*, sorry thing that it is now. The river has been "rectified" because it used to flood — and thereby nourish — the lowlands; that's how you farm one patch three hundred years and still get a crop. But, worse than flooding, the Rio Grande, like a wandering burro, would change course without warning, cutting off a slice of Texas and giving it to the Mexicans or handing over a chunk of Chihuahua and its residents to the Americans. What could immigration do about a *peón* who entered the country in an adobe hovel that had never moved?

El Paso was a pleasant city, but I felt I'd been in Texas for weeks, so I drove on west through the natural break in the Rockies that gives the town its name — the very pass Indians, conquistadors, and the Butterfield Stage used — drove around crumbling Comanche Peak, and headed up along the Rio Grande. On the opposite bank now was not Mexico, but New Mexico. I crossed the river. Eastward, the shattered Organ Mountains blocked off the White Sands country. The highway, straight and level, went into a land of tourist trading posts where yellow and black billboards repeated like a stutter: cactus jelly, Mexican black-velvet paintings, Indian dolls, copper bracelets, cherry cider, carved onyx, bullwhips, cactus candy, steer horns, petrified wood, Zuñi silver, Navajo rugs, desert blossom honey.

On the north, the mountains were worn pillows; but in the other direction, the Floridas (Flo-RYE-duhs) were treacherous jags tearing into the soft bellies of clouds. That barren inheritance of hostility, belonging to something other than man, would have nothing to do with him: no roads, no high-tension powerlines, no parabolic dish antennas, no concrete initials of desert towns. Mountains to put man in his place. By the time I got to Deming, New Mexico, the Floridas were covering themselves with long night shadows, the only thing that can embrace them entirely.

10

FLOORS, walls, counter, employees' uniforms — everything but the faces — were white at the Manhattan Cafe in Deming. From some place I recognized the beauty of the waitress, but I couldn't recall where. Later I realized she had the severe priestess beauty of high-bridged nose, full lips, and oblique eyes that one might see on a Mayan temple wall at Palenque.

She served a stack of unheated flour tortillas, butter, and a bowl of green, watery fire that would have put a light in the eyes of Quetzalcoatl. Texans can talk, but nowhere is there an American chile hot sauce, green or red, like the New Mexican versions, with no two recipes the same except for the pyrotechnical display they blow off under the nose. New Mexican *salsas* are mouth-watering, eye-watering, nose-watering; they clean the pipes, ducts, tracts, tubes; and like spider venom, they can turn innards to liquid.

I'd finished the tortillas when she set down *huevos rancheros* with chopped *nopales* (prickly pear), rice, and a gringo glass of milk to extinguish the combustibles. Solid cafe food without pretense. Maybe the time is coming, but as yet the great variety and subtlety of fine Mexican cuisine have not much reached the United States. Ten thousand taco stands peddle concoctions cooked by some guy who pronounces the *l*'s in *tortilla*, and, in the Southwest, cafes like the Manhattan serve a good but basic fare; yet, only a few places turn out the dishes that put a *cocinero* in a class with the chef: squash blossom enchilada, chicken in green pumpkin-seed sauce, tortilla soup, drunken octopus, sweet tamales, shrimp marinated in jalapeños, lime soup, chicken breast pudding, chicken-in-a-shirt.

Gritty as a lizard, I went looking for a bath and found a room (the first since I'd taken to the blue highways) for eight dollars at the edge of town. I showered and watched the last of a Gary Cooper movie on television. In fluent, dubbed Spanish, Cooper made his way through a romance:

> She: *Eres tú libre?*
> He: *Libre como el viento.*

Free as the wind indeed. A brave hope.

After dark, I walked into town for a beer. A choice of two bars: the Central where English was the language or the Western where it was Spanish. On the street outside the Chicano saloon — in living memory — a rustler was hanged, and in a basement next door was once an opium den. Now the Western got by on beer and eight ball. Until the game began, none of the seventeen customers spoke to me. I got the message, but I stayed anyway.

Five young workers for the highway department and their grizzled foreman, Ruquito ("Pops"), shot pool. The best player was the only person speaking some English: loud and cocky, he cried out, "AttabayBEE!" or "Holy *cojones!*" or "Dirty *bruja!*" He was a clever shooter who shepherded his stripes or solids in tight little flocks, and his friends didn't mind losing to him. At the bar, older and beefier men stood talking about work and women, but they kept an eye on the game. Then, from somewhere, someone laid a wager. Señor AttabayBEE! would play a gristly, angry man in his fifties. The older man took a few smashing warm-up shots and made them. A worker unplugged the jukebox, another adjusted the light over the table, and El Señor talked rapidly but only in Spanish. Ruquito took him aside to rub his shoulders and arms, all the while whispering fiercely to him. Two old compadres limped quickly out, tumbleweed blowing at their heels.

A man with three or four silvery incisors that gave his mouth the appearance of a steel trap said to me: "How much you bettin'?" I told him I was too poor to gamble. He sneered a laugh. "You come in just to watch us *mojados*?"

"Okay. I've got two bucks. Two on the young señor."

"You are a fool."

Ruquito pushed everyone away from the area except the two contestants, and the place went quiet but for the sharp click of the balls on the felt. With the precision of little howitzer shots, the balls found their marks and dropped from the table. El Señor won easily.

"Now you gonna bet good, Sir Gringo?" steel mouth said.

"Let it all ride. Haven't got any more." I pulled my pockets inside out.

He sneered again. Pool Game Wager Ends in Death. Either I got fished in or Señor AttabayBEE! forgot to herd his stripes. He lost five straight. I would have done better guessing the number of spots on a Dalmatian.

11

That a handcrank coffee mill helped kill off the Old West has not been widely appreciated. For five thousand miles I'd driven between fences, but along New Mexico 81, for the first time, there was none. At last I'd come to open range, a thing disappearing faster than the condor.

In 1874, an Illinoisan, Joseph Glidden, received the first patent for a barbed fencing wire he made on a converted coffee mill. Ranchers called the stuff "the Devil's hatband," but they saw their economic future in it: · the new fence gave means to control breeding and thereby upgrade stock, and it allowed a single well to water an entire herd. Before barbed wire, the West had few long fences because there wasn't wood enough to build them, and cattle trampled wooden fences anyway. No alternative to open range and cowhands existed. But a barbed wire fence was cheap to buy, erect, and maintain over the big acreages required in the West, and cattle shied from it once they ran against it. In the 1870s some animals cut themselves to death on it, and one rancher said that at first he could hardly drive a cow between two posts.

But Glidden's invention offered something even more important: a means of staking property claims, particularly on plats belonging nominally to the federal government. Ranchers fenced claims to establish ownership, and entire towns ended up encircled or cut off from access to public land. Neighbors tore out each other's fences, and President Cleveland ordered the Army to take down illegal ones. It was too late. What began as "range privilege" became an unlawful seizure that was the basis for many of the great cattle empires.

And so, from the prototype off the coffee mill, came the successors that partitioned the West and changed it forever: Glidden's Twisted Oval, Briggs' Obvious, Allis' Sawtooth, Scutt's Arrow Plate, Brinkerhoff's Riveted Splicer. Staples and pliers became more important than bullets and pistols, and the cowboy went from riding the range to riding fence and greasing the bearings on a windmill. No longer was there need to drive range cattle to pasturage and water or to sort out herds; the cowboy was on his way to becoming a feedlot attendant, and a piece of American history turned to legend. With the transport of cattle to market by truck, the shift was complete.

After fifteen miles of open range along state 81, I saw, lying along the roadside, threads gleaming like trails of mercury. Barbed wire. In a week, this piece of open range would be gone too.

Eastward, a dusty spume of wind created by thermal pressures spun wildly about the sage and thistle. People of the Old Testament heard the voice of God in desert whirlwinds, but Southwestern Indians saw evil spirits in the spumes and sang aloud if one crossed their path; that's why, in New Mexico and Arizona today, the little thermals are "dust devils."

Off to the south lay the Big Hatchet Mountains, their backs against the deserts of Mexico; under them, tiny Hachita sat almost squarely on the Continental Divide where it bends east and west. Before the Gadsden Purchase of 1853, this newest piece of the contiguous states belonged to Spain and Mexico for three centuries. The sight of Hachita's tin roofs simmering in the early sun gave me ease; although I'd filled the tank in Deming an hour earlier, I couldn't keep from continually checking the gauge, couldn't stop hearing the soft *knock-knock* of the water-pump.

Hachita, facing an abandoned railroad trackbed and locomotive water tower, turned out to be a conglomerate of clay bricks and wood and aluminum. In sandy lots between faded trailers and adobe houses, old cars mummified in the dry air. There were two businesses: a small grocery and the Desert Den Bar & Filling Station.

Here was a genuine Western saloon primeval, a place where cattlemen once transacted affairs of commerce and of the passions. The ichthyologist who first found the "fossil fish" coelacanth still swimming the seas could have had no finer pleasure than I did in coming across a buttressed adobe saloon that by all right should have been extinct.

It was a long room with a pool table, a circular poker table, and a nine-stool L-shaped bar. Claptrap hung on the east wall, antlers and inept oil paintings on the west, while calendars, beer signs, an old license plate, and stacks of things covered the backbar mirror. The countertop was pocked with shallow cavities where silver dollars once had been embedded and with deeper holes that had held turquoise nuggets. Now only a few worn pesos and pieces of malachite remained.

Virginia Been owned the saloon. Born in Oklahoma, she grew up within a hundred miles of Hachita. Her husband, George, worked "dirt construction" and left her to run the Desert Den most of the time. Each week she drove sixty miles into Deming to bank and pick up supplies. Her mother, Iva, sat at the poker table with a bag of tortilla chips by her elbow and stared into the glare of empty road. She said nothing.

"I'd have a beer," I said, "but I guess it's too early."

"Not in the desert." Mrs. Been set out a bottle.

"You have a fine old place."

"One time a *National Geographic* photographer came in and took pictures, but I never saw them in the magazine."

"How old is the bar?"

"Older than statehood. Late eighteen nineties. We've got liquor license number twenty-seven. One of the oldest in the state. We were here before Pancho Villa raided the county. We've always guaranteed one thing — this is the best bar in town. Anybody doesn't like it can drive fifty miles to the next one."

"I think I've been looking for it since my first Western."

She whistled at a sparrow that hopped through the doorway to peck about the sandy wooden floor. "Nothing wasted out here if you can eat or drink it. We've got a nice town — what's left. That's not much. You could put us all in a cattle truck now, but we used to be a thousand of us."

"Where?"

"Right here. Southern Pacific had a roundhouse across the road fifty years ago. That's the truth. We were on the route between El Paso and the mines at Douglas, Arizona. A roundhouse! But the railroad closed the line and came out and pulled up the tracks, ties, everything. The locomotive water tower and the cattlepens, that's all that's left of SP. I guess they didn't even want to be reminded of us down here on the border."

"How far's the border?"

"About ten miles by the crow, but fifty miles by car. I think the railroad hurried out too soon. Six years ago a copper smelter went in over west where it can smoke down the border. When they were building it, our place jumped again — people to the gills." She laid out a photograph of her at a phony teller's window she had built next to the bar. "We cashed paychecks. The Den was the town bank. Money poured in like wind. Copper money."

"Do smelter workers live here now?"

"Company built a new town by the smelter. We don't get good TV reception and people won't move in. I'm never home to watch so I don't care. To tell the truth, I'm glad they didn't settle. Don't want to see Hachita get any bigger because I like it this way. Wouldn't live anywhere else. And I don't mind if there isn't much to do except work."

"I've got the feeling I'm in the farthest corner of the United States. The word for your town is *remote*."

"We're the end of things down this way. This is where she stops."

A fellow with a face he'd gotten a lot of mileage out of sat down and drank off a beer like ice water and started complaining the electric company had billed him forty-eight dollars for an unoccupied house he owned. "Hell," he said, "place has been boarded up ten years. May have to clean your ceiling."

Dollar bills, folded to the size of postage stamps, clung like spiders to the ten-foot Celotex ceilings. "Why is money up there?" I asked.

"Road salesman in here years ago," Mrs. Been said, "started betting he could throw a dollar bill against the ceiling and make it stay. Got some takers — like everybody. So he pulls out a couple of quarters, heavy silver ones, and a thumbtack. Folds the bill around the coins and tack so the tack stuck through the paper. He tosses it up and it sticks like a dart. He made some money that night. So'd the ceiling. Don't ever bet a man against his own tricks. Every now and then, a dollar comes down. One stuck in a fella's boot couple years ago. Money from heaven."

A small man, tightly and neatly put together, his muscles wound around his bones like copper wire on an armature, his eyes faded turquoise, sauntered in. "Highway department's stringin' fence down eighty-one," he said.

11. *The Desert Den Bar in Hachita, New Mexico: Iva Sander, Virginia Been,*
and customer

"What's the need for a fence?" I asked.

"People are runnin' over cattle," he said. "Miners drive it like a racetrack. Folks used to slow down for stock on the road, and we didn't need no fences, but copper people don't respect nothin' smaller than a steamshovel. Always in a hurry. Afraid somethin's gonna get them out here."

"Those city boys don't believe what can happen if they hit a steer, but school's out when a half-ton of hamburger comes over the hood. That fence is for people, not cattle."

"Government's got things bassackwards again," the little man said.

Mrs. Been turned to me, "He's a real cowboy. Horse, lasso, branding iron."

"Not many of us left except you count ones that tells you they's cowboys. A lot them ones now. I been ridin' since the war."

"Weren't you up around Alamogordo when they tested the bomb?" the high-mileage man said. "Think I heard you were."

"Over west to Elephant Butte, up off the Rio Grande. Just a greenhorn, sleepin' out where we was movin' cattle. July of 'forty-five. They was a high wind that night and rain, and I didn't get much sleep. Curled up against a big rock out of the wind. I was still in my bedroll at daybreak when come a god-terrible flash. I jumped up figurin' one of the boys took a flashbulb pitcher of me sleepin' on the job. Course nobody had a Kodak. Couple minutes later the ground started rumblin'. We heard plenty of TNT goin' off to Almagordy before, but we never heard nothin' like that noise. Sound just kept roarin'. 'Oh, Jesus,' I says, 'what'd they go and do now?' Next month we saw wheres they bombed Heerosaykee, Japan. We never knowed what an A-tomic bomb was, but we knowed that one flash wasn't no TNT blockbuster."

"The day the sun rose in the wrong direction," the other man said. "They've been testing soldiers stationed at Alamogordo in 'forty-five for radiation poisoning. You know, Herefords up there turned white."

"Feelin' fine. Doctor told me once it was a good thing I was behind that rock. He says the wind saved me, but the wife says the bomb musta been why we never had no kids. Says it burned out my genetics."

"You never know."

"Truth is, bad genetics runs in the family. Dad never had no kids."

"Your dad didn't have children?" I said.

"Not a one. That's why he adopted me." He drained his beer. "You know what Spaniards called the valley where the bomb got blowed off?"

High mileage looked up. "Don't think I ever heard."

"Journey of Death," the little cowboy said. "That's the English for it."

12

THERE'S something about the desert that doesn't like man, something that mocks his nesting instinct and makes his constructions look feeble and temporary. Yet it's just that inhospitableness that endears the arid rockiness, the places pointy and poisonous, to men looking for its discipline.

Up along blue road 9 in the Little Hatchet Mountains — just desert hills here — I stopped for a walk in the scrub. Every so often I paused to listen. Like a vacuum. Pascal should have tried these silences. I yelled my name, and the desert took the shout as if covetous of any issue from life.

Walking back to the highway, I saw a coil of sand loosen and bend itself into a grainy S and warp across the slope. I stood dead still. A sidewinder so matched to the grit only its undulating shadow gave it away. And that's something else about the desert: deception. It can make heat look like water, living plants seem dead, mountains miles away appear close, and turn scaly tubes of venom into ropes of warm sand. So open, so concealed.

For the fourth time that day, I crossed the Continental Divide, which, at this point, was merely a crumpling of hills. The highway held so true that the mountains ahead seemed to come to me. Along the road were small glaring and dusty towns: Playas, a gathering of trailers and a one-room massage parlor ($3.00 for thirty-five minutes the sign said); and Animas, with a schoolyard of Indian children, their blue-black heads gleaming like gun barrels in the sun. Then the road turned and went directly for an immense wall of mountain that looked impossible to drive through and improbable to drive around. It was the Chiricahuas, named for the Apache tribe that held this land even before the conquistadors arrived.

I crossed into Arizona and followed a numberless, broken road. A small wooden sign with an arrow pointing west:

PORTAL

PARADISE

In the desert flatness, the road began twisting for no apparent reason, tacking toward the Chiricahuas. It had to be a dead end — there could be no opening in that sheer stone obtrusion, that invasion of mountain, looked as if it had stridden out of the Sierra Madres, had seen the New Mexican desert, and stopped cold in its Precambrian tracks.

The pavement made yet another right-angle turn, and a deep rift in the vertical face of the Chiricahuas opened, hidden until the last moment. How could this place be? The desert always seems to hold something aside. The constriction of canyon was just wide enough for the road and a stream bank to bank with alligator juniper, pine, sycamore, and white oak. Trees covered the water and roadway and cut the afternoon heat. Where the canopy opened, I could see canyon walls of yellow and orange pinnacles and turrets, fluted and twisted, everything rising hundreds of feet. More deception: in the midst of a flat, hot scarcity, a cool and wet forest between rock formations that might have come from the mind of Antonio Gaudi. I couldn't have been more surprised had the last turn brought me into Jersey City. And that was the delight — I'd never heard of the Chiricahuas. I expected nothing.

Portal consisted of a few rock buildings and not a human anywhere. Three miles up the canyon I forded Cave Creek and pulled in under some big juniper and sycamore. Ghost Dancing sat so my bunk was at the edge of the stream; I wanted to hear water that night and wash away the highway wearies. I took an apple and went to the creek. The place drowsed. I was sitting in the northeast corner of the great Sonoran Desert, while at my feet a pair of water bugs swam in slow tandem as if shadows of each other. Evergreens resinated in the air, and bleached clouds moved high over three rhyolite monoliths cut from the spewings of an ancient volcano to which the Chiricahuas are a tombstone. Before any men, wind had come and inscribed the rock, and water had incised it, but who now could read those writs?

I was in one of the strangest pieces of topography I'd ever seen, a place, until now, completely beyond my imaginings. What is it in man that for a long while lies unknown and unseen only one day to emerge and push him into a new land of the eye, a new region of the mind, a place he has never dreamed of? Maybe it's like the force in spores lying quietly under asphalt until the day they push a soft, bulbous mushroom head right through the pavement. There's nothing you can do to stop it.

13

SUNDOWN, taking color from the land, briefly spread it low over the western sky; then it was gone from there too. As the air cooled, I built a small fire and cooked some eggs and sausage, made coffee, and laced it with bourbon. Across the stream, a javelina sniffed and watched. The woods were full of small noises fusing with the purl of Cave Creek, and the fire loosed a thin column of blue, resinous smoke to curl around me before rising to the black sky; every so often an orange coal went cracking out into the stream, which extinguished it with a hiss.

Still looking for a pattern, a core, in what had been happening, I played a tape recording of the last few days and made notes. After a while I gave up on words and tried diagrams in hopes an image might shake free an idea. I cogitated, ergoed, and sumed, and got nothing.

A sudden movement in the darkness. A voice: "Writing a book?" I jumped and spilled coffee. I couldn't see anything beyond the pale of the fire. "Sorry to scare you. Figured an old chief like you would hear me coming."

A man, about forty, stepped into the light. He had a soft, kindly face, but it was terribly drawn, and he was bent slightly in the shoulders as if yoked to something. He wore flame-stitch bullhide boots and a Boss-of-the-Plains Stetson with an absurd seven-inch crown. He saw my notebook. "You into radio schematics?"

"That radio is my life."

"Hunting answers?"

"Ideas."

"I could write a book about my life," he said. "I'd call it *Ten Thousand Mistakes*. I've made them all: wife, kids, job, education. I can't even remember the first six thousand."

"Done a pretty good job myself." I was glad for the company, although I had thought I wanted to be alone. "How about a little coffee and bourbon?" His face moved around as if trying to come out of a fixed position of agony, but something was lacking, something of moment. Rather, he had the look of a man pulling on wet swimming trunks.

"I shouldn't be drinking. Got out of the hospital this week. Went in for those 'routine tests' people die from. Doctors thought I had a cancerous colon. Then they tried ulcerative colitis. Finally settled on a rectal polyp."

One minute after meeting me, he'd admitted to ten thousand failures and given a tour of his lower tract. I wondered where we'd be in half an hour.

"Sit down if you like."

"Are you just moving through?"

I gave a précis to distract any further proctological talk. When I finished, he said, "Your little spree sounds nice until you go back."

"Don't have to go back who I was."

"Can you get out of it?"

"I'll find out. Maybe experience is like a globe — you can't go the wrong way if you travel far enough."

"You'll end up where you started."

"I'm working on who. Where can take care of himself. A 'little spree' can give people a chance to accept changes in a man." I was sounding like some bioenergized group leader. I poured another coffee and bourbon. "Sure you won't have a sip of Old Mr. Easy Life?"

"Could you put some milk in it?" We introduced ourselves. He was from Tucson and worked in the loan department of a bank. "What you were talking about sounds like marital problems," he said.

"I guess, but my point was that what you've done becomes the judge of what you're going to do — especially in other people's minds. When you're traveling, you are what you are right there and then. People don't have your past to hold against you. No yesterdays on the road." I was doing it again.

He looked behind himself into the dark. "You have kids?" I said I didn't, and he nodded as if that explained something. "I have two girls, twenty and eighteen. When I was buried I forgot — "

"When you were *buried*?"

"Married. When I was married I forgot my family. Now I'm divorced, and I can't forget them. Wish I could. They've hurt me. I wish I'd bronzed the girls instead of their baby shoes."

"More corn mash in your milk?" We sipped in the darkness and talked of little things. He'd rented a trailer that afternoon and driven to the Chiricahuas to put the hospital out of mind. His hobby was the Old West, and he regretted not becoming a history professor — his true calling.

"I like to come here to read history. Reading Plutarch this trip. Been driving up for years. Always alone. My wife and daughters wouldn't ever join me. Their lives go as far as they can stretch their hair dryer cords."

To steer him away from marriage, I asked about his work. He disliked it and had looked into other things but found employers distrustful of anyone changing jobs outside his field.

"Once you're thirty, you're permitted to go up in your specialty or maybe sideways if you can make it look like up. But if you want out altogether, that's the same as going down. And after forty they think the bottom layers of your life have turned to coal."

The job problems had strained the marriage. He and his wife simply grew tired of sharing each other's struggles and losses, and when one had a success, the other became envious. And each feared aging — especially the other's. Things finally broke when his elder daughter took a job modeling for an advertising agency and her face and bare shoulders began appearing on condom machines around the city.

"You know: 'Ribbed Sensation! New Pleasure Delight!' The picture didn't really show anything. Actually, it looked like she was yawning instead of the other, but the condom — I mean the context — made it look like the other. My girls thought it was funny and went around telling people to go down to the Texaco and take a look. My wife and I argued over how to handle it. After that, we just fell apart as a family."

I didn't say anything. Questions led him back to the same topic, and I had nothing to say about marriage. He was starting to ruin Cave Creek. I poured another shot. Maybe he'd forget. "When you're driving," he said, "do you ever feel like swinging over in front of a semi that's really moving?"

"I know the urge."

He pulled off his Boss of the Plains and brushed it fastidiously with a sleeve. "I'd like to do what you're doing, but I don't have the guts for it right now — literally." He put the Stetson on, setting it at just the right pitch. "Lately, I've even wished I'd go broke so I could go for broke. I wish I'd get truly desperate." His words were coming as if strangling him.

Here's a man, I thought, who would change his life if he could do it by changing his hat. Maybe a .22 long rifle in a shirt pocket would help.

"The other day," he said, "I remembered something from when I was a little kid that I didn't understand then. I was six or seven. My dad was stuffing me into a snowsuit like parents do — this arm, that arm. When he had me in, he looked at me so long it scared me. Whatever he saw made him shudder." The boss cleared his throat. "Now I know what it meant."

"What did it mean?"

"He knew what I was going to know."

"Love can make fathers shudder."

We had another round. That might have been a mistake. The conversation started slipping as he began wallowing in crises. He said things like, "The whole bag just seems more and more of the same," and, "Other people make life so damned banal."

I suspected that the Boss embraced one crisis after another because they gave him significance, something like tragic stature. He had so lost belief in a world outside himself that, without crisis, he had nothing worth talking about. On and on, the tolling of words revealed his expertise in living a life that baffled him.

Occasionally, when the fire ignited a drop of resin, our twin shadows, absurdly big, would stretch to the edge of night, then shrink back with the dying flame. He noticed my attention wandering and asked a question that flabbergasted me: "So you say you're just driving through?" He wasn't that drunk. Maybe he wasn't drunk at all; maybe he just never quit thinking of himself long enough to listen. He made me tired.

"That's right," I said. "Just driving through to Utica."

I wanted to slap him around, wake him up. He had the capacity to see but not the guts; he mucked in the drivel of his life, afraid to go into the subterranean currents that dragged him about. A man concealed in his own life, scared to move, holding himself too close, petting himself too much.

"Time for some sleep," I said and yawned big to prove it.

He got to his feet, leaning a little this way and that. Then he delivered a lecture. I think he'd read too much Plutarch. After a sentence or two, I flipped on the tape recorder. Here is the essence:

"In eighteen eighty-five, the government of these United States took measures to prevent Apaches from manufacturing tiswin. Tiswin is a beer-like intoxicant Apaches had made for centuries. The great Chiricahua Apache,

Goyathlay — whose name translates as One-Who-Yawns — became angered at this additional infringement on Indian traditions and conducted several retaliatory raids here and in Mexico against the ancient enemy. One notes the government had appropriated most of the hunting grounds of the Chiricahua, forcing them to depend on the Army for sustenance, although the Army seldom gave Apaches their full allotment and often made them — even children, the aged, and infirm — walk twenty miles to get rations. Further, unscrupulous white men, who wanted Apache land for mines and ranches, incited the Chiricahua by telling them they were marked for extermination. They knew the subsequent unrest would give the Army an excuse to drive them off the reservation. Intelligent commanders like General George Crook saw this, but Washington rarely listened because the Congress knew all it needed to know about blood-thirsty Apaches. President Grover Cleveland based his judgment on headlines and yellow journalism and wanted Goyathlay hanged. General Crook understood that Goyathlay fought not out of hatred but out of fear and love for his heritage and — what's more — having nothing of significance to do any longer. This is all a footnote.

"After numerous raids and subsequent surrenders, Goyathlay's final surrender brought him incarceration in damp Florida, where so many desert Indians died. The chief saw the old wars were a losing game. A willingness to die no longer made a man free — it made him stupid. By fighting so hard for their old life, the Chiricahua forced the extinction of their ancient ways. There's the key. But the reactionary Goyathlay accepted some of the new ways after he was moved to a reservation in Oklahoma, where he became a successful farmer, wrote his autobiography, and joined the Dutch Reformed Church — the church which prays, 'All my works are as dirty rags in the sight of the Lord.'

"But I've gotten ahead of my story. After Goyathlay's many raids in this desert, he often escaped to these mountains — to this very canyon, a sacred place where Apaches heard voices of the dead. He camped by and drank from this very stream. Like the outlaws of Tombstone who also hid here, Goyathlay was a desperado — that is to say, a desperate man."

He stopped speaking. "Aren't we all?" I said and yawned again.

"The desperado who died aged and successful although deprived of his old life and homeland, One-Who-Yawns by name, you may have heard of."

"I don't think so."

"Think again, my countryman. The United States Army called him Geronimo. You see, there is hope for us all."

14

THE morning was the kind of day that makes a man doubt the reality of death: warm sun, cool air, clear water, bird notes flying out of the hardwoods like sparks from an anvil. I washed and got moving, heading up canyon. After four miles, the pavement stopped and the road turned to a horrendously stony slope that twisted sharply up into the mountain forest. A sign: IMPASSABLE TO TRAILERS. An intriguing road. Whitman writes:

> O highway I travel, do you say to me Do not leave me?
> Do you say Venture not — if you leave me you are lost?
> Do you say I am already prepared, I am well-beaten and undenied, adhere
>   to me?
> O public road, I say back I am not afraid to leave you.

Ready for anything that morning, that's what I got.

Onion Saddle Road, after I was committed to it, narrowed to a single rutted lane affording no place to turn around; if I met somebody, one of us would have to back down. The higher I went, the more that idea unnerved me — the road was bad enough driving forward. The compass swung from point to point, and within any five minutes it had touched each of the three hundred sixty degrees. The clutch started pushing back, and ruts and craters and rocks threw the steering wheel into nasty jerks that wrenched to the spine. I understood why, the day before, I'd thought there could be no road over the Chiricahuas: there wasn't. No wonder desperadoes hid in this inaccessibility.

Higher and higher the road, hanging precariously to the mountain edge as if tacked on; the truck swung around the sharp turns, and all I could see was sky and cloud. It was like flying. Then, far above the southern Arizona desert, snow lay in shaded depressions. Finally, at eight thousand feet, I came to what must have been the summit. Pines were bigger on the western slope, but the descent was no less rocky or steep. And it went on and on. I thought: Why couldn't this curse of a road just be a nightmare? Why couldn't I wake to find myself groggy and warm, curled like a snail in my sleeping bag?

No road signs, no indications that I was coming off the mountain; maybe I was on the way to a dead end. I could only trust in the blue-highway maxim: "I can't take any more" comes just before "I don't give a damn." Let the caring snap, let it break all to hell. Caring breaks before the man if he can only wait it out.

Sure enough, the single lane became two, the dirt macadam, and Pinery Canyon led out to Arizona 186, a crooked highway that dipped into arroyos rather than bridging them; but it was smooth beyond measure, and Ghost Dancing drove itself. I had crossed. No accomplishment at all, but it seemed like one. In the side mirror the powdery visage of a man embraced by the desert; I was wearing a layer of the Chiricahuas. As for Paradise, I never found it.

The towns were Dos Cabezas, a clutch of houses under worn twin peaks like skulls, and Wilcox, clean and orderly. Then another road choice: two days of rock and ruts through the Little Dragoon Mountains or I-10. It was Friday, and I wanted company. I weakened and took the well-beaten and undenied public road northwest toward Phoenix, where I hoped to find a man who knew my boyhood almost as well as I did.

The interstate, after the mountains, came as relief. I sat back. My encounter of the night before had been on my mind since morning. The Boss of the Plains bothered me — I didn't know why. Things outside himself he found banal and not worth his attention. Was that it? An empty man full of himself? Unlike other people of common coin I'd met along the road, he was separate rather than distinct; yet, unlike his, their commonality sang. They seemed parts of a whole. After traveling nineteenth-century America, de Tocqueville came to believe one result of democracy was a concentration of each man's attention upon himself.

The highway rose slowly for miles then dropped into wacky Texas Canyon, an abrupt and peculiar piling of boulders, which looked as if hoisted into strange angles and points of balance. Nature in a zany mood had stacked up the rounded rocks in whimsical and impossible ways, trying out new principles of design, experimenting with old laws of gravity, putting theorems of the physicists to the test. But beyond Texas Canyon, the terrain was once more logical and mundane right angles, everything flat or straight up.

I was thinking of Cave Creek again. The beautiful place seemed shadowy as if the Boss cast a murk. Black Elk says men get lost in the darkness of their own eyes, and indeed, the Boss had found a thousand ways to protect himself from a real confrontation with himself. And more: he listened for despair, then accorded himself with it. "Hell under the skull bones," Whitman calls it.

In Tucson, I stopped for gas along a multilane called Miracle Mile (they love that appellation in the West) congested like an asthmatic bronchial tube; then back to the highway. By last light, I came into the city named after the bird forever reborn from the ashes of what it has been.

Five

WEST BY SOUTHWEST

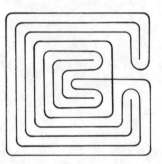

I DON'T suppose that saguaros mean to give comic relief to the otherwise solemn face of the desert, but they do. Standing on the friable slopes they are quite persnickety about, saguaros mimic men as they salute, bow, dance, raise arms to wave, and grin with faces carved in by woodpeckers. Older plants, having survived odds against their reaching maturity of sixty million to one, have every right to smile.

The saguaro is ninety percent water, and a big, two-hundred-year-old cactus may hold a ton of it — a two-year supply. With this weight, a plant that begins to lean is soon on the ground; one theory now says that the arms, which begin sprouting only after forty or fifty years when the cactus has some height, are counterweights to keep the plant erect.

The Monday I drove northeast out of Phoenix, saguaros were in bloom — comparatively small, greenish-white blossoms perched on top of the trunks like undersized Easter bonnets; at night, long-nosed bats came to pollinate them. But by day, cactus wrens, birds of daring aerial skill, put on the show as they made kamikaze dives between toothpick-size thorns into nest cavities, where they were safe from everything except the incredible ascents over the spines by black racers in search of eggs the snakes would swallow whole.

It was hot. The only shade along Arizona 87 lay under the bottomsides of rocks; the desert gives space then closes it up with heat. To the east, in profile, rose the Superstition Mountains, an evil place, Pima and Maricopa Indians say, which brings on diabolic possession to those who enter. Somewhere among the granite and greasewood was the Lost Dutchman gold mine, important not for whatever cache it might hide as for providing a white dream.

North of the Sycamore River, saguaro, ocotillo, paloverde, and cholla surrendered the hills to pads of prickly pear the size of a man's head. The road climbed and the temperature dropped. At Payson, a mile high on the northern slope of the Mazatzal Mountains, I had to pull on a jacket.

Settlers once ran into Payson for protection from marauding Apaches;

after the Apache let things calm down, citizens tried to liven them up again by holding rodeos in the main street. Now, streets paved, Payson lay quiet but for the whine of sawmills releasing the sweet scent of cut timber.

I stopped at an old log hotel to quench a desert thirst. A sign on the door: NO LIVE ANIMALS ALLOWED. I guess you could bring in all the dead ones you wanted. A woman shouted, "Ain't servin' now." Her unmoving eyes, heavy as if cast from lead, watched suspiciously for a live badger under my jacket or a weasel up my pantleg.

"This is a fine old hotel," I said. She ignored me. "Do you mind if I look at your big map?" She shrugged and moved away, safe from any live animal attack. I was hunting a place to go next. Someone had marked the Hopi Reservation to the north in red. Why not? As I left, I asked where I could water my lizard. She ignored that too.

Highway 260, winding through the pine forests of central Arizona, let the mountains be boss as it followed whatever avenues they left open, crossing ridges only when necessary, slipping unobtrusively on narrow spans over streams of rounded boulders. But when 260 reached the massive escarpment called the Mogollon Rim, it had to challenge geography and climb the face.

I shifted to low, and Ghost Dancing pulled hard. A man with a dusty, leathery face creased like an old boot strained on a bicycle — the old style with fat tires. I called a hello, he said nothing. At the summit, I waited to see whether he would make the ascent. Far below lay two cars, crumpled wads. Through the clear air I could count nine ranges of mountains, each successively grayer in a way reminiscent of old Chinese woodblock prints. The Mogollon was a spectacular place; the more so because I had not been anesthetized to it by endless Kodachromes. When the cyclist passed, I called out, "Bravo!" but he acknowledged nothing. I would have liked to talk to a man who, while his contemporaries were consolidating their little empires, rides up the Mogollon Rim on a child's toy. Surely he knew something about desperate men.

The top of the great scarp, elevation sixty-five hundred feet, lay flat and covered with big ponderosas standing between dirty snowdrifts and black pools of snowmelt. I began anticipating Heber, the next town. One of the best moments of any day on the road was, toward sunset, looking forward to the last stop. At Heber I hoped for an old hotel with a little bar off to the side where they would serve A-1 on draft under a stuffed moosehead; or maybe I'd find a grill dishing up steak and eggs on blue-rimmed platters. I hoped for people who had good stories, people who sometimes took you home to see their collection of carved peach pits.

That was the hope. But Heber was box houses and a dingy sawmill, a couple of motels and filling stations, a glass-and-Formica cafe. Heber had no center, no focus for the eye and soul: neither a courthouse, nor high church steeple, nor hotel. Nothing has done more to take a sense of civic identity, a feeling of community, from small-town America than the loss of old hotels to the motel business. The hotel was once where things coalesced, where you could meet both townspeople and travelers. Not so in a motel. No matter how you build it, the motel remains a haunt of the quick and dirty, where the only locals are Chamber of Commerce boys every fourth Thursday. Who ever heard the returning traveler exclaim over one of the great motels of the world he stayed in? Motels can be big, but never grand.

2

TUESDAY morning: the country east of Heber was a desert of sagebrush and globe-shaped junipers and shallow washes with signs warning of flash floods. I turned north at Snowflake, founded by Erastus Snow and Bill Flake, and headed toward the twenty-five thousand square miles of Navajo reservation (nearly equal to West Virginia) which occupies most of the northeastern corner of Arizona. The scrub growth disappeared entirely and only the distant outlines of red rock mesas interrupted the emptiness. But for the highway, the land was featureless.

Holbrook used to be a tough town where boys from the Hash Knife cattle outfit cut loose. Now, astride I-44 (once route 66), Holbrook was a tourist stop for women with Instamatics and men with metal detectors; no longer was the big business cattle, but rather rocks and gems.

North of the interstate, I entered the reserve. Although the area has been part of the Navajo homeland for five hundred years, settlers of a century before, led by Kit Carson, drove the Navajo out of Arizona in retribution for their raids against whites and other Indians alike. A few years later, survivors of the infamous "Long Walk" returned to take up their land again. Now the Navajo possess the largest reservation in the United States and the one hundred fifty thousand descendants of the seven thousand survivors comprise far and away the largest tribe. Their reservation is the only one in the country to get bigger — five times bigger — after it was first set aside; their holdings increased largely because white men had believed Navajo land worthless. But in fact, the reservation contains coal, oil, gas, uranium, helium, and timber; those resources may explain why Navajos did not win total control over their land until 1972.

Liquor bottles, beercans, an occasional stripped car littered the unfenced roadside. Far off the highway, against the mesa bottoms, stood small concrete-block or frame houses, each with a television antenna, pickup, privy, and ceremonial hogan of stone, adobe, and cedar. Always the hogan doors faced east.

In a classic scene, a boy on a pinto pony herded a flock of sheep and goats — descendants of the Spanish breed — across the highway. A few miles later, a man wearing a straw Stetson and pegleg Levi's guided up a draw a pair of horses tied together at the neck in the Indian manner. With the white man giving up on the economics of cowpunching, it looked as if the old categories of cowboys and Indians had merged; whoever the last true cowboy in America turns out to be, he's likely to be an Indian.

At the center of the reservation lay Hopi territory, a large rectangle with boundaries the tribes cannot agree on because part of the increase of Navajo land has come at the expense of the Hopis. A forbidding sign in Latinate English:

> YOU ARE ENTERING THE EXCLUSIVE
> HOPI RESERVATION AREA. YOUR
> ENTRANCE CONSTITUTES CONSENT
> TO THE JURISDICTION OF THE HOPI
> TRIBE AND ITS COURTS.

Although the Hopi have lived here far longer than any other surviving people and consider their mile-high spread of rock and sand, wind and sun, the center of the universe, they are now, by Anglo decree, surrounded by their old enemies, the Navajo, a people they see as latecomers. In 1880, Hopis held two and one half million acres; today it has decreased to about a half million.

Holding on to their land has been a long struggle for the Hopi. Yet for a tribe whose name means "well behaved," for Indians without war dances, for a group whose first defense against the conquistadors was sprinkled lines of sacred cornmeal, for a people who protested priestly corruption (consorting with Hopi women and whipping men) by quietly pitching a few padres over the cliffs, Hopis have done well. But recently they have fought Navajo expansion in federal courts, and a strange case it is: those who settled first seeking judgment from those who came later through laws of those who arrived last.

Because the Navajo prefer widely dispersed clusters of clans to village life, I'd seen nothing resembling a hamlet for seventy-five miles. But Hopi

Polacca almost looked like a Western town in spite of Indian ways here and there: next to a floral-print bedsheet on a clothesline hung a coyote skin, and beside box houses were adobe bread ovens shaped like skep beehives. The Navajo held to his hogan, the Hopi his oven. Those things persisted.

Like bony fingers, three mesas reached down from larger Black Mesa into the middle of Hopi land; not long ago, the only way onto these mesas was by handholds in the steep rock heights. From the tops, the Hopi look out upon a thousand square miles. At the heart of the reservation, topographically and culturally, was Second Mesa. Traditionally, Hopis, as do the eagles they hold sacred, prefer to live on precipices; so it was not far from the edge of Second Mesa that they built the Hopi Cultural Center. In the gallery were drawings of mythic figures by Hopi children who fused centuries and cultures with grotesque Mudhead Kachinas wearing large terra-cotta masks and jackolantern smiles, dancing atop spaceships with Darth Vader and Artoo Deetoo.

At the Center, I ate *nokquivi*, a good hominy stew with baked chile peppers, but I had no luck in striking up a conversation. I drove on toward the western edge of the mesa. Not far from the tribal garage (TRIBAL VEHICLES ONLY) stood small sandstone houses, their slabs precisely cut and fitted as if by ancient Aztecs, a people related to the Hopi. The solid houses blended with the tawny land so well they appeared part of the living rock. All were empty. The residents had moved to prefabs and doublewides.

I couldn't see how anyone could survive a year in this severe land, yet Hopis, like other desert life, are patient and clever and not at all desperate; they have lasted here for ten centuries by using tiny terraced plots that catch spring rain and produce a desert-hardy species of blue corn, as well as squash, onions, beans, peppers, melons, apricots, peaches. The bristlecone pine of American Indians, Hopis live where almost nothing else will, thriving long in adverse conditions: poor soil, drought, temperature extremes, high winds. Those give life to the bristlecone and the Hopi .

Clinging to the southern lip of Third Mesa was ancient Oraibi, most probably the oldest continuously occupied village in the United States. Somehow the stone and adobe have been able to hang on to the precipitous edge since the twelfth century. More than eight hundred Hopis lived at Oraibi in 1901 — now only a few. All across the reservation I'd seen no more than a dozen people, and on the dusty streets of the old town I saw just one bent woman struggling against the wind. But somewhere there must have been more.

To this strangest of American villages the Franciscan father, Tomás Garces, came in 1776 from Tucson with gifts and "true religion." Hopis permitted him to stay at Oraibi, looking then as now if you excluded an occasional television antenna, but they refused his gifts and god, and, on the fourth day of July, sent him off disheartened. To this time, no other North American tribe has held closer to its own religion and culture. Although the isolated Hopi had no knowledge of the importance of religious freedom to the new nation surrounding them, several generations successfully ignored "the code of religious offenses" — laws designed by the Bureau of Indian Affairs to destroy the old rituals and way of life — until greater bureaucratic tolerance came when Herbert Hoover appointed two Quakers to direct the BIA.

A tribal squadcar checked my speed at Hotevilla, where the highway started a long descent off the mesa. The wind was getting up, and tumbleweed bounded across the road, and sand hummed against the Ghost. West, east, north, south — to each a different weather: sandstorm, sun, rain, and bluish snow on the San Francisco Peaks, that home of the Kachinas who are the spiritual forces of Hopi life.

Tuba City, founded by Mormon missionaries as an agency and named after a Hopi chieftain although now mostly a Navajo town, caught the sandstorm full face. As I filled the gas tank, I tried to stay behind the van, but gritty gusts whipped around the corners and stung me and forced my eyes shut. School was just out, and children, shirts pulled over their heads, ran for the trading post, where old Navajo men who had been sitting outside took cover as the sand changed the air to matter. I ducked in too. The place was like an A&P, TG&Y, and craft center.

In viridescent velveteen blouses and violescent nineteenth-century skirts, Navajo women of ample body, each laden with silver and turquoise bracelets, necklaces, and rings — not the trading post variety but heavy bands gleaming under the patina of long wear — reeled off yards of fabric. The children, like schoolkids anywhere, milled around the candy; they spoke only English. But the old men, now standing at the plate glass windows and looking into the brown wind, popped and puffed out the ancient words. I've read that Navajo, a language related to that of the Indians of Alaska and northwest Canada, has no curse words unless you consider "coyote" cursing. By comparison with other native tongues, it's remarkably free of English and Spanish; a Navajo mechanic, for example, has more than two hundred purely Navajo terms to describe automobile parts. And it might be Navajo that will greet the first extraterrestrial ears to hear from planet Earth: on board each *Voyager* spacecraft traveling toward the edge of the solar system and beyond is a gold-plated, long-playing record; following an aria from Mozart's *Magic Flute* and Chuck Berry's "Johnny B. Goode," is a Navajo night chant, music the conquistadors heard.

Intimidated by my ignorance of Navajo and by fear of the contempt that full-bloods often show lesser bloods, I again failed to stir a conversation. After the storm blew on east, I followed the old men back outside, where they squatted to watch the day take up the weather of an hour earlier. To one with a great round head like an earthen pot, I said, "Is the storm finished now?" He looked at me, then slowly turned his head, while the others examined before them things in the air invisible to me.

I took a highway down the mesa into a valley of the Painted Desert, where wind had textured big drifts of orange sand into rills. U.S. 89 ran north along the Echo Cliffs. Goats grazed in stubble by the roadsides, and to the west a horseman moved his sheep. Hogans here stood alone; they were not ceremonial lodges but homes. For miles at the highway edges sat little cardboard and scrapwood ramadas, each with a windblasted sign advertising jewelry and cedar beads. In another era, white men came in wagons to trade beads to Indians; now they came in stationwagons and bought beads. History may repeat, but sometimes things get turned around in the process.

3

SOMEWHERE out there was the Colorado River perfectly hidden in the openness. The river wasn't more than a mile away, but I couldn't make out the slightest indication of it in the desert stretching level and unbroken for twenty or thirty miles west, although I was only fifty miles above where it enters Grand Canyon. This side of the Colorado gorge was once an important Hopi trail south, and, some say, the route Hopi guides took when they first led white men to the canyon. While the arid path followed the river cleft, water was an inaccessible four hundred feet down. Typically, the flexible Hopi solved the desert: women buried gourds of water at strategic points on the outward journey for use on the return.

The highway made an unexpected jog toward Navajo Bridge, a melding of silvery girders and rock cliffs. Suddenly, there it was, far below in the deep and scary canyon of sides so sheer they might have been cut with a stone saw, the naturally silted water turned an unnatural green (*colorado* means "reddish") by the big settling basin a few miles upriver called Glen Canyon Dam. Navajo Bridge, built in 1929 when paved roads began opening the area, is the only crossing over the Colorado between Glen Canyon and Hoover Dam several hundred river miles downstream.

West of the gorge lay verdant rangeland, much of it given to a buffalo herd maintained by the Arizona Game Commission; the great beasts lifted their heads to watch me pass, their dark, wet eyes catching the late sun. To the north rose the thousand-foot butt end of the Vermillion Cliffs; the cliffs weren't truly vermillion, but contrasting with the green valley in the orange afternoon light, they seemed so.

In 1776, a few months after white-stockinged men in Philadelphia had declared independence, a Spanish expedition led by missionaries Francisco Silvestre Velez de Escalante and Francisco Atanasio Dominguez, returning from an unsuccessful search for a good northern route to the California missions, wandered dispiritedly along the Vermillion Cliffs as they tried to find in the maze of the Colorado a point to cross the river chasm. They looked for ten days and were forced to eat boiled cactus and two of their horses before finding a place to ford; even then, they had to chop out steps to get down and back up the four-hundred-foot perpendicular walls. My crossing, accomplished sitting down, took twenty seconds. What I saw as a remarkable sight, the Spaniards saw as a terror that nearly did them in.

Escalante's struggles gave perspective to the easy passage I'd enjoyed across six thousand miles of America. Other than weather, some bad road, and a few zealous police, my difficulties had been only those of mind. In light of what was about to happen, my guilt over easy transit proved ironic.

I went up an enormous geologic upheaval called the Kaibab Plateau; with startling swiftness, the small desert bushes changed to immense conifers as the Kaibab forest deepened: ponderosa, fir, spruce. At six thousand feet, the temperature was sixty: a drop of thirty degrees in ten miles. On the north edge of the forest, the highway made a long gliding descent off the plateau into Utah. Here lay Kane and Garfield counties, a place of multicolored rock and baroque stone columns and, under it all, the largest unexploited coalfield in the country. A land certain one day to be fought over.

At dusk I considered going into the Coral Sand Dunes for the night, but I'd had enough warmth and desert for a while, so I pushed north toward Cedar Breaks in the severe and beautiful Markagunt Plateau. The cool would refresh me. Sporadic splats of rain, not enough to pay attention to, hit the windshield. I turned onto Utah 14, the cross-mountain road to Cedar City. In the dim light of a mountainous sky, I could just make out a large sign:

ELEVATION 10,000 FEET
ROAD MAY BE IMPASSIBLE
DURING WINTER MONTHS.

So? It was nearly May. The rain popped, then stopped, popped and stopped. The incline became steeper and light rain fell steadily, rolling red desert dust off the roof; I hadn't hit showers since east Texas. It was good. The pleasant cool turned to cold, and I switched on the heater. The headlights glared off snowbanks edging closer to the highway as it climbed, and the rain became sleet. That's when I began thinking I might have made a little miscalculation. I looked for a place to turn around, but there was only narrow, twisted road. The sleet got heavier, and the headlights were cutting only thirty feet into it. Maybe I could drive above and out of the storm. At eight thousand feet, the wind came up — a rough, nasty wind that bullied me about the slick road. Lear, daring the storm to "strike flat the thick rotundity of the world," cries, "Blow, winds, and crack your cheeks! Rage! Blow!" And that's just what they did.

A loud, sulphurous blast of thunder rattled the little truck, then another, and one more. Never had I seen lightning or heard thunder in a snowstorm. Although there were no signs, the map showed a campground near the summit. It would be suicide to stop, and maybe the same to go on. The wind pushed on Ghost Dancing so, I was afraid of getting blown over the invisible edge. Had not the falling snow taken away my vision, I might have needed a blindfold like the ones medieval travelers wore to blunt their terror of crossing the Alps. A rule of the blue road: Be careful going in search of adventure — it's ridiculously easy to find.

Then I was on the top, ten thousand feet up. UP. The wind was horrendous. Utah 14 now cut through snowbanks higher than the truck. At the junction with route 143, a sign pointed north toward Cedar Breaks campground. I relaxed. I was going to live. I puffed up at having beaten the mountain.

Two hundred yards up 143, I couldn't believe what I saw. I got out and walked to it as the raving wind whipped my pantlegs and pulled my hair on end. I couldn't believe it. There it was, the striped centerline, glowing through the sleet, disappearing under a seven-foot snowbank. Blocked.

Back to the truck. My heart dropped like a stone through new snow. There had to be a mistake. I mean, this wasn't 1776. The days of Escalante were gone. But the only mistake was my judgment. I was stopped on state 143, and 143 lay under winter ice.

I turned up the heater to blast level, went to the back, and wrapped a blanket around the sleeping bag. I undressed fast and got into a sweatsuit, two pairs of socks, my old Navy-issue watch cap, a pair of gloves. When I cut the engine, snow already had covered the windshield. Only a quarter tank of gas. While the warmth lasted, I hurried into the bag and pulled back the curtain to watch the fulminous clouds blast the mountain. That sky was bent on having a storm, and I was in for a drubbing.

At any particular moment in a man's life, he can say that everything he has done and not done, that has been done and not been done to him, has brought him to that moment. If he's being installed as Chieftain or receiving a Nobel Prize, that's a fulfilling notion. But if he's in a sleeping bag at ten thousand feet in a snowstorm, parked in the middle of a highway and waiting to freeze to death, the idea can make him feel calamitously stupid.

A loud racketing of hail fell on the steel box, and the wind seemed to have hands, it shook the Ghost so relentlessly. Lightning tried to outdo thunder in scaring me. So did those things scare me? No. Not *those* things. It was something else. I was certain of a bear attack. That's what scared me.

Lightning strikes the earth about eight million times each day and kills a hundred and fifty Americans every year. I don't know how many die from exposure and hypothermia, but it must be at least a comparable number. As for bears eating people who sleep inside steel trucks, I haven't been able to find that figure. It made no sense to fear a bear coming out of hibernation in such weather to attack a truck. Yet I lay a long time, waiting for the beast, shaggy and immense, to claw through the metal, its hot breath on my head, to devour me like a gumdrop and roll the van over the edge.

Perhaps fatigue or strain prevented me from worrying about the real fear; perhaps some mechanism of mind hid the true and inescapable threat. Whatever it was, it finally came to me that I was crazy. Maybe I was already freezing to death. Maybe this was the way it happened. Black Elk prays for the Grandfather Spirit to help him face the winds and walk the good road to the day of quiet. Whitman too:

> *O to be self-balanced for contingencies,*
> *To confront night, storms, hunger, ridicule, accidents,*
> *rebuffs, as the trees and animals do.*

I wondered how long I might have to stay in the Breaks before I could drive down. The cold didn't worry me much: I had insulated the rig myself and slept in it once when the windchill was thirty-six below. I figured to survive if I didn't have to stay on top too long. Why hadn't I listened to friends who advised carrying a CB? The headline showed darkly: Frozen Man Found in Avalanche. The whole night I slept and woke, slept and woke, while the hail fell like iron shot, and thunder slammed around, and lightning seared the ice.

4

DIRTY and hard, the morning light could have been old concrete. Twenty-nine degrees inside. I tried to figure a way to drive down the mountain without leaving the sleeping bag. I was stiff — not from the cold so much as from having slept coiled like a grub. Creaking open and pinching toes and fingers to check for frostbite, I counted to ten (twice) before shouting and leaping for my clothes. Shouting distracts the agony. Underwear, trousers, and shirt so cold they felt wet.

I went outside to relieve myself. In the snow, with the hot stream, I spelled out *alive*. Then to work chipping clear the windows. Somewhere off this mountain, people still lay warm in their blankets and not yet ready to get up to a hot breakfast. So what if they spent the day selling imprinted ballpoint pens? Weren't they down off mountains?

Down. I had to try it. And down it was, Utah 14 a complication of twists and drops descending the west side more precipitately than the east. A good thing I hadn't attempted it in the dark. After a mile, snow on the pavement became slush, then water, and finally at six thousand feet, dry and sunny blacktop.

Cedar City, a tidy Mormon town, lay at the base of the mountains on the edge of the Escalante Desert. Ah, desert! I pulled in for gas, snow still melting off my rig. "See you spent the night in the Breaks," the attendant said. "You people never believe the sign at the bottom."

"I believed, but it said something about winter months. May isn't winter."

"It is up there. You Easterners just don't know what a mountain is."

I didn't say anything, but I knew what a mountain was: a high pile of windy rocks with its own weather.

In the cafeteria of Southern Utah State College, I bought a breakfast of scrambled eggs, pancakes, bacon, oatmeal, grapefruit, orange juice, milk, and a cinnamon roll. A celebration of being alive. I was full of victory.

Across the table sat an Indian student named Kendrick Fritz, who was studying chemistry and wanted to become a physician. He had grown up in Moenkopi, Arizona, just across the highway from Tuba City. I said, "Are you Navajo or Hopi?"

"Hopi. You can tell by my size. Hopis are smaller than Navajos."

His voice was gentle, his words considered, and smile timid. He seemed open to questions. "Fritz doesn't sound like a Hopi name."

"My father took it when he was in the Army in the Second World War. Hopis usually have Anglo first names and long Hopi last names that are hard for other people to pronounce."

I told him of my difficulty in rousing a conversation in Tuba City. He said, "I can't speak for Navajos about prejudice, but I know Hopis who believe we survived Spaniards, missionaries, a thousand years of other Indians, even the BIA. But tourists?" He smiled. "Smallpox would be better."

"Do you — yourself — think most whites are prejudiced against Indians?"

"About fifty-fifty. Half show contempt because they saw a drunk squaw at the Circle K. Another half think we're noble savages — they may be worse because if an Indian makes a mistake they hate him for being human. Who wants to be somebody's ideal myth?"

"My grandfather used to say the Big Vision made the Indian, but the white man invented him."

"Relations are okay here, but I wouldn't call them good, and I'm not one to go around looking for prejudice. I try not to."

"Maybe you're more tolerant of Anglo ways than some others."

"Could be. I mean, I *am* studying to be a doctor and not a medicine man. But I'm no apple Indian — red outside and white underneath. I lived up in Brigham City, Utah, when I went to the Intermountain School run by the BIA. It was too easy though. Too much time to goof around. So I switched to Box Elder — that's a public school. I learned there. And I lived in Dallas a few months. What I'm saying is that I've lived on Hopi land and I've lived away. I hear Indians talk about being red all the way through criticizing others for acting like Anglos, and all the time they're sitting in a pickup at a drive-in. But don't tell them to trade the truck for a horse."

"The Spanish brought the horse."

He nodded. "To me, being Indian means being responsible to my people. Helping with the best tools. Who invented penicillin doesn't matter."

"What happens after you finish school?"

"I used to want out of Tuba, but since I've been away, I've come to see how our land really is our Sacred Circle — it's our strength. Now, I want to go back and practice general medicine. At the Indian hospital in Tuba where my mother and sister are nurse's aides, there aren't any Indian M.D.'s, and that's no good. I don't respect people who don't help themselves. Hopi land is no place to make big money, but I'm not interested anyway."

"You don't use the word *reservation*."

"We don't think of it as a reservation since we were never ordered there. We found it through Hopi prophecies. We're unusual because we've always held onto our original land — most of it anyway. One time my grandfather pointed out the old boundaries to me. We were way up on a mesa. I've forgotten what they are except for the San Francisco Peaks. But in the last eighty years, the government's given a lot of our land to Navajos, and now we're in a hard spot — eight thousand Hopis are surrounded and outnumbered twenty-five to one. I don't begrudge the Navajo anything, but I think Hopis should be in on making the decisions. Maybe you know that Congress didn't even admit Indians to citizenship until about nineteen twenty. Incredible — live someplace a thousand years and then find out you're a foreigner."

"I know an Osage who says, 'Don't Americanize me and I won't Americanize you.' He means everybody in the country came from someplace else."

"Hopi legends are full of migrations."

"Will other Hopis be suspicious of you when you go home as a doctor?"

"Some might be, but not my family. But for a lot of Hopis, the worst thing to call a man is *kahopi*, 'not Hopi.' Nowadays, though, we all have to choose either the new ways or the Hopi way, and it's split up whole villages. A lot of us try to find the best in both places. We've always learned from other people. If we hadn't, we'd be extinct like some other tribes."

"Medicine's a pretty good survival technique."

"Sure, but I also like Jethro Tull and the Moody Blues. That's not survival."

"Is the old religion a survival technique?"

"If you live it."

"Do you?"

"Most Hopis follow our religion, at least in some ways, because it reminds us who we are and it's part of the land. I'll tell you, in the rainy season when the desert turns green, it's beautiful there. The land is medicine too."

"If you don't mind telling me, what's the religion like?"

"Like any religion in one way — different clans believe different things."

"There must be something they all share, something common."

"That's hard to say."

"Could you try?"

He thought a moment. "Maybe the idea of harmony. And the way a

Hopi prays. A good life, a harmonious life, is a prayer. We don't just pray for ourselves, we pray for all things. We're famous for the Snake Dances, but a lot of people don't realize those ceremonies are prayers for rain and crops, prayers for life. We also pray for rain by sitting and thinking about rain. We sit and picture wet things like streams and clouds. It's sitting in pictures."

He picked up his tray to go. "I could give you a taste of the old Hopi Way. But maybe you're too full after that breakfast. You always eat so much?"

"The mountain caused that." I got up. "What do you mean by 'taste'?"

"I'll show you."

We went to his dormitory room. Other than several Kachina dolls he had carved from cottonwood and a picture of a Sioux warrior, it was just another collegiate dorm room — maybe cleaner than most. He pulled a shoebox from under his bed and opened it carefully. I must have been watching a little wide-eyed because he said, "It isn't live rattlesnakes." From the box he took a long cylinder wrapped in waxed paper and held it as if trying not to touch it. "Will you eat this? It's very special." He was smiling. "If you won't, I can't share the old Hopi Way with you."

"Okay, but if it's dried scorpions, I'm going to speak with a forked tongue."

"Open your hands." He unwrapped the cylinder and ever so gently laid across my palms an airy tube the color of a thunderhead. It was about ten inches long and an inch in diameter. "There you go," he said.

"You first."

"I'm not having any right now."

So I bit the end off the blue-gray tube. It was many intricately rolled layers of something with less substance than butterfly wings. The bite crumbled to flakes that stuck to my lips. "Now tell me what I'm eating."

"Do you like it?"

"I think so. Except it disappears like cotton candy just as I get ready to chew. But I think I taste corn and maybe ashes."

"Hopis were eating that before horses came to America. It's piki. Hopi bread you might say. Made from blue-corn flour and ashes from grease-wood or sagebrush. Baked on an oiled stone by my mother. She sends piki every so often. It takes time and great skill to make. We call it Hopi cornflakes."

"Unbelievably thin." I laid a piece on a page of his chemistry book. The words showed through.

"We consider corn our mother. The blue variety is what you might call our compass — wherever it grows, we can go. Blue corn directed our migrations. Navajos cultivate a yellow species that's soft and easy to grind, but ours is hard. You plant it much deeper than other corns, and it survives where they would die. It's a genetic variant the Hopi developed."

"Why is it blue? That must be symbolic."

"We like the color blue. Corn's our most important ritual ingredient."

"The piki's good, but it's making me thirsty. Where's a water fountain?"

When I came back from the fountain, Fritz said, "I'll tell you what I think the heart of our religion is — it's the Four Worlds."

Over the next hour, he talked about the Hopi Way, and showed pictures and passages from *Book of the Hopi*. The key seemed to be emergence. Carved in a rock near the village of Shipolovi is the ancient symbol for it:

With variations, the symbol appears among other Indians of the Americas. Its lines represent the course a person follows on his "road of life" as he passes through birth, death, rebirth. Human existence is essentially a series of journeys, and the emergence symbol is a kind of map of the wandering soul, an image of a process; but it is also, like most Hopi symbols and ceremonies, a reminder of cosmic patterns that all human beings move in.

The Hopi believes mankind has evolved through four worlds: the first a shadowy realm of contentment; the second a place so comfortable the people forgot where they had come from and began worshipping material goods. The third world was a pleasant land too, but the people, bewildered by their past and fearful for their future, thought only of their own earthly plans. At last, the Spider Grandmother, who oversees the emergences, told them: "You have forgotten what you should have remembered, and now you have to leave this place. Things will be harder." In the fourth and present world, life is difficult for mankind, and he struggles to remember his source because materialism and selfishness block a greater vision. The

12. *Kendrick Fritz in Cedar City, Utah*

newly born infant comes into the fourth world with the door of his mind open (evident in the cranial soft spot), but as he ages, the door closes and he must work at remaining receptive to the great forces. A human being's grandest task is to keep from breaking with things outside himself.

"A Hopi learns that he belongs to two families," Fritz said, "his natural clan and that of all things. As he gets older, he's supposed to move closer to the greater family. In the Hopi Way, each person tries to recognize his part in the whole."

"At breakfast you said you hunted rabbits and pigeons and robins, but I don't see how you can shoot a bird if you believe in the union of life."

"A Hopi hunter asks the animal to forgive him for killing it. Only life can feed life. The robin knows that."

"How does robin taste, by the way?"

"Tastes good."

"The religion doesn't seem to have much of an ethical code."

"It's there. We watch what the Kachinas say and do. But the Spider Grandmother did give two rules. To all men, not just Hopis. If you look at them, they cover everything. She said, 'Don't go around hurting each other,' and she said, 'Try to understand things.'"

"I like them. I like them very much."

"Our religion keeps reminding us that we aren't just will and thoughts. We're also sand and wind and thunder. Rain. The seasons. All those things. You learn to respect everything because you *are* everything. If you respect yourself, you respect all things. That's why we have so many songs of creation to remind us where we came from. If the fourth world forgets that, we'll disappear in the wilderness like the third world, where people decided they had created themselves."

"Pride's the deadliest of the Seven Deadly Sins in old Christian theology."

"It's *kahopi* to set yourself above things. It causes divisions."

Fritz had to go to class. As we walked across campus, I said, "I guess it's hard to be a Hopi in Cedar City — especially if you're studying biochemistry."

"It's hard to be a Hopi anywhere."

"I mean, difficult to carry your Hopi heritage into a world as technological as medicine is."

"Heritage? My heritage is the Hopi Way, and that's a way of the spirit. Spirit can go anywhere. In fact, it has to go places so it can change and emerge like in the migrations. That's the whole idea."

5

A THIRD of the land mass of earth is desert of one kind or another. After my bout with the mountain, I found that a comforting statistic as I started across the Escalante Desert west of Cedar City. Utah 56 went at the sage-brush flats seriously, taking up big stretches before turning away from anything.

A car whipped past, the driver eating and a passenger clicking a camera. Moving without going anywhere, taking a trip instead of making one. I laughed at the absurdity of the photographs and then realized I, too, was rolling effortlessly along, turning the windshield into a movie screen in which I, the viewer, did the moving while the subject held still. That was the temptation of the American highway, of the American vacation (from the Latin *vacare*, "to be empty"). A woman in Texas had told me that she often threatened to write a book about her family vacations. Her title: *Zoom!* The drama of their trips, she said, occurred on the inside of the windshield with one family crisis after another. Her husband drove a thousand miles, much of it with his right arm over the backseat to hold down one of the children. She said, "Our vacations take us."

She longed for the true journey of an Odysseus or Ishmael or Gulliver or even a Dorothy of Kansas, wherein passage through space and time becomes only a metaphor of a movement through the interior of being. A true journey, no matter how long the travel takes, has no end. What's more, as John Le Carré, in speaking of the journey of death, said, "Nothing ever bridged the gulf between the man who went and the man who stayed behind."

Within a mile of the Nevada stateline, the rabbit brush and sage stopped and a juniper forest began as the road ascended into cooler air. I was struck, as I had been many times, by the way land changes its character within a mile or two of a stateline. I turned north on U.S. 93, an empty highway running from Canada nearly to Mexico. I'm just guessing, but, for its great length, it must have fewer towns per mile than any other federal highway in the country. It goes, for example, the length of Nevada, more than five hundred miles, passing through only seventeen towns — and that's counting Jackpot and Contact.

Pioche, one of the seventeen, was pure Nevada. Its elevation of six thousand feet was ten times its population; but during the peak of the mining boom a century ago, the people and the feet above sea level came to the same number. The story of Pioche repeats itself over Nevada: Indian shows prospector a mountain full of metal; prospector strikes bonanza; town booms for a couple of decades with the four "G's": grubstakes, gamblers, girls, gunmen (seventy-five people died in Pioche before anyone died a natural death); town withers. By 1900, Pioche was on its way to becoming a ghost town like Midas, Wonder, Bullion, Cornucopia. But, even with the silver and gold gone, technological changes in the forties made deposits of lead and zinc valuable, and cheap power from Boulder Dam (as it was then) kept Pioche alive.

A citizen boasted to me about their "Million Dollar Courthouse" — a plain yet pleasing century-old fieldstone building sitting high on the mountainside — albeit a little cynically, since construction cost a fraction of that; but through compound interest and refinancing, the price finally hit a million. The courthouse was condemned three years before the mortgage was paid off.

The highway went down into a narrow and immensely long, thunder-of-hooves valley, then, like a chalkline, headed north, running between two low mountain ranges, the higher eastern one still in snow. A sign: NEXT GAS 80 MILES. In the dusk, the valley showed no evidence of man other than wire fences, highway, and occasional deer-crossing signs that looked like medieval heraldic devices: on a field of ochre, a stag rampant, sable. The signs had been turned into colanders by gunners, almost none of whom hit the upreared bucks.

Squat clumps of white sage, wet from a shower out of the western range, sweetened the air, and gulches had not yet emptied. Calm lay over the uncluttered openness, and a damp wind blew everything clean. I saw no one. I let my speed build to sixty, cut the ignition, shifted to neutral. Although Ghost Dancing had the aerodynamics of an orange crate, it coasted for more than a mile across the flats. When it came to a standstill, I put it back in gear and left it at roadside. There was no one. Listening, I walked into the scrub. The desert does its best talking at night, but on that spring evening it kept God's whopping silence; and that too is a desert voice.

I've read that a naked eye can see six thousand stars in the hundred billion galaxies, but I couldn't believe it, what with the sky white with starlight. I saw a million stars with one eye and two million with both. Galileo proved that the rotation and revolution of the earth give stars their apparent movements. But on that night his evidence wouldn't hold. Any sensible man, lying on his back among new leaves of sage, in the warm sand that had already dried, even he could see Arcturus and Vega and Betelgeuse just above, not far at all, wheeling about the earth. Their paths cut arcs, and there was no doubt about it.

The immensity of sky and desert, their vast absences, reduced me. It was as if I were evaporating, and it was calming and cleansing to be absorbed by that vacancy. Whitman says:

O to realize space!
The plenteousness of all, that there are no bounds,
To emerge and be of the sky, of the sun and moon and flying clouds,
    as one with them.

On the highway a car came and went, sounding a pitiful brief *whoosh* as it ran the dark valley. When I drove back onto the road, I saw in the headlights a small desert rodent spin across the pavement as if on wheels; from the mountains, my little machine must have looked much the same. Ahead hung the Big Dipper with a million galaxies, they say, inside its cup, and on my port side, atop the western range, the evening star held a fixed position for miles until it swung slowly around in front of me and then back to port. I had followed a curve so long I couldn't see the bend. Only Vesper showed the truth. The highway joined U.S. 6 — from Cape Cod to Long Beach, the longest federal route under one number in the days before interstates — then crossed the western mountains. Below lay the mining town of Ely.

Not everything that happens in Ely happens at the Hotel Nevada, but it could. The old place is ready for it. But that night the blackjack tables were empty, the slots nearly so, and the marbleized mirrors reflected the bartender's slump and a waitress swallowing a yawn. Yet I did see these things:

Item: a woman, face as blank as a nickel slug, pulling dutifully on the slot handles. She had stood before the gears so many times she herself had become a mechanism for reaching, dropping, pulling. Her eyes were dark and unmoving as if unplugged. The periodic jangle of change in the winner's cup moved her only to reach into the little coffer without looking and deposit the coins again.

Item: a man moseyed in wearing leather from head to toe; attempting cowpuncher macho, he looked more like a two-legged first baseman's mitt. With him a bored blonde. "I'm a very competitive person. I'm in it to win," he said, and the blonde yawned again.

Item: in a glass case hung a cross-section of bristlecone pine. At its center a card said: 3000 B.C. BUILDING OF THE PYRAMIDS. A seedling today could be alive in the year 7000. That put a perspective on things.

Over another beer I watched faces that would be lucky to see A.D. 2000. When I left, a man in a white goatee whispered, "No games of chance, cowboy?"

"Haven't finished losing the first one," I said.

6

TRADITION persists in Nevada. You can see it, for example, in the whorehouses of Ely. Prostitution is legal in White Pine County because miners, in order to work efficiently in the ground digging for this and that, traditionally require whores.

The next morning, I overfilled my gas tank, splattering no-lead around, because I was eavesdropping on a conversation about the going price of a trick. A man with a white beard (there are more per-capita white beards in Nevada than any state other than Alaska) said to a tourist with a prissy little mustache *à la mode,* "I don't know all the prices, but I heard girls at the Big Four are getting twenty-five simoleons for a straight."

Another white-beard said, "Used to be ten."

"Hell, it used to be five. We got old just in time, didn't we, Boyd? Could you do a dollar's worth of damage now?"

"Couldn't do a lick of damage."

A young man replacing a wiper on the tourist's Camaro said, "A lick's all either of you could do. You coots keep your jeans zipped. Last night couple girls got to swinging knives because one had more hours on her check."

"Calling them 'hours' now, are they?" Boyd asked.

The tourist, trying to be one of the men, said, "Got a friend in Denver whose wife charges him five bucks a jump. She's buying furniture with it."

"Now that's *real* whoring," Boyd said. "These girls are just trying to make a living. Why don't your friend take on the neighbors over the back fence. She could buy a Florida vacation too."

When I went to the road again, clouds obscured the sun and a damp wind came out of the north. The mountainsides along highway 50 west of Ely were shot through with abandoned mining tunnels, the low entrances propped open by sagging timbers; they were the kind of old-time mines that Walter Brennan might come limping out of, chortling his crazy laugh. Magpies, looking like crows dressed for a costume party, swooped from fencepost to post and flicked wings in the mist. The highway was a long, silver streak of wet. Up into the Pancake Mountains, driving, driving, wishing the day would dry off — after all, this was the desert. But the sky remained dark as dusk.

I looked out the side window. For an instant, I thought the desert looked back. Against the glass a reflection of an opaque face. I couldn't take my attention from that presence that was mostly an absence. Whitman:

> *This the far-off depth and height reflecting my own face,*
> *This the thoughtful merge of myself, and the outlet again.*

Other than to amuse himself, why should a man pretend to know where he's going or to understand what he sees? Hoping to catch onto things, at least for a moment, I was only following down the highways a succession of images that flashed like blue sparks. Nothing more.

The experience of the desert anchorite Saint Anthony is typical of men who go off into deserts: hunger, solitude, and vastness engender not awareness or redemption so much as phantasmagoria. Under desert bushes Saint Anthony saw naked girls, behind stones dragons, and in shadows the deformed demons of Satan. My guess is that he was finding the consequence of his own imagination.

I had only a vacancy of face on the window, so maybe a simple slice of salami would dispel it. At Hickison Summit, a long rise formerly called "Ford's Defeat" because a Model T needed to be pulled up it by real horsepower, I stopped at a wayside set back in a box canyon of wet juniper and sage. The scent of plants saturated the mist. Alexander the Great, I've heard, was preserved in honey, Lord Nelson in brandy, and Jesus in aloe and myrrh. If I can choose, I'll take my eternity in essence of sage and juniper.

After a sandwich and some wine, I walked up the canyon. In the evergreens, a pipping of invisible birds and the slow drip of rain. The stones were wet through and through, but their blanched surfaces didn't glisten; even the desert rocks seemed designed to hold moisture.

Wind and water had cut the canyon wall into peculiarly sensuous shapes, and on rocks the elements had left blank, Indians of a thousand years ago carved sacred designs. The Bureau of Land Management had fenced off the petroglyphs, but stick figures, concentric circles, and rectangles stood out clearly from the damp stone. To the Indian, these cuttings were not pictures or objects so much as events: they carried life.

At the west end, where the fence came close to a ritualistic chiseling, I reached over and traced my finger along an incised abstraction now polished by years of hands. A cryptic engraving. Then I saw that the design wasn't at all abstract, but rather a graphic rendering of a female pudendum, a glyph even Cro-Magnons carved. In a time so long ago no descendant can remember any of it, an Indian had cut his desire, or coming of age, or hope for regeneration into the pink sandstone. It was as if I touched another dimension — a long skein of men, events, places. *It was as if I had reused the image.*

I walked back to the Ghost and drove to the highway. The sky began to open and the mist to dissipate. On the map I noticed a thermal spring to the south. I wandered around side roads before Spencer's Hot Springs appeared on a knoll under the snowy Toquima Mountains east of Austin.

When I saw the blue pools steaming, there was no question in my mind. With only five Nevadans to the square mile (in actuality many fewer when you discount Las Vegas and Reno), I figured I could get by undisturbed. Behind a cover of thistle and spiny hopsage, I stripped and dished up the hot water, let it cool slightly, then poured buckets of it over me. I even slapped on hot, gritty, blue-gray mud to loosen the sinews. Then I rinsed clean as men before must have done, dumping over me water warmed by the molten heart of the earth.

7

THEY hanged a horsethief three times one day in Austin, Nevada, because the hangman couldn't get the length of rope adjusted properly; but he was a conscientious public official and kept at it until he got it right. About the only thieving going on now was syphoning gasoline out of automobiles by people who came through at night and found the stations closed. After dark, the next gas was a couple of hours away.

Austin, in a canyon on the west slope of the Toiyabe Mountains, was a living ghost town: forty percent living, fifty percent ghost, ten percent not yet decided. It was the seat of Connecticut-sized Lander County mainly because only one other place, Battle Mountain, could you honestly call a town. But now Battle Mountain, with six times the population, thanks to the interstate and new power plant, wanted the government up there, where old mines were starting to produce again as the price of silver rose. Time was working against Austin. Once the county seat went, so would Austin, they said. A man commented: "We'll be all but finished down here. Twenty-five years ago a fella wrote a book about us called *The Town That Died Laughing*. Stick your head out the window and listen to all that laughing. You ask me, I don't believe one damned bit in change."

On three sides of town, prospect holes riddled the mountains and dripped out mine tailings like ulcerated wounds; to the west, several hundred feet down, lay a flat desert valley disappearing into the Shoshone Mountains on the horizon. Main Street, also U.S. 50, made a straight and steep run through Austin, then down the mountain and off across the desert. The side streets were hard-packed, oily sand, some with gradients that would test a donkey, and the rutted sidewalks, washing down the slope, still had their Old West canopies. Because Austin is without level land, many of the houses had been built into terraced cutouts so that from their porches people looked down onto the roofs of buildings along Main Street.

I liked Austin. The house chimneys slipped a wispy smoke from juniper hearth fires, and the cracked brick and stone of the storefronts, more or less, had been left alone. An 1890 photograph showed things little changed other than the defunct one-car railroad running up Main. Here, too, the Nevada story: 1862, a Pony Express rider looking for a lost horse finds a rock loaded with silver ore; 1865, six thousand people and as many mining and milling companies, hundreds of them fraudulent; 1878, the mines virtually played out; a century later, three hundred people — about the same number as in the old cemetery at the edge of the mountain, where the names were English, Polish, Italian.

In a small backroom with walls, ceiling, and floor going off at a variety of angles, not one of which was ninety degrees, I had a hamburger. After dinner I walked the town over, but the damp night got to me, and I went into Clara's Golden Club — one of six bars — to shake the chill. It was a fine, worn place with trophy heads (the dusty deer wore a tie); against the east wall stood a century-old backbar supported by four Corinthian columns of mahogany. The silver on the mirror had cracked apart, breaking the faces that watched from it, and sections of brass bar rail were scuffed through.

Clara, toes snugged under a drowsing sheep dog, wore a shapeless lavender sweater and a clerk's green visor to hold back her gray hair. She wrapped coins at the empty blackjack table. Behind her a sign:

NO ONE UNDER 21 NEAR TABLE
MIN $1.00 FINE   MAX $5.00

The way her shoulders bent over the clinking coins brought to mind Madame Defarge, knitting needles clicking ceaselessly, overseeing the fates of men.

I ordered a draft. Everyone at the bar — cattlemen, sheepmen, miners — wore the Nevada uniform: a down vest. Periodically, someone threw a coin on top of the ten-foot backbar. I asked a man, whose brow opened and closed like a concertina as he talked, what was going on.

"Crazy," he said. "They been doing that to bring luck for years. No telling how many silver dollars behind that mirror. Who knows what else? One time, a double-eagle was the smallest piece of change you got in Austin." He shifted around to talk. "Go out to the mountain edge and look at Stoke's Castle. Everything's falling down now, but you can get an idea of the money we used to have here. Took fifty million dollars in silver ore out of these mountains before they went empty."

A man named Vern said, "Mines gonna come back, Johnny. Soon as the price of silver gets high enough."

"Been slinging that for a hundred years," Johnny said. He put his arm on my shoulder. "Right here's the only mine worth talking about now — these Californians and New Yorkers. Mining and ranching together don't equal half what these boys bring in to the state. I read that in print."

A woman playing the slots stepped to the bar for a rum. Her T-shirt once carried a message, but soap and sun had bleached it to unreadability.

"You wouldn't play those if you were deaf," Johnny said.

"I'd play them if I was dead." She returned to her relentless pulling.

I asked what he meant. "People play slots because of sound. Gears turning, money jangling like in an old trolley. Same reason pinball machines got noises. Bandits wouldn't turn a dime if they didn't rattle and roll."

Johnny and Vern took the bar dice and rolled horses to see who would plug the jukebox. Johnny won. "Don't play the dirty one, or my wife'll get wind of it again." Vern made the selections and went to the toilet. The music came on. Country and western. *Thump, thump, thump.* "Dang him!" Johnny said. "He played that dang song. Now he'll tell the wife I paid for it." Johnny yelled toward the back, "Dang it, Vern!" A cackle from the jakes. Johnny didn't talk during the music. I think he was listening. As best I could make out, this was the dirty part: "I got the hoss, she's got the saddle" . . . *dum-dum-dum* . . . "together we gonna ride, ride, ride" . . . *dum-dum-dum* . . . all night long."

We ordered another round. Johnny said, "Bag of flour sold here once for a quarter million dollars. That's why the town seal's got a bag of flour on it."

"What?" He repeated it very slowly. In my mind I saw a furred, aquatic animal balancing a sack of daisies on its nose. "I don't follow you."

"In bonanza days, after the Civil War, a grocer made a bet with a fella on an election. Whoever lost had to carry a fifty-pound bag of wheat flour up Main Street. Now just walking that street taxes a man. Grocer lost. So he carried fifty pounds up Main to the tune of 'John Brown's Body.' He was a Southerner. After he got to the top, he auctioned the bag off and gave the money to charity. Man who bought it auctioned it off and gave the money to charity. And so on. Made ten thousand dollars that day off the same bag. Later, another town got wind of it, and they wanted in. Last time that flour got auctioned was at the nineteen oh four World's Fair in St. Louis. That dang bag raised better than a quarter million dollars, and that's why the official town seal is a bag of flour. It's over in Reno now."

"You mean with all the great natural wonders around Austin, the town symbol is a sack of stale flour?"

"Tell me, mister, what's more unusual: a pine tree or flour at five thousand dollars a pound?"

We bought each other a third round, and Johnny said, "Think a smart New Yorker like you can tell a religion by the way people pay for their church?"

"Don't know what you mean."

"Three new churches built in Austin after the Civil War when the town had money. Methodist, Episcopalian, Catholic. This is a true fact. One church pays for the building with one pass of the collection plate on Easter Sunday. One pays with donated mining stock, which it sells in the East. And one makes the first mortgage payment by charging admission. Who did what?"

"All right," I said, "the Catholics charged admission."

"Okay."

"Episcopalians had the stock."

"Wrong. I said the church *was given* the stock. Episcopalians had the cash. Methodists had the investments. Businessman's religion. You oughta know that."

Just before I left, the woman at the slots gave the quarter bandit a perfect pull, and the machine clattered coins into the metal cup and onto the floor. One made a long, circling roll across the room and passed by the nose of the sheep dog. The animal half raised its eyelids, saw the coin, and went back to its snooze.

8

NEW Pass Station, under cliffs of the Desatoya Mountains and half an hour west of Austin, used to be a stagecoach stop. The cold morning I pulled in to make breakfast, it was a tumble of stone walls and the willow-thatch roof had long since gone to compost. These stations were crude shelters even when the Overland ran the route; a traveler in 1861 described Cold Spring, the next stop west, as a "wretched place, half-built and wholly unroofed." He spent the night in a haystack. What I took for a ruin was, perhaps, a reconstruction.

I found my cooler empty except for some sardines and the can of chopped liver, so I went on along the stage road, also once the Pony Express trail and the route of the first transcontinental telegraph. Add to those the journeys of Indians and Forty-niners, and highway 50 is one archaeological layer of communication upon another.

Regardless of the utter fierceness of desert winters and summers, the Pony Express riders, they say, always rode in shirt-sleeves; considering the real hazards of the job, that may be true. The Central Overland California and Pike's Peak Express (the actual name of the Pony Express) used to run notices that are models for truth in advertising. An 1860 San Francisco newspaper printed this one:

> WANTED
> Young, skinny, wiry fellows not
> over eighteen. Must be expert
> riders willing to risk death
> daily. Orphans preferred.

Despite or because of such ads, never was there a shortage of riders.

The only baggage the boys carried — in addition to the mail mochila — was a kit of flour, cornmeal, and bacon, and a medical pack of turpentine, borax, and cream of tartar. Not much in either one to keep a rider alive. A letter cost $2.50 an ounce, and, if the weather and horses held out and the Indians held off, it might go the two thousand miles from Missouri to California in ten days, as did Lincoln's Inaugural Address. But the primary purpose of the service was neither the speedy delivery of news or correspondence; rather, the Express comprised part of the Northern defense strategy during the Civil War by providing a fast, central link with California that Southern raiders couldn't cut. For the seventeen months the Pony Express existed, it helped to hold California in the Union; what's more, this last of the old-world means of communication before mechanical contraptions took over left a deep mark on the American imagination. The riders, going far on little, became touchstones of courage and strength.

9

FRENCHMAN, Nevada, population four, sat on the edge of a U.S. Navy bombing range. As if that weren't enough, it was also on a fault zone that still wobbled the seismographic instruments around.

Frenchman appeared on my map as a town, and, in the desert, it probably was a town, consisting as it did of a cafe-bar-filling station, four-unit motel, trailer, and water tower all huddled on an expanse of dry lakebed mudflats cracked into a crazed jigsaw puzzle of alkali hardpan. In a state abounding with uninhabitable places, Frenchman excelled. Without vegetation, suffering from unrelenting wind and extremes of temperature, no source of food or supplies closer than thirty-six miles, no medical care other than Band-Aids and Mercurochrome, frequently rattled by bombs and earthquakes, Frenchman somehow survived on a single source of income: highway travelers.

A little east of town, a road sign warned of low-flying airplanes in Dixie Valley. Since Ghost Dancing was not equipped with antiaircraft guns, I took cover in the cafe, where red neon tubes spelled out ICE CREAM and a scrawled sign said NO GUNS IN BAR. Just what you'd expect of a bombing-range cafe.

The warm knotty-pine room smelled of hot coffee and a baking cake. I ordered a standard road breakfast, then noticed the peppermint-green Hamilton-Beach mixer — the old drugstore model — and added a chocolate milkshake. A young woman poured coffee although I hadn't asked for it. "Better unthaw. Cold air's numbed you out if you're ordering a milkshake. I mean, it's fifty degrees and breakfast time."

"Any time is chocolate milkshake time." She stared at me. "The best part is the beaters hitting the metal cup. That's what puts the flavor in."

She went to the kitchen, and I heard her say to someone, "I believe the desert's got to that boy."

Two men sat down. One asked for an egg and a slice of lemon pie, the other a vodka and rootbeer. She didn't bat an eye at that order. The lemon pie man was a geologist who carried a trail bike in his pickup to check claims in the *real* back country the truck couldn't reach. He talked about a mountain lion someone had shot in the Toiyabes; he couldn't remember when that last happened.

Vodka and rootbeer said, "Why don't somebody shoot one them damn mustangs?"

"Guy down in Tonopah got acquitted for stealing mustangs," the woman said.

"Of course. He probably saved the horses. Hell, they's a place in Idaho where the wild herd went from a hundred to five hundred in seven years."

"What's the problem with the horses?" I asked.

"The mustangs are sick and starving because they've overpopulated," the geologist said. "Desert can't support but a few things. Takes fifty acres just to feed a steer, and horses crop grass so short they kill it. Worse than sheep. People get emotional about mustangs because they think they're wildlife. Horse apples. Half are strays — got brands on them. It's not even like coyotes that've been here all along."

"Ever damn thing now is this invarnmint shit," vodka said. "Gotta call Washington so you can cut sage on your own land. Shoot a sick horse and them invarnmentists sign a petition. Shoot a man and they smile."

"Those Eastern laws are creeping in," the geologist said. "Nine-tenths of this state is in the public domain. Let's keep out of each other's way, okay, buckaroo?" I nodded. "Sure, we got to have laws and we do. And I'm not supporting the snake-oil boys in Carson City wanting to legalize Laetrile and Gerovital so they can turn Nevada into the monkey-gland capital of America."

The woman brought my breakfast and whipped up the milkshake. Vodka said, "What the hell's going on with that goddamn milkshake?"

"Him," she said. The geologist asked her what the new powerlines coming out of Fallon were all about. "Navy's converting to television and computers along the bombing runs. No more observers in the towers."

"I'd feel safer if the Navy was sitting out here with me instead of just a camera," the geologist said. "They still drag out old trucks for targets?"

"Sometimes. But planes are dropping more flares now instead of bombs. Saving money. When they make night runs, those flares light up the whole valley. Fantastic show. Just as well they can see us, I guess. Plane dropped a bomb on the highway last year, and nearly killed some clown in a car."

"Exploded on the road?"

"Just bounced up on the pavement and rolled dead, and he almost ran into it. Came in here afterwards, white as salt. He said, 'Miss, I haven't been drinking, but I just got bombed out there.' We called the Navy, and of course they claimed it was only a dummy bomb."

"Trying to get off the hook and ease your mind."

"*Ease* my mind! When a plane off course actually bombed Fairview a couple months ago?"

"I never heard anything in the news about the Navy bombing a town," I said.

"Fairview's a ghost town up on the ridge above the valley. Nothing but kangaroo rats. Navy sent out a crew and piled rocks back on the walls and shoveled dirt in the craters and picked up the shell fragments."

"Don't tell me this isn't a crazy state," the geologist said. "A Navy jet in the desert bombing a ghost town."

"The planes used to fly off carriers in the Pacific for runs in here. Can you believe flying off the ocean to bomb Nevada? Now most of them fly out of the base at Fallon. They've changed it all over to electronic warfare — 'EW,' they call it. Planes come in on a bombing run, flying real low. Almost reach up and poke them with a stick. They try to slip in under the radar, and that's what worries me. Two T–twenty-eight trainers already crashed this year. I don't mind the bombs, but I don't want a jet in the cafe."

"Is the shelf booze behind chickenwire because of bombs?" I said.

"Not bombs so much, although when they go off, everything jumps pretty good, especially me. One explosion opened that crack." She pointed to an inch-wide fissure in the wall. "An explosion on Bravo Seventeen — that's the closest run — that's what did that. But the chickenwire's for earthquakes. The big one in 'fifty-four broke every jug in the house."

A miner who had worked at Sheelite Mill a few years ago came in. "I'll have a Wild Turkey on the rocks," he said loudly.

"Not here you won't," the woman answered.

"Why not? Law won't let you serve miners?" He guffawed at his joke. The woman said either, "Don't have any Turkey," or "Don't have any, turkey." I couldn't tell which.

"Make it a Beam then." He pushed his hat back. "I see Sand Mountain's moved across the highway."

Vodka and rootbeer looked up. "The hell you say."

"The hell *you* say! Used to be on the south side."

The geologist, who had pointed out earlier it was a crazy state, turned to me. "Hear that? Couple boys arguing about a mountain crossing the highway."

The men went silent, sipped their liquor, each convinced the other was wrong. A trucker came in for coffee. "You've lost weight, Lex."

"I'm working double shifts to pay for my new rig. Don't know if it's worth it. Guess it is for the little wife. Been up thirty-two hours now on a run to the coast and back. Just want to get home today."

When he left, one of the men said, "Sure hope the little lady knows Poppa's on his way. She's quite the little at-home entertainer."

I wasn't ready for the road so I stayed on after the others left and talked to the woman, whose name was Laurie Chealander. She had attended the University of Nevada for two years while working the night shift for Nevada Bell as a long-distance operator in Reno, but the calls from drunks and would-be suicides depressed her. Looking for change, she had arrived in Frenchman four years earlier with her husband, whose parents had owned the town since 1970.

"When I got married, friends said I wouldn't last two weeks out here. They made bets on it. Now I love Frenchman, maybe because no one else does."

"Do you get bored? Or lonely?"

"Let me put it this way: we've never plugged the television in. I work an eighteen-hour day with my mother-in-law. There aren't many people around, but we see ninety percent of the ones here. Always something happening because this is the only place to eat, drink, and buy gas for a long ways east or west and even longer north or south. If it gets too dull, we climb the water tower and watch bombing runs. Night strafing with tracer bullets is better than the valley mirages."

"I wouldn't want to be in the air during strafing runs."

"Safer up there than in here when miners from the tungsten pit come around. Maybe that stuff does something to the brain. They're animals. Not gentlemanly like cowboys. When I was pregnant, one came at me with a pool cue."

"What happened?"

"We ran him out. We've got guns hidden. Got to. Nearest law is a half hour away in good weather. Time the sheriff gets here, show's over."

"Sounds like a good place for a holdup."

"All they'd get is a few bucks and a lot of lip. Then they've got to drive east or west. If they take a back road, you'd see the dust trail for fifteen miles. Can't get away out here. Desert's our defense. The only thing I worry about is the diesel generator going out. But I hope we can tie into that new powerline."

"And another town of the Old West bites the dust."

"Talk about biting the dust, look at this." She handed me a photograph of the place in 1906. In front of the building was a stone well; painted on it: IF YOU DONT WANT TO PAY FOR WATER LEAVE IT ALONE. Chealander said, "That's the second cafe. First one was built in the eighteen fifties. We burn down about every thirty years. Ours is the fifth. That's a hand-dug well in the picture. Now we have to drill three hundred feet to get good water."

"I saw where the Overland Stage and Pony Express ran this route."

"Everybody who's ever had the station does the same thing: sell food, something to drink, and a bed. They used to sell oats for horses. We sell regular and unleaded. Paiutes and Shoshones used to come in for a drink, and they still do, except Paiutes call themselves Shoshones now because the Shoshones have a good name and a reputation of good-looking women."

"How did the name 'Frenchman' come about?"

"It used to be 'Frenchman's Station' when it was a stage stop operated by somebody with a French name. I've heard they couldn't pronounce it, so they just called him 'the Frenchman.' "

Margaret Chealander came out of the kitchen. She had moved to the

13. Margaret and Laurie Chealander in Frenchman, Nevada

station from San Francisco with her husband after he retired from General Motors. She said, "We were living here when my husband died, but I've never wanted to move. Strange how this god-forsaken place gets in you. In the summer it's a hundred and ten; in winter it's fifteen below. Telephone lines get blown down regularly — or they did before the microwave relay came in. When the lines went down, we were cut off, and I mean *off*. But you get to know yourself out here — you have to. And you get to know the others around because we all have to look after each other. Out here, sooner or later, all of us need help. Look out for yourself, look out for each other. The law of the land." She came around the counter to sit down. "I think it's the distance between us that keeps us close. Everything here is important because there isn't much of it — except weather and dust. Once you see that, you're not lonely."

"Loneliness is blindness?"

"We've got bar tabs three years old," Laurie said. "They'll get paid someday. Can't afford to write anybody off. Last year a man — seventy-two and with an artificial leg — he came in a little oiled and then got tighter than Dick's hatband. When he tried to get to his car, I told him I was going to pull his leg off. He griped but spent the night in the motel."

The isolation — " I was starting to say.

"You like it or you don't," Laurie said. "Callie, our daughter, is a fourth-generation Nevadan. That's something in a state where most people are from somewhere else. I wanted to have the baby on the pool table, but nobody would listen. So we had to make a ninety-mile-an-hour drive to Reno at three in the morning. God, what a ride!"

"On the pool table?"

"I don't think anyone's ever been born in Frenchman in a hundred and thirty-five years."

"A pool table on a bombing range?"

"It would have been something for her to remember."

10

THE argument whether or not Sand Mountain had crossed the highway made more sense when I saw the thing — a single massive mound of tawny sand, a wavy hump between two larger ridges of sage and rock. It was of such size that, while it wasn't perhaps big enough to be a mountain by everybody's definition, it was surely more than a dune. Nevadans once called it "Singing Sand Mountain" because of the pleasant hum in the blowing sands, but no one has heard the mountain since off-road vehicles from California took it over.

I crossed Eight Mile Flat, a stretch of alkali crusts and shallow winter run-off where a machine scraped up salt crystals. It was near here in 1907, they tell, that a cafe owner, preparing broilers for supper, found two chicken craws laden with golden gravel; he at once butchered all his yard hens and found more nuggets. Because the flat contained no gold, he began looking for the source of the chickens and learned they had been raised on four separate farms before he bought them. Although the search lasted years, the Chicken Craw Goldrush died as it was born.

I stopped for a beer in Salt Wells at a place called Maxi's. If there was more to Salt Wells than that entirely Chinese-red building, I didn't see it. An ornamental wrought-iron fence covered the front; the gate was locked. Turning to leave, I noticed an arrow pointing to a button. Push me. I felt like Alice in Wonderland. I pushed, a dark face peered from a circle scraped on a window (painted red too), the gate clicked open, and I went inside where walls, ceiling, curtains, and lightbulbs were bright red. A sign:

DANCE WITH THE LADIES
50¢
THREE FOR A DOLLAR.

Below was a sticker, GO NAVY. A saloon as peculiar as the desert. That's when I realized it wasn't a desert saloon. It was a desert cathouse. Bold and plain, directly on U.S. 50, and flagrantly red from top to bottom.

Everyone — two Indians, two Negroes, a Chicano, and the bartender — all of them watched me. I ambled to the bar as if I'd known all along. Mirror decals showed the management accepted Visa, Mastercharge, American Express.

"Hey, Joe, what's your name?" she asked. I don't know where she came from.

"Al," I said.

"How about a party, Al?"

"What's *your* name?"

"Tiffany. How do you like it, Al?"

"It's a fine name."

"Not the name, Al baby — your party. How do you like your party? Hot?"

Tiffany, with all due respect, was one of the most facially unfavored women I'd ever seen. Her features would have been woeful on a man, but on a woman who earned her way by sexual attraction they were calamitous. She was a good dose of saltpeter. Yet nature, not withholding everything, had recompensed her with two impressive advertisements that she rested flat on the bar. "How about a dance with a lady? Three for a dollar."

"Dances or ladies?"

"Don't be cute, Allie. Just name your pleasures."

Allie it was now. "I only stopped in to use the phone. You know, engine trouble with my rig. Got to report in to the dispatcher."

She looked at me sympathetically. "Are you gay, honey? Tiffany's helped a hundred of your kind. Your problems show up like the honeymoon virgin."

I think that woman must have been a terrific salesperson. She had backed me into a dialectical corner with three or four sentences and left me only two escapes: admit to deviance or prove a capacity to perform at her standard. The bartender edged over, insinuating a little pressure. Tiffany turned on her stool and one of her portions on the bar followed. Another dancing lady came in. She was quite pretty.

"That's Faith," Tiffany said. "Men prefer her. Maybe you would too. I'm used to it. I mean, it's no surprise to Tiffany." Another tack coming. "I just hope if you have a little girl, she's beautiful, because you men make it so tough on anybody who doesn't look like Debby Boone."

"Debby — I mean Tiffany — I'll tell you the truth. I walked in here not realizing it was — it was a place."

"Sometimes us girls call it a whorehouse."

"Right. When I finish my beer I'll have to get back on the road."

"So you're in a whorehouse. Too good for woman's company, Mister Allen?"

The woman had the tactical mind of General Patton. She blocked me at every move. The bartender leaned in. "Good buddy, let Miss Tiffany help you. She's cured worse cases than yours. Why do you think she's called Tiffany? Pure class. Twenty-four carat."

"My case is okay. I just don't have the money."

"Look, Joe," Tiffany said. "You talk money? It's costing me to sit here trying to give a good time. You think I like crapping around with tweeties?"

I drank my beer and took my case down the road, through the irrigated plain at Fallon, into hills, along the Truckee River, under a shelf of glowing clouds above downtown Reno, past signs offering CANDLE LIGHT WEDDINGS — NO WAITING — FREE WITNESSES. I stopped near the University of Nevada and put my case to bed. The geologist was right. It was one crazy state.

11

THE next morning on the desert I was awakened by the squeal of seagulls. I looked out the window. I should have been used to the vagaries of the desert, but I wasn't. Sure enough, a pair of gulls overhead.

While the radio played, I washed up. The big news that Sunday in Reno was of a seventy-three-year-old Canadian who had been coming to the casinos three times a year for twenty years. She had met with no success until last night when she won $183,000.

At breakfast in the university cafeteria, I sat by a student who, even with the orthodontics, had a face of ill-matched features. I mentioned the woman's win. "Rigged," he scoffed. "It's too good: a grandmother returning faithfully to Mecca for years, then finally hitting the big score."

"Why rig a loss?"

"Cheapest and best advertising casinos can get. It'll go out on the wire services and be reported as news. It's believable, and it'll bring in new suckers and keep the fixtures hanging around. Makes casinos look good."

"The lady didn't really win?"

"She probably won and still doesn't know how she hit a jackpot. The house had her checked out — knew how long she'd been coming here. I'll bet she's got a face sweet as a sugar bun. Of all the greasy scumbags down there every night, did you ever see any of them big winners?"

I headed north out of Reno, crossed into California at an intersection once called Hallelujah Junction because it meant arrival in Eurekaland, then turned west on state 70. At Beckwourth Pass, only a mile high and the lowest route over the Sierra Nevadas, I hardly knew I'd crossed anything. But the mountains rose again on the other side, and the day became a dim, sodden thing, damp without rain. Dismal. The weather saturated me, and it may have provoked a dark fit of musing I fell into.

While I had failed to put any fragments of the journey into a whole, I did have a vague sense of mentally moving away from some things and toward others. But in the Sierra gloom, even that notion seemed an illusion produced by motion down a highway, as if the road moved through me in a continual coming and going that was, in the long run, stasis. I was on a Ferris wheel, moving along, seeing far horizons, coming close to earth, rising again, moving, moving, but all the time turning in the same orbit. Black Elk says, "Everything the Power of the World does is done in a circle." A hope.

Missourians sometimes speak of a place called Hacklebarney: a non-existent town you try to get to that is forever just around the next curve or just over the next hill, a town you believe in but never get to. Maybe that's enlightenment — always a little ahead of perception.

Hindus represent their god of destruction, Shiva, by the yoni-lingam symbols of regeneration to suggest the cyclical movement of coming into and going from being that never ceases. Even if a man resists belief in the fixity of things, even if he discredits the scope of human understanding, even if he sees a hint of metaphysics between "cosmic" and "comic" (Yiddish proverb: Man thinks and God laughs), he still longs to arrive at a place of clarity.

Just outside Portola, I crossed Humbug Creek. I didn't believe it. Nothing that apropos happens in real life. I stopped and walked back to the brook to see whether I saw what I thought I saw. Humbug Creek. I could almost hear the laughter from on high.

The road made a long turn and headed northwest up a deep river valley of conifers where slab-pine houses with tin roofs leaked a blue vapor of wood smoke from stovepipe chimneys into the mist. Apple trees were in blossom, but the leaves, still closed, waited for the right slant of vernal light. It came to me that I didn't recognize the coming of spring in this mountain country. At home I could name the season by its angle of light, its color and shadow and sound and scent. But in the valley of the Middle Fork of the Feather River, the light and sound and smells were different.

Quincy was a clean mountain town, empty and quiet but for a church bell. It was Sunday with a vengeance. Sunday in the churches, yes, but also Sunday in the streets, alleys, fields, even in the heart of the pines. Sunday is the day bells toll, the day funny papers come out — and with good reason. While the citizens sat under arched ceilings and spoke with their various gods and saviors, I scuffled with humbug in the Laundromat.

By noon, outfitted with a full set of washed clothes, I went again into the mountains. North of Keddie, the road passed a spring spilling from the side of a broken cliff. I emptied my jugs of city water and filled them with purity from the rocks and drank a pint to clear the pipes, then walked up into the trees to dispel the jounce of miles. The sun, breaking through now and then, cast long slopes of light down the mists, and for a time, the vapors of humbug evaporated.

Route 89 followed the Indian River, a frothing green turbulence, up into higher mountains. For miles, the only bridge across it was a rusty cable chair, the only things visible the river and big firs and pines of the Plumas Forest. When I got to state 36, I had a choice of heading toward the Sacramento Valley farmlands or staying in the mountains. I took the road across Lassen Peak, a sharp ascent that disappeared in clouds. Halfway up, snowflakes the size of nickels dropped out of the cold. Cedar Breaks. Then a sign saying the road was closed for winter. I inched the van back and forth until turned around, all the while cursing a sign not at the bottom of the mountain. Arriving again at the foot of Lassen, I started around it.

Rain fell as I moved toward the valley, but on a ridge road between deep volcanic canyons, the showers stopped and a rainbow arched the highway canyon to canyon. The slopes were strewn with shattered "thunder eggs" ejected from Lassen, a volcano last violently active only sixty years before. I took a road not marked on my map toward Manton. Nowhere was the way straight, but the land it traversed looked like an illustration from a child's book: a whimsy of rocky shapes, a fancy of spongy bushes, a figment of trees. Two loping deer could have been unicorns, and the fisherman under a bridge a troll. The only reality was that somebody owned the land. At three-hundred-yard intervals, alternating signs hung from barbed wire: NO TRESPASSING. PRIVATE PROPERTY.

Wonderland stopped at Manton. I should have asked the way to Viola, but I didn't; instead I went hunting it up a highway through woods and new vineyards. The hills, unlike the weird rockiness I'd come from, looked softly rounded like full bellies. When the road became a narrow dirt trail, I turned around in the first clearing and headed back to Manton.

Travelers are supposed to ask directions, but I believed, as usual, that I could find the way. Encouraged by a sign pointing to Viola, I tried another road. I had only to follow. Sunset vanished as the pavement again went into the woods; it narrowed progressively to a pair of wet troughs, and pine boughs screeched against Ghost Dancing. Having backed away from two roads already that day, I wasn't retreating again. Besides, I couldn't have turned a unicycle around in the thick forest. Muddy holes a small man on a small unicycle would have disappeared in rocked the truck violently, and nothing gave evidence I was getting anywhere but in deeper. If a tree lay across the trail, I'd be locked in this blackness — this home of Sasquatch — for the night. On and on the pitching and squeaking. Why did I get into things like this? I wasn't going to get to Viola — give up on that. Maybe I wasn't even going to escape the woods unless I walked out.

But things got no worse. In fact, after a while, the wallows became shallower, the branches stopped screeching, the road widened, then the headlights bounced off striped pavement. Rain again. Ten minutes later I reached what must have been Viola, a few darkened houses. (Note to mapmakers: without a gas station, cafe, water tower, and stoplight, you don't have a town.)

I drove on in anger, then in weariness, and my eyelids drooped. Nothing for miles of darkness until something loomed in front of the truck and gave a toothy grin just before I smunched it. Fearing what it might be, I stopped and ran back up the road. It lay shuddering, its legs trying to push it off the highway. I dreaded it. Whatever else it was, it was black, fat, and wet. I played the flashlight over the body. There: an improbable bag of prickles, a big porcupine, all thirty thousand quills of it, its sleepy feeble eyes glazed with shock. The legs stopped pushing and it died. I rolled it off the road as its belly sloshed, full of whatever watery greens it had just eaten.

What a day. Seagulls on the desert, rigged payoffs, mountains, Hallelujah Junction, Humbug Creek, a volcano, fairyland, vineyards, forest, mist, sun, rain, snow, a rainbow, doubt, hope — and now a goddamned dead porcupine. And here I was trying to make sense of things. I wiped the rain off my face and went on. Ten o'clock and I hadn't eaten since noon. I understood that no highway went for long without getting rough, but I couldn't break myself of the notion that whenever I hit good road it would hold to the end. I just couldn't remember cycles, the circles.

A wooden sign in the headlamps pointed to a small state campground. I pulled in under the ponderosas, the rain dubbing hard. I got out some bread and put it back. Too tired. The truck was as dark as the inside of a stone, and I was about to sleep under a volcano that had exploded within living memory, and I kept seeing the yellow grin of a porcupine whose luck it was to have a path coincident with mine and end the day as a ball of bloody meat.

12

Two Steller's jaybirds stirred an argy-bargy in the ponderosa. They shook their big beaks, squawked and hopped and swept down the sunlight toward Ghost Dancing and swooshed back into the pines. They didn't shut up until I left some orts from breakfast; then they dropped from the branches like ripe fruit, nabbed a gobful, and took off for the tops of the hundred-foot trees. The chipmunks got in on it too, letting loose a high peal of rodent chatter, picking up their share, spinning the bread like pinwheels, chewing fast.

It was May Day, and the warm air filled with the scent of pine and blooming manzanita. To the west I heard water over rock as Hat Creek came down from the snows of Lassen. I took towel and soap and walked through a field of volcanic ejections and broken chunks of lava to the stream bouncing off boulders and slicing over bedrock; below one cascade, a pool the color of glacier ice circled in effervescence. On the bank at an upright stone with a basin-shaped concavity filled with rainwater, I bent to drink, then washed my face. Why not bathe from head to toe? I wet down with rainwater and lathered up.

Now, I am not unacquainted with mountain streams; a plunge into Hat Creek would be an experiment in deep-cold thermodynamics. I knew that, so I jumped in with bravado. It didn't help. Light violently flashed in my head. The water was worse than I thought possible. I came out, eyes the size of biscuits, metabolism running amuck and setting fire to the icy flesh. I buffed dry.

Then I began to feel good, the way the old Navajos must have felt after a traditional sweat bath and roll in the snow. I dressed and sat down to watch Hat Creek. A pair of dippers flew in and began feeding. Robin-like birds with stub tails and large, astonished eyes, dippers feed in a way best described as insane. With two or three deep kneebends (hence their name) as if working up nerve, they hopped into the water and walked upstream, completely immersed, strolling and pecking along the bottom. Then they broke from the water, dark eyes gasping. I liked Hat Creek. It was reward enough for last night.

Back at Ghost Dancing, I saw a camper had pulled up. On the rear end, by the strapped-on aluminum chairs, was something like "The Wandering Watkins." Time to go. I kneeled to check a tire. A smally furry white thing darted from behind the wheel, and I flinched. Because of it, the journey would change.

"Harmless as a stuffed toy." The voice came from the other end of the leash the dog was on. "He's nearly blind and can't hear much better. Down just to the nose now." The man, with polished cowboy boots and a part measured out in the white hair, had a face so gullied even the Soil Conservation Commission couldn't have reclaimed it. But his eyes seemed lighted from within.

"Are you Mr. Watkins?" I said.

"What's left of him. The pup's what's left of Bill. He's a Pekingese. Chinese dog. In dog years, he's even older than I am, and I respect him for that. We're two old men. What's your name?"

"Same as the dog's."

"I wanted to give him a Chinese name, but old what's-her-face over there in the camper wouldn't have it. Claimed she couldn't pronounce Chinese names. I says, 'You can't say Lee?' She says, 'You going to name a dog Lee?' 'No,' I says, 'but what do you think about White Fong?' Now, she's not a reader unless it's a beauty parlor magazine with a Kennedy or Hepburn woman on the cover, so she never understood the name. You've read your Jack London, I hope. She says, 'When I was a girl we had a horse called William, but that name's too big for that itty-bitty dog. Just call him Bill.' That was that. She's a woman of German descent and a decided person. But when old Bill and I are out on our own, I call him White Fong."

Watkins had worked in a sawmill for thirty years, then retired to Redding; now he spent time in his camper, sometimes in the company of Mrs. Watkins.

"I'd stay on the road, but what's-her-face won't have it."

As we talked, Mrs. What's-her-face periodically thrust her head from the camper to call instructions to Watkins or White Fong. A finger-wagging woman, full of injunctions for man and beast. Whenever she called, I watched her, Watkins watched me, and the dog watched him. Each time he would say, "Well, boys, there you have it. Straight from the back of the horse."

"You mind if I swear?" I said I didn't. "The old biddy's in there with her Morning Special — sugar doughnut, boysenberry jam, and a shot of Canadian Club in her coffee. In this beauty she sits inside with her letters."

"Letters?"

"Her hobby's writing threatening letters to the phone company, the power and light. Whoever. After the kids left home, she took up hollering down rain barrels to occupy herself. You get like that if you don't watch it. Got to watch how you get. She was complaining today about me spending my sunshine years just driving around and doing nothing constructive. She doesn't know that's what old men are *supposed* to do: stand and look. I told her so. 'Besides,' I says, 'don't give me that sunshine shit' — excuse me — 'I'm old and it didn't come easy.' I says, 'You call me "old" if you go talking about me, damn you.' Excuse me. If you ever get the choice of traveling with a German woman or a dog, don't make a silly mistake."

We talked about Lassen, and I told him about my dive in Hat Creek.

"When I first started coming over this way years ago," he said, "you could drink out of it. Maybe you still can, but I'm afraid to try. Might kill me." He laughed and the gullies in his cheeks changed courses. "I came out of the First War without a scratch. Lost a couple pals to whizzbangs, but I made it out. Just sick one time over there. We were camped in east France and took our water from a stream — real pretty little thing. Then, one after another, we commenced getting sick — deep sick in the guts. Few days later somebody found a dead German upstream. Water had washed away most of his hair and skin. What skin was left was horrible white and peeling off like wallpaper. I haven't had a sip of stream water since."

Mrs. Watkins shouted from the camper, "Where's Bill?" Watkins rattled the leash and White Fong either barked or coughed. "All right," she said.

"What kind of work you in?" he asked.

That question again. "I'm out of work," I said to simplify.

"A man's never out of work if he's worth a damn. It's just sometimes he doesn't get paid. I've gone unpaid my share and I've pulled my share of pay. But that's got nothing to do with working. A man's work is doing what he's supposed to do, and that's why he needs a catastrophe now and again to show him a bad turn isn't the end, because a bad stroke never stops a good man's work. Let me show you my philosophy of life." From his pressed Levi's he took a billfold and handed me a limp business card. "Easy. It's very old."

The card advertised a cafe in Merced when telephone numbers were four digits. In quotation marks was a motto: "Good Home Cooked Meals."

" 'Good Home Cooked Meals' is your philosophy?"

"Turn it over, peckerwood."

Imprinted on the back in tiny, fading letters was this:

I've been bawled out, balled up, held up, held down, hung up, bulldozed, blackjacked, walked on, cheated, squeezed and mooched; stuck for war tax, excess profits tax, sales tax, dog tax, and syntax, Liberty Bonds, baby bonds, and the bonds of matrimony, Red Cross, Blue Cross, and the double cross; I've worked like hell, worked others like hell, have got drunk and got others drunk, lost all I had, and now because I won't spend or lend what little I earn, beg, borrow or steal, I've been cussed, discussed, boycotted, talked to, talked about, lied to, lied about, worked over, pushed under, robbed, and damned near ruined. The only reason I'm sticking around now is to see
WHAT THE HELL IS NEXT.

"I like it," I said.

"Any man's true work is to get his boots on each morning. Curiosity gets it done about as well as anything else."

He wanted to look my rig over, which he did critically. "Not much here," he said. "Now, my camper has most anything you'd want. Because of her. Even one of those Ping-Pong TV games. She says we have to have it to entertain the great-grandkids. I says to her, 'Why can't they look out the window?' "

I laughed.

"You think I'm joking. Those kids won't have anything unless wires come out of it. If I ran an extension cord down my pantleg and let them plug me in, then they'd believe they had real great-granddad."

Mrs. What's-her-face whistled the call of the bobwhite out the door. "Well, boys, there you have it. That means come drink your Sanka and take your pill. Sanka! If I don't watch it, it's all going to come down to that."

Six

WEST BY NORTHWEST

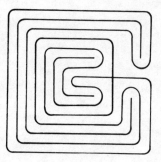

‎

LASSEN Peak is a kind of bookend to the bottom of the Cascade Range that runs single-file toward the Canadian border, where Mount Baker props up the other end. In between — preeminently — are Rainier, St. Helens, Adams, Hood, and Shasta. Their symmetric conical peaks average nearly twelve thousand feet and retain snowy summits all year; what's more, they are part of the most volcanically active range in the conterminous states.

Highway 89 wound among the volcanic dumpings from Lassen that blasted Hat Creek valley about three hundred times between 1914 and 1917. Scrub covered the ash, cinders, and lava as the wasteland renewed itself; yet even still it looked terribly crippled. Off the valley floor, California 299 climbed to ride the rim of the Pit River gorge. I ate a sandwich at the edge of a deep rift that opened like jaws to expose rocks so far below they were several hundred million years older than the ones I sat on. From the high edge I looked down on the glossy backs of swallows as they glided a thousand feet, closed their wings like folded fans, and plummeted into the abyss. It was a wild, mad, silent, spectacular descent of green iridescence that left me woozy.

Again on the road, I drove up a lumpy, dry plateau, all the while thinking of the errors that had led me to Hat Creek. The word *error* comes from a Middle English word, *erren*, which means "to wander about," as in the knight errant. The word evolved to mean "going astray" and that evolved to mean "mistake." As for *mistake*, it derives from Old Norse and once meant "to take wrongly." Yesterday, I had been mistaken and in error, taking one wrong road after another. As a result, I had come to a place of clear beauty and met a man who carried his philosophy on a cafe business card.

The annals of scientific discovery are full of errors that opened new worlds: Bell was working on an apparatus to aid the deaf when he invented the telephone; Edison was tinkering with the telephone when he invented the phonograph. If a man can keep alert and imaginative, an error is a possibility, a chance at something new; to him, wandering and wondering are part of the same process, and he is most mistaken, most in error, whenever he quits exploring.

The Boss of the Plains had said (after he mentioned his death wish) that his life had come to seem more and more of the same thing, and he called the story of his life *Ten Thousand Mistakes*. It stood to reason. To him a mistake was deviation from preconceived ideas, from standard answers, from wandering off the marked route. To him, change meant error.

Biochemists hold that evolution proceeds by random genetic changes — errors — and that each living thing is an experiment within the continuum of trial and error and temporary success. In nature, *correct* means harmony that breeds survival. Always to demand established routes, habitual ways, then, is to go against the grain of life; that is often the Indian impulse. But to engage in the continuing experiment is to reach for harmony. Hesse writes:

> I am an experiment on the part of nature, a gamble within the unknown, perhaps for a new purpose, perhaps for nothing, and my only task is to allow this game on the part of the primeval depths to take its course, to feel its will within me and make it wholly mine.

Whitman said it too: "A man is a summons and a challenge."

I had driven through Fall River Mills and McArthur, and I couldn't remember a thing about them. If I were going off on some blue highway of the mind, I should have pulled over. North of Bieber, on a whim, I followed the road to Lookout. In the high valley lay marshes filled with yellow-headed blackbirds, pintails, cinnamon teals, willets, Canada geese. The highway rose again into another volcanic region. Mount Shasta, sixty miles west, isolated by its hugeness, haloed in clouds, looked like a Hokusai woodcut of Mount Fuji. Perhaps it is the immensity of space around Shasta or the abundance of high peaks in the West that diminishes a mountain of such size and perfection in the American imagination, but in almost any other country, a volcano so big and well-made as Shasta would be a national object of reverence — as in fact it once was to the first men who lived under it.

I never found Lookout. In dry and dusty Tulelake, I bought groceries, then crossed into Oregon, where the Cascades to the west blocked a froth of storm clouds; but for the mountains, I would have been in rain again. A town of only fifteen thousand somehow spread across the entire bottom of a long valley; when I saw the reach of Klamath Falls, I kept going. U.S. 97 was an ordeal of cars and heavy trucks. I don't know whether Oregonians generally honk horns or whether they had it in for me, but surely they honked. Later, someone said it was part of the "Keep Moving, Stranger" campaign. I turned off into the valley at the first opportunity, an opportunity numbered route 62 that ran to Fort Klamath, a town that began in 1863 as an Army post with the mission of controlling hostile Klamath Indians, who had succeeded for years in keeping settlers out of their rich valley. Keep moving, stranger.

Drawn as always to the glow of neon in the dusk, I stopped at a wooden cafe. No calendars, otherwise perfect. In front sat an Argosy landcruiser (the kind you see in motel parking lots) with an Airstream trailer attached; on top of the Argosy was a motorboat and on the front and back matched mopeds. Often I'd seen the American propensity to take to the highway with as many possessions as a vehicle could carry — that inclination to get away from it all while hauling it all along — but I stood amazed at this achievement of transport called a vacation. Although the Argosy side windows were one-way glass (to look and not get looked at back), in the trailer I saw pine paneling, Swiss cupboards, and a self-cleaning oven. What the owner really wanted was to drive his 3-BR-splitfoyer so he wouldn't have to leave the garage and basement behind.

A man with a napkin tucked to his belt came out of the cafe. A plump woman, lately beyond the Midol years, face fearful like the lady who has just discovered the heartbreak of psoriasis, watched from the cafe.

"What's up, chum?" the man said.

"I couldn't believe this outfit. You are one well-prepared family. This little highway's not really big enough for you, is it?"

He relaxed at what he took as sympathy. "Tried a damned back road."

We went inside, and I heard the woman whisper, "His type make me nervous." She'd read about people like me and stared in a bold, contemptuous way she never would have used had she been alone. I tried to check my own irritation. She probably wasn't a bad sort; she had her good side. Surely she had studied the Gospel According to Heloise and knew by rote the six helpful hints for removing catsup stains.

The food was ordinary, prices high, the waitress unpleasant, and, on top of that, I got reviled by people who could afford life at six-miles-per-gallon. I paid and left. The couple came out, hoisted themselves into the Argosy, and clicked locks against my type. Just above the legal maximum, off they went, those people who took no chances on anything — including their ideas — getting away from them. After all, they read the papers, they watched TV, and they knew America was a dangerous place.

MOUNT Mazama may be the greatest nonexistent fourteen-thousand-foot volcano in the country. Actually, it isn't entirely nonexistent: only the top half is. From the upper end of the Klamath basin, you can still see a massive, symmetrically sloping uplift of the mountain base. Some six thousand years ago, geologists conjecture, the top of Mazama blew off in a series of ruinous eruptions and the sides collapsed into the interior.

Hoping for a place to pass the night, I took a highway up the slope. After a few miles, the road became a groove cut between ten-foot snow-banks, but stars shone, so I drove on to the top. I got out and looked around. A brilliant night. Trusting more than seeing, I walked through a tunnel in a snowdrift to the craterous rim of Mazama. There, far below in the moonlight and edged with ice, lay a two-thousand-foot-deep lake. Klamath braves used to test their courage by climbing down the treacherous scree inside the caldera; if they survived, they bathed in the cold water of the volcano and renewed themselves. Also to this nearly perfect circle of water came medicine men looking for secrets of the Grandfathers. Once a holy place, now Crater Lake is only a famous Oregon tourist attraction.

The next morning, the fog rising from the surface of the lake (the deepest and bluest in America) gave it the look of a hot washtub of Mrs. Stewart's Bluing. The lodge still lay piled under some of the six hundred inches of annual snowfall here, and the road down the other side of Mazama was not yet cleared, so I went back the way I'd come. Again. Oregon 230 followed a broad mountain stream called Muir Creek. When the morning warmed, I stopped along the banks to fill a basin and wash; after Hat Creek, the water was merely bracing.

Big, yellow-hooded blossoms of the Western skunk cabbage spread over the margins. Although the plant bears some resemblance in shape to the purplish skunk cabbage of the East, it is a relative of the jack-in-the-pulpit, and its flowers are virtually odorless. Looking nothing like cabbage, the leaves were used by Indians to wrap food for cooking; they pulverized the hot, peppery roots into a flour that helped save them (and the Lewis and Clark expedition) from starvation in early spring before other edible plants sprouted. Even today elk and bear, grubbing for the roots, will dig up whole patches of swamp.

I crossed the Cascades on Oregon 58. While the mountains were not particularly high, the road made steep climbs and drops over timbered slopes, and runaway-truck escape ramps looked like ski jumps. On the western side, humidity increased and ferns grew thick as jungle vines. For a time, desert lay behind.

At noon, the journey began a kind of sea change that started when I drove up an old logging road into the recesses of Salt Creek, a stream working hard to beat itself to a lather. In Missouri, when a man's where-abouts come into question, the people say he's "gone up Salt Creek." It's a place in which you disappear. Maybe I should have taken warning.

After a sandwich, I poked about the woods and turned up a piece of crawling yellow jelly nearly the length of my hand. It was a banana slug, so named because the mollusk looks like a wet, squirming banana. I wanted to photograph it, but a drizzle came on, so I bedded it down in damp leaf litter in a pail. I could drive out of the rain to take its picture.

Then, three things, quite unconnected, began to stack themselves like crystals into a pattern.

FIRST: Waiting on the rain, I studied the map. Where to go? South lay two towns of fine name — Lookingglass and Riddle — but I would have to backtrack sixty wet miles, and already the desert showers had left me prey to the "Oregon blues," that dissipation of spirit that accompanies the rainy periods when suicides noticeably increase. But Lookingglass! What a name!

SECOND: The town recalled to me a line from Walter de la Mare: "Things are the mind's mute lookingglass."

THIRD: Still waiting on the weather, I started reading a book I'd bought in Phoenix, *The Sacred Pipe*, Black Elk's account of the ancient rites of the Oglala Sioux. In contrast to the good and straight red road of life, Black Elk says, the blue road is the route of "one who is distracted, who is ruled by his senses, and who lives for himself rather than for his people." I was stunned. Was it racial memory that had urged me to drive seven thousand miles of blue highway, a term I thought I had coined?

That's when something opened like a windowshade unexpectedly rat-tling up in a dark room. A sudden, new cast of light. What need for a man to make a trip to Lookingglass, Oregon, when he'd been seeing his own image across the length of the country? De la Mare was right: a mirror may not reflect mind, but a man's response to landscapes, faces, events does. My skewed vision was that of a man looking at himself by looking at what he looks at. A man watching himself: *that* was the simulacrum on the window in the Nevada desert.

Hadn't I even made a traveling companion of the great poet of ego, the one who sings of himself, who promises to "effuse egotism and show it underlying all," who finds the earth his own likeness? Whitman:

To me the converging objects of the universe perpetually flow,
All are written to me, and I must get what the writing means.

Money half gone, I'd come up with a bit of epistemological small change.

Not knowing what else to do, I drove off westward. The highway rolled out of the mountains into the basin of the Willamette River, a broad trough with at least as many shades of green as the Irishman can count in Eire. The level and verdant valley should have soothed after so much aridness and stone, so much up and down, but I sat absorbed in my own blue funk.

Old Oregon 99 led into the clean college town of Corvallis. I had no heart for more road. At a grocery I bought six bottles of Blitz beer and six of Buffalo and a hunk of smoked salmon and drove to the campus of Oregon State University and pulled up under a flowering cherry tree of large girth. I walked in the rain, came back in the dark, sat in the truck, and drank a Blitz, then a Buffalo, ate some salmon, and drank another, and one more. I just stared into the morose rain and watched petals slip wetly down the windows.

That's when I remembered the slug. Too late for pictures now. I turned on the light to release the damn thing. It wasn't in the pail, and it wasn't in the box the pail was in; it wasn't anywhere I could discover. Impossible. With the van tightly sealed, the slug couldn't have gotten out, but the rain prevented me from emptying the truck.

Listing a little from the beer, I crawled around hunting one of the most primitive and unsightly creatures on earth. Nothing. I looked for the tell-tale glossy trail. No trail. Whether or not slugs have ears, I didn't know, but I called to it anyway. Finally, unsteadily, I undressed and went to bed.

Somewhere in Ghost Dancing was a slug — horned, fat, gelatinous with primeval slime, and free to ooze its footless way anywhere while I slept: up walls, onto bunks, over eyelids, across lips. Of all nights for this to happen.

The biggest hindrance to learning is fear of showing one's self a fool. But this was ridiculous. Never had I figured on this kind of humiliation.

3

For two days, two days of drizzle, I waited for the slug to make its move. In western Oregon it can rain a hundred and thirty inches a year, making weather so dismal that even a seadog like Sir Francis Drake complained about it four centuries ago when he sailed here on the *Golden Hind* in search of the Northwest Passage. Those two days I wandered around Corvallis more dispirited than edified by the blue-road perception. I walked and walked. "Nothing," Homer sings, "is harder on mortal man than wandering." That's why the words *travel* and *travail* have a common origin.

During those days, I was drawn to telephones, and on four occasions I dropped in coins and four times I put the receiver back. On the fifth I didn't.

"Hello?" the Cherokee said.

"It's me."

A quiet. "Could I call you back?"

Well, boys, there you have it. Struggling to put it all out of mind, I went to the university library to find how Lookingglass, the town I hadn't seen, got its name. One theory held that Lookingglass was a local Indian who so admired himself he always carried a small mirror. Well, boys . . .

Another etymology: *Corvallis*, a Latin combination meaning "in the heart of the valley." For me, it was more a valley of the heart. No wonder Pascal believed man's inability to stay quietly in his room is the cause of his unhappiness.

In darkness and rain I left the library. I began fighting the fear that I was about to lose heart utterly and head back. Oh, god, I could feel it coming. The old Navajos, praying for renewal of mental strength, chant, "In the ways of the past, may I walk," but my chant went the other way around.

Oregonians, also known as "Webfeet," learn to live with rain as Texans do wind. In front of me, a man walked a small white dog. White Fong. I remembered the old Californian and his business card. Up went a windowshade. What I needed was to continue, to have another go at reading the hieroglyphics, to examine (as Whitman says) the "objects that call from diffusion my meanings and give them shape."

I had been a man who walks into a strange dark room, turns on the light, sees himself in an unexpected mirror, and jumps back. Now it was time to get on, time to see WHAT THE HELL IS NEXT.

4

THE wind came in over the Coastal Range in the night and blew the sky so clean it looked distilled. As the sun cast long morning shadows, I went west into the mountains toward Philomath and Burnt Woods. Either the return of sun or a piece of cornpone etiology from a California cafe gave the feeling I'd begun the journey again. As for the slug, I hadn't found it.

U.S. 20: a scribble of a road, a line drawn by a palsied engineer. The route was small farms — one with a covered bridge — and small pastures and mountainsides of maple and fir and alder and wet green moss. Oblique sunlight turned blossoms of Scotch broom into yellow incandescence that illumined the highway; settlers brought the plant from Scotland to use in broommaking, but it had escaped cultivation and is now a nuisance to coastal farmers as well as a fine ornament of spring.

The road squeezed through a narrow pass, then dropped to Yaquina Bay with its long arches of bridging. In the distance, the blue Pacific shot silver all the way to the horizon. I had come to the other end of the continent.

Newport has been a tourist town for more than a century and it showed: a four-lane runway of beef-and-bun joints and seashell shops; city blocks where beach bungalows jammed in salty shingle to shiplap. On north to Agate Beach. Shoreline I had camped on fifteen years before was now glassy condominiums and the path to the ocean posted. Again northward to a pocket of shore between developments near Cape Foulweather. The surf rolled out an unbroken uproar like a waterfall rather than the intermittent crash I'd listened to in North Carolina. In the lee of a big tussock of beach grass I ate lunch, as gulls, slipping over the drafts and yawing and tilting in the stiff sea wind, watched me watch them. It's a curious sensation when nature looks back.

I stayed so long that dark clouds moved in and piled against the mountains like flotsam washed ashore. Then it began to hail. Cape Foulweather, named by Captain James Cook exactly two hundred years earlier, showed itself true, and I cursed and ran for the truck. By the time I reached Depoe Bay, a few miles up the coast, the western sky had cleared again, and the afternoon sun seemed to glare off the ocean all the way from the Orient. Cycles. The cold waves, coming unimpeded from Japan six thousand miles away, struck the rocks hard, and the high surf so struggled, it looked as if the sea were trying either to get out or pull the shore back in.

A high, concrete-arch bridge crossed a narrow zigzag cleft of an inlet leading to a small harbor under the cliffs. Depoe Bay used to be a picturesque fishing village; now it was just picturesque. The fish houses, but for one seasonal company, were gone, the fleet gone, and in their stead had come sport fishing boats and souvenir ashtray and T-shirt shops. In Depoe Bay the big fish now was the tourist, and, like grunion, its run was a seasonal swarming.

Several streets scotched the town but you could forget them all except the big one: U.S. 101. What happened economically happened on 101 or the water. Two restaurants faced the highway: one called the Happy Harpooner or some silliness; the other had no sign visible. A beanery needing no name had to be good. As if suspended above the harbor, it sat on a cliff with all comings and goings of men and boats and tide and wind in complete view.

I took a plate of fresh bottomfish, chowder, and slaw. At the next table four charterboat seamen, watch caps pulled tightly to their skulls, bent into the vapor of coffee mugs and talked about snapped shafts, leaking holding tanks, environmental regulations, creosoted timbers. Down in the harbor, cabin lights blinked on and bobbed in the dusk. I asked a seaman who sat alone if I could park overnight on the waterfront. "Coast Guard station down there surveys things close," he said. "Why don't you take a state campground?"

"I'd rather see Oregon than trailers from Ohio."

The man operated a charterboat company that catered to tourists. He said this: "Depoe Bay used to be a good commercial fishing town, but they overfished this corner of the Pacific. Then they polluted the spawning streams. Maybe the big schools will come back, maybe not. I don't care. My sport boats are easier and income's more predictable — can't always land greenling, but you can always hook a Californian. But there was a time when all those wood buildings on the bay processed our catch, back when the commission gave out commercial fishing licenses to anybody. Then we started getting irresponsible jackbats ruining the grounds. Next year, to get a license, you'll have to earn sixty percent of your income from fishing. Going to keep out the exploiters."

"Changes everywhere."

"This coast is a story of one thing after another disappearing. Except people. We don't have sea otters much now, but you used to see them floating on their backs with a flat rock on their stomachs, cracking open shellfish on it. Razor clams hard as hell to find now. Beach used to have agates, petrified wood, Japanese net floats — those colored glass balls, you know. Pieces of broken-up schooners too. Coast was full of skookums. That's what the Chinooks called ghosts. Know what you'll find beach-combing now? Clorox-jugs. The highway department even dug into old Indian shell piles to get material to build beach roads. Now people are fighting over somebody trespassing on the beach. Christ-to-mighty, Supreme Court even got into it."

"What happened?"

"Don't know all of it, but the Court declared the whole Oregon coast open to the public. Amazed me. Who'd want to go down there now anyway?"

"People who don't remember the way it was."

"I'll tell you about the people. 'The people is a beast.' Alexander Hamilton said that. Too many people catching fish, digging clams, buying up the coast. Too much crud in the streams. More and more people, less and less of everything else except regulations."

"Can regulations bring fish or clams back?"

"What's left to try?"

I went down to the harbor, slipped past the Coast Guard station, and pulled up at the wharf. I counted on my delivery-wagon appearance not arousing attention. Cold wind stirred the surf, but the little harbor lay quiet. I heard laughter and a card game on a boat, and from out in the Pacific came the deep-throated dolor of sonobuoys groaning in their chains (seamen say) the agony of drowned sailors.

5

In 1788, the *Lady Washington*, the first American ship to visit the Northwest coast, anchored inside Tillamook Bay so that a party could go ashore to gather fresh fruit for a crew suffering from scurvy. During the mission a Negro sailor attempted to recover a cutlass stolen by Indians. The mate, Robert Haswell, recorded the incident:

> [There] was a very large group of the natives among the midst of which was the poor black with the thief by the collar loudly calling for assistance, saying he had caught the thief; when we were observed by the main body of the natives to hastily approach them, they instantly drenched their knives and spears with savage fury in the body of the unfortunate youth. He quieted his hold and stumbled but rose again and staggered towards us but having a flight of arrows thrown into his back and he fell within fifteen yards of me and instantly expired while they mangled his lifeless corpse.

Nearly two centuries later, Fort Stevens to the north of Tillamook Bay earned the distinction of being the last place in the forty-eight states attacked by a foreign power when the Japanese shelled it in June of 1942. The four-hundred-mile Oregon littoral, as much as anywhere in the country, has been an area of confrontation and conflict.

In the morning I took U.S. 101 up the blue coast of high headlands and broken sea stacks that demark the old shoreline. The route was a far stretch of history and beauty ("romantic," Meriwether Lewis called it in 1805) if you ignored clapboard-by-the-sea motels, Jolly Whaler buffets, and clear-cut mountain slopes with tall stumps bleached into tombstones by the salt wind. Years ago, loggers tried to reduce the heavy flow of pitch by cutting trees higher than usual. Yet it was this abundant pitch in coastal firs that made clearing the land easy for settlers: a farmer would bore two holes in the trunk, one horizontal and a second slanting into the other to provide a draft; he fired the pitch in the first hole, and a two-hundred-foot fir became a living wick.

Only after the Federal Highway Act of 1921 coordinated, standardized, and encouraged road construction did 101 appear on the coast; but for thousands of years, the level beaches, and the hazardous tidal waters too, were routes for Clatsops and Tillamooks, Coos and Siuslaw, and later for Spaniards coming in search of the mythical Straits of Anian that would give passage east.

The long view south down the coast from the steep headlands near Neahkahnie Mountain seemed to reach the length of Oregon. Northward stood Haystack Rock, a three-hundred-foot domed skerry topped by a mantle of snowy bird stain, looking like a chipped whale's tooth. And, in fact, it was near the great monolith that a whale swam ashore in 1806; Lewis and Clark, camped to the north, got word of the sea beast. Saca-gawea, the Shoshone guide for the Corps of Discovery — as Jefferson called the expedition — who had never asked the captains anything for herself, insisted on making the hard trek to see the whale. She and the explorers sampled the blubber and found it, in Lewis's words, "white and not unlike the fat of pork, though the texture was more spongy and somewhat coarser." Clark thanked Providence that he got to swallow a piece of leviathan rather than having it Jonah's way. Years later, the story goes, after Sacagewea returned to the Shoshones, of all things she saw in her twenty-three months with the corps, the Bird Woman never tired of telling about the great beached "fish" that gave milk.

North of Haystack, at the old resort town of Seaside, was the site of a firepit where the expedition, in preparation for the long return east, boiled down seawater to make salt, a commodity they ran out of coming west. Lewis writes:

My friend Captain Clark declares [salt] to be a mere matter of indifference with him whether he uses it or not; for myself, I confess I felt a considerable inconvenience for the want of it; the want of bread I consider trivial, provided

I get fat meat; for as to the species of meat I am not very particular, the flesh of dog, the horse, and the wolf having from habit become equally familiar [as] with any other, and I have learned to think that if the cord be sufficiently strong, which binds the soul and body together, it does not so much matter about the materials which compose it.

Although Clark believed the party healthiest on a subsistence of dog flesh, the favorite meat of the explorers, when they could get it, was beaver tail.

Inland some distance from Seaside, near the base of the northwestern prong of Oregon that sticks into the Columbia estuary, Lewis and Clark made winter camp, their last outpost before returning home. Here at Fort Clatsop they celebrated the first American Christmas in the Northwest. The men who smoked received a gift of tobacco, the others handkerchiefs; Sacagawea gave Clark two dozen weasel tails, and Lewis gave him a pair of socks. Their dinner on that "showery, wet, and disagreeable" Christmas, Clark said, was "poor elk so much spoiled that we ate it through mere necessity, some spoiled pounded fish, and a few roots." All without salt. Despite the pester of fleas and mosquitoes, the group was "cheerful all the morning."

The great sea reach of the Columbia ranges in width from about three miles to ten miles and was bridged just recently at Astoria. When it comes to fall and force, no other American river can match this one; near its mouth, sudden whirlings of water will suck logs under only to spit them forty feet into the air. The Columbia, once called the Oregon, gets its name from the ship of Captain Robert Gray, the first American to sail over the dangerous bar at the mouth. The Bostonian thought the new name would help claim the territory for the United States then contending Britain for it. Gray's primary mission, however, wasn't to stake claims; rather it was to buy valuable sea otter skins (an iron spike for a beaver pelt, but a sheet of copper for an otter skin) to use in the lucrative China trade. In that way, the Chinese helped Americans claim Oregon territory — the only parcel of the United States never under European dominion. The Northwest came directly from the Indians.

Astoria, the oldest city on the river and now an industrial center, began as a trading post established by John Jacob Astor's fur traders. Soon after the founding, Indians gathered to annihilate the white men; one of Astor's partners, a devious man named Duncan McDougal, thought to save the company by threatening to uncork a black vial that he said held smallpox; the tribes quickly agreed to peace and Astoria survived. It was smallpox, of course, that did more than repeating rifles to subdue the American

Indian. But McDougal's ruse came back to haunt later settlers. The story of the vial spread among the natives, and years later when smallpox did break out (partly from infected blankets deliberately given tribes), Indians began massacring pioneers in an effort to eradicate little black bottles.

McDougal sought to solidify the company's position — and his own — by marrying an esteemed daughter of the Chinook chief. On the wedding day, the princess arrived made up in red clay and anointed with sacred fish oil. The horrified whites, ignoring the affronted Indians, scrubbed her down. Washington Irving describes it in his book *Astoria*:

> By dint of copious ablutions, she was freed from all adventitious tint and fragrance, and entered into the nuptial state, the cleanest princess that had ever been known, of the somewhat unctuous tribe of the Chinooks.

U.S. 30 bent where the Columbia bent, but for much of the way, hills blocked any view of the water. On occasion I could see sandbars, where in times gone, old horses from the Portland streetcars and fire wagons walked belly deep, pulling thousand-foot seines filled with the silver violence of salmon. Now horse seining is illegal.

St. Helens, Oregon, high above the river, was remarkable that day for splendidly clear views of the white summits of four great volcanoes: Rainier, St. Helens, and Adams northward across the river in Washington, and Mount Hood southeast in Oregon. Each has its distinction: Hood is the most notable American mountain named after an enemy military leader (Admiral Samuel Hood, second in command of the British fleet during the Revolutionary War); Mount Rainier, even after blasting away two thousand feet of summit, is still the highest volcano in the country; Mount St. Helens (Lord St. Helens was an English ambassador to Spain), youngest of the peaks, was quiet again but perking; Klickitat Indians have a better name for St. Helens: Tawonlatkla, "Fire Mountain." And there's Mount Adams; poor Adams, second in height only to Rainier. Easily as imposing as the others the way it rises so separately from the land, it remains the greatest unknown American mountain. The anonymity, if you ask me, results from the name (after the second President). They might as well have called it Mount Jones or Schwartz Peak.

To citizens of St. Helens, the names were insignificant anyway. I asked three people to confirm which mountain was which; while all agreed on the location of Hood, they argued over the peaks in Washington. To live so uninformed before such grandeur is the hallmark of a true native son.

BUT for the flip of a coin, Portland, Oregon, would be Boston, Oregon. Asa Lovejoy of Massachusetts and Francis Pettygrove of Maine, owners of land along the Willamette River, each wanted the name of their new town to honor the leading city of their home states, so they tossed a coin. A man told me: "Two Portlands cause confusion, yes, but nobody here complains. We could have ended up living in Lovejoy, Oregon."

The river road came off the hills into the industrial bottoms of Portland and left no way but through the city; once committed to it, I went looking for oysters downtown in the area where drinking (Erickson's Saloon formerly had a bar running nearly eight hundred feet), whoring, and shanghaiing sailors were the main after-dark endeavors a century ago. It was here that five-foot-tall Bunco Kelly kidnapped, by his own count, a thousand lubbers through his standard method of knockout drops, although his easiest haul was eight tramps he found drinking formaldehyde in an undertaker's basement; Kelly gathered them up and got them aboard ship by passing the dying men off as intoxicated.

In Kelly's time, the wharf area of Portland was known as Skidroad, a logger's term for a timber track to drag logs over. Forgetting the history and thinking the word referred to rundown buildings and men on the skids, people began calling the squalid section "skid row."

Portland, working now to eradicate the skid-row image, calls the area "Old Town," even though many businesses are new. But Louie's Oyster Bar was one of those rare things in America: a restaurant serving the same menu in the same building on the same location for more than a generation. If you wanted a private table, you waited in line on Ankeny Street; or, if you would take one of the long, ship's mess tables, you could be seated immediately. The communal tables were, of course, more fun, more companionable, but not many customers wanted community with strangers.

The menu, shaped like an oyster, said "Eat 'em Alive," but I took my Yaquina Bay oysters panfried on the recommendation of a student from Lewis and Clark College who sat across from me. His face, smooth as a new glove, sported a beard of eleven perfectly groomed whiskers. On weekends and days he had no classes, he picked up spending money by returning rental cars to Boise, Idaho, a nine-hour drive one way. "That cuts into the education a little," I said.

"Got to have the money. Car payments, clothes, my girl. You know. I need fifty bucks a week above Pop's money just to hold steady."

"That's the most depressing thing I've heard on this trip. How old are you?"

"Twenty. What trip?"

His eyes burned with wanderlust and the fever of adventure as I recounted the journey with the narrative flourish of the Ancient Mariner. Undermining routine and consumerism at the source. He listened intently. I had him.

"God, I wish Pop was here," he said. "I wish he could hear this."

"Don't be afraid of Pop's disapproval."

"Disapproval? You're doing what he'd give a nut to do. He goes on all the time about selling the house and quitting his job and traveling around the country. Or going back to school. He's seriously proposed I take over the house and run it for two years while he and my mother go off to school. No lie! His theory is I need to learn what he knows and he needs to learn what he says I'm throwing away. He claims if I had his life for a year I'd know what the ballgame's about. I'd do it, but my mother won't approve because she knows I'd move my girl in."

"You'd trade lives with a middle-aged couple? Your parents of all people?"

"With their buying power, sure. The economy's about to hit bottom."

"Don't you know kids are supposed to rebel against their parents' values?"

"I am. They hate their life."

"You don't want to take off for England or Japan? How about a little warm-up trip to Yonkers?"

"Maybe — if I had enough money, but I'd lose my girl if I did."

"Oh, my god."

"What's wrong? The oysters?"

7

After breakfast at Lewis and Clark College, I felt like Paleolithic man. It wasn't anything I ate — it was what I heard from students. The only sensible thing for me, it seemed, was to take my ancient Black Elk and old Whitman and give up on the times. Student conversations had one theme: Grab! Time was running out on the good grabbing; you had only to look at the dollar, resources, the world, the country. The students believed in a gospel of surfeit and followed two rules: (a) anything less than more than enough was not enough; and (b) anything not taxable was of dubious use: community, insight, and so on. Goodbye, Portland.

I headed for Vancouver, Washington, once the Hudson's Bay Company's major outpost in the Northwest with lines of commerce reaching to Russian Alaska and Spanish California. In spite of a headstart, the old town had not been able to keep up with the new settlement across the river that got named by a coin toss. In Vancouver I lost the highway, found it again, and drove east on state 14 to follow the Columbia upriver until it made the great turn north. I could have accomplished a similar goal by taking I-80N on the south side of the river and driving the famous Columbia Gorge Highway ("Kodak As You Go," the old slogan said, and even Meriwether Lewis wished he'd carried a camera obscura to capture the beauty); but I would have had to breathe truck fumes. Instead, on blue highway 14, I breathed a fresh odor of something like human excrement. Near Camas, I stopped where a farmer had pulled his tractor to the field edge to reload a planter. "What's that terrible smell?" I said.

"What smell?"

"Like raw sewage."

"That's the Crown-Zellerbach papermill."

"How do you stand to work in it?"

"I don't work there."

That answered my question. Running the steeply buckled land, the highway curved up and down again and again, giving horizon to horizon views of river and mountains. The strength of the Columbia shows in the deep, wide gorge it has cut through the massive uplift; river bottom here lies two hundred feet below sea level, yet the Columbia keeps out the Pacific. Although mountains stretch away north and south from the riverbanks here for hundreds of miles, nowhere else in the Cascades is there an opening like this one.

At Skamania the road climbed so far above the river valley that barns looked like Monopoly hotels and speedboats were less than whirligigs. East stood Beacon Rock, a monumental nine-hundred-foot fluted monolith of solidified lava. Lewis and Clark camped here both going and returning. In Portland, I had bought De Voto's abridged edition of their journals so I could follow that singular expedition of men and one woman, white, red, and black, upriver. Readers who see a declining literate expression in America will find further evidence in the journals. Meriwether Lewis and William Clark presented their permanently important historical and anthropological record clearly and poignantly, often writing under trying and dangerous conditions. In our time, who of the many astronauts has written anything to compare in significance or force of language?

Volcanic bluffs along the highway were flittering with cliff swallows, their sharp wings somehow keeping them airborne. High ridges came down transverse to the Columbia in long-fingered projections perforated by narrow tunnels, some with arched windows opening to the river. Above each tunnel the same date: 1936. To drive state 14 in the snow would be a terror, but on a clear day it was good to find road not so safe as to be dull; it was good to ride highway Americans wouldn't build today.

At North Bonneville, the first of the immense dams that the Corps of Engineers has built on the Columbia at about fifty-mile intervals, thereby turning one of the greatest rivers of the hemisphere into staircase lakes buzzing with outboards. Unlike the lower river, Lewis and Clark would not recognize the Columbia above Bonneville. Rapids and falls where Indians once speared fish lay under sedimented muck; sandbars and chutes, whirlpools, eddies, and sucks were gone, and the turmoil of waters — current against stone — that ancient voice of the river, silenced.

There was, of course, a new voice: the rumble of dynamos. The Columbia and its tributaries account for one-third of all hydroelectric power generated in the United States. The dams also provide other things, the Corps says: irrigation, flood control, backwash lakes for navigation and recreation. But they say nothing about turbines maiming and killing ten percent of the young salmon swimming downstream or about mature fish returning from Alaska and Russia to spawn and suffering burst blood vessels in the eyes and ulcerated blisters under the skin from a high nitrogen content spillways put into the deep pools. Dams are necessary, the Corps maintains, and you can't argue necessity; nevertheless, I don't think Lewis or Clark or the old Chinooks would care much for Bonneville. But then, like the wild river, they are dead.

During lunch in White Salmon, I noticed the map showed a town up on the northern plateau almost in the shadow of Mount Adams called Liberty Bond. No question about where to go next. The highway had no number, and, after several miles, no pavement either. Elevation and trees got higher, but the land began looking like the desert, and the road remained a dusty, lonely thing.

I tried to get directions in Appleton, a fading place of three or four fading houses and a fading school. Had anything else been there, it would have been fading too. No one about. I started on. Then a sudden clatter of hooves and a long "Halloo!" A horse whickered as a woman reined up at my window. "What are you looking for?" she said.

"I'm looking for Liberty Bond."

"Who?"

"Not who — where. A town. Liberty Bond."

She had long, black hair loose over her shoulders. Muscular and pretty. About thirty-five. Very pretty.

"I thought you said 'Liberty Bond,' but I didn't figure you could know about it. Only a few of us up here know about Liberty Bond."

"What's the secret? It's right here in the Rand-McNally."

"You're joking."

"See for yourself." I passed the atlas. She certainly was pretty. Skin smooth and polished and dark like a butt-worn saddle.

"That's something all right," she said. "Very strange."

It was taking some time to get simple directions. Thank heavens.

"Why is that something?"

"Liberty Bond doesn't exist."

"You knew about it."

"It's gone. Fallen down. Looks like Joshua went up there with his horn. All picked over and not a doorknob left. Even carried off the keyholes. Anything they didn't swipe has evaporated. Things don't rot on this side of the Cascades — they evaporate. I know, our ranch is just over the hill."

"How long's it been gone?"

"Years. Years and years. What'd you want up there?"

"Just wanted to see what goes on in a place called Liberty Bond."

"Afraid you're too late for that one." She flicked the reins and the horse walked off. I drove alongside. With neither brazenness nor incivility, she was a woman capable of returning a man's direct gaze.

"How about taking me home to the ranch?"

She laughed. "What've you got in mind?" For a moment I saw a ranch-house parlor, low light through shades, the glow of whiskey in tumblers, a deep cleave and merge of thigh. She smiled. "Too late there too."

"You don't look evaporated."

"Might as well be." She snapped the horse to a trot.

"Tell me one thing, then. Will this east road get me to highway four-teen?"

"If you're patient and don't make any wrong turns." She cracked the reins and the horse bolted across a meadow. Black hair to the wind, she waved without looking around.

Where in hell were the old men who sit on porches and whittle, the ones you're supposed to get directions from when you're in the back of beyond? Since Salt Creek, I'd been working to keep the loneliness down. Now I'd lost my grip. The girl in Tennessee was right: if you're going to run away from home, take a dog along. Even a German woman would be better than this.

8

I was low. The loneliness of the long distance traveler. Try to forget it. Look at the land; it too is medicine. Here were firs shrinking as the desert neared, here open hills of sage and rabbit brush and purple lupine. Then a deep break in the highlands, where far below lay a blue-green strip of the Klickitat River coming down from a glacier on Mount Adams.

Something darkened the windshield just as I came to the edge of the high slope. I ducked, braked hard, and leaned out to see what it was. Should have guessed. A man had just jumped off the mountain in a hang-glider.

He cut slow circles over the Klickitat and the rooftops of the village of Pitt eight hundred feet below, then spiraled a prolonged ascent, a thousand feet above the town. Prone under the canopy, leaning and banking, he swept out a figure eight, then wheeled down, passing a few feet above two men standing nearby. "Piece of cake until I lost my draft!" he shouted. With each turn of the helix he was lower until we were looking into the canyon at the top of the glider. Only his feet showed from beneath the red canopy puffed into a gullwing-like airfoil.

"A tremendous performance," I said to the men.

One nodded. "The flyingest flying. No noise, no pollution."

They drove off down the crest, with me in pursuit, into the canyon and through the village and across the Klickitat to an alfalfa field where the flier was swooping in for a hop, skip, and bounce of a landing, toppling over only at the end. It looked like the crazy tumble landing of a gooney bird. We all ran toward him. When we got there, he was still laughing.

The pilot, Alba Bartholomew, talking quickly, picked up his glider and carried it out of the field. His "kite" was a Wills Wing Cross Country with a "sail" of fifty-five-pound Dacron over an aluminum frame. The only instruments were a variometer and altimeter.

"Did you see the hawk above you, Al?" one of the men, Garland Wyatt, asked.

"Heard him. They stay on your blind side until they dive on you. Glad he wasn't gunning for my face today." The other man, Bob Holliston, asked about the wind. "Not bad, but I couldn't find a warm draft blowing steady."

Wyatt said, "That highwire walker who fell not long ago, Wallenda, he used to say the wind was the worst enemy always."

"Enemy and friend," Holliston said to me. "Our necessary evil. Rising currents make soaring possible. They also make it risky. We fly or die by the same force."

"How'd you get started with this?" I asked Bartholomew.

"Saw a man on television sailing. I knew then I had to try it, so I bought a glider kit, put it together, and jumped off a hill."

"That hill?" I pointed to the high slope he'd just swooped from pterodactyl style. Everybody laughed.

"Pitt's a hang-three incline. Hang-four is the ultimate — like Grand Canyon," Bartholomew said. "My first glide was off a hang-zero-point-one bump."

"Eighty-some people died last year hang-gliding," Wyatt said.

"How do you get yourself to make that first leap?"

Bartholomew shook his head. "Don't know. Guess I didn't want to waste the couple hundred dollars I'd spent on the kit. I remember being scared out of my brains. Actually, it turned out all right until I landed and mowed down about twenty yards of alfalfa. I was just ridge gliding then — running off a hill and gliding to the bottom. In the air twenty seconds on a good flight, but I took a lot of sled rides in those days, bouncing down hills. What you saw is soaring."

Holliston, a contractor who also soared, motioned toward Pitt Hill. "Those cumulus clouds indicate thermal updrafts. Catch a cumie burning hot and you can almost corkscrew out of the atmosphere. We call it 'skying out.' "

"What's it feel like?"

"Hard to describe," Bartholomew said. "Maybe free is the word, or magical. You can't believe you're doing it. I think it's what a bird feels. Or Superman. But ridge gliding's different; it's a carnival ride. Zoom, boom!"

"You feel like a wounded goose before you take off," Holliston said, "but once the sail fills and you're stable, then it's like you've grown wings. You can't see the kite — all you see is ground or sky."

"Are you scared?"

"Always edgy until you're airborne and even a little then. You've got to be a little nervous or you get cocky and careless. Then it's stuff-it time."

"It's a balance," Holliston said. "We've got to risk a little more each time to improve and go beyond what we've done in the past. But if we take on too much at once, it could be the last lesson. The problem is we don't always know when we get in over our heads. We've got to trust our gut reactions without giving in to them. That's what's hard."

"Tell me," I said, "what would happen if I got into your glider right now and jumped off Pitt with only a few minutes' instruction?"

"Off Pitt?" Bartholomew shrugged. "You might live if you made yourself follow natural instincts, but I think you'd get bent up pretty good coming in. That's nearly a thousand feet up there — about the same as jumping off the observation deck of the Empire State Building."

"I don't think you'd be able to climb or soar because of the turns," Holliston said. "You'd stall in the first turn, and that would be the show. Turns take time to catch on to."

"I learned turning from watching buzzards," Bartholomew said. "I saw how they hesitate on the downwind leg."

"Put it this way," Wyatt said. "Al was the first ever off Pitt, and he'd been gliding two years before he tried it. The launch has to be almost perfect."

"My first real soaring ended me up in a lake," Bartholomew said, "which may have been the safest landing place considering the way I came in. My first two years I was banged up a lot: sprained neck, twisted ankles. But I haven't been hurt the last four years. Of course, I'm not a real acrobatic type either. I *would* like to glide off Mount Adams though. Now that would be highly interesting. The problem there is severe winds. I'd have to pack my kite six thousand feet to the top, which is twelve thousand feet, and hope the wind was up, but not *too* up. If I ever think I've got a fifty-fifty chance of getting off, I'll try it. Watch for it in the newspaper: dead or alive."

"That first jump off Pitt must have been hellacious."

"Worse than my first glide. Mountain air is rough — much rougher than California-style ocean gliding. I'd read you've got to have good airspeed to counteract turbulence, so I knew I had to run off the mountain, not just jump. I stood up there a long time, sort of accepting the possibility of whatever. I promised myself I'd run hard. Gliding's not like motorcycling; for us, the more speed, the more safety. I'd read everything there was on gliding and that wasn't much then. I hoped I'd remember it when I needed it. I saw people watching down on the highway, and I knew I'd have a good audience if I stuffed it. Might as well die in a spectacular crash."

"We hate audiences," Holliston said. "Damned applause from beautiful girls."

"Anyway, I took my run and jumped. My heart got a good rest up there when it stopped beating. My whole body said, 'How could you do this to us?'"

"The technology was crude then. The glide ratio of early kites was about three to one — three feet horizontal for every foot vertical *if* you knew what you were doing. Those kites were flying rocks."

"This glider," Bartholomew said, "has a glide ratio of ten to one. Eight years ago it was something for anyone to stay up an hour. Now time aloft depends more on weather and your biceps than on the machine."

"How high can you go?"

"No one knows yet. One pilot did ten thousand feet, but if you don't get a good thermal, you sink about a hundred feet a minute. With a long burner, who can say? I've ridden a hot column up two thousand feet above The Dalles."

"Two thousand feet hanging onto a piece of Dacron? No parachute?"

"After a hundred feet, it's all the same if you lose it. Except for a new model, parachutes are too heavy and restricting. I wouldn't buy one anyway because I'd be tempted to try it, and I've never parachuted. Lose my kite too if I jumped."

"Hang-gliders aren't as flimsy as they look," Holliston said. "They're stressed for six G's whereas a Boeing Seven Forty-seven is stressed for three. Of course, there's some relativity in there."

Wyatt went home, and Bartholomew rolled up the glider and lashed the twenty-foot bundle to his pickup. He said, "Come on back with us."

Holliston rolled his eyes. "Trophy time."

Alba Bartholomew lived in Klickitat, a company town of seven hundred in the narrow vale of the Klickitat River. His little frame house was like the others on the street except for the windsock blowing on the roof. He worked at the St. Regis sawmill, where he ran a stacker. It wasn't the most interesting of jobs. The mill got much of its timber from the Yakima Reservation twelve miles north. St. Regis was the reason for Klickitat, and when the Yakima's big ponderosa were gone, people feared the company would pull out and Klickitat would go the way of Liberty Bond.

Bartholomew's wife grilled hamburgers, and we sat talking and drinking Olympia in the front yard. At first the topics were technical — wing stress, nose altitudes, load factors — but after we'd eaten and had some more beer, the conversation took a different cast. Maybe it was the Tumwater in the beer.

Bartholomew drew a sketch of an airfoil. "Today, hang-gliders are variations of one a man named Francis Rogallo made about 1949, although most of the changes came in the early seventies, after NASA decided not to use them to bring down space capsules. A new technology for a new sport."

"The Wright brothers started out with hang-gliders, but the concept's older," Holliston said. "Leonardo da Vinci sketched something that looks like early gliders. Five hundred years before the idea became a working thing."

"When I first got into it," Bartholomew said, "you almost had to buy a new kite every year just to keep up with the aerodynamic changes. New models were much better and safer." He got out a pamphlet on hang-

14. *Bob Holliston, Al Bartholomew, and Garland Wyatt near Pitt, Washington*

gliding. "Man who wrote this is paralyzed now from a crash." He offered that as if he'd told me the man was left-handed.

"If you stay at it long enough, something's bound to go wrong," I said.

"If I flip a coin ninety-nine times and it comes up heads every time, the odds are still fifty-fifty when I flip the hundredth time. Besides, each flight I learn something, and learning makes for safety."

"That's probably true," Holliston said, "but I think the real answer to why we fly is because it's addictive. It's a buzz to put everything on the line. Whenever we go up, we're subconsciously asking the most important question in the world — asking it real loud — 'Is this the day I die?' "

"You're really pumped up when you come back down; it's great to be up, but afterwards the earth feels so good and you think how you've gotten away with it one more time. Still, it took me a year of flying before I could relax enough to call soaring a pleasure. Even water's a more natural place for a man than the sky."

"You're not a bird just because you fly like one," Holliston said, "but it seems like you are. There's no compartment around you so you feel and hear the wind just like the birds. Man's oldest dream."

"You hear the wind when you're in it?"

"You'd better hear it, otherwise you're into a stall and it's time for the last thrill. You gauge safety, which is airspeed, by the sound of the wind."

"It's hard to explain how good it feels to be totally alone up there, where everything depends absolutely on yourself. Until you've felt the freedom of that, and how your senses come alive, you really can't understand soaring."

"Freedom's a misleading word, though, because we're only free as long as we balance gravity and thermals. It's like both sky and earth want us. They're both pulling. We get to fly as long as we keep things balanced, and that's where the sensation is — when we're hanging between up and down."

"Sometimes it seems like — I don't know," Bartholomew said abstractedly. "Sometimes I just get to thinking I can stay up forever if I can only keep the balance. You can get so outside yourself, you start believing you belong in the sky. Like you were born up there. That's when it's most dangerous — and the best."

"You sound like Icarus."

"Of course, you never can maintain the balance," Holliston said. "Something always comes along and changes things. Mr. Down gets you every time."

9

I FOLLOWED the road, the road followed the Klickitat, and the river followed the rocky valley down to the Columbia. At The Dalles another dam — this one wedged between high walls of basalt. Before the rapids here disappeared, Indians caught salmon for a couple of thousand years by spearing them in midair as the fish exploded leaps up the falls; Klickitats smoked the salmon over coals, pulverized the dried flesh, and either packed it in wicker baskets lined with fishskins for use during the winter or they tied the cooked salmon in bundles for trading to other tribes. The fish kept for months and some even ended up with Indians living east of the Rockies.

The cascades provided such a rich fishing site that Lewis and Clark called The Dalles "the great mart of all this country." Natives found a new source of income in the falls when white traders came with boats to be portaged. One fur trader complained, as did many early travelers, that the Indians were friendly but "habitual thieves"; yet he paid fifty braves only a quid of tobacco each to carry his heavy boats a mile upriver.

East of the dam, the land looked as though someone had drawn a north-south line forbidding green life: west, patches of forest; east, a desert of hills growing only shrubs and dry grasses. The wet coastal country was gone. A little before sunset, in the last long stretch of light, I saw on a great rounded hill hundreds of feet above the river a strange huddle of upright rocks. It looked like Stonehenge. When I got closer, I saw that it was Stonehenge — in perfect repair. I turned off the highway and went down to the bottomland peach groves, where a track up the hill led to the stones. They stood a hundred yards south of several collapsed buildings.

In truth, the circle of menhirs was a ferro-concretehenge, but it was as arresting on its hill as the real Stonehenge on Salisbury Plain. From it, I could see the river Lewis and Clark had opened the Northwest with and awakened a new consciousness of nationhood; I could look across to a far riverside section of the Oregon Trail now buried under I-80N. The setting sun cast an unearthly light on the sixteen-foot megaliths and turned the enormous pyramid of Mount Hood, fifty miles away, to a black triangle. I felt again the curious fusion of time — past with present — that occurred at the Nevada petroglyphs.

A flaking wooden sign said a highway engineer and rail magnate, Sam Hill, whose grave was just down the slope, had built the replica in the twenties as a memorial to doughboys "sacrificed to the heathen god of war." Over several smooth declivities in the concrete slabs appeared almost imperceptible notations from other travelers: A. J. WILSON NYC. HELLO STUPID. KT 1936. BOB AND JANEY WAS HERE. The monument had become a register, and the scribbles gave a historical authenticity that masked its bogus one. The twentieth century had made the stones an equivalent to the petroglyphs.

I picked up a peel-away Polaroid negative — the totemic offering of the American tourist. Barely visible was the reversed image of a woman standing against a monolith, her arms upraised, head bent to the left as if in sacrificial posture. She was unclad. A joke — it must have been. But in the half-light from a disappearing sun completing one more day of a two-hundred-fifty-million-year circle around the galaxy, the stones looking more and more genuine in the shadows, and a cold stillness dropping onto the desert plateau, the pendulous-breasted woman suggested something more.

The hills went dark, the volcano vanished against the black sky, blue ice stars shone as thick as mottles on a trout. A few lights from Biggs, Oregon, several miles across the river, gleamed off the slick water.

The loneliness again. Now I had only the idea of the journey to keep me going. Black Elk says it is in the dark world among the many changing shadows that men get lost. Instead of insight, maybe all a man gets is strength to wander for a while. Maybe the only gift is a chance to inquire, to know nothing for certain. An inheritance of wonder and nothing more.

Stars shone with a clarity beyond anything I could remember. I was looking into — actually seeing — the past. By looking up into the darkness, I was looking into time. The old light from Betelgeuse, five hundred twenty light-years away, showed the star that existed when Christopher Columbus was a boy, and the Betelgeuse he saw was the one that burned when Northmen were crossing the Atlantic. For the Betelgeuse of this time, someone else will have to do the looking. The past is for the present, the present for the future.

Astronomers say that when telescopes of greater range can be built, ones that can look down the distant curves of the universe billions of light-years away, they might show existence at the time of creation. And if astrophysicists and countless American Indians are correct in believing that a human being is composed of exploded bits of heavenly matter, billions of galactic atoms, then astronomers may behold us all in the stellar winds; they may observe us when we were something else and very much farther away. In a time when men counted only seven planets, Whitman recognized it:

> Afar down I see the huge first Nothing, I knew I was even there,
> I waited unseen and always, and slept through the lethargic mist,
> And took my time.

There came a dry rustle in the desert bush — a skunk, rabbit, coyote, I didn't know what, but it pulled me back to Sam Hill's Stonehenge, now just an orbit of shadows. The people who built the British Stonehenge used it as a time machine whereby starlight — the light of the past — could show them a future of equinoxes, solstices, eclipses. Across America I had been looking for something similar. An old urge in man. It seemed the journey had led here.

What was this piece of ground I stood on? Fifty miles away rose the ancient volcano like those that puffed out the first atmosphere, and under me lay the volcanic basalt ridge the old river had cut through. For thousands of years, chinook and chum and bluebacks swam upriver to regenerate, and Indians followed after the salmon; and then new people came down the river after everything. South lay the Oregon Trail under four lanes of concrete marked off by the yellow running lights of the transports; south, too, were glinting rails of the Union Pacific. North a ghost town crumbling, and around me a circle of stones for the dead of the first war called a "world war."

Astronomer Edwin Hubble observed a galaxy moving away from Earth at nine hundred million miles an hour and concluded that the universe is dispersing itself to emptiness. Perhaps so, but the things I saw on the mountain — and more that I didn't — all had come together briefly while I stood as witness. Now atomic physicists, those who watch the dance of the universe, were saying that in the pursuit of matter one ends up not so much with things as with interconnections — interconnections that give the particularities not merely definition but (even more) their moment, their meaning. Whitman: "A vast similitude interlocks all."

Who can say how a man comes to see? I appeared surrounded by tombstones: the volcano dead, the basalt solidified, the fast river of cataracts drowned, the Indians and explorers and settlers and thirteen doughboys and Sam Hill too (his tombstone said "Amid nature's great unrest, he sought rest"), all in their graves. That's how a man sees the continuum: by the tracks it leaves.

All of those things — rock and men and river — resisted change, resisted the coming as they did the going. Hood warmed and rose slowly, breaking open the plain, and cooled slowly over the plain it buried. The nature of things is resistance to change, while the nature of process is resistance to stasis, yet things and process are one, and the line from inorganic to organic and back again is uninterrupted and unbroken.

The Ghost Dancers showed both man's natural opposition to change he doesn't understand and his natural failure in such opposition. But it is man's potential to try to see how all things come from the old intense light and how they pause in the darkness of matter only long enough to change back into energy, to see that changelessness would be meaninglessness, to know that the only way the universe can show and prove itself is through change. His job is to do what nothing else he knows of can do: to look about and draw upon time.

A man lives in things and things are moving. He stands apart in such a temporary way it is hardly worth speaking of. If that perception dims egocentrism, that illusion of what man is, then it also enlarges his self, that multiple yet whole part which he has been, will be, is. Ego, craving distinction, belongs to the narrowness of now; but self, looking for union, belongs to the past and future, to the continuum, to the outside. Of all the visions of the Grandfathers the greatest is this: *To seek the high concord, a man looks not deeper within — he reaches farther out.*

THE light, spreading slowly that morning, came over the hills as if on foot, filling in a hollow here, pushing out a shadow there, working gradually to bring on the colors and forms of day. It bleached the gray eastern sides of the megaliths and rolled a shadow like a great spoked wheel down the scarp; snow on Mount Hood shifted on the spectrum from yellow to ice white.

I walked around what was left of the streets of the ghost town: a stone fountain, a few fireplugs, four rock buildings. A monument out here in the isolation made some sense, but not a town, so I went back up the highway to the Maryhill Museum of Fine Arts (made no sense here either) to ask how come.

Sam Hill had many plans — some shrewd, some cockamamie — and he had money to try them. His plan for Maryhill, Washington (first called Columbus), was to find a narrow zone where coastal rains met desert sun; that belt, he believed, would be an agricultural Eden. Early in the century, he decided the Columbia Hills was that place and laid out a town of thirty-four city blocks, built a reservoir and a few buildings. He talked some Belgian Quakers into considering settlement, but when scouts for the group came, they saw and left. To them, Hill's ideal zone was the fiction of a creative road engineer more adept at theory than practice when it came to agronomy and climatology. And they were right. The town lay in the rain shadow of the Cascades.

Hill continued building the big and costly stone manor, often called, with some accuracy, "Maryhill Castle." At one time he said it was for his wife Mary, but she apparently refused even to visit the place. At various other times he said Maryhill would be (a) a fortress to stop foreign invaders, or (b) a cultural center served by his Northern Pacific railroad running down alongside the Columbia and cross river from the competing Union Pacific, or (c) "a universal school for all the people . . . where farmer folk could find solutions to their problems," or (d) an international museum, which it turned out to be if you consider America and Rumania to constitute "international."

As for the town, Hill finally gave the meetinghouse to a couple of English women for their years of service in his employ, and they opened the Meadowlark Inn, a place of good food and quiet. But Hill died, the other buildings fell down, the reservoir silted up, the women died, and in 1958 the inn burned. Hill's dream had passed, and now, but for the museum, monument, and the ruined rock walls, the desert slope was as vacant as ever.

On the highway again: at a cluster of closed buildings called Roosevelt, I noticed my gas was low. The next town, according to the atlas, was Moonax five miles away. Ten miles on, McCredie; fifteen, Alderdale; twenty, Whitcomb. I drove unconcerned. But Moonax was another Liberty Bond. Same with McCredie. Down went the needle. I could see stations along the interstate a mile south across the bridgeless river. No Alderdale. I locked the speedometer needle on forty-five and my arms to the steering wheel. A traveling salesman once told me that if you tense butt muscles tight enough, you can run on an empty tank for miles. And that's what it was going to take. Whitcomb was there, more or less, but the station was closed on Sundays. Paterson, the last hope. If it proved a ghost town, I was going to learn more about this deleted landscape on foot. I drove, tensed top to bottom, waiting for that sickening silent glide. Of the one hundred seventy-one thousand gas stations in the country, I needed one.

Paterson, under the Horse Heaven Hills, had an open station, where I pumped in a kilderkin of gas. The odds paid off. I told the attendant — a surly fellow who could have raised mushrooms in the organic decay of his front teeth — about looking for Moonax. Two obese women with faces they might have bought at K-Mart burst out laughing from their aluminum chairs.

"Moonax! Moonax! Moonax!" each crowed one after the other.

"Moonax," I repeated. I might just as well have said "Mongolia." I didn't have the heart to mention McCredie.

"You're about fifty years late, tootsie," one said. "Moonax ain't but a hole in the ground."

I climbed into my truck. From the greasy room somebody said, "Moonax!" and the laughter began again. Maybe I knew about Betelgeuse, but Moonax I didn't know from a hole in the ground.

Across the Columbia at Umatilla, Oregon, and up the great bend of river into country where sage grew taller than men. The highway swung north once more into Washington to join U.S. 12 at new Wallula, a town forced to move when McNary Dam turned a segment of the Columbia into Wallula Lake.

Old Wallula was one of those river settlements you can find all over the country that appeared destined to become key cities because of geographical position. Sitting at the confluence of the Walla Walla with the Columbia and just a few miles downstream from where the Snake and Yakima meet the big river, old Wallula was a true joining of waters (the name may be a Nez Perce word meaning "abundant water"), although if you lift your gaze from the rivers you see desert. Astride the Idaho gold rush trail, Wallula began well: riverboats, stagelines, railroads, two highways. But money and history came through, paused, and went on.

The future passed eastward to Walla Walla ("little swift water") with its many small streams instead of navigable rivers. Outsiders may laugh at the name until they consider the original one: Steptoeville. Walla Walla, a pleasant little city of ivied college buildings, wasn't at all what you'd expect of a town with a name that sounds like baby babble.

The road went around the Blue Mountains into the Palouse, one of the most visually striking topographical regions in America. The treeless, rounded hills, shaped by ice and wind and water to a sensuous nudity, were sprouting an intensely green fuzz of winter wheat. These fertile highlands, the steepest American cropland, are so vast and rich, special machinery has been built to work them: twelve-wheel, self-leveling tractors and combines that can ride the thirty percent gradients.

Into the Palouse I took state 126, a graveled and slender and precarious piece of aerial roadway running the hills and grassy chasms with bravado, affording magnificently long views of the undulating land, before dropping once more to U.S. 12 along Pataha Creek. Then over the low mountains and down to a shallow basin where the Clearwater River joins the Snake. All the way, chukars crouched along the shoulders only to blast to cover as I approached.

A few miles south of the highway, the Snake River came out of five-thousand-foot-deep Hells Canyon, a place as inaccessible as any in the country. North of the road, the river, called by the voyageurs *La Maudite Rivière Enragée*, "The Accursed Mad River," went back into a canyon two thousand feet deep and almost as inaccessible. It was as if the Snake, which travels such difficult terrain that explorers proved its true source only in 1970, crawled from underground to see sky before disappearing again.

At the east end of the Clearwater basin lay the twin towns of Clarkston, Washington, and Lewiston, Idaho. Clarkston used to be Jawbone Flats, until it became Vineland, then Concord (the grapes, you see); in 1900, the town took the present name to parallel Lewiston across the river. The historical pairing is nice, but give me Jawbone Flats.

A few miles upstream on the Clearwater, eastward-bound Lewis and Clark stopped for a meal with the Nez Perce, Clark's favorite tribe. The explorers, trade goods nearly exhausted, had resorted to eating bear-grease candles and to cutting off coat buttons to barter for a dog or horse they could butcher when their huntsmen returned empty. But more in demand among Indians than buttons or tobacco was Clark's ability to dress a wound or drain an abscess or soothe a lesion. Clark wrote, "In our present situation, I think it pardonable to continue this deception [as a physician] for they will not give us any provisions without compensation in merchandise."

After treating one Nez Perce, Clark sat down with the party to eat roasted dog, dried roots, and root bread. He described the meal:

> While at dinner an Indian fellow very impertinently threw a half-starved puppy nearly into the plate of Capt. Lewis by way of derision for our eating dogs and laughed heartily at his own impertinence; Capt. Lewis was so provoked at the insolence that he caught the puppy and threw it with great violence at him and struck him in the breast and face, seized his tomahawk, and showed him by sign that if he repeated his insolence that he would tomahawk him; the fellow withdrew apparently much mortified, and we continued our dinner without further molestation.

Through such combinations of boldness and humanitarianism (and a little magic with friction matches, magnets, and magnifying glasses), Lewis and Clark moved their small group for twenty-six months through eight thousand miles of wild land with only the loss of two Indians and one soldier (apparently to an appendicitis; Lewis almost became a casualty when the half-blood boatman, Peter Cruzat, mistook him for an elk and shot him in the rump). For three-quarters of a century after the two visits by the Corps of Discovery, the Nez Perce did not fight white men because the captains had conducted the first encounters so well.

Lewiston, some residents think, looks like a European mountain town, what with its old brick buildings pressed in the valley. Maybe so, although a yellow pother over it from the Potlatch particle-board mill on the Clearwater gave it the appearance of a one-industry town anywhere. A potlatch, by the way, was a Northwest Indian ceremonial feast in which the host either distributed valuable material goods or destroyed his own to prove his wealth. Which conclusion the Potlatch company had in mind I couldn't say.

Old U.S. 95 up barren Lewiston Hill, two thousand feet of grinding steepness, is such a fearsome thing travelers often carry an extra pair of undershorts when forced to drive it. Even the engineers of the new route approached the "hill" most reluctantly, tacking evasively as if ascent and descent weren't their goal. But once on the summit, the rider sees the highways turn to mere dribbles trying to gain the great basin below.

Above the hill, the land again took on the soft face of the Palouse, fields alternating green wheat with tilled brown fallow. A few trees stood in the deep glens now going blue in the dusk; otherwise the horizon was a smooth concatenation of hills as fertile as the valleys. When pioneers arrived, they found the Palouse covered with tall bunchgrass, which Indians of the plateau wove into huts, baskets, and clothes. The settlers cleared the grass, planted wheat, and reaped huge yields despite a usual annual rainfall of less than twenty inches. The secret of this land that has never known a crop failure, in addition to good soil, is that seventy-five percent of the precipitation occurs between October and April when it helps most. Now farmers, still reaping harvests double the national average, sow in alternate years and control weed growth during the fallow period so that each crop gets two years of moisture. The Palouse is that ideal blend of rain and sun that Sam Hill dreamed of but looked for in the wrong place.

Seven

NORTH BY NORTHWEST

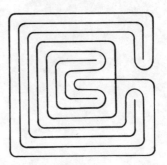

1

I SPENT the night in Hog Heaven, as early settlers called Moscow, Idaho, after they saw the gustatorial excitement pigs got into snorting up camas roots. Although settlers refused to eat the tubers, they were an Indian staple that helped sustain the Lewis and Clark expedition.

Citizens later tried to counteract the swinish name by changing it to Paradise, but that was much too unbelievable. In 1877, a transplanted Easterner applied for a postal permit under the present name to honor Moscow, Pennsylvania. That ended the silliness; but, as best I could tell, many residents, unable to agree whether the last vowel is long or short, don't like the toponym Moscow any better than Hog Heaven.

The night before I had left on the trip, I met Fred Tomlins. He and his wife, Peggy, lived in Moscow. He had said, as people carelessly do, "If you ever get out to our corner (ho-ho), give us a call." So I did.

Tomlins flew two hundred twenty-five combat missions in the F-100 Super-Sabre in Viet Nam and received three Distinguished Flying Crosses. After his tour, he finished his Air Force hitch as a test pilot in Georgia. He moved to northern Idaho, where he tried to earn a living by making wooden toys, but it didn't work out. He talked with several airlines about flying for them, but, at thirty, he was too old. So Tomlins began studying for a master's degree in Wildland Recreation Management at the University of Idaho. Someone had said the night I met him that he and his wife watched more television — especially game shows — than any two-member family in the country. Tomlins told me privately that was a lie. They had come in third in the district regionals.

After breakfast, I called. He suggested we meet for lunch at a new Mexican cafe housed in an old filling station. "Can't remember the name," he said, "but you won't miss it. It's the only gas station on Main serving enchiladas. No Margaritas though." He liked Margaritas very much.

At Moreno's we took a table about where the grease pit had been. The owners served a good lunch but had grown tired of the "get gas" jokes. "How do you like the Palouse?" Tomlins said.

"A strange piece of land. Beautiful."

"Want to fly over it this afternoon?" He was not an indirect man.

After his afternoon class, we drove nine miles out to the airfield at Pullman, Washington. Pullman, home of Washington State University, and Moscow are the "U cities." We rented a Cessna 150 and flew southeast toward the lower Snake River Canyon.

"I read today that topsoil in the Palouse can be a hundred feet deep!" I yelled over the engine and wind.

"Not true. Up to two hundred feet. First farmland in the country to sell for a thousand dollars an acre."

"How do you get two hundred feet of topsoil?"

"It's not all topsoil in the usual sense, but three layers. The first is silt, the second's a lighter soil, and the third layer is loess — windblown glacial dust, old topsoil. An absorbent stuff that holds water. Under all that you've got volcanic rock. Weird, isn't it? Glacier dust over lava."

Much of the time we were flying so low I could see the men on tractors plowing stubble under and raising tall spumes of dust. The rigs, riding the high swells of land, looked like smoky ocean freighters.

Tomlins pointed at a drove of Appaloosa. "The breed gets its name from the Palouse. Indians invented the Appaloosa and white men discovered it. The strain almost died out after the Nez Perce were forced out of here in the eighteen seventies and the Army sold off their horses. But in the thirties, some Anglos started working to save the breed by using pure stock the Nez Perce still had. Lots of Appaloosas now."

The man was a good pilot and didn't mind showing his skill. The horizon tilted on its axis like a teeter-totter, the altimeter needle swung back and forth like a windshield wiper, and my stomach crawled up my throat.

"The thing I like when I'm up here," he said, "you know what it is?"

"Your parachute?"

"Simplicity. Up here life has just one clear purpose: get back down."

"Using the wings and wheels, I'm hoping."

He rolled the Cessna on its side to show me the hills. "The tan fields are lentils and peas. The Palouse grows ninety-nine percent of the lentils in this country and ninety-five percent of the dry peas. Also a good share of the wheat which they rotate with the beans."

He flipped the 150 on the other side, and I checked both wings to make sure they had followed after. We were twelve hundred feet above the fields, but at least we weren't hanging under fifty-five-pound Dacron.

"Can't believe it," he said. "Not now anyway. But sometimes I miss Viet Nam. Not the war — I'm talking about the flying and how things were

15. *Fred Tomlins in Moscow, Idaho*

clear cut. Like the work. We all wanted just one major thing — stay alive long enough to get back home.''

He locked the right wing in place as we pinwheeled above a silvery barn roof. Around and around, down, down. ''You haven't lost wanting that, have you, Fred?'' We were in a sharp descent. ''Fred?''

"What? Just thinking."

"Are you thinking about great things living men do on the ground —
like watching *Tic Tac Dough* and drinking Margaritas? Things that make
life worth living?" We were still dropping. "Captain?"

He pulled out and leveled off. "I'll show you the Snake River Canyon.
One of our great rivers and almost unseen because it's so hidden." He
nosed around toward the setting sun. "I was just thinking about one
Christmas Day in Viet Nam. Sounds piss-poor to tell it, but we were on a
bombing run to Laos because Nixon said we couldn't bomb in Nam on
Christmas. The nape — napalm cans — had been painted like candy canes.
On the ADF radio they were playing Creedence Clearwater singing 'Rollin'
Down the River.' I sang along all the way." He looked at the altimeter and
pulled the nose up. "I guess the war was a hundred-thirty-billion-dollar
waste, but it was a hell of a time if you lived."

The Cessna went *whump-whump* when we reached the Snake. "Normal
turbulence over a river," he shouted. We were a thousand feet above the
green rim of the gorge and three thousand feet over the river, a twisted
strand of tourmaline.

"Take a good look," Tomlins said. "Next time you see it, it may be a
lake. Corps of Engineers has plans for hydroelectric dams all the way from
the Columbia through Hells Canyon and on up. They've already built a
couple dozen. Half the river's drowned and so are a lot of Indian picto-
graphs. Lewiston's four hundred miles from the Pacific and now it's a
seaport because of the dams."

"The Corps' job is to keep free rivers from going to waste. That and to
replace every salmon and sturgeon with carp," I said.

We crossed and recrossed the great Snake, a task virtually impossible
on the ground. "Steamboats used to run this lower section," he said. "Hard
to believe when you look into that crooked thing."

We turned back toward Moscow. Later, driving into town, Tomlins said,
"I hate going slow. You know what fun is? Fun is flying ten feet off the
ground at Mach one." He shook his head. "Oh well, *Twenty-Thousand-
Dollar Pyramid* is on tonight. I'll make it through another day."

2

THE thing that finally got my attention was his little aluminum suitcase.
Except for the "spiritual material" consisting mostly of typed testimonials

in the satchel, everything he owned was in the aluminum case. But I didn't really see it until later.

Early afternoon: overcast, cheerless. A few miles north of Moscow I saw him hitching. The crosswind pulled his gray beard at a right angle to his face so that he looked like Curry's painting of John Brown standing before the Kansas tornado. I stopped, and the small man quickly limped up the road with a hobble that reminded me of Porfirio Sanchez. Pushing the aluminum case ahead, he climbed in, smiling, introducing himself. His name was Arthur O. Bakke. The O stood for Olaf. He spelled the last name, asked mine and how to spell it.

Now the first question from a hitchhiker never varies: "How far ya goin'?" After making certain of spellings, Arthur O. Bakke's first question was, "Do you want a free Bible course?" Oh, god, not this, I thought. "Jesus is coming," he said. Save me, I thought and started working on a reason to turn back and head the other way. There's little you can do to stop a soul claimsman; even aluminum siding salesmen run out of words before these guys. He was saying something about "God's strategy."

"I've got nothing against God's strategy, but let's not talk about it now."

He looked out the side window. "We're coming into the forest," he said. "You start to miss trees on the Palouse. And rocks — you don't see rocks or fences much there." He looked over the truck. "Do you smoke?" I said I didn't. "I don't like to ride with smokers. The Spirit's moving in you, but never mind that." He pulled out a palm-size notebook made of two pieces of linoleum. "Where did you pick me up?"

"Near Potlatch, Idaho."

He wrote that down, making sure of the spelling, then scribbled my name and the year and manufacturer of the van. When I pulled in for gas, he checked his watch and said aloud as he wrote: " 'Fueling stop at Tensed, Idaho. Rain imminent.' Would you spell Tensed?"

I did. "How do you know about the rain?"

"My hip. The affliction's good for that."

"What happened?"

"Car wreck. Rolled off a mountain in a snowstorm. Jesus allowed me to almost get killed to get me into His work."

I wasn't up to asking what work he referred to.

Tensed is on the Coeur d'Alene reservation. As a young Indian scrubbed the windshield, Bakke leaned out the window. "Would you like a free Bible course?" The boy never stopped wiping, but he looked in at me. I shrugged. "Jesus is coming soon," Bakke chirped.

The Coeur d'Alene said, faltering, "No read white man word."

Bakke thought for a moment. The Indian finished wiping, and I followed him inside to sign the credit slip. Filling out the form in a precise hand, he said, "What's wrong with your buddy?"

"He's okay. Just a friendly fellow."

"That's what they say at the funny farm."

Bakke and I went up the road. He talked happily about the fields, clouds, his travels. He was fifty-eight years old and a Seventh-Day Adventist. Some years ago he lost in a divorce most of what he owned and had never bothered to gather more. After recuperating from the car wreck, he went on the road to serve Jesus. Several times he said, always softly, "My! How we need Jesus!" He had a bank account in southern California and one in Virginia; otherwise, all his material goods were at his feet or wrapped around him.

"Where are you going now?" I said.

"To El Salvador."

I thought before I spoke. "Do you understand we're a couple of hundred miles from the Canadian border and heading due north?"

"Most certainly. I'm stopping off along the way."

"You're stopping off in British Columbia on the way to El Salvador?"

"No, no. I'm stopping off in Coeur d'Alene tonight on my way to Missoula, Montana. But I have to go to Virginia before I leave the country."

Bakke knew of an Adventist church in Coeur d'Alene and figured on finding a place for the night there. It began to rain — waving sheets of water the wipers couldn't handle. He took out his notebook to record the weather change and our arrival time. "Is Coeur d'Alene hyphenated?" I stopped at a gas station for directions to the church, and Bakke went into his routine again. "Salvation's just around the corner, brother."

The pumpman lighted a cigarette and looked helplessly at me to see if it was a joke. "I'm already done up with the Presbyterians," he said, retreating, watching us carefully as if Bakke had said, "Is the safe just around the corner?"

I was getting interested in the way people reacted to the offer of a free Bible course. Whatever the response, Bakke's directness unnerved them.

"The Lord will get you off that tobacco."

The man kept stepping backwards, reaching behind to feel where he was going. I thanked him and drove away. "Don't think he's ready yet," I said. "Catch him next time through."

Bakke took out his pad and noted the station. "Good idea." I stopped again at a supermarket to get bread and fruit for the next day. He bought a can of beans and two bananas. As I fumbled my change, Bakke said to the checker, "How's your faith today?"

That same uneasy smile. "Pretty good." Then quietly, "I don't know."
She rang up the sale, and I gave no helping shrugs.

"Jesus is coming sooner than you realize."

"Maybe I'd better go home and clean house," she mumbled.

The rain had eased when we got to the church, but it was still a wretched
night, and I told him I would wait until he found a place. Bakke was inside
some time. When he came out, the rain had stopped.

"I've found a home for the night," he said. "You're included too."

"I'll stay in my rig, but maybe I could wash up there."

"We're supposed to follow a red pickup truck. He'll be out in a while.
The service was slowed by an intoxicated man who's seen his error. He's
still on his knees crying."

"They're not going to convert a drunk, are they?"

"No, no. This is just his first step. Let's have something to eat while we
wait." He pulled his twelve-by-fifteen-inch case onto his lap and opened
it. "I have a cheese sandwich and an apple we can share," he said. "And
a corn muffin. Students at Walla Walla College gave me the food."

"I've got something here too."

Bakke said grace over the cheese sandwich, then ate quickly, paying
attention to his meal. "Good cheese," he said. "Praise Yahweh." Then he
went at the apple, holding it in both hands, turning it, eating it from end
to end the way people eat corn on the cob. He looked up once and smiled.
"This is a sweet apple. I got a lift from a man and he gave it to me. I meet
some beautiful people, praise the Lord."

Bakke's host tapped on the window, and we followed him to a house
so new there wasn't yet a lawn. His wife had recently died, and I think
he was lonely, although he seemed a little uneasy about two wayfarers
coming into his living room. It was a small, orderly home without a single
book visible except a phone directory, Bible, and one called *Philosophical
Thoughts*, which I picked up. A clay bank.

The men talked and reached agreement on several points:

(a) Constantine set us all back in A.D. 321 by passing a law forcing people
     to observe the first day of the week instead of the true Sabbath — the
     seventh day, Saturday.

(b) Nations are cursed because they won't tithe ten cents on the dollar, but
     they can't get away with it much longer.

(c) Television is a serpent both men were guilty of peeking at. Movie houses
     are palaces of make-believe, but they weren't guilty here.

(d) God is a He, not a She (Genesis 1:26–27).

Bakke, at the request of our host, led a kneeling prayer during which I suffered the embarrassment of losing my balance in the deep-pile shag carpet and having to lunge for the coffee table. Bakke asked for strength for us all, and I hoped he wasn't referring to my tumble.

3

"I SURE ate that breakfast," Bakke said. "Praise Yahweh."

In some Christians of strong conviction there is a longing never to be hungry, to have no appetites; but he was one who enjoyed filling the hunger.

The morning sun cast bars of light across the road. Bakke had offered to ride with me into western Montana as he worked his way toward Missoula.

"I just finished a national tour — something like the one you're on," he said. "The Master impressed me to undertake the mission while the rate by Greyhound was still fifty-five dollars cross country, unlimited stops."

I felt up to it that morning, so I asked about his work.

"Jesus hitchhikes in me. That's the work. Luke fourteen: twenty-three."

"I don't know the Bible by numbers."

From his breast pocket he drew a small limp book marked over in ballpoint: red, green, and blue. Red markings pertained directly to Deity, green to man, while blue tended toward the "Satanic area." Bakke held his Bible softly, as if it were alive, and never did he thrust it threateningly.

He read: " 'And the Lord said unto the servant, "Go out into the highways and hedges, and compel them to come in, that my house may be filled." ' Probably ten thousand people have been enrolled by Christ through me in the Voice of Prophecy Bible course."

"Enrolled by Christ? Am I talking with Jesus?"

"You're trying to make me look foolish. That's an easy thing to do. Paul says, 'We are fools for Christ's sake.' My words are my own. I don't credit myself so much. If we only knew the mind of God, oh, my!"

"Tell me how you came to believe. Is it too personal?"

"I was a jack-of-all-trades at Boeing Aircraft in Seattle, Washington. That was before Jesus claimed me, so what happened isn't important now. But my wife left me. I missed her so very much for three years." He seemed to lose himself recollecting. After a few moments he said, "I wonder how

I escaped so long. I guess God looked ahead and saw my service, like with Paul."

Bakke opened his briefcase and took out one of his personal testimonies — a legal-size, marginless sheet dense with typed words — titled "A Fateful Night — December 9th, 1966. True Story by Arthur Olaf Bakke, R.P."

"You could keep this and read it," he said with diffidence. "I'm the first to admit I don't know the mechanics of English. Don't know how to paragraph."

"Why don't you read it aloud as we ride? Start with what R.P. stands for."

"Royal Priest. First Peter two:nine." He wrote the citation on his testimony and turned to the passage and read: " 'Ye are a chosen generation, a royal priesthood' and so on 'that should show forth the praises of Him who hath called you out of darkness into his marvelous light.' But I've dropped the R.P. now and just use I.M.V. for International Missionary Volunteer."

Bakke's voice, an unsubstantial contralto, rose as he read his testimony. The nub was this: he had been living alone near Wenatchee, Washington, where he made a little money selling windfall apples. One morning he loaded his Plymouth with so many boxes of windfalls that there was room only for him and a blender he used to make apple and carrot juice. He had become a vegetarian. To make his deliveries he drove west on U.S. 2 toward Everett. It was snowing in the Cascades. On the west slope of Stevens Pass, he overtook a pickup and lost control on the slippery downgrade. Here is his account:

I slid into the snowbank and crashed thru. At that split second, I called upon the name of the LORD for help, to spare my life so I can do the work I'm doing now: Missionary Work. After rolling over and over down the hillside approximately 200 feet, an old snag about two feet thru stopped the car (I had no seat belt on — maybe if I had had one on, I'd have snapped my neck?) and spun it around right side up on an angle, nose down. I felt my hip give. Then I noticed the windshield was missing (no doubt the juicer went through it). Then I squirmed out of the wreckage and crawled onto the hood. I looked up and saw a flashlight up on the road and cried out for help. The man said to hold on an hour or so and he'd get help. I was so happy to be alive. I put my fingers in my mouth to keep them from freezing off. Later they came down the hill with a rope and stretcher and tied me on. They offered me a cigaret, but I told them a Christian doesn't smoke. "An ungodly man diggeth up evil; and in his lips there is a burning fire." Proverbs 16:27.

Bakke began walking again six months later with three steel screws holding his pelvis together.

"I kept my word. I serve the Lord full-time. I started witnessing in the hospital. Then in California I witnessed to the hippies at Berkeley."

"How do you support yourself?"

"I get a Social Security disability check every month for two hundred eighteen dollars and seventy cents. And people like you contribute along the way."

"Does the Adventist Church help out?"

"They send the free Bible courses."

"And you keep moving all the time?"

"Sometimes I stop in a place awhile. In Virginia, outside Bowling Green, I built a tree temple on I-ninety-five. Stayed there about six months."

"What's a tree temple?"

"Like a tree house in a pine grove. I built it out of scrap lumber to about the size of your van. It was for hitchhikers — to give them shelter and the love of Jesus. This country's tough on hitchers, not like Canada. I wanted to open tree temples all over the country, but the Baptists got sore because I was teaching a different doctrine. They said the temple would attract tramps, and they got the state to come out and run me off and tear it down. That's another instance in American history of showing spite for the underdog. But it proves there are a lot of ways to beat the rat race."

"You should write a book about it."

"I'd never write about that. This world isn't worth it. Stories are fine, but salvation is everything. I'll tell you, though, I might write a book about salvation. I'd call it *Hitching for Yahweh.*"

In a mountain valley full of greenness and blue water, we stopped to stretch. A historical marker explained the geology of the basin.

Bakke said, "That sign has a mistake. It says this valley was formed a million years ago, but the earth is only six thousand years old."

At Bonner's Ferry, where U.S. 2 ran a long, deep break in the Bitterroot Mountains, we turned toward Montana. I asked why he was going to El Salvador.

"My fiancée lives in San Salvador. I'm going there to get married and bring Carmen back if I can raise the money. She's a wonderful woman. Her love freed me from a ten-year obsession with a gospel singer. She's sixty and can't speak English and I don't speak Spanish so we have to get our letters translated. But I think maybe we could witness along the Mexican border."

He took out an envelope addressed to her. Inside was a letter and a paper placemat with a map of Idaho on it furnished by the state beef association. He marked our route for her and drew heavy X's through the word BEEF and the color pictures of rump roast and prime rib.

"What's going on there?"

"Just reminding Carmen we shouldn't eat things that hurt us: beef, pork, clams, oysters, prawns. Paul says, 'Meat commendeth us not to God.' "

I said, " 'Whatsoever is sold in the shambles, that eat, asking no questions for conscience' sake.' That's Paul too. Somewhere."

"You know Scripture?"

"Here and there. I know that one from arguing with a friend who became a vegetarian for a time."

"Well, then," Bakke said and buried me in quotation. I had fired my single salvo but hadn't sunk him.

"When the Bible has so many interpretations, how do you know your view is right?"

"I don't interpret. I read the Word as it is and trust the Lord to make me understand. And another thing: understanding depends on how well you know the whole Bible and how the parts fit in."

"You seem to know all the Bible well."

"I know the New Testament better than the Old. I read four Old Testament chapters and four New Testament chapters six days a week, so I get through the whole Bible about twice a year. But the New Testament is less than a third as long so I get through it more often." Bakke turned toward me. "I saw you reading this morning. Was it the Bible?"

"The journals of Lewis and Clark. Lewis was recounting his thirty-first birthday, which he spent not far from here. He surveyed his life and found he'd done very little with it. He vowed right then to live for others the way he had been living for himself."

"Some worldly books have the Spirit moving in them."

We rode silently for several miles, and Bakke dozed off. A bird swooped the highway and slammed into the hood. The clunk woke him. "What was that?"

"I hit a bird."

"Why are you stopping?"

"Want to see what kind of bird it is. Or was."

He got out too. I picked it up, a warm crumpled fluff limp in my hand, its talons clenched into tiny fists. "A sparrow hawk," I said.

"Throw it away."

" 'There is no object so soft but what it makes a hub for the wheeled universe.' The poet, Walt Whitman, said that."

Bakke smiled. We drove on along the Kootenai River, and he pointed out places that would be certain death if you slid off the pavement.

"I want to ask you something personal," I said. "Everything you own — other than your testimonies and typing paper — is in that aluminum suitcase?" He nodded. "Would you show me what's in there? I'm interested in how you've reduced your goods to that box."

"Never call them 'goods.' " He opened the little case and held up the contents one by one: two shirts, a pair of pants, underwear, toothbrush and paste, bar of soap, flashlight, candle, toilet paper, a corn muffin, and a bag of Jolly Time popcorn. "I try to 'live of the gospel,' as Paul says."

"I envy your simplicity."

"Paul says, 'Set your affection on things above, not on things on the earth.' Colossians three:two. The idea is to come away from things, away from ourselves, come away from it all toward God. Buying things is an escape. It's showing what you aren't. It's loving yourself."

I was still looking at the suitcase. "You've got necessities in one box, your work in a briefcase, a creed in your shirt pocket. I admire the compression of it. I wish I could reduce it all to a couple of boxes. I like your self-sufficiency."

"Don't give me so much credit. Paul preached how pride separates us from God." He opened his small Bible and read: " 'Walk not as other Gentiles walk, in the vanity of their mind, having the understanding darkened, being alienated from the life of God through the ignorance that is in them, because of the blindness in their heart.' Ephesians four:seventeen."

"Maybe so, but for basic necessity, you come close to material self-sufficiency." Bakke sat quietly. "The college students you talk to, they must admire your on-the-road work, your freedom."

"I don't think many would trade places with me. Would you?"

It was a terrible question.

"I don't have your belief or purpose. But I wish I knew what you know."

" 'Knowledge puffeth up, but charity edifieth. If any man think that he knoweth any thing, he knoweth nothing yet as he ought to know.' First Corinthians eight: one and two. Knowledge of the Lord is the knowledge worth knowing."

"Walt Whitman says, 'Be not curious about God, for I who am curious about each day am not curious about God.' " Bakke smiled again. "Now you're going to say mortal life is a troublous shadow, aren't you?"

" 'For what is your life? It is even a vapor, that appeaseth for a little time, and then vanisheth away.' James four:fourteen."

"I like little appeasing vapors."

16. Arthur O. Bakke outside Kalispell, Montana

" 'Let no man deceive himself. For the wisdom of this world is foolishness with God.' First Corinthians three: eighteen and nineteen."

" 'Why should I wish to see God better than this day?' Whitman, 'Song of Myself.' Here's another one from a Sioux medicine man called Black Elk: '*Whatever* you have seen, maybe it is for the good of the people you have seen it.' "

"Errors. To know God, to know the City of God — that's the only true life."

"Maybe this is the City of God."

"How could it be? The City of God has streets paved with transparent gold."

"Sounds pretty worldly. That's the standard account in Revelation, isn't it?"

"Yes, Revelation."

We rode on in silence to Kalispell, and Bakke dozed off again. I looked at him. He seemed one of those men who wander all their lives. In him was something restless and unsatisfied and ancient. He was going everywhere, anywhere, nowhere. He belonged to no place and was at home anyplace. He understood that the Bible, in spite of its light, isn't a particularly cheerful book, but rather one with much darkness, and he recognized that is where its power comes from.

Yet the word he carried to me wasn't of the City of God; it was of simplicity, spareness, courage, directness, trust, and "charity" in Paul's sense. He lived clean: mind, body, way of life. Hegel believed that freedom is knowledge of one's necessity, and Arthur O. Bakke, I.M.V., was a free man hindered only by his love and conviction. And that was just as he wanted it. I don't know whether he had been chosen to beat the highways and hedges, but clearly *he* had chosen to. Despite doctrinal differences, he reminded me of a Trappist monk or a Hopi shaman. I liked Arthur. I liked him very much.

Near Kalispell he woke up. I said, "I'll let you off at the junction of ninety-three so you can hitch toward Missoula."

"I could ride on with you. I know a friend in North Dakota."

"I've got to go alone, Arthur. For now, I have to go by myself. There'll be times when I'll wish for your company."

He hobbled out and came around to my window as gusts again pulled his beard sharply. We shook hands, and he said, "Carry God's blessing, brother."

"You'll be all right in this wind?"

" 'For I have learned, in whatever state I am, therewith to be content.' Phillippians four:eleven. Hardships are good. They prepare a man."

"I believe you."

4

THE boy was severely handicapped. Trying to fill a big thermos from a spring spewing out of the mountain east of Kalispell, near Hungry Horse, he laughed as the cold water splattered him, and he burbled something.

I had no idea what he said. "Very cold water indeed," I answered.

He burbled again, then lost his footing, and fell hard on the wet rocks. The gush hit the flask and kicked it away. I went to help him.

"Leave him alone!" someone shouted over the crash of water. A man who looked as if he'd swallowed a nail keg came toward us. "Let *him* do it. You'll make him weak if you do it for him. He's my son. He understands."

The boy struggled up and slipped and struggled again.

"I'll hand him the thermos."

"Let him get it." The boy retrieved the jug and went back to the big spout. He fell again, got up, and tried again.

"Grab on to the pipe!" I shouted, but he couldn't do it and hold the jug. The thermos bounced over to me. I picked it up and handed it to him.

"He'll never survive if he gets turned into a pussy," the father said.

"He'll never survive if he dies filling a thermos jug."

"Malarkey! We're on our way now to float a branch of the Flathead. That river's a bad-tempered horse, and you'd better stay on top of it, or it'll beat your liver out. This little gimp's got more white-water time than most of those canoe daredevils, and he can't even swim. Just never learned fear."

The boy succeeded in filling the jug. I filled mine and drank off a pint. My teeth ached from the cold, and I grimaced. The boy watched and did the same thing, but his grimace was too real.

"Glory is that cold!" I said to him. "And good!"

"Golden gud!" he repeated.

The father stepped in to fill a jug. "On our way home," he said with authority, "I'll fill a five-gallon can. I'll tell you something. I used to go through sixty suppositories a month — two a day. Last year, I started mixing this water with a teaspoon of cayenne and equal parts of nutmeg and flour. Now I don't even use six tablets a month."

"You attribute healing power to this water?"

"Water's got nothing to do with it. It's the cayenne, nutmeg, and flour."

"That's different."

"Nobody believes me. If you ever get hemorrhoids, try it, and don't worry about thanking me. I never could thank the old boy I got it from."

Eastward: U.S. 2 up the long canyon of the Middle Fork of the Flathead River. To the north, gusts scoured gritty snow from one wind-shorn peak to another: Mount Despair, Mount Rampage, Mount Scalplock, Mount Doody. In a crevasse I stopped to watch six mountain goats cling to the canyon wall. The mountain goat isn't a goat at all, but rather a relative of the antelope, and one proved it by bounding ledge to ledge, each time sticking like an arrow.

The highway ascended the west slope of the Continental Divide. In the middle of the pavement at the top of Marias Pass stood a tall limestone obelisk marking the divide and also commemorating Teddy Roosevelt. Your basic double-duty monument. Then the great mountains of the west lay behind, and, sweeping ahead, mile after terribly visible mile of roadway across a grandly canceled plateau, were the grasslands of the Big Sky country.

The state of Montana had marked spots of fatal car crashes with small, pole-mounted steel crosses: one cross for every death. Along the highway, as it traversed the Blackfeet reservation, the little white crosses piled up like tumbleweed: a single, a pair, a triple, a half dozen, a group of nine. What began as an automobile safety campaign, the Blackfoot — once among the best of Indian horsemen — had turned into roadside shrines by wiring on plastic flowers. Somebody later told me the abundance of crosses around the reservation was "proof" of chronic alcoholism.

The reservation town of Browning, unlike Hopi or Navajo settlements, was pure U.S.A.: an old hamburger stand of poured concrete in the shape of a tepee but now replaced by the Whoopie Burger drive-in, the War-bonnet Lodge motel, a Radio Shack, a Tastee-Freez. East of town I read a historical marker that said the Blackfeet had "jealously preserved their tribal customs and traditions." Render therefore unto Caucasians the things which be Caucasian.

At Cut Bank, the rangeland and wheat fields and oil wells began. Montanans call U.S. 2, paralleling the Canadian border all the way to Lake Huron, the "High-line." The most desolate of the great east-west routes, it was two lanes of patched, broken, rutted, mind-numbing pavement running from horizon to horizon over the land of god-awful distance.

I stopped at Shelby. Shelby used to be on the old Whoop-up Trail, a route followed by Missouri River whiskey traders who sold to Indians. What the U.S. Army could not accomplish — the destruction of tribal organization — whiskey traders did with help from Christian missionaries who suppressed the old rituals. The white settlers, moving in after tribal disintegration opened this land, should have erected a monument to the whiskey bottle. The Blackfoot, for example, once hunted an area about twice the size of Montana; now their reservation of steel crosses and Whoopie Burgers doesn't occupy even all of Glacier County. It isn't that Indians lost their land because of whiskey — that stuff they called the Great Father's Milk — they just lost it faster because of whiskey.

The Husky Cafe truck stop, glowing warm in the spring wind, was one of those places with a rack of joke postcards about fishing weekends, outhouses, mule cruppers ("I'm the one on the left"), and full-color photographs of spotted fawns and antlered jackrabbits. At the counter and tables sat the diesel boys in their adjustable, ventilated caps that said MACK, GMC, KENWORTH, WHITE.

I seldom go into truck stops. When I hear teamster cant about being the self-professed "son-of-a-bitches of the highway," when I hear stories of retreads shredding at seventy, when I watch drivers trying to recuperate on coffee and chili, and look at faces with eyes bloodshot from "pocket-rockets," and witness their ludicrous attempts to be folk heroes, I get very nervous the next time I see one pushing forty tons seventy miles an hour at me. But that night in Shelby, I didn't have much choice.

One eighteen-wheel stud said to the waitress, "Hun, you know, don't cha, that old truckers never die — they just get a new Peterbilt."

"I've heard that about a goddamn million times." She had the skin of a Dresden figurine and the mouth of a Fruehauf driver. "They say the drive in your shaft's about shot." Automatically she pushed a mug of coffee under my menu. "What's it for you, hoss?" Someone cracked another joke at her. Looking at me, answering him, she said, "Teach your old lady to suck eggs."

I ordered two eggs anyway, a slab of hashbrowns, and a cut of ham. The conversation next to me was about a trucker killed in a wreck. He had been pulling a "fatload" of fifty thousand pounds of hanging beef in a reefer well above legal speed.

"Heard Bouncer bought pork over to Black Eagle," one said. "Was he up?"

A garrulous teamster whose handle was Rubberlip said, "That wasn't it. Half-ton come on the other way and tossed a brick straight in the air and let him run into it. Half-ton was probably doing eighty so that brick come through the windshield at a hunerd and fifty mile an are."

"He had union problems all along."

"Ain't no tongue gonna tell for sure now, but that union bull is coverup. Some seatcover's old man finally got word on him. He'd pornicate a snake if you held its head."

The waitress slid a platter of three eggs down her arm.

"Only ordered two," I said.

"The eggs was small tonight."

5

WHAT does the traveler do at night in a strange town when he wants conversation? In the United States, there's usually a single choice: a tavern.

The Oil City Bar was north of the railroad tracks near the spot where the Great Northern accidentally founded Shelby in 1891 by dumping off an old boxcar. From it the town grew, and the antecedents still showed.

One of the authors of the Montana Federal Writers' Project describes Shelby in the 1890s as

> the sort of town that producers of western movies have ever since been trying to reproduce in papier-mâché. . . . The town playboys were featured in the *Police Gazette* after holding up an opera troupe passing through on a railroad train. . . . The men shot out the engine headlight, the car windows, and the red signal lights, and forced the conductor to execute a clog dance.

I was out looking around to see how the old Wild West was doing when I came across the Oil City Bar. Although the night had turned cold and gusty, only the screendoor was closed; the wooden one stood open so men in down vests wouldn't overheat. A shattered pool cue lay in the corner, and to one side was a small room lighted only by the blue neon flicker of a beer sign — the kind of light you could go mad in. Left of the ten-point buck trophy and above the gallon jars of pickled pig's feet and hard-boiled eggs hung a big lithograph of a well-formed woman, shotgun in hand. She was duck hunting. Other than her rubber boots, she wore not a stitch.

A man, somewhat taller than the barstool and dressed in yellow from shoulders to cowboy boots, drank with assembly-line regularity. He leered wobbly-eyed at the huntress, tried to speak, but blew a bubble instead.

I blame what was about to happen to him on the traditional design of the American bar: a straight counter facing a mirrored wall, which forces the customer to stare at himself or put a crick in his neck looking at someone else. The English build their bars in circles or horseshoes or right angles — anything to get another face in your line of sight. Their bars, as a result, are more sociable. For the American, he stares into his own face, or at bottles of golden liquors, or at whatever hangs above the bar; conversation declines and drinking increases. If the picture above the bar is a nude, as is common in old Western bars, you have an iconography for creating unfulfilled desire: the reality of a man's own six o'clock face below the dream of perfect flesh.

I turned away from the huntress to watch a pool game. There was a loud *flump* beside me. Knees to his chest, the man in yellow lay dead drunk on the floor. He looked like a cheese curl. His friend said, "Chuckie's one good little drinker."

A woman of sharp face, pretty ten years ago, kept watching me. She had managed to pack her hips into what she hoped was a pair of mean jeans; a cigarette was never out of her mouth, and, after every deep draw, her exhalations were smokeless. She was trying for trouble, but I minded my own business. More or less. The man with her, Lonnie, walked up to me. He looked as if he were made out of whipcord. "Like that lady?" he said.

"What lady is that?"

"One you been staring at."

"Without my glasses, I can't distinguish a man from a woman." That was a lie.

"The lady said you were distinguishing her pretty good."

Well, boys, there you have it. Some fading face trying to make herself the center of men's anger, proving she could still push men to their limits.

"Couldn't recognize her from here if I did know her."

He pressed up close. Trouble coming. "Don't tell *me*," he said. "Happens all the time. She thinks men stare at her."

"Look. No offense, but I've no interest in the woman."

"I can see it, and she can see it, and that's the trouble. But let's talk."

It was an act he had been coerced into. He was faking it. He called for two beers and set one in front of me. "Take it," he said. "When I sit down, I'm going to tell her you apologized for staring but you just thought she was one hell of a fox. Don't make a liar out of me."

He walked off. That was the silliest row I never got into.

I went to the restroom. When I came out, Lonnie was standing at the bar and the woman had gone to sit with three other women. She didn't buy it, I thought. DRIFTER BLOWN AWAY IN BAR.

"Trouble?" I said.

"Forget it. She works with those broads. Casterating bitches every one."

There was a commotion that got loud and moved outside to the windy street. Two men from Mountain Bell, the phone company, were going to fight. They came at each other, locked outstretched arms and pushed, circling slowly as if turned by the prairie wind. They tired and revolved slower, but neither let go or fell down. A police car drove up and honked. The fighters went to the squadcar, both leaning on the window to listen. After a while, they slumped off in opposite directions, and that was the end of it.

Lonnie and I watched from the bar. After it was over, he said, "Jack Dempsey had a real fight here."

"A fight in this very bar?"

"Not a bar fight — heavyweight boxing. Shelby built a grandstand for it. Forty thousand seats. Seven thousand people showed up. Town almost went bust."

The woman came over to Lonnie and said, "Let's go." She was mad. I left soon after, walking out into the streets of the new Wild West.

6

THE first thing I knew that morning in Shelby was that I was catching cold. My throat felt like a cat had got a paw down it and scratched out a strip. Then I saw the day: blustery and foul. I went back to the Husky grill and let them fill me with potato-skin hashbrowns and eggs and their hot, fierce coffee. I was trying to burn out the cold, the weather, trying to get ready for a long passage across the Great Plains of the North.

A man wearing denim — hat, jacket, pants, boots, and probably even his shorts — sat down beside me. "Is that your truck with the Missouri tags?" he asked. I told him it was. He said, "Shoulda named the Missouri River 'the Montana,' you know. That dammed river, and I'm not cussing, is born, you might say, due south of here a ways. And we got more miles of it than you people down south."

"Might as well call the Mississippi 'the Minnesota' then," I said. "Anyway, explorers named the Missouri after Indians who lived along it."

"So where'd those Indians live?"

"In Missouri."

"That's what I'm saying. Doesn't stand to reason."

"The men who named it didn't know where the river came from. They saw the bottom end first."

"That's how the jackass got named."

I asked where he was from. "Next county over. Liberty County. Only three other Liberty counties in the country. For the talking Americans do about freedom, I'd say that's interesting. Tell me a county not named after a man or an Indian tribe."

"Well, you have . . . there's . . ." I couldn't do it.

"Three thousand and some counties in the country and half are Jefferson, Jackson, Johnson, Monroe, Madison, Washington, or Lincoln. What's your county?"

"Born in Jackson but I live in Boone."

He smiled. "I've studied it. In Montana we got Beaverhead, Deer Lodge, Silver Bow, Petroleum, Sweet Grass, Wheatland, Rosebud. Even one called Musselshell. But the nation's got a problem — no counties left to name things after. No rivers or mountains either. Got to use freeways now."

He started to say something else when a woman put her head in the door and blasted us with cold, wet air. "Clay! Late again!" she shouted.

"Coming," he said. "So long, Jackson."

"Talk about names," a man who sold potato chips said and pushed a receipt in front of me:

FIRST AND LAST CHANCE LIQUORS
202 BRONTOSAURUS BLVD.
DINOSAUR, COLORADO

"Try spelling Brachiosaurus Bypass or Triceratops Terrace in the morning," he said.

Time for the road. People who equate travel with getting the miles behind them love U.S. 2 as it strikes a more or less flat, straight line for a thousand miles across the north. The great ice sheets cut the tops off the hills and dumped glacial debris in the valleys so that nothing interrupts the rush of wind off the east slopes of the Rockies.

On that May morning the wind came strong at my back, and the square stern of Ghost Dancing served as sail; even resting easy on the accelerator, I blew past clusters of buildings that had got in the way of 2 so they could call themselves towns: Joplin, Rudyard, Hingham, Gildford, Kremlin. Russian settlers, half mad from the vast openness and the sway of prairie grass, thought they saw the Citadel of Moscow. Tractor-trailers, noses to the wind, hammers to the floor, highballed west, drivers rapt in the CB chatter of their cabs. The mountains would slow them, but they had the Great Plains behind.

What little topographical relief there was came from creeks notching the tablelands. Cottonwoods, like cattle, followed the streambeds for water and escape from the wind. Indian children used to twirl leaves of the holy tree of life into toy tepees, and women made a brew from the inner bark to soothe stomach disorders; sprigs fed Indian ponies in winter, the catkins lured grouse in spring, and in summer everyone searched hollows of the trunks for wild honey. A white, inner pulp furnished a delicacy later called "cottonwood ice cream." When settlers arrived, they cut the biggest cottonwoods for lumber although it was prone to warping; and Missouri rivermen fueled steamboats with it. White men learned they needed the tree too, so they set out thousands of seedlings, but today the cottonwood still keeps to the streams as if it knows the primogeniture of the grasses.

Clear Creek, typically, ran full with an earthen goo the ducks could walk more easily than swim, but it was the only surface water for miles. Yet the language of the plains harks to the ocean: pioneers came in "prairie schooners" (some even rigged with sails) and spoke of the "sea of grass" and the "prairie ocean," and they cured hangovers with calf ballocks they called "prairie oysters." Maybe the sodbusters saw seascapes in the undulations of the grasses or in the immensity of sky or in the lack of refuge from wind and storm. Perhaps a sea crossing was still in the minds of the newest immigrants. And maybe also, their words expressed a prescient awareness of the tug between coming and going; for the buffalo grass, the wheat and rye spring from the limestone bones of ichthyosaurs and plesiosaurs lying under stony blankets of the ancient seabed where molecules turn to soil and cellulose. Perhaps those people of the land knew the cycle (Whitman's "perpetual transfers"): that time mineral, this time vegetable, next time animal, sometime man.

The grasses. Mile after mile after mile. Miles. Then mile marker 465. By afternoon, half of Montana still lay ahead, with the even flatter plains of North Dakota yet to come. For a state whose name is "mountain," Montana shows thousands of miles of level prairie. I've read that if all the space *within* the atoms of the earth were pressed out, the planet would have a diameter of three hundred twenty-eight feet — not even the distance of a good major league homerun. I don't know whether it's possible to believe that figure, but I do know if you're driving across Montana you'll never believe it.

Pock-pock went the tarred road cracks. *Pock-pock*. The day remained dark, showers fell and stopped and came again, the uneven roadway collected water, the van hydroplaned every few minutes. The clamor of wind numbed my ears; the fever made me woozy. *Pock-pock*. First the highway held me, then it entered me, then I was the highway. *Pock-pock, pock-pock*. Prairie hypnosis. I drove miles I couldn't remember, and the land became a succession of wet highway stripes, and I wished for a roadfellow. I sat blindly, dumbly like a veiled stone sphinx. Finally, to dispel the miles, I stopped, got out, and held my face to the rain. I shook myself. But, once more on the road, I again became part of the machine: generator, accelerator, humanator. I knew nothing. A stupefied nub on the great prairie.

East of where the muddy Milk River begins rubbing its back against the highway, I stopped again, climbed a fence, and walked out to a pair of rusty boulders that an ice sheet dropped on its northward retreat. Stones like these the Indians carved into billboards, scorecards, boundary markers, prayer books. I hoped for a message from the first people, but the stones sat as featureless as the land.

Back in the truck, I fired my little stove to heat water for coffee. I threw in some cocoa for energy, and sat, and watched, and sipped. The prairie was blowing and gray, interrupted here and about by the white faces of Herefords. A century ago the Sioux tribes — Assiniboines ("stone boilers") and Gros Ventres ("big bellies") — who hunted bison on these plains, found in those descendants of the mastodons a four-legged grocery, hardware, and dry goods store. For generations the people stalked buffalo and dried and pulverized the meat and mixed it with bone-marrow grease and wild berries and packed it in buffalo skin bags. The pemmican lasted indefinitely and had ten times the nutrient value of fresh meat. Tanned bison hides gave the Sioux shelters and bedding, moccasins, leggings, shields, boats, buckets, even vessels to boil food in. Horn and bone gave spikes, drills, knives, scrapers, axes, and spoons. Ribs and jawbones provided children with snowsleds. The hooves furnished glue, the scat heat. When a Sioux finished with a buffalo, he had used all of it, even its spirit, for it was the bearded buffalo, alive and dangerous, weighing nearly a ton, snorting and short-tempered, that stood at the heart of the rituals and religion of the Plains Indians. Until the ghost dance generation — the one that kissed the old life goodbye to face an enemy future — the tribes that dominated these grasslands for eight thousand years fought most of their battles over hunting territory. The red man ate buffalo (transubstantiation in the Indian manner), he dressed in buffalo, he imitated and talked to it, and he died for and by the sacred buffalo.

Then the future came wearing shoes cut out of cows and pants woven on a machine. It found bison a nuisance. The beasts took valuable grass from cattle, stampeded crops, interrupted trains, knocked over telegraph lines. And so the American bison, a symbol to both red and white, disappeared even faster than the way of life it engendered.

I put my mug away as the unsexed Hereford steers chewed blankly in the grasses where once buffalo bulls, shaggy pizzles almost touching the ground, red eyes glaring over their females, had roamed. I remembered reading that one out of nine beef cows ends up in a McDonald's hamburger. The sky had been cloudy all day, and now I'd just heard a discouraging word.

Again to the *pock-pocking*. The road shook and pounded me, the seat slammed my spine, the steering wheel rattled my knuckles. I felt like a watch in a Timex commercial; I could hear John Cameron Swayze: "We strapped this man in a truck on a Montana highway for two days. He took a licking, but . . ." etc. I turned on the radio. Amidst the crackles, a revivalist was at work on a sermon shot through with real thunderbolts. Between heavenly interferences, I heard his amazing-grace voice: "Thou knowest, O Lord, we shall pass this way but once." Amen.

Darkness came early. At Wolf Point, a lightning storm struck the benchland, rain dropped in noisy assaults, and I took refuge in town. Dim houses, bound in by nothing but the Missouri River on the south, huddled each to the other, and streets were slick with mud and full of brown pools. I had to go back to the highway for dinner at a truck stop. Something moved in there — I couldn't say what. Six people sat in the cafe, in the light and warmth, almost assured by the jukebox, and filled their stomachs; yet there was an edge to the voices, to the faces. From a thousand feet up, the prairie storm, pouring cold water on the little cafe glowing in the blackness, held us all. Even as we ate our soup and steak and eggs, we felt the sky.

Again into town. A foot of oily water swirled in a railroad underpass where two cars had collided. A police light twisted, turning raindrops crimson, and a man's still face pressed against the window. I slipped past and found a street for the night. The rain, hostile and forbidding, thundered on the steel roof. Unable to see anything in the deep black, I crawled into the sleeping bag and listened to the tumult.

One November in another century, before Wolf Point had a name, the citizens complained of wolves. They got together and set out poison, and the varmints died all over the prairie, and townsmen stacked a thousand frozen carcasses into high mounds that stood all winter. When spring came, the mounds thawed and rotted. One man thought the stink drove away the remaining wolves. Whatever it was, nobody saw a wolf alive, and nobody since has seen one here. On my night in Wolf Point, Montana, I couldn't imagine man or beast contending for the place.

7

In Poplar, Montana, where Sitting Bull surrendered six years after the Battle of the Little Big Horn, I stopped for groceries. Having resisted a chewing hunger for five days — before meals, after meals, in moments of half-sleep — I gave in to it east of Wolf Point and bought a pound of raisins, a pound of peanuts, a pound of chocolate nibs and mixed them together. By the time I got across North Dakota, the bag was empty, the hunger gone.

U.S. 2 followed the Missouri River for miles. At the High-line town of Culbertson I turned north toward treeless Plentywood, Montana, then went east again down forsaken blue highway 5, a road virtually on the forty-ninth parallel, which is the Canadian border in North Dakota. In a small flourish of hills, the last I was to see for hundreds of miles, on an upthrusted lump sat a cube of concrete with an Air Force radar antenna sweeping the long horizon for untoward blips. A Martello tower of the twentieth century. Below the installation, in the Ice Age land, lay a fine, clear lake. Fingerlings whisked the marsh weed, coots twittered on the surface, and at bankside a muskrat munched greens. It seemed as if I were standing between two worlds. But they were one: a few permutations of life going on about themselves, each thing trying to continue its way.

East of Fortuna, North Dakota, just eight miles south of Saskatchewan, the high moraine wheat fields took up the whole landscape. There was nothing else, except piles of stones like Viking burial mounds at the verges of tracts and big rock-pickers running steely fingers through the glacial soil to glean stone that freezes had heaved to the surface; behind the machines, the fields looked vacuumed. At a filling station, a man who long had farmed the moraine said the great ice sheets had gone away only to get more rock. "They'll be back. They always come back. What's to stop them?"

The country gave up the glacial hills and flattened to perfection. The road went on, on, on. Straight and straight. Ahead and behind, it ran through me like an arrow. North Dakota up here was a curveless place; not just roads but land, people too, and the flight of birds. Things were angular: fenceposts against the sky, the line of a jaw, the ways of mind, the lay of crops.

The highway, oh, the highway. No place, in theory, is boring of itself. Boredom lies only with the traveler's limited perception and his failure to explore deeply enough. After a while, I found my perception limited. The Great Plains, showing so many miles in an immodest exposure of itself, wearied my eyes; the openness was overdrawn. The only mitigation came from potholes ice sheets had gouged out; there, margins and water were full of stilt-legged birds — godwits, sandpipers, plovers, dowitchers, avocets, yellowlegs — and paddling birds — coots, mallards, canvasbacks, redheads, blue-winged teals, pintails, shovelers, scaups, mergansers, eared grebes, widgeons, Canada geese. Whenever the drone of tread against pavement began to overcome me, I'd stop and shake the drowsiness among the birds.

You'd think anything giving variety to this near blankness would be prized, yet when a Pleistocene pond got in the way, the road cut right through it, never yielding its straightness to nature. If you fired a rifle down the highway, a mile or so east you'd find the spent slug in the middle of the blacktop.

Here the earth, as if to prove its immensity, empties itself. Gertrude Stein said: "In the United States there is more space where nobody is than where anybody is. That is what makes America what it is." The uncluttered stretches of the American West and the deserted miles of roads force a lone traveler to pay attention to them by leaving him isolated in them. This squander of land substitutes a sense of self with a sense of place by giving him days of himself until, tiring of his own small compass, he looks for relief to the bigness outside — a grandness that demands attention not just for its scope, but for its age, its diversity, its continual change. The isolating immensity reveals what lies covered in places noisier, busier, more filled up. For me, what I saw revealed was this (only this): a man nearly desperate because his significance had come to lie within his own narrow ambit.

Onward across the appallingly featureless yonder of North Dakota where towns, like the poor verse of Burma Shave signs, came and went quickly; on across fields where farmers planted wheat, rye, barley, and flax, their tractors sowing close to fences marking off missile silos that held Minutemen waiting in the dark underground like seeds of another sort. As daylight went, the men, racing rain and the short growing season, switched on headlights to keep the International Harvesters moving over cropland that the miracles of land-grant colleges (cross-pollinated hybrids resistant to everything but growth and petrochemicals) had changed forever. The farmer's enemy wasn't a radar blip — it was the wild oat.

At last the horizon ruptured at the long hump of Turtle Mountain, obscurely scrubby against the sky, and a pair of silent owls (Indians called them "hush wings") swooped the dusk to look for telltale movements in the fields.

I needed a hot shower. In Rolla, on the edge of the Turtle Mountain reservation, I stopped at an old house rebuilt into a small hotel. Despite a snarl of a clerk, it looked pleasant; but the floors smelled of disinfectant and the shower was a rusting box at the end of the hall. The nozzle sent one stinging jet of water into my eye, another up my nose, two others over the shower curtain, while most of the water washed down the side to stand icily in the plugged bottom. I lost my temper and banged the shower head. The Neanderthal remedy.

In a hotel room at the geographical center of North America, a neon sign blinking red through the cold curtains, I lay quietly like a small idea in a vacant mind.

8

EAST of Rolla. After breakfast in the city park at Langdon, a Nordic town of swept streets and tidy pastel houses with pastel shutters at the picture windows, a town with the crack of Little League bats in the clear Saturday air, a town of blond babies and mothers wearing one hundred percent acrylics and of husbands washing pastel cars to kill time before the major league Game of the Week, this happened:

In the park, a man walking with a child saw me staring at a "retired" Spartan missile that now apparently served the same function as court-house lawn fieldpieces with little pyramids of cannonballs once did. The white Spartan, a skeletal finger pointing into the beyond, was undefaced by initials, lovers' notations, graduating class years, or spray-can anarchy. The only blemishes were a smudgy ring of handprints from children who had tested the reality of the thing and, penciled small near the bottom as if to hide it, this:

> WARNING: THE SURGEON GENERAL HAS DETERMINED
> THAT SMOKING ICBM'S ARE DANGEROUS TO YOUR HEALTH.

"She's a nuke," the father said with proprietary pride. His shirt-sleeves were rolled to the elbows, and he carried a full complement of ballpoint pens in a plastic pocket protector above his heart. "We're lucky to have her here. Came from a silo down at Nekoma. Air Force selected our town."

"I've seen a lot of missile installations along the highway."

"Make you feel good, don't they? Proud and taken care of, like."

"Taken care of — that's it."

"From a distance, in the right light, this bird looks like a church steeple. And I promise you, if these things ever start flying, she'll be the mother we'll be praying to."

"Our Lady of the Unholy Boom?"

He ignored me. "I don't mean these old Spartans, of course. I'm talking about the new Minutemen. Or the MX when it gets approved — and it will. Ten nuke warheads on the MX."

His daughter fell in the grass. Without a drop of irony, he cautioned her to be careful.

"Do you believe they'll be used?" I asked.

"This one's deactivated, of course. But I promise you we're ready for the Soviets up here. That border is only seventeen miles away. You ask if they'll ever be fired. As long as Moscow is insane for conquest, don't bet against it." He waited for a response, then flagged his arm to the northeast. "Wahalla's the next town over, and you know what that is."

"What is it?"

"The home of warriors slain in battle. The place the Valkyrie carry heroes to. We're ready here on the perimeter."

"The Air Force is ready, you mean."

"I don't tell tales out of school, but some of us are personally equipped."

"With what?"

"Let's just say we have basements stocked for whoever crosses that border."

"I hope you don't have the other cast-off ICBM's in your rumpus rooms."

"Everybody worries about ICBM's. We live on top of them up here. We grow the bread you *and* the Russians eat right over the missiles. You want to worry? Worry about IBM. Worry about bug bombs. But with what the generals got over there in the Ukraine — those ICBM's that carry ten times the kilotons of our biggest — don't fret yourself about this baby." Parentally patting the Spartan, he dislodged the ballpoints in his pocket protector, then repositioned them precisely to make sure he would reach the aftermath free of ink stains.

9

THERE was something stretched about the landscape as if all dimension but length had been pulled from it. It seemed incapable of hiding anything. That may be why I was surprised when route 5 dropped sharply off the Drift Plains into another dimension of the tree-filled valley of the Tongue River. The buffy western soil was now the color of hazelnuts, and I knew I was nearly across the prairie.

The nickname of North Dakota is the "Flickertail State." That morning I saw why. Mile after mile, the small ground squirrels stood at attention along the highway. As my truck approached one, the little rodent would make a madcap, high-tailed dash for the other side, only to stop a couple of feet from the shoulder before turning around and making a last-ditch dive for the side it had started from. Again and again it happened. It looked like some sort of crazy game in which the losers were mashed clots of fur. Over many of the flattened rodents, a second one stood; I thought they mourned, but someone later told me flickertails have a keen tooth for flickertail flesh.

A sign pointed north to Backoo. Backoo, North Dakota, may not be the only town in America named after an Australian river (the Barcoo), but then again, maybe it is. I went to see it, or, as it turned out, to see what was left, which was: the Burlington Northern tracks, a grain elevator, grocery, boarded-up school, church, and a thimble of a post office. The town had closed for Saturday, so I started back to the highway when the smell of gasoline stopped me. I lifted the hood. The fuel line below the gas filter had split and was arcing a fine jet of no-lead into the sunlight. I tried to wire it closed, but it didn't work.

I made for Cavalier, the nearest town. Had I not gone to Backoo, the line would have ruptured *in* Cavalier instead of miles up the road. So logic would dictate. The fact is, engine malfunctions happen only in places like Backoo, North Dakota. Axiom of the blue road. The gauge — visibly — dropped toward E, and the long miles went on. Damn, did they go on.

I couldn't remember how much money I had left, but I did know strangers with stalled vehicles get soaked in isolated towns. Axiom of the blue road. That two-inch plastic gas line, of course, should cost no more than a quarter, but in the realm of high technology you don't figure the simplicity or inexpense of an element, you calculate availability.

At Cavalier I pulled into the first garage I saw, and a teenaged boy with the belly of a man came out and stared. People don't just throw words around in the North. I lifted the hood to show him the line. I didn't speak either.

"Sumbitch's likely to catch fire!" he said.

"I know that. Can you fix it?"

"Pull the sumbitch in the bay fast and shut her down. Goddamn!" He backed off a safe distance as I drove in.

"Have you got that hose?" Here it comes, I thought.

He pointed toward a big coil of hose hanging on the greasy wall. "Fix every sumbitch in the state if we had to." The boy's blackened hands grappled with the connection. He struggled, cut himself, cursed, and took off on an analgesic tour of the grease pit, blood seeping from his oily finger. I picked up the pliers and tried to free the clamp. My hand slipped as the connection popped loose, and I cut my finger. The boy sliced a piece of hose off the coil and clamped it in place. "That'll take care of the sumbitch," he said.

"Very speedy service. What do I owe you?" Here we go.

"A dime for the hose and two bucks for labor — that'll take care of the leak. But it won't do nothing about the real problem under your hood." Here it comes for sure. "Water pump's about to go." He grabbed the fan blades and pulled them back and forth. "Shouldn't be no play in the fan. When those bearings give, fan's coming through your radiator and that'll be all she wrote."

"I've been keeping an eye on it."

"How long's it been like that?"

"About nine thousand miles, I guess."

He slapped his forehead to indicate my stupidity. "Suummbitch!"

"Trying to buy a little time."

"You're gonna buy a lot more than time when that sumbitch goes. I wouldn't even drive the sumbitch to Hoople."

"How far's Hoople?"

"Eighteen miles."

"Can you fix it?"

"Wouldn't try. Take the sumbitch to the Ford dealer."

So I did. The service man said, "Can't get parts on Saturday. In fact, I couldn't get a pump before Monday afternoon — if then. All of our parts come out of Grand Forks, so you might as well drive down there yourself."

"Can I make it?" For nine thousand miles I hadn't worried, but now I worried about seventy.

"*Quién sabe*, podnah? You know? Maybe you make it home. Then again, maybe you won't make it to Hoople."

I went down state 18 toward Grand Forks and wondered what this Hoople place was that figured as a basic guide to distance in Pembina County, North Dakota. I couldn't get to Grand Forks before five o'clock, so I drove slowly, relaxed in my fate. The truck had carried me to the Atlantic Ocean and then to the Pacific and halfway back to the Atlantic. But now, of course, the sumbitch might not make it to Hoople.

10

WHO in America would guess that Grand Forks, North Dakota, was a good place to be stuck in with a bad water pump? Skyscrapers from the thirties, clean as a Norwegian kitchen, a state university with brick, big trees, and ivy. On Monday morning the pump got replaced in an hour for $37.50. I had expected to be taken for three times that figure, but I met only honest people.

I drove up the valley of the Red River of the North (which empties into Hudson Bay) and crossed into Oslo, Minnesota. Near Viking, tall stalks from the sunflower crop of a year earlier rattled in the warm wind. For miles I had been seeing a change in the face of the Northland brought about because Americans find it easier to clean house paint out of brushes with water than with turpentine. This area once grew much of the flax that linseed oil comes from, but with the advent of water-base paint, the demand for flax decreased; in its stead, of all things, came the sunflower, and now it was becoming the big cash crop of the Dakotas and Minnesota — with more acreage going each year to new hybrids developed from Russian seeds — because "flower" is a row crop that farmers can economically reap by combine after the grain harvest.

Thief River Falls, another town of Nordic cleanliness, reportedly got its name through an odd mingling of history and language. A group of Dakota Sioux lived on the rich hunting grounds here for some years. Although the bellicose Chippewa controlled the wooded territory, the Dakotas managed to conceal a remote settlement by building an earthen wall around it and disappearing inside whenever the enemy came near. They even hunted with bows and arrows rather than risk the noise of guns. But the Chippewa finally found them out and annihilated them. Because the mounds hid a portion of the river, the Chippewa referred to it as "Secret Earth River." Through some error, early white traders called it "Stealing Earth River"; through additional misunderstanding, it came to be "Thief River." As for Crookston downstream, it took its name from a railroad man.

South of Thief River Falls, on U.S. 59, I crossed the Clearwater River; but this one, unlike a dozen others of that name I'd seen in the past weeks, was true to its description. It drained a country that became increasingly heavy with aspen, birch, pine, and spruce. I had come to the western edge of the North Woods. The prairie was gone.

On the Clearwater River and upstream from Clearwater Lake and down the highway from the hamlet of Clearbrook was the seat of Clearwater County: Bagley, a village with pines and a blue lake, a village where the names on the buildings were Lukkasson, Olson, Peterson, Lundmark. I stopped for the night and went to the Viking House Cafe for a Viking omelette (cheese, ham, green peppers, onions) and a chocolate milkshake. To the waitress in long flaxen braids, I said, "Who's the most famous native son of Bagley, Minnesota?"

"Oh, my golly! I'll ask the cook." When she returned with dinner, she said, "That would be Richard Davids, author of *How to Talk to Birds*."

Two old men, spectacles like dusty windows, sat slurping broth and arguing about Indian net fishing on the Lake of the Woods Reservation in the Northwest Angle, the northernmost part of the lower forty-eight.

"I never cut an Indian net," one said, "but I never discouraged a fishing partner from cutting. No redskin should have to buy a license to fish reservation land, but he ought to fish fair."

The words came slowly, with long pauses; in the silences, the soft clacking of dentures. "Indians got first rights," the other said. "They fish for a living. You fish for fun."

"Law's law or it ain't law."

The waitress said, "You boys on the fishing rights again?"

They had trouble hearing her, although she spoke louder than either of them. Maybe, after so many years, they didn't need to hear each other.

Louder, she asked, "Who won the argument tonight?"

"I did," they said.

"It's a good friendship where everyone's a winner."

"What's that, honey?" they said.

I walked down to the bakery, the one with flour sacks for sale in the front window and bowling trophies above the apple turnovers. The people of the northern midlands — the Swedes and Norgies and Danes — apparently hadn't heard about the demise of independent, small-town bakeries; most of their towns had at least one.

With a bag of blueberry tarts, I went up Main to a tin-sided, false-front tavern called Michel's, just down the street from the Cease Funeral Home. The interior was log siding and yellowed knotty pine. In the backroom the Junior Chamber of Commerce talked about potatoes, pulpwood, dairy products, and somebody's broken fishing rod. I sat at the bar. Behind me a pronghorn antelope head hung on the wall, and beside it a televised baseball game cast a cool light like a phosphorescent fungus.

"Hear that?" a dwindled man asked. He was from the time when boys drew "Kilroy-Was-Here" faces on alley fences. "Did you hear the announcer?"

"I wasn't listening."

"He said 'velocity.' "

"Velocity?"

"He's talking about a fastball. A minute ago he said a runner had 'good acceleration.' This is a baseball game, not a NASA shot. And another thing: I haven't heard anybody mention a 'Texas leaguer' in years."

"It's a 'bloop double' now, I think."

"And the 'banjo hitter' — where's he? And what happened to the 'slow ball'?"

"It's a 'change-up.' "

The man got me interested in the game. We watched and drank Grain Belt. He had taught high school civics in Minneapolis for thirty-two years, but his dream had been to become a sports announcer.

"They put a radar gun on the kid's fastball a few minutes ago," he said. "Ninety-three point four miles per hour. That's how they tell you speed now. They don't try to show it to you: 'smoke,' 'hummer,' 'the high hard one.' I miss the old clichés. They had life. Who wants to hit a fastball with a decimal point when he can tie into somebody's 'heat'? And that's another thing: nobody 'tattoos' or 'blisters' the ball anymore. These TV boys are ruining a good game because they think if you can see it they're free to sit back and psychoanalyze the team. Ask and I'll tell you what I think of it."

"What do you think of it?"

"Beans. And that's another thing too."

"Beans?"

"Names. Used to be players named Butterbean and Big Potato, Little Potato. Big Poison, Little Poison. Dizzy and Daffy. Icehouse, Shoeless Joe, Suitcase, The Lip. Now we've got the likes of Rickie and Richie and Reggie. With names like that, I think I'm watching a third-grade scrub team."

The announcer said the pitcher had "good location."

"Great God in hemlock! He means 'nibble the corners.' But which of these throwing clowns nibbles corners? They're obsessed with speed. Satchel Paige — there's a name for you — old Satch could fire the pill a hundred and five miles an hour. He didn't throw it that fast very often because he couldn't make the ball cut up at that speed. And, sure as spitting, his pitching arm lasted just about his whole life."

The man took a long smacking pull on his Grain Belt. "Damn shame," he said. "There's a word for what television's turned this game into."

"What's the word?"

"Beans," he said. "Nothing but beans and hot air."

11

WERE it not for a web-footed rodent and a haberdashery fad in eighteenth-century Europe, Minnesota might be a Canadian province today. The beaver, almost as much as the horse, helped shape the course of early American history. Some *Mayflower* colonists paid their passage with beaver pelts; and a good fur could bring an Indian three steel knives or a five-foot stack could bring a musket. But even more influential were the trappers and fur traders penetrating the great Northern wilderness between the Mississippi River and Rocky Mountains, since it was their presence that helped hold the Near West against British expansion from the north; and it was their explorations that opened the heart of the nation to white settlement. These men, by making pelts the currency of the wilds, laid the base for a new economy that quickly overwhelmed the old. And all because European men of mode simply had to wear a beaver hat.

That morning in Clearwater County, I was thinking about the beaver after one surfaced near where I had knelt to taste a stream coming from a dark, slick lake leaking spirals of mist. In a narrow strip of sky opening above the brook, a great blue heron somehow got its bulk airborne without snaring immense wings and long dangling legs in the close mesh of branches.

The lake was Itasca and the stream, a twelve-inch-deep rush of cold clarity over humps of boulders, was the Mississippi River. I crossed it in five steps. The Father of Waters, beginning a two-thousand-mile journey to join the source of all waters, was here a newborn — small and pure.

The name "Itasca," despite its Indian sound, came from two Latin words, *veritas caput* ("true head"), that Henry Rowe Schoolcraft assembled. Schoolcraft — led by the Chippewa, Yellow Head — traced the Mississippi to Itasca in order to settle an old dispute about the source of the river (the fact is, several ponds feed Itasca). He recorded in his log that the area was full of "voracious, long-billed, dyspeptic mosquitoes," and another explorer wrote that a swarm extinguished his lantern flame. A century and a half later, the dark timber still sounded with their whine, their proboscises were still alarmingly large and powerful. With every swat, I splattered a dozen bloody bugs over pants and shirt. An ordinary mosquito can penetrate the tough scutum of a rattlesnake, but Northwoods species can pierce the rind of stones.

Highway 200 took me eastward into the forest, past No Name Road. Late spring had been creeping north, and suddenly that day it pounced. Nobody was ready for the eighty-two degrees. At Walker on the south shore of Leech Lake, I stopped at the county museum; it was closed, but the handyman, John Day, let me in to fill my water jugs. He was half Chippewa and half French, and his son was legal counsel to the litigious Chippewa tribe living on the big reservation here. Day had been in the fifth assault wave on Iwo Jima and still limped from shrapnel he caught on the island.

"This could be July," he said. "It can hit a hundred and five in July, and forty-five below in January. One hundred and fifty degrees of temperature is how we keep the riffraff out. When that doesn't do it, then it's up to the mosquitoes and leeches. If it wasn't for them, and another thing or two, this piece of God's country would be overrun with people."

I took a slug of cold water from my jug and nearly choked. I'd just found one of the other things: drinking water that tasted like a mouthful of raw pig iron. Day said, "You see?"

He had retired from his job as a school custodian and lived now on Social Security, a Marine disability pension, and another from the school system. He worked at the museum for the occupation of it.

"I never worried about making a living," he said, "but I've done thinking about making a life. It's hard to know the difference sometimes, and it must be getting harder, judging by all them that don't know the difference now."

"What is the difference?"

"Best way to tell it is that if you're trying to make a killing, what's going to get killed is your life."

The highway out of Walker went through Whipholt, past the roads to the Indian towns of Boy River, Federal Dam, and Ball Club. The land alternated between marsh and aspen woods filled with white blossoms of wake robin. I came to the Mississippi again at Jacobson and stopped to get off the hot asphalt. The river was wider here, and it took me three attempts to shy a rock across. I walked up along the banks. The Mississippi, not a hundred water miles from its source, already flowed in olive murkiness.

Late afternoon. Downtown Duluth, if you ask me, hangs a little precariously to a volcanic bluff that drops six hundred feet to Lake Superior. The city revived in cool air that began to move off the blue lake stretching far eastward, finally so blending with sky that a horizon was almost indiscernible. It was as if Duluth sat on an edge of infinite blueness. The largest fresh water lake in the world (its volume is considerably greater than all the other Great Lakes combined), Superior is so big it has a three-inch tide.

Before the St. Lawrence Seaway made Duluth the most western Atlantic port, people used to say it was an old maid city looking under the bed each night for an ocean. Now Duluth has its ocean, and some citizens dream of a new Chicago here, although a lake that can freeze over for twenty miles out one-quarter of the year is something of a hindrance.

On Superior Street I ate smoked cisco, then crossed the bridge above St. Louis Bay into Superior, Wisconsin, then down broad and empty Belknap Street running from the ore docks past old walk-ups and corner taverns, on to route 35, and out of the city. It was dark when I turned south, and I couldn't find a place for the night. Pattison State Park drove me away with a board full of regulations. The map promised Moose Junction, Dairyland, Cozy Corners — towns that proved either no longer to exist or to be three houses and a barn. Somewhere in Douglas County I began falling asleep at the wheel. I pulled up a side road.

Combing fingers through my dusty hair, my thumb struck a growth near my temple. I pushed back the hair and looked in the mirror. A goddamned tick. Another of those little things that keeps the riffraff out of God's North country. I tweezered it out, undressed, and looked for more. One crawling my leg, one my shirt. I put a match to them. If you pull a tick in the first couple of hours, you have little to fear from the transmission of blood-borne diseases. So they say.

Lying atop the sleeping bag in the hot night, I heard the first mosquito. I put the screens in place but it was too late. Under the pinching bites I lay sweating and cursing. Unable to stay awake driving, now I couldn't sleep lying down. I was living someone's nightmare. "These are the days that must happen to you," Whitman says.

It was here, during the Depression, that Douglas County, after acquiring through tax delinquencies thousands of acres of logged-out land, offered a homestead plan intended to relieve unemployment in the cities and put the land back to use. You could buy an acre for two dollars cash or three dollars on time. The land sold, but mostly to people who already had it; of the few new residents moving in for a try at reclaiming the clear-cut barrens, not a single one was an unemployed city dweller. A generation later, trees had returned, but not many people. Hunting a cool spot on the bag, swatting the thirtieth mosquito, I understood why.

Finally, I gave up and pulled off the screens, and, with windows wide open, drove flat out down the highway to blast away the insects. At Danbury I parked by the town hall, put the screens in place, and again went to bed. I slapped a mosquito and fell asleep.

Before I left home, I had told someone that part of my purpose for the trip was to be inconvenienced so I might see what would come from dislocation and disrupted custom. Answer: severe irritability.

12

WITHOUT ever getting out of my rig the next morning, I left bleak Danbury for blue highway 77 and what is left of the Wisconsin Northwoods. West of Minong, at a small lake, I packed a knapsack, pulled on a swimsuit, and went up the shore to a wooded inlet for a cold, brief swim with a bar of Ivory ("It floats") to scrub out everything that wasn't me.

I built a little fire, cut some sausage, and put it in the skillet with two eggs. The pine popped and snapped in the flames, the sausage hissed like serpents, the warm air moved, and I was washed. Nights like last night made for mornings like this. I could stay on the road forever.

Scouring the skillet with wet sand, I heard a branch crunch behind me. I turned and stepped back into the lake. At the treeline stood a man in a fringed buckskin coat and a leather hat pulled low. An open knife glinted in his left hand. I was armed with a collapsible Boy Scout skillet. He raised his arm, the knife flashing again.

"Been watching you," she said. The knife was the cellophane of a Hostess Ding-Dong. "Camping here?"

"You startled me to hell." I stepped out of the lake. "Want some coffee?"

"It makes my arms break out." She spoke fast and her movements were jittery. Pushing back her hat, she scratched a forehead swollen with mosquito bites.

"Did you sleep in the woods last night?" I asked.

"I don't know. Maybe. Why?"

"You've got bites." I folded the skillet and put it away as she took a can of Pepsi-Cola from her backpack, opened it, and flipped the tab in the lake. "Fish swallow those tabs and cut their guts open."

"So who cares? Are you some big environmentalist?"

I picked up my gear. A perfect morning disappearing before a bug-bitten teenybopper. I doused the fire.

"Like I was into ecology," she said, "but it got boring." She looked uneasy. "You leaving?"

"Moving on." I hiked to the truck, washed the windshield, did a U-turn, and there she stood along the highway. Now she looked frightened.

"Hey! Sir! Going toward Green Bay?"

"So who cares?" I drove off, turned around at the top of the hill, and came back. She stood there, a pitiful mess of mosquito bites and stringy hair. "Are you asking for a lift?"

"I guess." She was frightened, all right.

"Do you live in Green Bay?" She shook her head. "Look, I'm not picking up some teenage roadie unless I know what you're doing." I kept checking the rearview mirror. "Where do you live?"

"Eau Claire." She was trying not to cry.

"What are you doing up here?"

"Come on, man!" I put the truck in gear. Her face red with rage, she screamed, "I split!"

"What's in Green Bay?"

She took a few steps up the road. "Christ! I don't need a ride this bad!"

"And I don't need your trouble." I put the van in gear again.

Through gritted teeth she said, "My grandmother's in Green Bay!"

I checked the rearview mirror again. The truth was I thought she might be the bait on some scam. "Hey!" she said. "I'm the one's supposed to be scared."

"Don't know how far I'm going."

"So who cares?" She got in, and I couldn't prevent one more glance at the mirror. PARENTS FILE CHARGES AGAINST UNEMPLOYED MAN.

Her name was something like Stacie McDougald, and she had run away two days earlier with another girl who returned home by bus after the first night. Stacie then hitched a ride with a boy who brought her down the back road.

"He never said anything, but when he stopped by the lake I got scared and ran. He looked for me in the woods and stuff, but the mosquitoes were like real terrible, so he gave up."

She had hidden in the trees all night, eaten a couple of Ho-Ho's, and finally put her head in the knapsack to escape the very mosquitoes that had saved her.

"Sorry my clothes are so gross." She took a vial from her jacket. "Only three left." Vacantly she stared at the vial, shook out a pill, and swallowed it with a swig of Pepsi.

"What's the pill?"

"Gotta take them. I'm hyperactive. They're Ludes."

The vial had no label. "Prescribed?"

"Oh, sort of. Like they used to be. I took Ritalin when I was little."

"Have you eaten anything besides the kiddie junk and Quaaludes?"

"If I eat too much I get gross and fat."

East of Hayward we drove into resort country where billboards and small, tacky motels lined the highway. The pavement rose and dropped, up and down, and the van rode like a cockboat. The girl fell asleep. At Park Falls, I stopped for gas. She woke up and disappeared into the restroom with her backpack. She came out wearing clean clothes, her long blonde hair wet and tied behind. Except for the insect bites, her face was smooth and bland and of an unnatural pallor like the underside of an arm. I suggested she telephone her grandmother, but she refused. At Fifield we went east toward Minocqua. The Chequamegon Forest was trees and sandy soil blooming with trillium. "Can you tell me why you took off?"

"I guess. I mean, so who cares?"

She opened another can of warm Pepsi and — furtively — took another pill, this one from a labeled bottle. Boasting of Ritalin and Quaaludes, she hid her Midol.

"Angus lost his ass in a taco franchise and things got really bad at home. I mean, you know. The business got worse, and me and Kevin started catching hell worse."

"Who's Angus and Kevin?"

"Black Angus is my dad. Kevin's my brother. Anyway, like Angus was losing it. I mean, he'd always find an excuse to beat up on us like maybe a low grade or using a buttertub lid for a Frisbee in the house, so he'd punch us because he was losing his ass. Like, Kevin's real smart. I mean, he aced everything. If he messed up a test, Angus would slap him around and pull his hair. Call him things like 'donkey' and 'yellow belly.' Anyway, the night his partners and him gave up the franchise, Black Angus's face started twitching like it does when he's tense. Mom told us to look like we were studying even if we weren't. God. Two days later he was trying to parallel park, and Kevin didn't tell him he was getting close to a pole, and Angus dented the fender. Right there in the shopping center, he starts yelling and slapping Kevin. Kevin didn't say anything then, but he ran off that night. He's in New York now, but I'm the only one that knows where. He's into Hare Krishna."

"He's had a hard go of it."

"When he was little, he fried out on acid. Then he found Jesus. He saw Jesus in a phone booth."

"A telephone booth?"

"He said Jesus was arguing with the operator for cutting off his call to God. He wrote last month and said he couldn't communicate with me anymore unless I dumped my false values. I told him that was cool, but I don't know what my false values are. I mean, like I'm not into first-promise rings."

We turned south onto U.S. 51 at Minocqua. Motels and restaurants gimmicked up like barns and country stores the whole way; most had gift shoppes and some had caged animals for petting. Then the supper clubs, each named after its owner. Looking for the land again, I turned east at Merrill.

"I'm not going to ever get married," the girl said. "But if I do, and Mom says don't marry the guy, I won't. I mean, if she'd listened to Nana, I'd be somebody else's kid."

"Angus won't be around forever."

"Nana says Angus never forgave us kids for changing his life. We kept him from becoming a famous writer. But Nana says it's because he was too scared to really do it on his own. I mean, he can't even get to work without Mom, but he likes people to call him Big Mac. It's all bullshit. The only way he's big is pushing little people around."

"He must have treated you fairly sometimes."

"Yeah? Like he calls us 'hundred-thousand-dollar jerks' because he read that's what it costs to raise a kid. Or he calls us 'unfeathered, two-legged arguments for abortion.' Anything good we did, he played it up to make himself look good. Always himself. He's got a drawing of himself dressed like Superman by his chair, and like all the time he lectures us for being conceited. He doesn't know anything about us. Kevin's not conceited — he hates himself."

"Time for lunch." She didn't hear me. She couldn't get all the bane out.

"Kevin used to call him Anus. I guess you know what that is. One night Anus heard him say it, and he slapped him around pretty bad. Later, Kevin was laying on his bed crying. Then he starts laughing. I got scared. I thought he was freaking out. I go, 'What's wrong?' and Kevin goes, 'I'm hungry.' I go, 'Jesus!' I mean he had blood and stuff on his shirt. And he goes, 'Yeah, I just had a Big Mac attack.' God, we laughed."

While we were eating, she said, "Last year, when I started going out on dates alone, Angus would always say to me before the guy got there — this is gross — 'Just remember, a stiff prick has no conscience.' He said that every time I went out. The other night when he said it, I screamed at him. I couldn't take it anymore. I mean, it's so sick. He started punching me with his thumb, and he told the guy I couldn't go out. That was cool because the guy was kind've a nerd. I guess I finally got to where Kevin got. I split that night."

She nibbled a French fry, then said abruptly, "Hey! Can we change the subject? I mean, like what are you doing in Wisconsin?"

I gave a half-minute outline.

She looked at me absently and said, "Hmmm," her curiosity easily satisfied. "If you took me on to Green Bay you could get the ferry across Lake Michigan. You wouldn't have to drive through Chicago. Please?"

I agreed to it although now I would be across Wisconsin without really seeing Wisconsin. Later, as we drove along state 29 through the moraine country of dairy farms and fine old barns, across the Embarrass River, it occurred to me that I *had* seen something of Wisconsin. What I hadn't seen was the Wisconsin of my blue highway preconceptions. Little is so satisfying to the traveler as realizing he missed seeing what he assumed to be in a place before he went.

At Green Bay the smell of Lake Michigan blew in strong. The girl directed me to her grandmother's house. When we arrived, she became excited and jumped down and ran to the bungalow. Then she ran back to the truck.

"Hey! What's your name?" I told her. "Okay. Keep on truckin'."

Ghost Dancing seemed empty, and I was lonely as I was after every rider left who shared some miles. It would pass, but for a while the quiet always bothered me.

Kewaunee, sitting on the eastern base of the peninsula that separates the inlet called Green Bay from the open lake, had a business district just a few feet above the water, with homes a hundred feet higher on sheer cliffs that dropped to the shore. It was as if someone had broken a mixing bowl in half, built a toy town in the bottom, and put little houses on the rim.

At the ferry slip I checked the schedule. I didn't want a night crossing, but I could take one at noon the next day. On a breakwater near where Father Marquette celebrated a mass in the seventeenth century, I ate a sandwich as killdeer made long glides down along the beach. I was quite alone.

13

THERE's something to be said for banal conversation. After paying the grocery clerk for the yogurt, I commented, "It's a fine day."

She smiled. "Anything else?"

"That's it, thanks. I'm taking the ferry today."

With a nod, she went back to stamping prices on aspirin bottles. I walked to the breakwater to eat breakfast. A man was fishing. "Any luck?"

"None."

"What're you fishing for?"

"Perch."

"What's your bait?"

"Minnows."

And so on. When I ran out of questions, the exchange was over. Across the central North, conversations had been difficult to strike up. The people were polite but reserved; often they seemed afraid of appearing too inquisitive, while at other times they were simply too taciturn to exchange the banalities and clichés necessary to find a base for conversation.

When I walked the North towns, people, wondering who the outsider was, would look at me; but as soon as I nodded they looked down, up, left, right, or turned around as if summoned by an invisible caller. "Stranger," Whitman says, "if you passing meet me and desire to speak to me, why should you not speak to me?" I even tried my old stratagem of taking a picture of a blank wall just to give a passerby an excuse to stop and ask what I could possibly be photographing. Nothing breaks down suspicion about a stranger better than curiosity — except in the North; whatever works better there, I didn't discover. The effect on me was that I felt more alone than I ever had in the desert. I wished for the South where any topic is worth at least a brief exchange. And so I went across the central North, seeing many people, but not often learning where our lives crossed common ground.

At noon the ferry rocked Kewaunee with her air horns and pulled into the slip just as one had done since 1892. She was the three-hundred-sixty-foot *Viking*, built in 1925 and converted from steam to diesel-electric in 1965. The boat swallowed a batch of boxcars, a few automobiles, then Ghost Dancing, small against the big steel wheels of the railway cars. Pivoting like a compass needle, the *Viking* made a ninety-degree turn in the harbor, sailed past the stubby lighthouse, and cut a straight line over the smooth water toward Elberta, Michigan. The temperature dropped twenty degrees, and the water changed from occluded green to indigo.

No one is pulling three-hundred-pound sturgeon out of Lake Michigan as the Indians once did, but municipal pollution and industrial contaminants have been reduced significantly since the sixties, and sport fishing is coming back; yet, levels of insecticides, PCB's, and mercury are still too high to allow a resumption of commercial fishing.

On the aft deck I took a seat and watched Wisconsin get smaller. I had long wondered whether all shorelines disappear on a clear day in the middle of Lake Michigan (the name means "big water"). I would soon find out. When the ferry had loaded at Kewaunee, an infestation of gnats and midges had swarmed in and with maddening accuracy whizzed into eyes and ears. But, once we were under way, thumb-sized flycatchers flew aboard and hopped and flitted and ran down the bugs. One bird alighted on the arm of my chair, cocked an eye at me, nipped a midge, wiggled its minuscule mustache, peeped, and flew to the next chair. I was guessing the number of gnats it took to fill a flycatcher's belly, an organ that can't be any larger than a pinto bean, when a man at the rail pulled an unshelled peanut from his pocket and set it on the deck to lure another bird.

"The peanut's almost as big as the bird," I said.

He just looked at me, his brown eyes shining like pocket-worn chestnuts, his head a creased, leathery bag that might have been dug from a Danish peat bog. The man took a seat and explained that flycatchers followed the ferry from shore to shore. "The peanut is a joke." He lived in Muskegon and had been visiting a daughter in Menominee. Born in Bavaria, he immigrated to Detroit with his mother in the thirties. For a number of years he had operated a double-crank-toggle-fender-stamping press at Chrysler Motors. "She push a million pounds against steel to make the fenders. But the boom-boom-boom damage the hears." He pulled his large, Buddha ears.

There came a terrible clanging from below, and I said I hoped the boxcars hadn't crushed my van. His eyes widened, and he said, "Boxcars? I tell you boxcars." There followed a long, entangled tale, full of details about the old German rail system and about trout fishing.

The essence, as I understood it, was this: Karl (he so called himself), a boy of fourteen, went fishing with a comrade. They caught four trout, but it took all day to do it. In the growing dusk, they chose to use the railway tracks as a shortcut home. The comrade had heard the route was easy if you weren't frightened of trestles over four deep gorges. The boys soon came to the first bridge; hoping not to meet a train at mid-bridge they crossed as fast as they could. It was terrifying to look between the ties.

"On the bridges," he said, "was no place to go if train is coming."

Trying not to look down, they crossed the second one; the tracks went into the forest and came out again to the third gorge, deeper than the second; they crossed quickly and again went into the forest and out to the last bridge. By that time it was too dark to see even their feet.

"We hold hands and feeled our way. Across almost, a big light blind us."

It was a locomotive rounding a curve. The boys turned and started back, but they couldn't hop from tie to tie quickly enough in the dark. Only one thing to do: laying poles and fish across the timbers, they slipped between the ties and hung by their arms. The engine, roaring above, knocked cinders in their eyes and nearly shook them loose. The cars kept coming, coming. Then the last clacked over. They started to pull up, but their arms were too tired.

"We can only hang like chickens at market."

The comrade tried to swing his feet up, but nearly lost his grip, so they hung and argued whether to drop in hopes of hitting the river.

"When we cross, we are not afraid to take a chance to die, but when we hang, we become afraid to take chance to live. Life is so."

"How long can a boy hang by his arms?"

"When it is all things you hang for? Who can answer?"

The comrade was in favor of dropping, but he couldn't get the nerve to go first. They settled on a course of yelling alternately every several minutes. They hung and they hung. The train had shaken the stringer of trout through the ties, and four dead fish dangled in their faces. "If we move, the fishes kisses us." They kept hanging. The next locomotive would shake them loose.

"I tell my comrade, 'Soon we will be dying.' "

The boys whimpered and Karl wished he had been a better son to his poor mother and had not lied so often to the priests. He promised God he would change his ways. Then a beam from under the bridge played over them.

" 'Schnell,' we call, and a voice say, 'What's this happening here?' I see big eyes looking into mine. Eyes blink and I see a man's face and it say, 'What are you stupid boys doing?' We look down and see his boots. He is standing in marsh. We was hanging with our fishes ten inches off the ground."

Whether the man's story was truth or tale, it had held me, and I had forgotten to see about the shore disappearing from view. I jumped up. We were almost across. It would remain a mystery. When I turned around, the old fellow was gone.

The sandy dunes of Michigan glowed pink in the late sun, and at the mouth of the Elberta harbor, there was a marvelous sight: little slivers of silver jigged on their tails over the blue water. They were alewives looking for all the world like dancing spoons. These were the fish that had washed ashore to foul beaches in the days of high pollution.

The *Viking* let loose with her horns, the crew tied up and sprinted across the dock and into cars and roared off to supper, and I wished the *Viking* were sailing all the way to the Atlantic.

14

SOME evenings on the road were like this one:

East of Elberta, across the Betsie River, and down route 115, I got choosy about where to spend the night. Looking for a town whose primary business was not tourism, I drove on through stands of birch girdled for souvenirs by sightseers, through a countryside of motels and sewer-hook-up camp-grounds. Nothing satisfactory. In an hour, I was unexpectedly on U.S. 27, a limited-access highway. Insisting on multi-access roads and resisting controlled-access living, I had driven right onto a no-U-turn, minimum speed, tractors-with-lugs-prohibited mainline. I was irritated, but things were to get worse.

Through the oilfields of middle Michigan and into Mount Pleasant with the last drop of light, and onto the campus of Central Michigan University. I opened the cooler and found a butt end of bread, a wrinkled orange, and the can of chopped liver. Off I went for a calendared cafe serving Michigan pasties and ended up at an assembly-line sandwich hut.

I stood with the other ambulatory digestive tubes reading the wall-mounted, internally lighted menu showing full-color photographic representations of hamburgers and French fries twelve times life size. A slice of potato big enough to lay steel track over did not look appealing. All prices ended in nine. I ordered, and the cash register hummed, spun its mechanism, glared a red number, and an agent pushed me my texturized substitute in its polystyrene sarcophagus. I joined the other diners, some of whose gizzards had already begun wrestling hamburgers named for their weight.

Sticky from the heat, I faced another warm night in the truck. I went back to the campus and stopped at an old stone dormitory. Although spring term had ended and summer session hadn't begun, somebody was living in the building. No one around. I heard a noise from a shower room, so I went in and started to call out when I noticed a tampon dispenser. TRESPASSER JAILED. Backing out quickly and quietly, I turned and bumped into a nude body. "What's going on?" A young man's voice.

"The person," I fumbled. "The resident assistant. Looking for him."

"He's out. What do you need?"

"Wanted to buy a shower."

"Help yourself."

"Isn't this a women's dormitory?"

"Usually. Right now it's for some businessmen taking a seminar."

When I came out of the shower, the student offered a vacant room. It would be cooler. I was almost asleep when the light went on, and in walked a man, about forty, wearing a baby-blue terrycloth hat — the kind you can wipe a sweating face with — and a blinking, multimode, programmable, digital chronograph that gave him a continuous readout on what microsecond, second, minute, hour, day, and month he was currently in, as well as his lap time, split time, and whether he was in first or second place. He set down two monogrammed suitcases, looked at me, said nothing, opened a case, undressed, wrapped a personalized towel around his looseness, locked the suitcase, stuck his billfold in his towel six-shooter style, and walked out, leaving the light on. After ten minutes I got up and turned it off.

He came back smelling of baby powder, turned the light on, studied his fret of a face in the mirror, got his shaving kit, and walked out, leaving the light on. After five minutes, I got up and turned it off. He came back, turned the light on, sat down, belched, wiped his tasseled shoes, lighted a Vantage Menthol, took out a *Consumer Reports, Penthouse,* and a plastic binder with North Central Assurance Group or something like that embossed on it. A man laughed in the hallway, and he walked out again.

"Larry," a voice said. "You fly in?"

"Drove the stationwagon. Say, who's the creep in my room?"

"The jigaboo?"

"No. Tonto."

"Don't know."

I got up and turned off the light. I was almost asleep when the door banged open and a flashlight blinded me. That was it. I jumped up.

"What the hell is this? Get that light out of my eyes."

"What's your name, buddy?"

"Sparkle Plenty. What the hell's going on?"

"Are you registered?"

"I'm not a Communist. What is this?"

A blinking readout reached over and switched on the light. Larry had brought a watchman. I explained the student's invitation, but the watchman didn't believe it and told me to get out. I pulled on clothes and rolled up my sheet. As slowly as possible. As I left, I said to Larry, "Be sure you call Sam Spade here if those two beds aren't big enough for your fat ass."

"Shut your own ass, you freak."

The watchman interrupted the exchange, and I went to the hot truck and lay down in a cold anger. I couldn't get to sleep so I wrote out a little report. When I finished, I went back and pinned it to the door:

AUTOPSY FINDINGS ON

LARRY ANONYMOUS

THE EXAMINATION: It was found that the life of the deceased was given over to the concerns of surety bonding, net profit margins, and total shareholders equity. As a student of actuarial statistics (i.e., letting the dead tell you where to put your money), the deceased formulated Larry's Law, which has become a leading piece of desk-plaque philosophy: RISK NOTHING.

CAUSE OF DEATH: Acute myocardial infarction due to the continued gathering and piling of material good upon material good and desire upon vain desire, aggravated by an ongoing fear that the deceased would one day find himself without his driver's license and wristwatch.

SUMMARY: Like a poorly written policy, the Primal Underwriter has declared this man of trifling sorrows null and void.

Respectfully submitted,
S. Plenty

15

ACROSS her T-shirt was SKI. She leafed through *Stalking the Wild Asparagus* in the college bookstore. I was in the middle of Michigan and looking for a place to go next; so I asked whether she lived in Mount Pleasant, but she didn't look up. I tapped her arm.

"I'm from Missouri. Traveling. I'd like to find a good place to visit in Michigan." She watched but said nothing. "Maybe you know a nice spot." She just stared. Northerners really carry taciturnity too far, I thought.

A clerk came up and said, "She's deaf. Probably having trouble reading your lips." He repeated what I'd asked.

She said, "Oh," and put the book down. Holding up her right hand as if to say "How" in Hollywood Indian fashion, she said, "Dumb."

"Dumb?" the clerk repeated. I didn't know whether she meant me or herself.

"Dumb Miss Ginn," she said and wagged her right thumb.

"Thumb of Michigan?" the clerk asked.

The girl smiled, wagged her thumb again, and nodded. "Berry bootful."

"It's very beautiful," the clerk translated.

Looking at her SKI T-shirt, I said, "Do you ski on the Thumb?"

"Dumbs due plat. By dames car water ski."

"Thumb's too flat to ski,". the clerk said. "Her name's Karworski."

So that was how I ended up on the Thumb of Michigan.

On a map, lower Michigan looks like a mitten with the squatty peninsula between Saginaw Bay and Lake Huron forming the Thumb. A region distinctive enough to have a name was the only lure I needed, but also it didn't hurt to have towns with fine, unpronounceable names like Quanicassee, Sebewaing, Wahjamega, or other names like Pigeon, Bad Axe, Pinnebog, Rescue, Snover, and — what may be the worst town name in the nation — Freidberger. People of the Thumb have come from many places, but Germans and Poles predominate.

I headed due east across the flat country, past the great industrial pile of Dow Chemical at Midland, past the Victorian houses in Bay City. Near Quanicassee, canals draining the wet land to make farming possible flanked the highway. In the ditches, mile after mile, violent flashes of polished bronze roiled the murky water. I stopped to see what it was. The hot, muddy banks frothed with the courtship of eighteen-inch carp. Males, flicking Fu Man Chu mustaches, metallic scales glittering like fragments of mirrors, orange tails thrashing, did writhing belly rolls over females as they demonstrated the right of their milt to prevail.

Away from the bay and lake, Thumbland was agricultural land: sugar beets, navy beans, silage; but on the bay from Caseville to Port Austin, the Thumb was an uninterrupted cluttering of vacation homes, tourist cabins, motels, and little businesses selling plastic lawn-ornament flamingoes and used tires cut into planters. The houses and cabins and businesses pressed in tightly, and in the few places where beach delivered itself to the road were "no trespassing" signs.

Whoever called Americans a "rootless" people never saw the west shore of the Thumb, where houses used eight weeks a year block off the lake every day of the year. If Americans are truly rootless, why weren't a few lodges and hotels built to leave the shore undeveloped as the "rooted" Europeans might do it? As it is, the rootless family drives up from Ypsilanti to spend its allotted time cutting grass, painting the boathouse, and unplugging the septic tank.

But the northeastern shore was another story: open. Farms and fields came down to the edge of Huron, and the people had collected into towns rather than stringing out along the lake. If west Thumbland was unrestrained America, the east Thumb was the best of rural England — settled yet uncongested.

Harbor Beach, a factory village and a pleasant one, had both a harbor and a beach inside a long stone breakwater; it also had a plant manufacturing plastics, one making food seasonings, and another producing pharmaceutical goods, as well as a big power station. People who argue that pretty towns and industry cannot live together should look at Harbor Beach.

A very long wooden pier ran out toward the breakwater. That Friday evening the whole village must have been fishing from it; although nobody was having any luck, the night before a crazy run of perch had swum in.

"This water was something to see," an angler said. He had that blankness of expression that comes only from years of watching eight-pound-test monofilament disappear into placid water. "Fish assaulted our bait."

He usually fished for whatever was running — perch, steelhead, chub; in the winter, he opened the ice and fished for pike. Most of his life he had worked in Detroit as a machinist turning parts for gasoline blowtorches.

"Now kids don't know what a gas blowtorch is, but they were beautiful things that built the country. Precision brass fittings machined to critical tolerances. Blew like thunder and ran like steam engines, and they lasted forever because they were designed and built and not just assembled. The throwaway propane bottle put us out of business. Those things are designed as junk and built accordingly. But the true blowtorch! A son inherited his dad's torch. I loved the work because I knew somebody would keep what I made."

He reeled in a nibbled-over minnow and reloaded. "The war changed things. During the forties, our shop converted to making brake shoes for Jeeps. There wasn't satisfaction in the job except for good money and helping our boys. When the war ended, things began breaking down, you might say, and that's when I and the wife started spending time up here."

In 1942 he had bought a small farm on the Thumb. "It was a good time to buy because I had money and land was available and going at a low price if you were white. People, you see, were afraid Coloreds were going to move in to do war work at the factory — a gunpowder plant I think it was — so they sold low to whites. It worked to my advantage. But I don't think any Coloreds ever came up to work anyway."

He jigged his bait and said to the water, "Hello?" then reeled in the dead minnow. "I like my role now — of no consequence whatsoever." He looked down the pier for activity. "I decided to buy the place up here on a Friday evening similar to this one. Went home from the shop and realized when I got home that I was just waiting for Monday. Funny thing was, I didn't like the job anymore."

As he packed up his gear, he asked why I was in Harbor Beach. I told him I was looking for a good hamburger. "That would be the Crow's Nest if you get out before ten," he said. "Be sure to see the painting. That thing stirs up almost as much commotion as a fast run of perch."

16

AT the Crow's Nest we drank "America's Only Fire-Brewed Beer," a brew remarkably interchangeable with any other American beer. Maybe that was why a man called Stitch took his Stroh's with a nip of ginger brandy. He wore coveralls and a herringbone sportcoat with a Buddy Poppy in the lapel. He was old and looked older. Before he lost coherent speech, I heard several things in his gargle of words. This was one: "I got healed when I was sixteen. Healed in a church basement on Wednesday night. Never been a religious man, but I been a believer since."

"What were you healed of?"

"An affliction to bear. I had feet flat as waffles."

He told a story about tracking down a pair of coyotes that were eating his mother's chickens. A long tale of the chase he'd recounted many times before, it was one of those events by which a man comes to define himself; no matter where else he'd failed, he'd killed the coyotes.

Above the bar hung the painting the fisherman had mentioned. On black velvet was a stacked, shimmering-haired, bronzed-bodied blonde in Indian-style headband and loincloth. That's all she wore unless you counted the expression on her face. Just another backbar nude, more silly than indecorous, I thought. I asked the bartender, a comely blonde herself, if the fuss about the painting was due to the mocking of Indian traditions.

"Indian traditions? What's with Indians? It's the bare tits, dearie."

"I see."

"Some people have gotten on my case because of a rumor that I posed for it." She stared at the painting as she pulled a draft. "Of course it isn't me. No woman's built like that. Those are fantasy knockers. They look like muscles."

Indeed they did. At nine o'clock, five post-adolescents with cigarettes rolled in their T-shirt sleeves came in and began setting up a band. They had speakers the size of closets, an amplifier control panel like the Kalamazoo switchboard, a siren to alert all of Lake Huron, enough strobes to light an airfield, and more drums than the Indian nation. I wondered what the group would do if they had to make music from cow bones and a washtub.

At ten o'clock they cut loose. I saw why I was supposed to be out before ten. I heard the band through my elbows on the bar, heard them against my forehead. The guitarist took off his shirt and flaunted a curved chest white as the gut side of a catfish. He was singing. I knew that because his mouth opened and closed, and he wasn't eating.

Sidling to the bar came a fellow in a blue suit large enough for a dancing partner to step in with him. He puffed a Swisher Sweet and didn't cough much. To the barmaid he said, "Pretty lady, this man's here to boogie."

"Anybody else know that, Shorty?"

Two young women drinking Scotch and Coke sat and waited to dance. The one with deep, dark eye sockets relentlessly worked a stick of chewing gum. The other, wearing snakeskin knee boots and golden slacks that fit as if gilded to her, was slender and had the eyes of a lynx. Boys in yellowed shirts took her to the dance floor one after another. They were stumps. Dancing out of her pelvis, she swirled around them like smoke, moving across the floor, inching back, sliding away. The siren went off, and the strobes flashed her into a wispy possibility. The boys were dying for her, but they got drunk and sat down. She danced on alone against the amplified drums and moved through the shadows of other dancers. Six college boys from Ann Arbor came in to drink Heinekens, and one had a few turns with the lynx, but only his shoulders and hands danced. No one else even tried.

At eleven-thirty the doors flew open and a couple dozen people — men wearing plaid slacks, the women billowy dresses — rolled in. I asked the barmaid who they were.

"Weekenders. Housewives and dentists and things. One guy's a chiropodist. They're the people that never dance with their own husbands and wives."

The men moved like the college boys, but with a little more effort and a little less result, while the women assumed strange postures as they danced: one placed both hands between her thighs and pulled her legs back and forth; another danced with an arm upraised as if calling for a fair catch; a third moved with arms perpendicular to her body as though greeting someone just off a boat; but the best danced with hands in pockets, her legs moving as if hot-wired to the drums. In the women there was a desperate sexuality, although I don't think the husbands — unlike the carp in the ditches — knew what was going on.

At midnight, a spinning dancer pulled a string at her waist, her dress billowed open like a parachute, and she stepped out of it and whirled it above her head. She wore a bikini swimsuit made with less material than the washing instructions in her husband's shirt. But the men lost interest as soon as they realized it wasn't her underwear.

The noise and smoke finally drove me to cover. When I left, the lynx had at last found a fit partner behind the bandstand: a full-length mirror.

And that's what went on one Friday night in May in Harbor Beach, Michigan.

Eight

NORTH BY NORTHEAST

THE wipers were useless. A black squall line had moved in so quickly, I could only pull off the road until the worst of the storm passed. I was on state 142, just west of the farm town of Bad Axe, and looking for Ivanhoe. Later when I was — apparently — in Ivanhoe, I had found only a church, so I headed east through Ubly, then down the edge of the Thumb, past more shoreline houses, to Port Huron. The rain eased but continued.

I had to decide. Either the eastward route lay through Detroit, Toledo, and Cleveland, or it was a shorter northeast jog through Canada. I crossed the St. Clair River into Sarnia, Ontario, and stopped at Canadian customs to assure officials I carried none of this or that, had enough money for my stay, was unarmed, had no live animals, and would be in the country only a few hours.

"Describe the purpose of your trip," the inspector said.

"Passage."

"Enjoy it, then."

But I didn't. The showers kept at it, the traffic ran heavy, I got lost in London, and again in Brantford; finally I was just driving, seeing nothing, waiting to get off the road. But it was a long haul of two hundred fifty miles through the province. By the time I reached U.S. Customs, the rain had stopped and, as I crossed the bridge over the Niagara River north of the falls, with quite unbelievable timing, the Canadian sun turned the eastern cliffs orange.

I was in New York: land of Texas hots, beef-on-a-wick, and Jenny Cream Ale, where hamburgers are hamburgs and frankfurters frankfurts. I was also within minutes of running out of gasoline. I took a guess that Lewiston would be a left turn; if not, I was in trouble again. But it was there, looking a century older than the Michigan towns I'd come from.

In fact, Lewiston was two centuries older, although the oldest buildings now standing were ones built just after the British burned the town in 1813. I filled up next to an old stone hotel where, the gas man told me, James Fenimore Cooper wrote *The Spy*. "It's some book, they say. Understand," he added, "our station wasn't here then."

Ten thousand miles of blue highways had wearied me, especially after driving the last three hundred of them in rain. I wasn't tired of traveling, and I had no reason to go home, but I wanted to put the wheel aside, to get off striped pavement for a few days. Near Canandaigua Lake, a friend I hadn't seen in several years had built a log cabin in the woods. Whether he would be home I didn't know, but that's where I headed.

With what remained of the light, I followed the Niagara River toward Lake Ontario, then picked up New York 93: through Warrens Corners (next to Wrights Corners), through Lockport (an old Erie Canal town and former home of Merchant's Gargling Oil, "Good for Man or Beast"), through the old Heinz 57 Varieties vegetable farms, onto state 5 and into Batavia (where the Old Snake Den Inn of the early 1800s advertised beds with "clean sheets only slept in a few times since new"), to Le Roy (former home of J-E-L-L-O), and on through darkness to the west edge of Canandaigua Lake.

I knew the road name where my friend lived and nothing more, so I stopped at a farm on route 21 for directions. The farmer got me to the road and the road took me to the house, which was lighted from top to bottom with no one around but the dogs. I went back to my bunk. Later, when trees obscured the moon, there was an uproar of metallic banging against the Ghost.

"Hey in there! Dammit! Open up this sardine can!"

It was my friend.

Scott Chisholm said, "I'm not going to wake you up by asking why you're sleeping in my woods. I'm only going to ask if you want to sleep inside."

"Too tired to move."

"All right, breakfast it is then. I'll tell you only this: I won't be able to sleep knowing you're here."

"I'm quite harmless."

2

AT breakfast, Linda, Chisholm's wife, told me he had slept like a fallen log. "I knew he would," I said, "but I liked thinking he thought he wouldn't."

Scott Chisholm, a Canadian citizen of Ojibway and Scotch descent, had lived in this country longer than in Canada and liked the United States but wouldn't admit it for fear of having to pay off bets he made years earlier when he first "came over" that the U.S. is a place no Canadian could ever love. He was a teacher in the Empire State College system.

In 1975 he built a two-story log house in the hills west of Canandaigua Lake, the "thumb" of the Finger Lakes. Chisholm drilled a well and hit sweet water at thirty-five feet. It produced six gallons a minute. Even though a human being needs only a pint of water a day to survive, Chisholm decided his family couldn't live on 8,640 gallons a day. So he drilled to sixty-eight feet and got fourteen gallons a minute — fourteen gallons of gassy, sulphurous stuff. Probably the most American thing he ever did.

He and Linda and their two children, Sean and Caitlin, shared the house with a three-legged dog named Teddy, a four-legged dog that had lost its fur named Chops, and Murray, a plump guinea pig that had just cut a foot and left red fleur-de-lis rodent prints all over the *New York Times* in the bottom of its cage. The family also had two cats. They were complete and unimpaired.

Chisholm fixed breakfast: a large mound of "secret ingredient" (forgot what went in) scrambled eggs, link sausage, muffins, melon, milk. The fellow talks or he doesn't talk — that is, he talks intensely or is intensely silent. He is the noisiest silent man I've ever known. That morning Chisholm was talking, something he does well (he planned to become a Mormon preacher before he lost the call).

"I'm writing a film treatment for a Western about Asa T. Soule, a man who gave Rochester a baseball team," he said. "In his day, Soule was to Rochester Kodak and Xerox combined. He manufactured patent medicines. The big seller was Hop Bitters, which he claimed to be, I'm quoting, 'the Greatest Blood Purifier, Liver Regulator, and Life and Health Restoring Agent on Earth.' He also made the Indian Cough Cure, Autumn Leaf Extract for Females, Ocean Weed Heart Remedy, and Swamp Root. Became preposterously rich. Some people even got well taking Soule's concoctions. Be all that as it may, what do you want to do?"

"Don't entertain me."

"I have to build my stone retaining wall."

"Let's build it then."

We began. There was nothing but an eroded bank, and the stones were still in the creek, on the hills, in the woods. We rolled, pushed, shoved, and piled rocks along the road, then loaded them into the back of his Fiat wagon. It was hot and tent caterpillars swarmed the ground like the Chinese army and bees hummed in the horse chestnut blossoms. While we worked, Chisholm talked: a friend who collected and drove nothing but Studebakers

17. Scott Chisholm near Cheshire, New York

got rear-ended by a man admiring the old car; Harold Outhouse had a
dog that could pull a bull down by the nose; a black family once moved
out here and began building a home before being run off — although the
area had been a stop on the Underground Railroad.

A young woman rammed past in her Dodge, covering us with dust, and
I asked what the hell was going on. "She's been living hidden away up
this little road all her life. She's judgmental and vicious and has it in for
what she doesn't understand, which is almost everything."

The pulling and hoisting and sweating stretched out the kinks of sitting
behind a steering wheel. I couldn't recall labor feeling so good. Chisholm
rolled a fat, round stone out of the trees. I grabbed and pulled. I was
capable of lifting it, but it was so close to the limits of my strength, I didn't
want to try. Working with someone I knew less well, I would have picked
it up, but with this old friend I could concede my limit and let the boulder
take my measure. Nothing showed our friendship better than that rock I

walked away from. Chisholm picked it up, tottered, and bounced it in the Fiat. Then he dragged an even bigger hunk out of the creek. He was getting curious about what size stone he could lift. This one was too risky. "Don't pull that Atlas routine again. Let me help." But he bent around the granite like a question mark and put it in.

We dumped the stones in front of the embankment, then quit for lunch. There was little talk; mostly we poured down ice tea and hung in our chairs like damp rags. At two o'clock we started again. Laying the stones was easier. Then a strange thing began to happen. We could feel an urging in the rocks, a behest to be put in just so, to be set where they would hold against the shifts of the earth, against the twists of the roots. They fit one way and not other ways. It was as if the stones were, as Indians believed, alive. The rocks were moving us. "Are you a determinist?" I said.

"How could a man live in this country and be a determinist?"

"Neither am I, but this wall is proof if you ever change your mind. It knows where it has to go. We aren't the ones making the decisions."

Chisholm stopped. "I've felt it too."

We just followed the will of the wall, whatever came from the stones, and the raw, eroded bank began to pull its cover of rock over. We worked like men possessed — Chisholm with a fever, I more slowly as I paused to watch him, to watch the sweat bead and drip through his beard. The dust stuck to us, and we smelled more of soil than men. We couldn't quit. My legs were turning to noodles, my hands cramping, and we began to drop stones, but we worked on. When the light came in low under the trees, we straightened to look. No more granite. We had laid twenty feet.

Chisholm wanted to wash the stones, to clean them, to set them, and he should have. It was his wall. He had worked harder. But I, an opportunist, got the hose first. Grit and dust flushed from the rocks, the round ones shining like men's skulls, the flat ones like their tombstones. The wall would be there until other men came, and, with effort, moved it. Maybe nothing else he or I had done or would do would last as long as that wall.

In the evening, fireflies switched on and off, crickets tweetled, and Caitlin lay next to Murray and held a sterling spoon to a bruise on her leg to take out the tenderness. We sat on the pine porch, Chisholm's cigar glowing in the dark. We felt full. It was as if we had done something.

Later, lying in bed, I was glad I'd stopped to see him. I had needed work and familiar faces around a dinner table; I needed stories that embarrass because they are undeniable, stories that only old friends can tell because only they know them. And it appeared then as though I wouldn't have been able to travel another mile had it not been for these people. I suppose that wasn't true, but it seemed so.

3

PETE Marvin was also Pierangelo Masucci — they were one and the same. Well, almost the same. He said he thought more like an Italian when people called him Masucci, but that didn't happen often now. His brother had changed the name in the late thirties when, as a schoolboy, he tired of teachers fumbling Masucci and kids laughing. Pete said, "If nobody can speak the name, you got no name."

He lived on a seventy-five-acre farm high on the glacial hills above Canandaigua Lake. In his garage workshop he was tinkering with a new Buick he'd just bought for a good figure because the front end had been damaged in a test drive. While barn swallows slid in and out, Pete chewed Winter's Cigar Clippings and worked on the car. There had been trouble with the dealer in the transaction and Pete had asked Chisholm, his neighbor, to write a letter of complaint for him. Chisholm had gone into Rochester and turned the project over to me. "Language-wise," Pete said, "if it's writing, I'm not so good." He gave me a pad and pencil.

"Who's the letter to?" I asked.

"Ralph Nader."

It wasn't a joke, so together we wrote the letter — a hot, fuming thing as Pete wanted. Then we talked and drank lemonade.

He and his wife, Pauline, were born in Rochester; Pete in 1910, she in 1914. His mother, Filomena, was born in Naples, Italy, in 1884. The three lived in a one-hundred-five-year-old farmhouse. Pete and Pauline had moved from Rochester to the New York vineyard country between Cheshire and Naples in the late forties and rebuilt the big house over the years — tearing down a shed to build a kitchen, installing heat and plumbing. It was an accomplishment, the more so because Pete had walked with crutches since he was a small boy. The carpentry required Pauline to lift, climb, and hold; Pete measured, cut, and drilled holes for her to drive the nails home. But when he put a new roof on the big garage, she would have none of it, and he crawled up and shingled it alone.

At the suggestion of his brother-in-law, Pete had moved the family to the farm for a go at raising chicken broilers. "What did I know about chickens?" He bent a thumb and finger to say zero. "So you learn what you want to do." He went to the library to find out how to build a rain shelter for poultry. "Jeez, the first year the price was two dollars a chicken. Good money. I thought we had it made. But the buyers came out and took the best stock and left me the junk. We fed the hell out of the others, fattened them, and sold them door to door for about three-fifty and made a little money. So I bought seven hundred more. The next year, the price hit bottom. I finally said shit on chickens."

In those early years of farming, he and Pauline took jobs in Canandaigua factories to meet the mortgage payments. First they worked at the Velo-King plant making tricycles for Sears, Roebuck. Then they worked at the F. A. Smith Company making electric motors. But Pete didn't like working inside, and he couldn't get the noise of punch presses out of his ears. Even in the fields, he heard the presses.

In the early fifties, they quit the factory jobs and began farming full-time. They put in a garden and vineyard and grew blackberries and grapes and built up a herd of fourteen dairy cows. They stayed with the Holsteins until the sixties.

"The government started coming around making you put in equipment if you sold your milk. New techniques like keeping the milk away from the air. You had to tube the milk from tits to tank. We couldn't afford nothing like that. We couldn't get a herd big enough to make bulk-making pay. Couldn't keep up with regulations. You remember that Butz, that Secretary of Agriculture? He said, 'Get big or get out.' We got out. I finally said shit on cows."

Pete cursed the Buick. "Engineers. Fifty thousand bucks a year to make things lousy and five years in college to learn how to do it. I had a 'twenty-seven Chevy coupe — old, busted thing with a cracked block. You think we had money to get it welded? We pulled the engine and set it on the kitchen table and filled the crack with solder. Drove it five more years. They engineered then."

He gave up on the Buick for a while and closed the hood.

"We tried blackberries, but picking was too hard on the old people and kids horsed around. We paid pickers a dime a quart and sold for twelve cents. Is that profit? A blackberry bush lasted three or four years after it started bearing. I finally said shit on blackberries."

"You're down to grapes."

"Grapes we picked by hand. Now they have a mechanical picker that shakes them off. Five or six acres of grapes in them days gave you a living. Six hundred plants to an acre. You can't live off them today unless you got a hundred acres. Sixty thousand plants to support a man. My fields have gone back wild like a lot of the other old vineyards. We planted Concords by the thousands. Growers around here used to dig the holes by hand. I couldn't do that, so I used a posthole digger on the back of the tractor. You know what? People got word of it and they said, 'This Pete's got an idea!' Did I ever get any money for it? Shit. But that's how they plant grapes today."

He looked over the letter to Ralph Nader and said nothing.

"We raised Concords and sold them to the Widmer and Taylor wineries. Widmer's just down the highway at Naples. Then, in the early seventies, Widmer quit buying. They started bringing in California grape juice in tank cars because it was cheaper than buying here. Vineyards went to hell all around. A lot of good stock died out, and growers went to planting peas and beans. Generations of the best root stock just torn out. A grape root can live a hundred years. Then the New York legislature — or somebody — said they couldn't call it New York wine if it was made from California juice. So the wineries started buying again from around here. Too late for me. Nitrate and potash for fertilizer got too expensive. I was sixty-six years old, and I couldn't baby the plants anymore. So I said shit on grapes. But hey! We used to make our own grape juice and wine and pie and jelly. We ate and drank grapes in any way you name. I got a purple gut like Pa."

Pete started tinkering with his old Ford tractor. The only modification on it for him was a hand clutch.

"You got to get up pretty early in the morning to keep up with those winery boys," he said. "During Prohibition, Widmer's sold grape juice to stay in business. But who wanted grape juice? So they put a label on the bottle that said the juice might ferment if it didn't get kept cold. That's upholding the law."

As Pauline came out to the workshop, she talked softly in Italian to the swallows. She wanted to show me the garden orchard they had just planted. The trees — cherry, plum, apple, pear — were nothing but fishing poles. "I look out kitchen window when I cook and see leafs," she said. "Someday, God letting me, I see apples and plums." We walked around to the well, and she pumped up a sample. "Taste this water sweet like candy and tell if this is a good place."

Pete said, "We play with farming now. I rent the fields to a young guy. Nice Italian boy. He's put in kidney beans this year. I wouldn't sell the farm. I wouldn't as long as nobody waves big money in my face." He pointed toward the lake. "Good vineyard country. The hills let cold air slide down to the water, and we don't get so many late spring freezes."

"We used to make our wine," Pauline said. "Pete, his father teached him."

"Now, Pa was a champeen winemaker. He learned in Naples, Italy, the old-country way. Back in Rochester he made wine in the basement out of Little Black Joes. We call them Zinfandels now. Always kept the wine-cellar locked and the key around his neck. He'd come upstairs and say,

'*Il vino fa'l sangue sano!*' Wine makes good blood! The old man's breakfast was a big glass of red with two raw eggs in it."

Pete had a long smile, and he smiled often, and always he smiled when he spoke of his father.

"You know how we knew when to bung up the bottles? The way we knew the fermenting was finished?"

"I couldn't guess."

"Then you're learning, my friend. This is the old Italiano way: we pulled a penny balloon over the neck of the bottle to keep air and dirt out and let gas escape into the balloon. When the balloon didn't get bigger, we'd start bunging up."

"Those darned old days," Pauline said, and she smiled at them.

"They're gone, honey." Pete waved a crutch skyward. "My grandfather planted his grapes according to the stars and moon. Now the boys out here plant according to Cornell University."

We went in for lunch. Pete poured out two jiggers of Seagram's Seven Crown and passed me one. "No good blood in it; only just some heat."

Filomena joined us. The conversation covered many things: crops, carpentry, machines, Italy, food. At times the talk was about someone who had failed a promise or pulled a shenanigan — they condemned the man then.

Pauline made the lunch from what she had taken from her garden and the edges of the field: a salad of dandelion and wild mustard greens served with olive oil and vinegar, boiled cardoon deep-fried in a garlic egg batter, boiled and sugared rhubarb, and a small piece of fried venison from a quart jar.

"Never eaten canned deer," I said.

"Does it taste like more?"

"That's the cardoon."

"And you have some more rhubarbs too," Pauline said. "You know, we hear about this place called McDonald's. Two weeks ago we drive there for a hamburg sangwich." Her face pinched up. "Meat was thin like cheese-cloth. 'This is no hamburg sangwich,' I say. 'This is joke.'"

Filomena couldn't have the dinner. She took boiled spinach and bread, dipping the bread into the spinach and eating all of it. She had her health, but the hearing wasn't so good now. "She's ninety-four," Pete said.

"I'm ninety-four."

"I just told him you're ninety-four, Ma."

"I was lucky all my life," she said.

"She came to America when she was eighteen."

Pete spoke in a kind of Bronx accent, his wife and mother with deep Italian accents. Sometimes I asked questions just to hear their words.

"When we talk about American things, we speak American. When it's Italian things, we talk Italiano," Pete said. "I don't speak it so good, but Pauline, jeez, she really talks the old language. They out-talk me in Italiano, but I take care of them in American."

Filomena, whose common name was Fanny, finished her meal and sat back listening as best she could, looking at nothing in particular. Her hands, spotted and veined like moth wings, fluttered up and down from time to time and landed softly on the table, in her lap.

I asked her, "Did you like the old days?"

"Ha!" she said. "They think more of horse or jackass than human person. They never teach me to read!"

"We womens was brought up to be just like mouse," Pauline whispered. "We was so quiet."

"Work all time because we got to make everything," Filomena said. "Couldn't buy no cookies, no cakes. Got to make it all. Couldn't buy nothing."

"You had two choices for dinner and supper," Pete said. "*Pasta fasol* or nothing. Every day we ate *pasta fasol*. Always on the stove *pasta fasol, pasta fasol*. Macaroni and beans. Shit on it."

"You got tired of it?"

"What can you do, my friend? We ate poor, lived poor, slept poor."

"How do you sleep poor?"

"Five to a room."

"My mother she had eight childrens," Pauline said. "They was all delivered by midwife. She go to doctor for first time in her life when she is sixty-five. Poor was not all things bad."

Pauline cleared the table and got the risen dough ready for the oven. Just before she pushed the pan in, she made the sign of the cross and kissed her first two fingers and touched them to the dough. I asked her what it meant.

"I don't know, but my mother used to bless the breads. If she throwed bread away, she kissed it. It was sin to waste."

"Rough living," Pete said.

Pauline smiled. "But life was good. You had your band."

"My band? Hell! The only good thing was eating on Sunday."

"We call Sunday a little special," Pauline said.

"Sunday was spaghetti day. But there were other hard things in Rochester, even if you were born in America like us. If your name ended in a vowel, you didn't go to college."

"What's a vowel got to do with it?"

"Masucci, Zambito, Gambrini, Barsetta. You were Italian, my friend. All they would say to you was 'Shut up' or 'Go to hell.' "

"Polish peoples come in our garden and steal our garlics," Pauline said. "We have nothing extra."

"Rochester was tough. If you were a German off the boat, you got a good job. Kodak or Bausch and Lomb wanted Germans. They thought just being Kraut made a good worker in lenses and film. But if you were Italian, you got the shovel and pick. No questions asked, no answers given. My brother finally got a job with a master carpenter, but the old man hid the skills from him — afraid the kid would take his trade away."

"Work all the time," Filomena said. "Work, work."

"Work was their god. Pa was a machinist for the Rochester streetcar company. The whole family worked. I drove a dump truck to help out."

"You was driving the truck when you first find me," Pauline said.

"I saw her washing clothes in a tub under a tree. I was hauling dirt in a hundred-twenty-five-dollar truck. I had a truck, a straw hat, and a cigar. Big man, you see. I honked and she smiled and that was it."

"Pete and me we go to the park. My brother and sister go with us always."

"It was courting then," Pete said. "Her father, Sam Zambito, he watched and approved everything. No messing around. The old Sicilian he knows when the pear's ripe it falls to the ground by itself." Pauline grinned at that. "But after I married her, Sam encouraged me. Without him, I wouldn't ever got this place. See, he came out here first. He lived up the road, up at the dead end where the undertaker lives now."

"The undertaker lives at the dead end?"

"Hey," Pete said. "Leave the jokes to me. I'm the fifty-third card."

He passed a whiskey. I asked, "Were you ever bitter about the crutches?"

"Bitter? Where was time to be bitter?"

"I prayed for him," Filomena said.

"It didn't help, Ma."

"Could a doctor have helped?"

"Who knows? My parents had no money, no education. They believed anything."

"I prayed for him. I prayed, yes."

"Okay, Ma." Pete poured himself another. "They wheeled me two miles in a kid's wagon one time to see Aimée Semple McPherson, the faith healer. I was seven or eight. We were up on a stage. She made a cross on my forehead in oil, and she looked at me and said, 'Throw away those crutches! Throw them down!' I knew I couldn't do it. You think I hadn't

18. *Pete, Pauline, and Filomena Masucci near Cheshire, New York*

tried a thousand times? 'Throw away those sticks, boy!' She yelled at me. I didn't, though. The audience called out. Jeez, they were crazy for a miracle.''

Pete's mother looked distressed as he told the story. "I prayed for him," she said quietly.

"And they took me to another healer. An Indian he claimed to be. The seventh son of the seventh son. They got him for fraud too. Now the Jehovah's Witnesses knock on the door and want to heal me. I tell them, 'Shit on this healing!' ''

We went outside to the edge of the fields. Pete said, "With the garden and wild food and the orchard, we got our retirement. There's a grocery in the cellar with what Pauline's put up. We always had our own meat, but we butchered the last steer a year ago and the last hog three years ago. Now that's finished for us too.''

Pauline pointed to the cardoon growing along the fence, and said, "God's green earth."

Pete shook his head. "There was a time when we made our own cheese and sold it door to door and grew our own wheat and had it milled over in Pittsford. We took apples down to Canandaigua to get made into cider. We raised ducks and turkeys. Tried them all. Old MacDonald had a farm."

"E-I-E-I-O," Pauline sang. "We never have sheeps though. When we have dairy cows, I wash the barn insides every day. You could eat in there, it was so clean. And when Pete drived the tractor, I ride on back behind him so I can be out of the wind. Where he go and work, I go."

"All that stuff is gone, honey."

"Now we don't move so good, and I got the sugar."

"She means sugar diabetes."

"The best was the childrens. We have twenty-four foster childrens come live with us since we move here in nineteen forty-five, but we never have childrens out of us."

"Cheaper by the dozen," Pete said. "One time we had seven all at once. Some had problems, but they were good pups when they got out here. We have a Puerto Rican boy coming back to see us Memorial Day."

Pauline looked at her watch and hurried into the house.

"Soap opera," Pete said. "I don't care for any of that. I work. What else can you do? I was born all over again when we came out. I'd be dead now if we didn't move to this place." He stopped and poked a crutch at some cardoon. "There's one thing though I've looked for here. I thought I'd find it."

"What's the thing?"

"I been put on this land for something, but I don't know what the hell for."

"You just told me."

4

I STAYED in the old vineyard country three days. Chisholm and I talked and worked, I wrote a few letters, cleaned cameras, we ate, we drank some Genesee. We disagreed, agreed, and said where we might be in a year or ten years and where we wouldn't be if we could help it.

My last evening with him, we walked down the road and he pointed out a spring in the hill high above the lake, where Indians had camped for many years. Under the grass, big dark rings, the marks of Seneca huts, still remained. "It seems they left nothing behind," he said, "as if they never were, but their signature is still here when you know where to look."

He talked angrily about the Sullivan-Clinton campaign George Washington sent through New York in 1779 to punish local Indians for siding with the British and also to clear the region for white settlers. The Iroquois tribes, led by the Onondaga Hiawatha, lived in houses, farmed the land, and, by most definitions, were civilized. Yet some settlers found that idea intolerable and saw to the destruction of the Iroquois. To encourage new settlement, the government even gave veterans of the Revolutionary War tracts of Indian land, but most of the soldiers sold it to speculators for a few cents an acre.

We turned to head home. "This has been a strange part of the country," Chisholm said. "Something around the lakes brings out the mystical in a person. These counties have been full of prophets, religious zealots, and spiritualists who had hot-lines to God. Or the dead. Joseph Smith, Jemina Wilkinson, the Fox sisters. There was a pair. They rapped to spirits in seances and got them to tap back. Under investigation later, they admitted making the noises from the other world by cracking their toe joints."

In the moonlight, we walked over an abandoned vineyard. The posts had fallen down, and vines inched about for something to crawl up on; one had twisted around a rusting baler and another climbed a broken plow. We passed a foundation of a barn that had collapsed, a toppled chimney, and a weedy depression where an icehouse had stood. "These are all dreams we're walking over," I said.

Chisholm looked at me strangely and went quiet for some time. When he spoke again it was about the dogs. Afterward, I thought I understood his silence: I had undercut the stone wall we had built, our accomplishment. The wall looked enduring, and it would serve for a while, but there would come a time when it would be a pile of rock to no end. I had undercut the biggest dream of all — the one for permanence. Maybe that's what we really felt in the stones: how man is the tool of his dreams, dreams that rise only to fall back to earth.

Wednesday afternoon I left. "Going?" Chisholm said. "You've got wings on your feet." I drove up along Canandaigua Lake, past the summer houses of the company men from Kodak and Bausch & Lomb and Xerox, past houses with names like Bide-a-Wee and Summer Daze, past the Roseland amusement park of sno-cones and fudge ripple, past pink and aquamarine motels, through Canandaigua with its wide main street of brick buildings from another century.

At the top of the street, among the Greek Revival houses, stood the old

Ontario County Courthouse — nearly as big as a state capitol — where Susan B. Anthony was found guilty of voting; to one side, in the same architectural style, the Masonic Lodge. Chisholm had said the similarity and proximity of the two buildings indicated something about the administration of justice here in the nineteenth century. It was western New York where, in the 1820s, a Masonic Lodge in Batavia turned down William Morgan for membership even though he claimed membership in Rochester. He threatened to reveal the highest secrets of the order. The last time a non-Mason saw him alive was in Lewiston; a few days later, Lake Ontario washed up a body that may have been Morgan's. The issue mobilized a group into a political party called the Anti-Masons. "That," Chisholm had said, "was the power Masons used to have here."

5

JOSEPH Smith, an eighteen-year-old with small hands and big feet, a quiet and "unlaughing" boy, encountered the Angel Moroni, son of Mormon, on a drumlin alongside a little road south of Palmyra in 1827. The road is now New York 21 and the drumlin, a streamlined hump of glacially drifted soil, they call Hill Cumorah. It is not a Mount Sinai or an Ararat, but rather a much humbler thing, yet apparently of sufficient majesty for angels and God to have chosen it as the place to speak to Smith. There he unearthed the golden plates that he said were the source of the *Book of Mormon*. With the aid of an ancient pair of optical instruments, the Urim and Thummin, which Smith found with the plates, he was able to translate the "revised" Egyptian hieroglyphics, although he insisted on dictating his translation to scribes from behind a curtain.

I looked at Hill Cumorah and tried to envision it as it was in Smith's day. The Mormons have built a shaft depicting witnesses who attested to the reality of the plates and the heavenly pronouncements, but, to my mind, the tower protested too much. Somehow monuments more entomb history than mark it. To see Bunker Hill (in fact Breed's Hill) today rising unimposingly from the workers' houses is to put historical imagination to the test, because Bunker Hill now belongs more to a notion of the past than to actuality.

Palmyra was a clean town of three-story brick buildings where I turned east on New York 31 and went down along the route of the Erie Canal, through villages, over fields of deep green, under blooming locust trees, and past barns collapsing next to mobile homes that looked depressingly immobile yet also impermanent. At Savannah, I found the unmarked road to Conquest (down the highway from Victory) easily enough, but staying on it was another matter. Trying to distinguish the main line from the tributaries by playing compass against the worn, yellow stripes was blue roading at its perplexing best. After some miles, I had no idea where I was. I called out to five fellows pouring something into the crankcase of a Trans-Am. These were the men who believe in the restorative power of STP as the Chinese believe in rhinoceros horn. "Is this the road to Conquest?"

They answered almost together: "Yes! Where? No! Conquest?" Then, pleased to be considered authorities on the country, they all came to my window. Each answered the question at length, and sometimes at the same moment as another. They corrected, modified, amplified, clarified, and repeated each other's directions. At last I came to understand nothing. "All right," one said, "here it is: run this road straight through, and you can't help but miss it."

Off I went, hoping Conquest would find me. In the dairy country, chewing Holsteins and Guernseys switched their tails and flicked their skins. On the other side of Johnny Cake Road lay Conquest. Then I began the game again, looking for Cato. Along the roads were cottage industries selling clothesline poles, purple martin houses, potted plants, AKC pups.

I stopped for a sandwich at an old hotel in Cato, but the only food was pickled sausage at the bar, so I had sausage with a glass of beer, and that, as it turned out, was dinner. Through the wavy panes of old windows, I could see children standing along the main street, jerking their arms up and down at trucks. Each time a driver pulled on his air horns, the children jumped and cheered. That evening in Cato, it was the only game in town.

Just after dusk I arrived in Central Square and couldn't find a place to park for the night. I finally drove up a quiet side street. In ten minutes the police joined me. "What's your business here?" one said.

"Got sleepy on the highway."

He gave a lengthy explanation about recent burglaries in the neighborhood. "In other words, Missouri, better move tail along."

"I'm going to fall asleep at the wheel."

"Get a motel."

"I don't want a motel. I live in the truck. I don't like motels. You've got my license number. I'm not going to pull off a heist now."

"Can you prove ownership of this vehicle?"

In irritation, I snapped open my wallet, sending credit cards flying. An older cop, a large pile of beef on the hoof, joined in.

"What's all the jawing about?" His hands were truncheons itching to clobber something.

"He wants a place to sleep."

"Has he got money, or do we have a vagrant here?"

"He's got money," I said, "but he's not going to prove it unless you book him. He just proved his identity and ownership of his vehicle and that's enough, considering he's broken no law."

"Go down to the park next to the cemetery," the beef said. "You'll be all right there."

"Is the night shift going to come around and run me off?"

"We are the night shift. We'll keep an eye on you."

For whose protection I didn't know, but I went to the tiny park and pulled up equidistant between homeplate and the tombstones. I'd traveled ten thousand miles and had not encountered a single hoodlum. But I'd been taken for one several times.

6

THE menu said: "Check Our Snowmobile Weekend Package Deal." I skipped it and ordered a standard road breakfast. The shingled cafe, Ben and Bernies, afforded a broad view of Lake Oneida. The placemats were maps of Italy, and the man beside me ate bagels and cream cheese. No question: this was the Northeast.

The Oneida shoreline road was warm — too warm — for May, although maples by the highway had opened to a cooling shade. The perpetual spring I'd been following around the country was about done. On a map Lake Oneida looks like a sperm whale, and my course that morning was down the spine, from the flukes to the snout. All along the shore, old houses, big houses, were losing to the North climate, and for miles it was a place of sag and dilapidation.

The lake once formed a twenty-mile link in the Erie Canal, and just east of Oneida, excavation for the waterway began on the Fourth of July, 1817. I stopped near the spot at an abandoned section of canal and walked down the old towpath, now a snowmobile trail. The canal, only four feet deep in its early years, had become a rank, bosky, froggy trough. But it was that forty-eight inches of water that did so much to open western New York and the Midwest to settlement and commerce. "Clinton's Folly," the popular name for the canal as it was being built, followed the Mohawk Valley, the only natural break at this latitude in the Appalachians.

From Lake Erie to the Hudson River (363 miles, 83 stone locks, 13 aqueducts) the canal moved people and things between the middle of the nation and the ocean; it was this watercourse, as much as anything else, that made New York City the leading Atlantic port. Travelers who had some money could take a packet boat with windows and berths, while poorer immigrants heading into the Midlands rode cheaper and drearier line boats. Ten years after Clinton's Folly opened, the populations of Syracuse, Rochester, and Buffalo increased three hundred percent; the canal, having paid for itself in that decade, had changed the northwest quarter of America. No paltry accomplishment for a scheme that even the visionary Thomas Jefferson saw as a little short of madness.

On down the highway to Rome, New York. From its appearance, it could have been London in 1946: the central section gutted but for a few old brownstone churches, a new shopping mall with triple-tier parking lot, and the National Park Service reconstruction of eighteenth-century Fort Stanwix covering several blocks on the east side. While the palisaded fort had been elaborately rebuilt, it did not turn Rome back into a city, and while ribbon development along the highways gave an economic life, it didn't give Rome a center. The place looked as if it had died of heart rot — from the inside out.

I went up into the Adirondacks at a point where they form a virtual wall, and Ghost Dancing labored making the ascent. No sun in the forest and twelve degrees cooler. The ancient Adirondack Mountains are much older than the old Appalachians they merge with; consequently, they tend toward roundness with few sharp outcroppings. Adirondack ("bark eaters") was a contemptuous epithet Mohawks gave to some degenerated tribe so poor it had to eat trees.

I bought gas in Alder Creek and asked the pumpman what winter was like in the mountains. "This," he said and held up the stump of a little finger. "Frostbite. Snowfall of a hundred forty-two inches last year, forty-five below, wind chill seventy below. That's what we call winter."

The forest became heavier, sky darker, mountains higher, settlements farther apart. What few people were here the black flies and weather kept indoors that day. Low clouds sailed around under a high overcast and broke up like schooners on the summits. Although moose and caribou disappeared long ago, I was at the heart of a great wilderness second only to the Northwoods of Maine in the eastern United States. An occasional woodsy gift shop or burger stand built like a chalet did not prevent the forest from being pervasive, ominous, and forbidding; nor did they quiet the strange cries of birds from the dark hemlock. Then a cold rain blew down, turned to hail, then eased to a drizzly fog. It was early afternoon, yet headlights vanished after twenty yards as if the damp extinguished the beams. Birch, alder, conifers — nothing but trees and water and fog for miles.

East of the village of Blue Mountain Lake, dominated by a bluish hump of the Adirondacks, the road descended to a small building — part house, part tavern — snugged against a wooded hill and surrounded by vaporous mountains. The mist glowed orange from a neon beer sign. The building, white clapboard trimmed in red with a silvery corrugated tin roof, was the Forest House Lodge. In fact, it wasn't a lodge, but something even better: an antique roadhouse. The roadhouse — institution and word — has nearly disappeared from America.

I ate a ham and cheese sandwich and drank Genesee Cream Ale. The pallid barmaid talked quietly to an old woman; when there would come a deep rumble of thunder, the women paused in conversation. There were no other sounds, no others about. The room was almost entirely of pine — immaculately scrubbed, hand-polished pine gleaming like lacquerware. Each table top, each wall, every stool and bench shone warmly in the soft incandescent light, and bottles of rum and brandy and whiskey glowed from within. It was as if the faded woman had given her life to buffing everything to a soft lustre and, in doing so, lost her own. Across from a photograph of an awakened hibernating bear hung an 1885 picture of the first Forest House Lodge when it was a stage stop. The present building, dating from the thirties, seemed to have absorbed the continuum of history.

Every so often a logging truck hissed wetly down the highway and rolled the mists before they settled in once more against the polished windows. I sat a long time in an event of no significance beyond simple joy. It lacked only the dimension of sharing.

A young man and woman came in carrying a tension as though an unexploded grenade had just dropped between them. He was a swelling of veins across the forehead and his speech a gnashing of teeth, but she was a light and airy woman, one who would move easily in loving. I was grateful for the company and forced a conversation about the Adirondacks that I ended up turning into an Izaak Walton League lecture.

The man said, "Wilderness! It's all a crock now. I rafted the Blue Nile in Ethiopia three years ago. After a couple of days, we got into country where the natives dressed like the old pictures you see — men almost naked, carrying spears. Women bare from the waist up. You know, darkest Africa. I was taking pictures when a girl wearing a necklace made out of the cap of a BIC pen held out her arm. She had a broken Timex on. She said, 'No *teek-teek.*' That almost ruined the trip. It's the same here — a bootprint on every square yard of Adirondacks.''

"Wilderness doesn't mean untouched.''

"Then it doesn't mean anything worth anything.''

"If you knew a place that had never been walked over by civilized man, would you stay out of it?''

"I would. Of course I would.''

"You wouldn't either,'' the woman said. "You'd walk every foot of it and brag about your experience and refuse to tell anyone else where it was.''

"That's it,'' he said. "Get your coat.''

7

OUR beginnings do not foreshadow our ends if one judges by the Hudson River. A few miles east of the Bad Luck Ponds, the Hudson came down between the ridges to race alongside route 28; it was a mountain stream: clear, cold, shallow, noisy. A few miles from its source in Lake Tear-in-the-Clouds a mile up on Mount Marcy (the Indian name for the mountain is better: Tahawus, "Cloud-splitter'') and three hundred river miles from the thousand oily piers of Hoboken, Weehawken, and Manhattan, here it was a canoer's watercourse. Above the little Hudson, spumes of mist rose from the mountains like campfire smoke.

Route 8 dropped out of the Adirondacks to Lake George, the way lined with resort homes and summer camps that advertise in the back pages of the *New York Times Magazine.* At Hague, I turned north and followed the water up a narrow valley to Ticonderoga and cut through town to the shore of Lake Champlain where, under the dark brow of the fort built by the British against French and Indian raids, I waited for the ferry.

A ferry, interrupted off and on only during the Revolutionary War, had crossed the long lake at this narrow point since the 1740s. The boat of 1759, large enough to carry a stagecoach, had a sail, but on windless days, boatmen walked the length of it and pushed with a single, thirty-foot oar. After Ethan Allen and Benedict Arnold captured Fort Ticonderoga in 1775, the crossing became a critical link in holding the northwestern portion of the colonies, even though Redcoats recaptured the fort and ferry two years later before it came again into American hands. When the British finally left after two wars, they returned as tourists. One, James Buckingham, wrote in 1838:

> We descended to the ferry across Lake Champlain, where we passed over in one of the rudest boats I had ever seen. It was little more than an oblong trough. . . . With single sail, the helmsman steering with a long oar, we soon crossed the lake, and landed at the station of Shoreham.

Almost a century and a half later, I made the same crossing with only a few technological changes here and there: the sail and oarsman had given way to a modified, Navy-surplus landing craft attached to a cargo barge. On the other bank, the Old Stone House that Buckingham had passed, built in 1823 of big blocks dragged across the frozen lake from ruined Fort Ticonderoga, still stood, although now an antique shop.

The storm blew on west, and a soft amber light fell over Vermont to give the rise of wet fields deep relief and color. Through the villages of Orwell, Sudbury, and Goshen Corners, past the old groceries with SALADA TEA lettered in gold on front windows, and into the Green Mountains (which, some say, *Vermont* means in French despite cynical literalists who insist on "Worm Mountain").

The White River led through highlands to route 12. Before realizing it, I was nearly across the narrow state. I drove past the Delectable Mountains (from *Pilgrim's Progress*) to a village surrounded on all sides by still more mountains and opened only by two rocky brooks. It looked like the set for an Andy Hardy movie — things quaint in the manner of Norman Rockwell. A small green encircled by Georgian and Federal houses with white picket fences and hitching posts joined the town center of two- and three-story granite buildings, each with many muntined windows. Around the green, along the pickets, lilacs and apple trees blossomed. Maybe the town wasn't the prettiest village in America, but if the townspeople wanted to make the claim, I wouldn't have disputed them. It was Woodstock, Vermont.

The streets spread from the green into wrenching twists that defied even compass reckoning as they played between Mount Tom and Mount Peg and between the Ottauquechee River and Kedron Brook. There wasn't much level ground in the dell, so the old firehouse hung over the brook, and another building stuck a foundation corner into the water. In spite of its smallness, the town had seven bridges — one of them a fine, covered structure. Most of the big elms were gone, but by intermixing species the town still retained tall maples, which prevented the barrenness of other New England villages that have lost elms.

Although the current population of twelve hundred was the largest ever, the town once had a medical school and five newspapers. In those early days, citizens manufactured combs, haut-boy reeds, Rumsford firedoors, pianofortes, brandy, and pottery. Today, except for a small ski-lift assembly plant, Woodstock was a citizenry of clerks: the shop windows displayed Vermont cheese, maple candy, maple syrup, hand-painted wallpaper, Williamsburg reproductions, Hickey-Freeman suits, period furniture, early ironwork, primitives, pewter ware, Chinese Export porcelain, English antiques, Izod pullovers, new wooden toys, antique dolls, tinware, kitchen collectibles, old prints of grouse, brass candlesticks, and copper pots. There were inns, restaurants, and a dozen real estate offices (outsiders own half of the residential and agricultural land in Vermont). About the mountains were ski slopes and hiking and horse trails, and in the south end of the valley, tennis courts, a skating rink, and a golf course. In other words, the village lived by the tourist — the well-heeled tourist. But few places in the country fused tourism and town life so well. In Woodstock, they were parts of the whole.

Any New England town worth its colonial salt has at least one bell cast in Paul Revere's foundry; like a DAR certificate, it's a touchstone of authenticity. Here, they boasted of four.

Yet things were not always so civilized in Woodstock. The first white man to see the site, Ensign Richardson, wrote in 1761 that the dingle was a "spruce hurricane" unfit for habitation other than by Indians. But settlers came anyway and cut out a green for grazing and put up stocks and a whipping post and cleared the lower hills for raising Merino sheep. Now the sheep were gone and the forest had taken back the mountains; gone too was any indication of where on the green lies buried the boiled heart of a child thought to be a vampire.

Ensign Richardson's view notwithstanding, the town had been blessed with its wooded setting and the resources around it. From Massachusetts and Connecticut, the first settlers brought along an established culture because the remoteness of the village forced them to grow and manufacture most of their necessities; but after the railroad came through, they began losing their self-sufficiency and depended more and more on goods made elsewhere, and the little independent industries disappeared. Then the railroad started carrying in people looking for spruce hurricanes: upland game-bird shooters, deer hunters, trout fishermen, horsemen, skiers (the first ski tow in the country was on old man Gilbert's farm outside of town), and hikers following the Appalachian Trail, which passes just to the north. And still more: golfers, tennis players, summer camp children, students for the equestrian and photographic "country" schools. And shoppers.

A chamber of commerce flier claimed that the citizens had "zealously guided Woodstock's development and growth past the hazards of change that overtook much of the country"; perhaps, at least for now, that was true. Indeed, the town was free of golden-arch strip development and shopping centers (one nineteenth-century textile mill had been remodeled into a shopping arcade), and the core of the village remained where it has always been — on the green. At night, when automobiles left the streets, Woodstock had the appearance of another century because, in place of the old businesses that died — the hatter, baker, saddler, tinsmith, fuller, foundryman, wheelwright, miller, wainwright — new businesses had come to use the old buildings in new ways so that Woodstock wasn't a restoration or even a renovation, but rather a town — like the best English villages — with a continuous and evident past.

The careful Yankees, overseeing both their past and their future, managed to lure a class of vacationers who came to stay for a week or a month, and they came with money, although Woodstock wasn't noticeably more expensive than a gimcrack tourist dive.

If the village had a fault, it lay in both a hubris about its picturesqueness and in its visitors with new money and new facades. While I walked the streets, I had the sense that the men, still wearing their club ties, had sung in collegiate glee clubs and that the women attended colleges where one's serviette was kept in a napkin cubby.

8

IF you keep a mental list of things in America that you can kiss goodbye, add the tourist home to it. As an institution it isn't extinct, but nearly so, thanks to the insistence of the American vacationer for star-burst-in-the-sky motels. You might as well ask him to share his toothbrush as his bathroom. Yet a proper tourist home is a third the expense and twice as clean as any cellblock motel. It can be like staying with Grandmother.

In Woodstock I took lodgings in the Bagley Tourist Home, a tall frame house on a hill with a high view of the Ottauquechee and the Green Mountains. An armoire and spool spindle bed filled most of the wallpapered room; at the window, an apple tree sprinkled petals against the screen. The bathroom, a clean and flowery pink place, was down the hall.

Raymond Bagley was a retired machinist and his wife a former schoolteacher who managed things and sold jams and jellies. For a time, I thought the quaintness might overwhelm me, but, as I sat talking with the Bagleys on the front-porch glider, the feeling passed. Much of what I learned about Woodstock came during two evenings on the porch. He and his wife both grew up in Woodstock; unlike some of the villagers — many from other states — the Bagleys showed no animosity toward "flatlanders" (anyone from outside the Green or White Mountains) who kept the town prosperous.

After sunset I went down to the village for dinner at Bentley's, a place, the menu said, with "the dignity of old wood and lush tropical plants." The diners wore heels and Von Furstenberg signature dresses or plaid shirts and L. L. Bean hiking boots. The men had pointy, thrusty names like Dirk and Derek and Pyke. I heard conversations about Grand Marnier crepes and glacé fruit and the problems of paying for a daughter's ballet lessons. An engaged couple dithered over whether to polish their shoe soles for the wedding — after all, they would kneel in front of the congregation. Because I'd never eaten a shad roe omelet before, I ordered one, figuring I could write it off to experience, but I almost ordered a second.

Around and up and down, I walked through town and watched Kedron Brook have its go at the rocks. The splashing and roe gave me a thirst, so I went to the Woodstock Inn, a big posh place of high-polish maintenance with an eighteen-hole putting green off the garden terrace. Laurance Rockefeller, who married a local woman and still helicoptered in to relax, owned the inn.

Cars parked in front were either elaborate hood-ornament models or Saabs, the Volkswagen of the Ivy League. On a BMW was a bumper sticker: POLO AT SKIDMORE. On a Mercedes a vanity license plate: STYLE. Throughout I saw a compulsion toward panache, a thing these people needed as the peacock needs its iridescent plumes.

In the piney taproom I sat near a table of two men and their wives who wore the colors for that spring: pink and Kelly green touched up with white. The women were in perfect trim like mortuary lawns, and the husbands wore clothes for the man who knows where he's going. They drank cranberry liqueur and Harvey's Bristol Cream with creme. The conversation was about suitable gifts to take the children at home with grandmothers. The decision: volleyballs for the boys, stuffed kangaroos for the girls, brandied apricot cakes for grandmothers.

I wondered what the boys were doing at Sonny's Place in Dime Box, Texas.

THE dreams were the kind I would have welcomed the police to rouse me from: twisted distortions of fact and desire all turning on the Cherokee offering a new marriage. At last I woke to find myself alone in the wall-papered tourist room. The desolation seemed to have velocity it hit so hard. I poured a whiskey, watched apple petals tap the screen, and waited out the night.

I spent the day on Mount Tom. Had I owned a ghost shirt, I'd have danced madly all over that mountain. Instead, I tried to keep from looking inward, tried to reach outward, but, as Black Elk says, certain things among the shadows of a man's life do not have to be remembered — they remember themselves.

By evening my judgment had given way, and I called home. I was talking fast, talking, talking, trying to find where we stood, how our chances were. She talked. No matter how we tried, our words — confounded — ran athwart and, as usual, we ended up at cross-purposes. Neither of us knew where to go from there. Nothing to do but hang up. When I put the receiver down and heard the line ding dead, I tried to excuse the failure by thinking that nothing ever works out over a telephone.

The door of the booth stuck, and I went into a rage, slamming the thing, yelling. People looked around. I went off waiting for insight, but all I got was desolation again.

Black Elk on seeing his people on the blue road: "I did not know then how much was ended."

10

SOME men take their broken marriages to church-basement workshops. I took mine to the highways and attempted to tuck it away for nearly eleven thousand miles. I had poked into things along the byroads, all the while hiding from my own failure. I hadn't forgotten it — I'd merely held down certain thoughts the way a murderer might hold under a person he's trying to drown.

Not so much to eat as to occupy myself, I went into a no-name, three-calendar, ten-stool cafe with walls of linoleum. Idling, I asked the cook who lifted hot lids with her apron ends, "What's the name of your diner?"

"The Wasp," she said in a Green Mountain voice.

"You mean like white-Anglo — "

"I mean like the high school mascot. First owner was a teacher."

"It's a nice, simple place."

"We try. Woodstock's gettin' a little too high pollutin' for me." She meant "highfalutin."

Two men, one carrying a small Crescent wrench on a key ring, were talking about a new son. I wasn't paying attention until the father said, "That's what saved the marriage." My head snapped up as if someone shouted my name.

"Babies don't save marriages," the friend said.

"This one did. I got down on myself when we found out Claudia couldn't get pregnant because of me. She was sorry, but she coulda lived with it. Not me. That's when I started running around proving."

"So how'd she get knocked up?"

"I changed my drawers."

The friend laughed. "Then you ate a gallon of oysters."

"Doctor found out I was low on sperms. Said my drawers was too tight — too much heat. Tight pants don't allow the animal heat to escape, and the high temperature kills off sperms. When I started wearing my old Army drawers again, Claud was pregnant inside three months."

I finished breakfast and drove up highway 4 in full envy of a man who could correct his marital problems by changing his shorts. The road crossed Quechee Gorge, an unexpected hundred-sixty-five-foot-deep sluice cut through stony flanks of the mountain; a couple clutched the bridge railing as they uneasily peered down into the gloom. Then over the Connecticut River and into Hanover, New Hampshire. The morning was hot — the hottest yet — and I had no mind for the road.

I killed off most of the day by wandering around the Dartmouth campus. The Reverend Eleazar Wheelock founded the college with his own library and a log hut in the woods and a goal of providing "for the education and instruction of Youth of the Indian Tribes in this Land in reading, writing, and all parts of Learning which shall appear necessary and expedient for civilizing and christianizing Children of Pagans." The Dartmouth motto reflects its origin: *Vox clamantis in deserto*. But now the voice crying in the (semi)wilderness was that of the tribal Americans who comprised one percent of the enrollment and who were decrying the unofficial nickname of the athletic teams — the Indians — as well as the "Scalp 'em" cheers, the faculty dining room murals depicting Indians in various states of carousal, and a popular rally song:

Oh, Eleazar Wheelock was a very pious man;
He went into the wilderness to teach the Indian,
With a Gradus ad Parnassum, a Bible, and a drum,
And five hundred gallons of New England rum.

As best I could tell, the students, faculty, and administration would gladly put the Indian rah-rah to rest by using the other nickname, "The Green." But alums — there was the problem. They might tolerate women graduates, but to give up their official Wah-hoo-wah!, that was too much. And so the murals got carefully boarded over but not taken down.

In the afternoon, I went on again. Near West Canaan, I stopped at Al's Steamed Dogs & Filling Station. A hand-painted sign: EAT HERE AND GET GAS. Al's was closed. The sky darkened, a shower doused the road and cooled things in the White Mountains. The villages seemed to seep down the slopes to settle in the valleys along streams where people of another time built multiwindowed stone and brick factories and mills. Most of the old buildings and mill dams had been done in by cheap electric power and centralized industry. But there was talk of again tapping the unused energy in the New England streams with small, computer-designed turbines.

I took route 104 up to the motel congestion of the west side of Lake Winnipesaukee — the lake with a hundred thirty different spellings and almost as many translations from the Indian (the best is "the smile of the Great Spirit") — and then around to the north shore into quieter country. On this corner of the lake, instead of stationwagons with wet swimtrunks tied to antennas and door handles, there were worn pickups, each hauling at least one rusty something.

It was sundown when I reached Melvin Village, a tiny place between the Ossipee Mountains and the northeast shore of the big lake. Among the old, white clapboard and black-shuttered houses lay an almost absolute calm. The only noise came from the diminutive Melvin River — in truth, a brook — sliding over a dam of commensurate size. Behind the dam, the water darkly translucent and nearly encircled by maples and the steep slopes of the Ossipees, a pair of bufflehead ducks paddled silently, then beat a long ascent into the twilight.

The town, pure New England, was so plain it was almost stark. I drove up and back the main street, New Hampshire 109, and looked for a place to pull in for the night. At the edge of town, I stopped at the Snack Bar, a wooden building with a porch screened against mosquitoes. It was late May, but the evening pressed close like midsummer.

I ate a grinder — elsewhere called a hero, hoagie, poorboy, submarine, sub, torpedo, Italian — and drank a chocolate frappe — elsewhere called a milkshake or malted velvet or cabinet. Although the true milkshake doesn't exist east of the Appalachians, the grinder was the best thing to happen to me in a day: thinly sliced beef and ham, slivered tomatoes, chopped lettuce, and minced hot peppers, all dressed down with vinegar and oil. I went back to the window to order another.

"You like my sandwich?" the proprietor said.

"Decidedly delicious."

The owner, Bert LaFrance, once lost a talent contest to Danny Kaye and used to sing and dance with his brother in traveling tent shows playing the New England mill towns and later the gold-mine section of Ontario where streets were mud and everything was wide open. "Twenty bucks a week," he said. "So who cared about money? We did. But work meant more. I was a poor man's Desi Arnaz: sang and danced to 'Night and Day,' 'That Old Black Magic.' All played on the conga drums. We performed with Benny Goodman, Sarah Vaughn, the Three Sons. Later when I was working with a couple of girls, we had a twelve-minute routine with six costume changes. But by then tent shows were dying out. They held their own against movies, but not television. It was good while it lasted, even during the war. I was a Marine and got assigned to a show-biz unit that performed to sell war bonds. I thought I had it made. Then one day an officer comes up and tells us we're going overseas. I asked where. 'Don't ask,' he says. In four weeks, we went from the boards to Guadalcanal." LaFrance shook his head. "Life! But what the hell, Melvin Village is a place called lovely."

"Who's Melvin?"

"Melvin? Oh, you mean Melvin like in Village. Don't know. Ask Len."

"Who's Len?"

Len was standing behind me. He and his wife had moved from Boston to take over the Hansel and Gretel Gift Shop. "Don't know either, I'm afraid," he said, "but I know who does. If you're staying, I'll introduce you tomorrow. She is — if anyone is — Melvin Village. A real live Yankee Doodle Dandy."

"Born on the Fourth of July?"

"She goes back farther than that."

11

MARION Horner Robie had not been Melvin Village for all her eighty years; the first seven decades she was just another citizen of fewer than five hundred, although when she ran the post office, grocery and dry goods store, telephone switchboard, and the fire dispatch all at the same time, she was (admittedly) "the big cheese."

Her white clapboard house, a long two-story building with a wooden sidewalk porch and boxes of red geraniums, thrust its north foundation into the Melvin River just downstream from the dam. The west half of the place was now a fabric and yarn shop; on the other side Mrs. Robie lived.

She sat on her sofa, the one bedecked with history books and a pair of stuffed animals, in the old room with pressed-tin ceiling, tall windows, fireplace, china cabinet, and the slow tock of a pendulum. Her longtime friend, Mrs. Ramsbotham, pottered about in the kitchen as she rattled up beef stew.

In broad New England vowels, Mrs. Robie said: "I never planned on becoming the big cheese, you see. It fell about that way as chance does. In fact, when I was a young woman I left the village for the more exciting life at the YWCA in Boston. More exciting compared to farming our hills. I attended Bryant and Stratton Business School in Boston for two winters, nineteen eighteen through nineteen twenty. Then I worked in the city as a bookkeeper for the Chester I. Campbell Company. We put on industrial exhibitions. After my Boston time, I ended up back here, not because of excitement in Melvin Village, but because of other things, like a sense of belonging — to the land and to history. I tried teaching school a year, but never was I cut out to be a teacher, so I became a shopkeeper with my father. And postmaster later. If you can believe it, we had three general stores in town then, and the post office got passed back and forth across the street depending on whether the President was a Democrat or Republican. Mr. Roosevelt appointed me in nineteen thirty-nine even though I wasn't of his persuasion. The post office was an honor, and good for business, but our excitement was the switchboard. My father founded the Tuftonboro Telephone Company in this very building, and later, we became the first company in Continental Telephone, third largest in the country today."

"What was the excitement?"

"Fires. When one broke out, I'd crank the magneto with my right hand and pull all the keys down with the left and set every phone in town to ringing — three long, three short. Whoever could, went off to fight the fire."

"You've spent most of your life right here in this house?"

"I and Continental Telephone, born in this very house. Hope to die here. And why not? First and last memories in the same place. My parents kept me as a baby in a box under the counter, down with the Uneeda biscuits."

"It's a fine old place."

"The oldest part dates from eighteen sixteen. In those days, they rolled casks of rum into our cellar. Nearest rum now is Wolfeboro, and that's just as well. Our store, from the earliest days, was the gathering place for hunting yarns and entertainment. Always a checkerboard glued to a table. When a wagon arrived with new barrels of flour, the men amused themselves by seeing who could lift the heaviest barrel. Would that amuse you?"

"Where's the ladle, dear?" Mrs. Ramsbotham called in. "Oh! Never mind. It's in my hand."

"I'll tell you something about Melvin Village in the days of flour barrels — say eighteen fifty," Mrs. Robie said. "It wasn't as pretty as it is now. Not so quaint, I'd say. Yes, we had the pond up where the gristmill was — a lovely place to ice skate, but a freshet came off the mountain about nineteen fifteen and washed it away. We have the salmon dam and pond there now. Other than that, not such a pretty town then. Paving the road got rid of the dust and mud. And a curious thing helped. The men who worked up at the new Bald Peak estate — quite a luxurious place — those men saw what a little carpentry and planting, a little paint and cleaning could do. Things began to look better down here, too, after a while. But most of all, educating the children improved our village."

"Don't forget the new families," Mrs. Ramsbotham called between vigorous stirrings.

"It's better when people choose to live in a place rather than having to live somewhere out of necessity. Newcomers have built nice homes and maintained old ones. Brought in pride of ownership. They've seen the special quality about our village is that things abide a little longer here."

"Someone told me you're the voice of the past in the town."

"Live long enough and you turn into history regardless of what you know. But what I haven't seen, I've studied. Take our lake. Two-thirds of its history I've read, the other third I've lived. Used to be big log rafts moving down the lake to the sawmills. And fine lake steamers like the *Cork Leg*. When I went off to Boston, I took the *Governor Endicott* down to The Weirs. Good steamer service then up and down the lake and even to some of the islands. More than three hundred islands out there — one for every day of the year we say." She laughed. "Now you've got this old lady remembering. The overland stage used to come through. Boats and coaches were important to us because we've never been on any main route. People tried to change that, but nothing came of it. Now, I can see that our — our apartness, let's call it — our apartness has preserved us."

"Tell him about the crowds when the salmon start migrating," Mrs. Ramsbotham said over a clatter of utensils.

"Salmon Stripping Sunday every November. Puts us on the map. You see, Winnipesaukee has more volume than surface — deeper than it is wide and long. Three hundred feet deep. Clear water with enough dissolved oxygen to support a landlocked species of salmon. When the water begins to cool, they go upstream, but they don't die after spawning like ocean salmon. The conservation commission comes out to trap salmon in pens below the dam and strip eggs for hatcheries. Gets busy here then, and we have some affairs down at the schoolhouse that turn into hog wrassles. But, once a year, we can survive it."

"This corner of Winnipesaukee's much quieter than the south and west sides."

"We have summer people, but we don't get tramps for the simple reason you have to entertain yourself here. On the other side, you can get entertained. We cultivate the idea that we're a reserved village."

"Summer visitors must be something new. The town looks so unchanged."

"Heavens no. Since the eighteen eighties. Families would come up by train and steamer from Boston to get out of the heat. The fathers just for weekends, but the rest of a family for the whole summer. John Greenleaf Whittier summered here in those days. Visitors have been important to the village ever since the Civil War. You see, our soldiers found out there was land in the West that contained more soil than rock, and our population fell. We've grown only a smidgen since. Still don't have home postal delivery."

Mrs. Ramsbotham called from the kitchen, "The saltshaker has walked off again, but I'll soon find it."

"We're a peaceful place now, but this land has been troubled," Mrs. Robie said. "The French once paid Indians to kill British and American settlers who came in here. That's part of the reason we're a newer town than some in Kentucky or Tennessee. People were slow to arrive."

From Mrs. Ramsbotham: "Tell him Whittier visited us."

"Whittier, yes. And Robert Frost. Whittier's poem 'The Grave by the Lake' is about Melvin Village." She recited:

> "Where the great lake's sunny smiles
> Dimple round its hundred isles,
> And the mountain's granite ledge
> Cleaves the water like a wedge,
> Ringed about with smooth, gray stones,
> Rest the giant's mighty bones."

"Sounds like Whittier."

She took down a book so I could read the whole poem. "Do you like it better?"

"I like the line, 'Kindled in that human clod.'"

"Not a Whittier lover! But don't you see, he expressed that sense of belonging you can feel here? Listen:

> *But somewhere, for good or ill,*
> *That dark soul is living still;*
> *Somewhere yet that atom's force*
> *Moves the light-poised universe.*

"Whittier must have felt the pull especially strong when he heard about the old Indian giant they found in eighteen eight when they were cutting the river road to the shore. The excavations exposed a large grave with an Indian of tremendous proportions sitting bolt upright in it. No one knew archaeological science then, and diggers could only make fanciful guesses about the man and the significance of the grave. The archaeology we have now is Whittier's poem. All we know is what a man from another time said about a man from yet another time. Even if the verse falls wrong, the notion is important, I should say."

From the kitchen: "Have you talked about Robert Frost yet?"

"He lived up on the mountain when his sweetheart spent the summer of eighteen ninety-five with her sister here. Up in the old Ossipee Mountain Park Hotel, the girls were, but Frost was too poor to rent a room, so he worked out an arrangement with Henry Horne. Frost received free lodging in a nearly forsaken house on the mountain in exchange for guarding a large stock of hard cider that old Horne kept in the cellar. Frost wrote a play about his guardianship called, I believe, *The Guardeen*, but I don't think it's ever been published."

Mrs. Ramsbotham brought in a jelly glass of lilies-of-the-valley. "We'll soon be ready, dear," she said. "I'm afraid the ladle's gone off again."

To me Mrs. Robie said, "If you really want to get the feel of our place, take the road up to the foot of the mountain. To Bald Peak Farm. Talk to my cousin — second cousin in point of fact — Tom Hunter. He's a sugar-maker and one of the few old-line families still farming their original land. Up there's the feel. And maybe the end of an era."

I was at the door when I remembered why I'd come. "Who's Melvin?"

"Whoever could answer that has been in the grave almost as long as the Indian giant. But we do know, after Lovewell's War — "

19. *Marion Horner Robie in Melvin Village, New Hampshire*

"A war called Lovewell?"

"I said we're a special place. But the history. During the war with the Indians in the seventeen twenties, some settler apparently explored upriver and found a sign or a tree carved with the word *Melvin*. Maybe something left by one of Lovewell's soldiers. From that word the river took its name. As for Melvin, he had no idea what he was starting. And that's what I mean by abiding. Things remain even when we think they don't."

12

TOM Hunter said Bald Peak in the Ossipee Mountains was not so bald as it was after a forest fire in the early part of the century exposed the granite crown. As trees edged back, the logic in the name "Bald Peak Farm" was less evident; in another generation or two, it was possible only the old residents would understand it. But not probable. "Always'll be more lightnin' up there than trees," Hunter said.

I had found my way through the heavy woods to the farm north of the village and under the peak. Hunter was showing me his sap house where he made maple syrup. Full of pots and outdated calendars, it was across the road of stone fences — walls laid by the first three generations of Hunters — west of the old Hunter farmhouse, and concealed in a grove of big sugar maples; everywhere soft fiddlehead ferns uncurled to the light.

Piled on and around a flatbed trailer hitched to his worn McCormick tractor were fifteen hundred three-gallon galvanized sap buckets, some washed for next spring, others still sticky from this year's run; in heaps lay washed and unwashed galvanized spiles, the spouts that drain the sap from the tree. Hunter's father built the sugarhouse in 1922. The building, really just a twenty-foot shed, had a corrugated tin roof and sides of pine shingles weathered to the color of grade-C maple syrup. The white-trimmed jamb and back of the sliding door carried a written history of Hunter syruping operations since 1925, the sap yields penciled in year by year for each of the "orchards": 1936, 305 buckets; 1924, 226; 1947, 434. The leanest year was 1945 and the best 1965. These were more than historical records — they noted achievements like dates and scores inscribed on an annual tournament trophy. As family albums are to some men, that doorjamb was to Tom Hunter.

His speech was a pronounced upland Yankee. "I'm the fifth generation to sugar on this land. But the sixth generation, all nine of them, come out to help durin' the season. Even the boy on the old Maine place. The seventh generation is developin'. We're tappin' trees my grandparents' grandparents tapped. We look at it like this: a corn farmer can eat corn from the same fields his great-grandfather planted, but he can't eat from the same stalk. But an old syrupin' family eats from the same tree."

"That's a long continuity."

"Even longer. When we cut up an old rock maple at our sawmill, sometimes the saw hits a spout that one of my grandfathers left in the tree by accident and the tree grew over. But more thrillin' is to cut into Indian sappin' scars — slashes like big V's or sometimes 'tis a burned-in hole. White men haven't improved on syrupin' the Abenaki did. We've just speeded it up."

"I'm surprised you cut your maples for lumber."

"Lumber? Only if the tree's goin' by. There's no forgiveness for a man who cuts into a healthy sugar bush. We got plenty others to cut — oak, pine, spruce, hemlock, poplar, beech, ash. But we're cuttin' just cordwood now. Closed down the commercial lumberin' end of our mill. Workmen's compensation, OSHA, FICA — 'twasn't worth the hassle. So we only cut twenty-five cords of wood for the syrupin' these days. And a little firewood for home."

"I wouldn't think you could make a living off maple syrup."

"Pays the taxes. We have a barge business transportin' materials and equipment to the islands. And there's our business excavatin' with bulldozers and backhoes, and a twenty-five-pad trailer park down on the lake."

"What about your cattle and fields?"

"Farm just for our own use now. Crop and cattle farmin' here are about gone. These mountain fields are too small to be economical. But they were more than big enough when I was a boy and had to plow them."

"You've lost land?"

"We've added land. But I used to have to plow with oxen or horses."

"Does all that mean maple syrup doesn't pay much?"

"It can pay. High-grade syrup's about twelve dollars a gallon this season, and I'll gross about five thousand dollars off syrupin'. I'm satisfied with the price. We had a good year. Four-hundred-gallon average this year and last. But two years ago 'twas only two hundred fifty gallons."

"What changes the yield?"

"Spring weather mostly. You got to have freezin' nights and warm days to get a good run of sap. But the number of leaves on the crown the year before makes a difference. Age and health of a tree too."

"In a good run, can you keep ahead of fifteen hundred buckets?"

"Durin' a top run, we're all rollin' up and down the mountains, pullin' the collection tank full of three hundred gallons of sap. Our sugar orchards go halfway up Bald Peak, so there's some overflow and spillage. We tried a new method where the sap runs from the trees through plastic tubes to a central collection tank and then gets pumped to the sugarhouse. But you have to keep patrollin' the lines. We didn't like it. No matter how you do it, from the tenth of March to the twentieth of April, 'tis awful hectic, and the evaporator's burnin' day and night until the frogs begin chirpin'. Then sappin's finished."

The evaporator, built in 1930, was an eighteen-foot contraption of plated tin mounted above a long firebox that burned four-foot pine slabs. From a holding tank, the raw, clear sap drained into the upper end of the evaporator pan where it heated to a foamy boil of two hundred nineteen degrees; if the foam began to inhibit evaporation, Hunter would throw in a piece of salt pork or a dollop of milk; the thickening liquid then moved down the pan through numerous little troughs to the strainer and outlet. Once the firebox reached temperature, the sap of two to four percent sugar became syrup of eighty-five percent sugar in about four hours. It is the critical evaporating process that creates the color and flavor of maple syrup and determines the profit. Fancy-grade pure maple, the light-amber premium syrup, brings the best price. Grade A is darker, more pungent, and B darker and more potent yet. It's a peculiarity of history that the milder tasting grades are the most expensive: in the early days when the primary purpose for maple syrup was to furnish sugar, women didn't want all their baked goods tasting like maple.

A five-foot-tall chair overlooked the evaporator and the big temperature gauge; whoever sat in it not only determined the profit but also whether the operation would continue — if the fire got too hot and boiled off the sap, it would melt the tin coating and soldered joints of the evaporating pan.

We went outside where Hunter pointed out a big sugar maple (also called a hard rock maple because of the tough wood and the rocky soil it grows in). Many kinds of trees produce syruping sap, but none gives a greater or sweeter flow than the sugar maple. To get his average annual yield of three hundred gallons of syrup takes about twelve thousand gallons of sap from twelve hundred tapped trees.

"A big rock maple like this could take four or five taps. Two men with twelve-volt electric drills and battery packs can tap three hundred holes a day, so our tappin' takes four or five days. Ours isn't a real big orchard, but 'tis all sugar maple and all natural. We don't have any planted groves like a pecan farm."

"What happens to the tree after you pull the spile?"

"Hole closes over and forms scar tissue. It's dry forever. Takes twenty-five years before you can even tap next to it. That's where snowfall helps out. In years when the fall's heavy, we can tap higher on the trunk. Other years we tap lower. We get snow years and we get mud years. Don't like either."

We went back to the road where Bald Peak showed clear.

"Sugarin's a business to us if you look only at the ledger. But in all other ways, sappin' season's the time when the kids come home and my wife cooks for two hours to prepare a meal for eleven of us. We live the life of the old-day Hunters then. I can tell you, the sweet smell of syrup at boil and the cold wind outside and the pine burnin' in the box — it gets in your blood. I'll bet you could tap me and get five percent. At the end of it all, we have our sugarin'-off party. Pancakes, waffles, French toast, snowball fights, basketball, and all the maple syrup a waffle can carry.

20. Tom Hunter near Melvin Village, New Hampshire

Maple cream too. If there's something better to eat, I never ate it. Twice-boiled syrup almost to crystallization it is." Hunter shook his head. "To tell the truth, I could make more money at things other than syrupin', but I'd be lost in the spring. I'd be out of whack the whole year."

"You can sell all you make?"

"Haven't advertised since the Depression. All of our syrup's spoken for. Got a waitin' list. Some families been buyin' from us for forty years. Only change in that time is the jugs — from crocks to tin cans to plastic."

As we walked up the road, air began whiffling down off Bald Peak and pushing invisible biting midges ("mingies" Hunter called them) downwind. He slapped at them once for every ten of my slaps. "Rain's comin' in with that breeze."

"It's a beautiful mountain," I said.

"I lived under it all my life and just found out a year ago it's an old volcano — a broken-down volcano. Nobody knew. We been climbin' it to picnic for years, up to a place where you can shake blueberries off the bush. What a place up there! I like to look down and see all our land. The fields we cleared, the trees we sap. Each generation of us has added a little more land and now we hold six hundred *connected* acres. That house up the road is my mother's. Been there since eighteen fifteen. From where we're standin' now, I can look up or down the road and see only our property. Nothin' I like better than to stand here and just look. But I used to look at these hills when you could buy them for almost nothin' and wonder who besides me would want them. Now, I couldn't afford to buy my own land."

"Would you sell it?"

"I could sell off pieces for house lots, and I wouldn't have to work anymore. But I'd lose more than just our land. The old families of the township are pretty well gone and dispersed, and the old homesteads keep disappearin'. Younger people almost have to go away to find proper work. 'Tis a beautiful place, but not a good one for an intelligent young person. I took the college preparatory course at Tilton School and went to the University of New Hampshire for two years. But I came back. Didn't seem like anything special returnin' home then. Now it looks like somethin' you may not see happen again."

We had been almost sauntering, but Hunter began walking fast. Then he stopped. "When I'm up on the peak lookin' down, sometimes I try to imagine the orchards and pastures a generation from now. Or in five generations. I imagine different ways it'll turn out, but the thing I always end up with is those fields I raked hay on when I was a boy. We're takin' timber off them now. People — outlanders — get upset because we cut trees. They don't see that those trees are growin' in an old field. I know this, what you think comes down to your point of view. Don't know where theirs is, but mine's from up on that old volcano."

Nine

EAST BY NORTHEAST

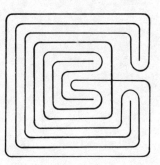

1

BLUE highway 109 ran out of Melvin Village, out from under the Ossipee Mountains, down toward the sea, all the way twisting like snarled fishline as it unreeled through an eerie spruce forest. I crossed into Maine, where evergreens absorbed the heat and the sky darkened. Lakes glowed luminescent in the last light, the water sending wisps of condensation into the cool air.

Although I was still miles from the ocean, a heavy sea fog came in to muffle the obscure woods and lie over the land like a sheet of dirty muslin. I saw no cars or people, few lights in the houses. The windshield wipers, brushing at the fog, switched back and forth like cats' tails. I lost myself to the monotonous rhythm and darkness as past and present fused and dim things came and went in a staccato of moments separated by miles of darkness. On the road, where change is continuous and visible, time is not; rather it is something the rider only infers. Time is not the traveler's fourth dimension — change is.

The towns — Springvale, Sanford, Kennebunk — watery globs of blue light, washed across the windows in the cold downpour that came on. I pushed the wipers to high speed, but the rain had its way.

I drove on until the road crossed a small drawbridge over an estuary at Kennebunkport, the fifth oldest village in Maine. Just above the sea reach, I stopped for the night. I'd come again to the Atlantic.

2

KENNEBUNKPORT was a town coming and going, a place in that way like any other. A quarter of a mile up the estuary from the ocean, the citizens once built large wooden ships on the north side of the river and unloaded fish downstream on the south. At Government Wharf they still unloaded fish and lobsters, and the boat-building continued too but on a smaller scale.

In that earlier time, the Baptists constructed a fine wood-frame church that looks down the estuary, and on the steeple they put a weathervane in the form of a golden fish. I asked four people what kind of fish it was. One said, "What fish?" One said it was merely a generalized Christian symbol; two others said cod. I don't suppose the Baptists prayed to fish, yet it did look that way. But cod giveth and cod taketh away, and cod fishing is no longer what it was. Were the Baptists to put up a weathervane today, they might erect a great golden traveler's check.

The storm passed inland, and by morning the sky was clear and warm and squealing with gulls scratching themselves in flight. In 1830, some of the townspeople sighted a sea monster, but things now were quieter, except during the summer, and that was the way it had been for almost a century. I did what you do in Kennebunkport: walk the odd angles and sudden turns of alleyways and cul-de-sacs among the bleached shingled buildings, climb the exterior stairs to the old lofts, step around lobster pots and upturned dinghies.

The summer season was coming on, and already middle matrons in nonskid-soled shoes and wraparound skirts were leading middle-level husbands into shops rigged out in macramé and down counters of perfumed candles, stained-glass mobiles, Snoopy beach towels, brass trivets, ceramic coffee mugs from Japan, music box cheeseboards, ladybug jewelry. Clerks, a generation younger, watched with expressions stuck on like decals.

Most of those visitors stayed on the north side of the river with the gift shops and galleries selling paintings by artistes, with the motels, restaurants, and tour-boat docks; but a few found the southside eateries, small and slanty, the ones on pilings out over the river; and some people even wandered into the boatyards where winches and cranes clanked out the old music of the harbor.

I went down to the shore. People lay in the sand of a narrow beach blocked at both ends by big broken mounds of glaciated rocks. Children dug holes, mothers read fat novels by women with three names, and fathers read the coeds' damp T-shirts. Later the women would stretch out on towels, the men doze off under *The Wall Street Journal*, and the children look for something to do away from the blowing sand, cold water, and six hundred yards of salted humanity.

I drove a hilly back road a couple of miles up the coast to Cape Porpoise, a white picket-fence village bent around a little balloon of an inlet off the Atlantic. Here, in 1629, Englishmen made the first so-called permanent settlement in Kennebunkport. Sixty years later, Indians "depopulated"

Cape Porpoise. That first settlement was on Stage Island, now an overgrown rise that loons and gulls rallied on.

At the edge of the town pier sat a lobster house. Lobsters were beyond my means, but I bought two pounds of steamed quahogs (also called "littlenecks" and "cherrystones" when small), walked to Bradbury Brothers grocery for a stick of butter and two bottles of Molson Ale. I packed up my dented aluminum pot and Swedish stove and headed down through the sumac and wild beach roses to a rocky coign of vantage just above a tidal cove Vikings likely saw. While the tide went out, I melted the butter and warmed the clam broth, dipped the steamers into the broth and hot butter, and ate, sitting against the granite, drinking the Molson's, watching the water.

The tide drained the flats with their sea-worn things that once belonged in the air now returned to it for a short space: sunken punts, busted lobster pots, barnacled timbers, pop bottles. And there were banks of shining, steely blue mussels closed tighter than the lips of God. At one time, only gulls harvested the black mussel, but when tidal-flat clams and lobsters became harder to find, people began gathering mussels for steaming, and now they, too, were not so plentiful.

Herring gulls, flashing white in the sun, circled down and let loose their usual hullabaloo, picked over the flats, and cocked a careful eye at little tidal pools full of orange rockweed and iridescent froth washing gently back and forth. They stitched the rank, black ooze with an embroidery of gull feet.

I went again to the pier. Old men had come down in Valiants and Dodge Darts and stood watching the fishing boats. Somebody said they came every day just like the gulls. Always when one died off, another took his place to do the watching.

A westerly had blown in strong, and the little Cape Porpoise fleet was returning early, each boat carrying into the pier an attendant flapdoodle of gulls circling as sternmen gutted the catch, then swooping the water for the pitched entrails. Trucks from Boston fish houses waited under the hoist as the fish tubs came up. Gill netters tore mackerel loose from nets and threw them into baskets. The mackerel is a beautiful piece of design: a sleek body of silver touched with indigo. An old watcher said, "A mack looks better than it eats, unless you're a cat."

The trawler *Allison E* tied up to unload her catch of flounder, cod, haddock, and hake. The skipper climbed the pier ladder and said, "It's steak and potatoes for me, boys." He kept an eye on the trawler as his crew cut the last of the catch, and he counted the baskets of fish coming up to the truck. The whole time, I stood at his side and asked questions.

Finally he said, "If you really want to see how a flounder gets from twenty leagues down to the A and P, be on the pier tomorrow morning at three-thirty. If you won't get seasick, you can go out with us."

The *Allison E* was the last to unload. When she moved off to tie up in the little basin, the pier emptied. In late afternoon, schoolboys came down with their Zebcos to fish for pollock. They filched chunks of cod and flounder from the foul shed where lobster bait festered in barrels; the stronger the bait, the better to lure a lobster. One small boy struggled out with a massive codfish head, its jagged maw, a good fourteen inches across, gaping wide enough to swallow him. In the harbor, red-throated loons paddled and dived and gulped, but the boys had no luck and went home when the eastern sky and sea turned inky in the dusk.

I parked Ghost Dancing on a flat outcropping of rock just above the pier; circles of yellow lichens lay over the stone like doilies, and broken mussel and crab shells, dropped by gulls, were all about. From my bunk, I could see out the back window the blinking light on Goat Island, a rocky ribbon once fought over by the British and colonists. On beyond, from deep water, the sorrowing drone of a sonobuoy.

To be able to get up at three, I went to bed early but couldn't fall asleep. I kept hearing music, an old kind of music, coming over the harbor from the village. The melody sounded so much like another time, I thought I imagined it, but it kept drifting softly across the basin like a dream. I got up and followed the sound along the road to Atlantic Hall, a last-century clapboard building that was the town meetinghouse, library, and dancehall. Parked around were Volkswagens, Saabs, Peugeots, Renaults, and an old camouflaged truck with a canoe rack. Each bumper carried a message: SPLIT WOOD NOT ATOMS, SAVE THE WHALE, EXTINCT IS FOREVER, VIVA LA BICI-CLETTA!

From the second floor of the hall, music and the thump of feet. Under the roof timbers, a band — upright piano, fiddle, flute, and banjo of immense size — was letting go with a barndance piece while dancers went up and down, stopping only to drink water from enamelware pitchers. The cool sea wind blew through the loft and pushed the sweaty air into the night.

Resting on the stairs was a student from Boston University who had come to Kennebunkport to do research on tide mill design. "I'm studying the old gristmill on the Kennebunk River," he said. "It's a restaurant now, but up until a few years ago, it was still milling. Same family ran it for two hundred years. Simple engineering, but ingenious. Yankee all the way."

He explained how it worked: a rising tide entered the pond through a gate in the mill dam. At high tide, the miller closed the gate to trap the water. As the tide ebbed, the pond drained through a turbine connected to the millstone.

"It worked only twice every twenty-four hours — once at night — but the energy was free, endless, and nonpolluting. I'm interested in a model that would operate with the tide coming *and* going so there's ready power most any time. The Bay of Fundy, maybe you know, is not far north of here. Twice a day there you have a hundred billion tons of water rising and falling fifty feet. Two hundred million horsepower every day."

He drew a sketch of the old mill turbine with his modifications.

"People think hydropower is a Grand Coulee Dam — big. But little is valuable too, especially in New England where heating oil is expensive and falling water is cheap. A lot of tide and streams get wasted now. And you wouldn't believe the number of little hydroplants on town dams that have been abandoned in the last thirty years. If we developed only ten percent of the small existing dams in the country, we could save a couple hundred million barrels of oil a year. As I see it, that gristmill may be the oldest thing in Kennebunkport, but it's also the most futuristic."

3

Three-thirty A.M.: Sky black, sea blacker. Goat Island light blinking every five seconds through a quiet rain. Tide full. Wind off the sea and into the beach roses and sumac. Smell of blossoms and brine. Squeak of a hull against the pier, the far clang of a bell buoy.

Three-forty: Because of small-craft warnings, there has been almost no lobstering for three days, and the bait shed smells like the ass end of some great unwashed creature. The old watchers wait nearby in their Valiants as fishermen arrive in crumbling trucks and discuss the forecast: winds easterly five to ten miles an hour, shifting to westerlies by afternoon. It's the westerlies you have to watch. The seamen head for the boats.

We take the punt, riding low with the four of us, out to the *Allison E.* On board: skipper Tom West; his brother and chief sternman, Ken; and assistant sternman, Ron Jeffers. I am chief observer.

Three-fifty: Still so early even the gulls are silent. Under way. The running lights show pocks of rain on the water, and our faces glow green from the navigational instruments. The engine gives more noise than heat.

For three centuries, white men have gone down this way to pursue the bottomfish — those peculiar species that loll in half somnolence on the ocean floor.

Four o'clock: On the open sea. Making ten knots, fast enough to raise a wake as high as the transom. The forty-foot *Allison E* rides up the swells and down the other side. Up, down, up, down. Although a new stern trawler, she is built the old way — cedar planks over oak ribs, keel, and stem.

In the forward compartment, Ron lies sleeping wound in among the two-gallon jugs of fresh water for the radiator, the coolers of food, a case of Seven-Up, three five-gallon drums of engine oil, a pair of life preservers, and a first-aid kit. Ken beside him, neither asleep nor awake.

In the small wheelhouse, Tom checks the gauges with a flashlight and watches the double set of six-digit LED numbers on the loran. A funnel above his head makes him look like the Tinman. "We're going to build in a couple of bunks, but the inclination and opportunity haven't struck at the same time yet," he says. "We're doing the cabin fitting ourselves to keep the expense down."

Around him hang fifteen thousand dollars in electronic gear: Wesmar Scanning Sonar, Si-Tex Fish Finder, marine radio, CB, radar, and the Loran C. Also binoculars, five Dexter fish knives, whetstone, half-dozen rolled charts (the good fishing coordinates terribly smudged), penciled figures on the bulkheads and overhead.

On the deck, stacked behind the wheelhouse and around the winch, stand thirty plastic fish crates furnished by fish brokers: John Nagle & Co., P. Markos Seafoods, H. R. Drake & Sons. Looking like laundry baskets, the rectangular containers are of several colors, but only one is blue. Also on the deck: two propane bottles, the mast, boom, gallows frame, net, holding box, and the Hathaway winch — a twin spool model, each drum wound with two hundred twenty-five fathoms of chain and steel towing cable. The cable runs through three sets of bollards, then up the gallows where it attaches on each side of the sixty-five-foot Yankee 35 net. At the front end of the net are the "doors" — a pair of four-hundred-pound steel-rimmed oak pieces that serve to keep the mouth of the long net open as it moves over the sea bottom. Atop the wheelhouse is a Givens four-man enclosed life raft with a hydrostatic release.

Four-fifty: Lights of Cape Porpoise gone from the horizon. Eastern sky cold and gray. Tom says, "We can fish in a good year only about two hundred days. Whatever income from dragging we'll earn, we've got to earn then. We can't ever make up for a day lost. The only alternative is hauling sport fishermen, but they get demanding. They've put down four hundred dollars and — fog or wind — by God they're going out. They don't know what the sea is. So you take them a half mile offshore and let them think they're deep-sea fishing. You hope they catch a rock cod so they'll go home happy, and you can keep your life, theirs, and your boat. I don't like that business. We fish twenty miles out with the inshore fleet. The *Allison E* isn't big enough for overnight runs."

Five-ten: The sternmen pull on rubber boots and yellow oilskins. Ron wins the race to dress first — no mean feat in the violent pitching. He crows as he puts on his sou'wester. Everyone animated. The crew sorts through an impossible twining of nylon net, and Tom holds the wheel with his left hand while watching an image flicker across the Fish Finder and listening to the *chat-chat-chat* of the sonar. Occasionally he peers into the screen of the depth sounder housed in a long tube like an Edison peep show to see an electronic cross-section of the sea bottom a thousand feet ahead. As soon as the *Alison E* passes over a ridge of jagged rocks, he waves, and the crew, staying clear of the wildly swinging doors, drops the net. Ken goes to the winch and evenly plays out the tow wire by releasing or braking the drums independently of each other. The cables crackle and thump as they unwind; the tension on them is terrific; should one part, it could cut a man in two. The left drum hangs up, and Ron beats the line free with a hammer. In eight minutes, one hundred twenty-five fathoms of cable is out, and the net rides forty fathoms below.

Five-thirty: Rain stops. Ten miles offshore and towing at three knots over an area in the Gulf of Maine known as Perkins Ground of Bigelow Bight. Two hundred forty feet below on the mud, sand, and gravel, the net rouses bottomfish as they bump up into the "sweep" and on back into the rear bag called the "cod end."

Five-forty: Crew out of oilskins. We open the coolers. The coffee and sandwiches for a few moments cover the smell of the sea. A squiggle blips across the Fish Finder: a school of herring. "Sardine fishing's gone to hell in Maine," Tom says. As we eat, he gives the news off the marine radio: the relative calm won't hold till evening. From the CB we hear the day's prices for "flats" (flatfish): flounders (yellowtails or lemon sole, blackbacks, dabs or plaice, gray sole or witch flounder) are selling at thirty-five cents a pound on the New Bedford market, the earliest auction. Less abundant groundfish — halibut (a flounder), cod, haddock, hake, whiting — are going at forty to fifty cents a pound. What the fisherman will sell for a half dollar a pound, the supermarket will sell for two dollars after the fish passes through the trucker (add ten percent), the broker (another ten), and cutting house where the fish will become a filet.

"In the winter when the weather cuts down on the fishable days," Tom says, "the supply drops and prices will triple. But the catch is smaller, and we have to fish at twice the depth, so our income stays level."

"Do you sell your catch in Boston?"

"Mostly, but it goes all over. Some of it, like the sand sharks, even goes to England for fish and chips. Flats that are too small to take to market — the ones we call 'windowpanes' — those fish end up on the pier as lobster bait at six dollars a box."

The four cylinder GM-Detroit diesel, sounding like an overloaded bus, works hard and covers over our words. The shouting keeps talk to a minimum.

"Driving a truck up a mountain is less strain than towing," Tom says, "especially when we go against the tide. You tow with or against the tide. If you pull across it, your doors are going to foul and close up the net. We're burning five gallons an hour now, and we'll try to keep the gear down for ten miles or three hours. We like to get three long tows in by sunset. Night dragging isn't very productive. If we get a good tow, we'll heist a ton or more of fish. A dragger never knows how well he's doing until the bag comes up. That's why you've got to tow by the clock. If you tow by feel, the tide can make you think you've got a full bag."

West usually trawls in a spiral pattern from the inside out. The big worry is to keep from getting the net (fifteen hundred dollars) or the doors (eight hundred dollars) or the cable (seven hundred dollars) hung up on an obstruction, often rocks, but sometimes other things. A few weeks earlier, he got entangled in the ribs of an old sailing ship; when the net broke free, it brought up a forty-foot timber and coal clinkers. He figures it must have been a wooden steamer. "A friend hooked up on a sunk German submarine from one of the wars, and another fisherman got bollixed up in an old airplane and had to cut his net. You can't always jerk it free. I overdid it once and blew a gasket. Another trawler gave me a tow. When you're dead in the water, the sea does what she wants with you."

Six o'clock: Ron forward again and napping. Ken explains the operation of the winch and gallows. He graduated from the "dragging college" conducted by the University of Rhode Island at Wickford, where he studied diesel engines, net design, marketing, navigation, deck gear, and sea survival. For graduation, his parents gave him a three-hundred-dollar neoprene survival suit constructed to prevent hypothermia. At any time of the year, the water temperature is the enemy. His education helps produce a better catch, but it also may help a bank to look favorably on a loan for a boat of his own one day.

Tom attended one semester at Parsons College in Iowa, then taught skiing in New Hampshire, and later worked five years as a contractor in house construction. Before buying the *Allison E* (named after his daughter), he operated his own lobster boat and made his traps in the Maine tradition and learned the rudiments of seafaring. But lobstering is a restricted, touch-and-go way to earn a living. Although the investment and risks are greater in dragging, so are the profits. He sold the small boat. With the trawler, he tried a new fishing method using a Scottish seine that required him to change all his deck gear to accommodate it. It didn't work well and became an expensive experiment.

Ron, born in Philadelphia, has lived in Maine off and on for ten years. During bad weather, he repairs oil heaters and drives a truck, but he prefers the sea. He hopes one day to buy his own lobster boat.

A day of good tows can bring a gross sale of about two thousand dollars; the crew takes forty percent and the boat sixty; the skipper pays operating costs. A good sternman on a good boat during a good year can bring in forty thousand dollars. But the work is not only rigorous, it's dangerous. "According to insurance companies," Tom says, "it's the second most dangerous occupation. I heard the only thing worse is a bomb squad."

Eight o'clock: Sun out. Ken and Ron back into oilskins. Ron says, "In fifteen minutes, we'll find out if this pond's got any damn fish in it." Tom throttles back, and swells come up under the stern, lift the trawler, slide under, and drop her *kerplunk* back down. Ken begins winching in the net as Ron pries with a length of pipe at the cable on the drums to keep the lines from snarling. The cable jerks and flings water. "If she's going to part, now's the likely time!" Tom shouts from the wheelhouse. The weight of the net pulls the boat backwards until we are above it. An aura of anticipation. A crew gets paid only for its share of the catch. There are no salaries.

Gulls, spotting the activity on deck, come from invisibility and plunge to the ocean to bob and wait. White on blue. Then the orange floats break the surface, then the doors, then the forward portion of the net called the "square" is up. Caught in it are several small starfish — white and brown ones — and a herring. Ron jumps to secure the deadly crash of the doors against the gallows. The net is entirely out of the sea and swinging like a giant pendulum above the deck. Ken reaches under the cod end to pull a line tied in a slip knot, and the bag opens and seven hundred pounds of bottomfish pour all over the deck. We stand ankle-deep in marine quicksilver and opalescent eyes. There isn't a thrash anywhere.

I ask, "What's wrong with these fish?"

"They're dead."

"Not already."

"Look at them."

The rapid decompression has bulged their eyeballs into spheres. Stomachs swell out of some mouths, and guts dribble from anuses.

"The bends," Tom says. "You should see the bag surface with a big load of cod. It explodes from the water when the fish blow their pokes. Their air sacs bust like balloons — and all at once."

Most of the catch is flounder, but there are also haddock, hake, a few cod and monkfish, two skate (some dealer will punch circular tidbits from the "wings" and pass them off as scallops), a lobster, a crab, two sea horses, four kinds of starfish (one palm size, another no bigger than a thumbnail), and two Coca-Cola cans.

As Ken resets the net, Ron hoses down the fish with seawater, then the gear again goes over the stern. Tom takes the wheel, and off we go once more.

Eight-thirty: In a single motion, each sternman swings his fishpick (a sawed-off broomhandle with a nail through one end) into a fish, mentally grades it, and flips it into the appropriate crate.

Bottomfish tend toward the primitive and primeval. It's as if the net had scooped up a big dipper of antediluvian broth and poured it over the deck. The old-world cartographers who mapped the unknown western ocean and inscribed on their charts "Here be strange beasts" might have had groundfish in mind. Take the flounder: this fossil imprint of a fish, rarely more than an inch or so thick but often fourteen inches long, spends a lifetime lying on its left side; consequently, the left side becomes a kind of belly. And that's good, because the flounder is so flat (hence the name "flatfish") it has no belly worth talking about. When born, the flounder has eyes positioned normally. But soon the left eye migrates to the "top" so that the right side carries both eyes, and the mouth pivots in order to open and close horizontally as mouths do. The new bottomside loses its gray pigment of camouflage and turns fish-belly white.

Even more primordial is the monkfish, also called the "goosefish" and "angler fish" — the latter name deriving from the flexible spine tipped with a fishtail-shaped appendage that the creature dangles in front of its mouth. When a smaller something swims in to eat the "bait," the monkfish gulps hugely to swallow whatever is near. The death-trap mouth is a cavernous thing, full not so much of spiky teeth as stalagmites and stalactites. But more: around the top half of the body are strange growths of skin resembling sea plants that give a resting monkfish the look of an old weedy stone. Under the mouth, where the pectoral fins should be, are two little finny, clawed hands that it uses to scrape out a depression to hunt from. If you've ever seen *Creature from the Black Lagoon*, then you have an idea of a monkfish.

Ron, a big man, struggles to pick up a four-foot specimen so I can look in its mouth. "They come six feet and longer. This one's just middle size." He drops it to the deck, pulls out his knife, cuts away the bony head to leave only the considerably smaller tail that contains a single bone. "Nobody would eat a head that can eat you. Especially when it's this ugly."

"Who's going to eat that tail?" I ask. The flesh is loose, almost like jelly. "Damn, that's revolting!"

"Ever had a franchise fishburger? Did you think you were eating red snapper? Monkfish take on the taste of what you cook with them."

The lobster goes overboard although it will almost certainly be eaten before it reaches the bottom. A trawler cannot legally keep lobsters because dragging is such an efficient means of harvest, trawlers could clear out the species in a year or two. "Biggest lobster ever found came up accidentally in a drag net. Forty-four pounds."

The flounders, looking like speckled, pointy Ping-Pong paddles, do not need to be cleaned even though two-thirds of the fish is waste; but the cod, hake, and haddock — heftier fish — must be gutted to keep them fresh. The transom is wet with slime and blood and entrails. Seabirds rise in a tremendous whirling and milling as they grab guts and the small fry that get shoveled overboard. One bird, flying off with a whole fish that it cannot quite get down, gulps frantically to keep it, until a larger one swoops and yanks out the half-swallowed herring.

The last of the catch to get cleaned is a big vicious-looking thing with rows of fangs rather than teeth. I prod it with my boot.

"Want to lose a toe?" Ron shouts. "Don't get nosy with a wolf fish."

"It's dead."

"It's the only one that might not be dead. They'll bite your ass right here on deck. They'll snap as you cut their goddamn heads off."

"Who eats wolf fish?"

"I don't know. Ask Mrs. Paul."

With the catch cleaned and stacked, Ron picks up the Coke cans. One has a return-for-deposit imprint. The other goes overboard. "Five cents," he says.

"I never guessed a deposit law would work at forty fathoms."

Nine-twenty: The day is cold enough there's no need to carry a hundred pounds of ice as the trawler must do in summer. The crew hoses down deck and oilskins. Gulls make one more pass at the floating guts, then disappear.

Ron and I climb atop the rocking wheelhouse to lie back in the sun as the *Allison E* unwinds her course over the swells. Before he falls asleep,

Ron sniffs and says, "Amazes me. When you're on shore you smell the sea. When you're at sea, you smell the land."

Eleven-ten: Sternmen don oilskins and again haul in the net. A small catch, maybe four hundred pounds. There is little talk as they sort and clean. Ron picks up a three-foot cod by the tail and shakes a half-dozen shrimp from its mouth. "That's breakfast. Let's see what Big Mama had for supper." He slips the knife in below the anal fin and slits open the belly. "Look." Inside lies a whole lobster as red as if just out of the steampot.

I say, "Can you eat a lobster cooked in a cod's stomach?"

"Take a bite and let me know."

Eleven-thirty: Ron calls in to Tom for permission to throw overboard the blue fish crate. Tom nods. Over it goes, floating off like a little barge.

"What's wrong with that crate?" I ask.

"It's blue."

"So?"

"Never bring things blue aboard," Ken says. "Bad luck. Almost as bad as sticking a knife in the deck or leaving a hatch cover upside down. Or saying p-i-g or eating walnuts on board."

"You mean you believe if I say pig — "

"Nobody believes it. We just don't do it."

Twelve-ten: Tom watches the sonar apprehensively. He says, "We may be in trouble, lads." He throttles back, and no one speaks. The moony eyes of the fish goggle blankly through the slots in the baskets. Finally, Tom says, "Get ready to haul in." The crew dresses and hurries astern. The catch is again small because of the abbreviated tow. Ron mutters a single word: "Blue."

I ask Tom what happened. "I steered into a canyon — rock piles on both sides. No room to turn around without hanging up the gear. There goes four hundred dollars."

A hundred and sixty million years ago, according to plate tectonic theory, the Atlantic didn't exist; this water was land. For a dragger, it still is.

One-twelve: The *Allison E* trawling a new location. I ask Tom what the future of bottom fishing is for Maine.

"Good, bad, so-so. All of that. In 'seventy-six, the government extended the old three-mile territorial limit to two hundred miles to keep foreigners out. Had to do it. Russians and Germans and Japanese were coming in with armadas of trawlers and factory ships that process and freeze the catch. Once they found a good coordinate, they'd sit on it until they cleaned it out. A factory ship can hold six-months' catch so their draggers don't have to return to port to refuel or off-load. And they used roller nets so they could drag bottom we couldn't, and they fished with two-inch mesh nets, whereas we have to use five-inchers to let the little ones escape. The Europeans and Japanese lost all their boats during the war so their governments subsidized new ones in the sixties. Their fleets are newer and more efficient than our Yankee one. We couldn't compete. But since the two-hundred-mile limit, our catch is way up."

"That's the good. What's the bad?"

"About the same thing — the government. They watch over everything out here now. That helicopter that passed a while back was observers. We've got quotas imposed by marine biologists although nobody has an accurate idea how many fish are below. You can't count them like elephants. A year ago, we caught the entire East-coast quota for haddock in two days. Some of the regulations are just out of line with reason. This is one of the richest fishing grounds in the world. It's why New England got so prosperous in the early years. It's why they hung a gold codfish in the statehouse in Boston in seventeen-and-when."

"Is the government your main problem?"

"Government, the sea, weather, rocks, a flounder's brain, dogfish tearing open nets to get your catch. Hell. Even the church giving up meatless Fridays. Guinea boats up out of Gloucester — old boats that go down all the time. Not long ago one dragged across the courses of fifteen of our trawlers and tied everbody up. Tell me that wasn't bedlam."

Two-forty: Wind strong off the coast. Sea a deep blue-black. As the westerlies grow stronger, Tom waves and shouts, "Heist the gear!" Another tow cut short. What began as a good fishing day has turned sour. The sternmen, cutting the fish, struggle to stay upright on the wet, pitching deck. The return to port at twenty knots over the surge of sea is a harum-scarum carnival ride of bouncing and salt spray and following gulls. "Find a smoother street, captain!" Ron yells. "I'm about to slip with this knife and cut a tallywhacker off!"

With everything hosed down and secured, Ron pulls out a couple of big yellowtails. In quick strokes, he slices behind the gills, down the spine, flips the fish and does the same thing, then, with two final quick cuts, frees the filets. "Put your nose here," he says and holds up the flounder.

"All I smell is sweetness."

"Sweetness is right. It's fresh. Once you eat a real, honest fresh flounder, you won't like what lubbers call fresh seafood. You'll be like the woman after the French tickler — never satisfied again."

He drops a filet in a bag. Kens says, "Cook it up in your truck tonight. Eat it tonight, or you'll never know what fresh fish is."

Four-twenty: The *Allison E* warped to the pier. Tom and I watch the catch come up to a broker's truck. Tom calls down, "Save a nice haddock

21. Tom West in Cape Porpoise, Maine

for the mother-in-law." To me he says, "We had to heist early three times and that cost us about a thousand dollars. Our check for this haul will only be about eight hundred dollars. Anytime you pull less than a thousand, it's costing you money." As we wait for the truck to finish stowing the crates, I ask Tom what's the most unusual thing he's encountered at sea.

"Breath of a whale," he says.

I laugh. "Seriously."

"That's it. When they sound and blow, it's like the mouth of Hell opened."

Four-fifty: Tom moves his trawler to anchorage in the harbor and returns to the pier in the punt.

"What will you do now after a day on the high sea?" I ask.

"What anyone else here does — watch television."

Five-ten: But for the whelm of tide, the pier is quiet and empty of boats, gulls, trucks, fish, and the men that go down to the sea in ships and come home to watch *The Price Is Right.*

I walk to my rig, sauté the flounder in butter and pepper, and eat. Ron is right. I've become the woman after the French tickler.

4

THE main thing here was concrete. Trying to find blue highways down the Northeast seaboard wasn't going to be difficult — it was going to be impossible. Using the theory (which had worked in the South, West, and North) that an expressway relieves a paralleling road from congestion, I tried U.S. 1, a highway so famous there is a book called *U.S. One,* which gives a virtual mile-by-mile description of the route as it was in 1938. From New York to Eastport, Maine, much of 1 follows the old Boston Post Road, which itself followed Indian trails.

Highway statistics: since 1930, American road and street miles have increased only eighteen percent while car traffic has grown by fifty percent, truck by seventy. But most of that increase in roadways has come in surburban streets. Even though there is about one road mile per square mile in the contiguous states, highways take up less than one percent of the three million square miles in the country.

I knew U.S. 1, stretching from the Canadian border to Key West, was capable of putting a man in an institution of one kind or another — at least it once was — but I hoped things had changed.

They hadn't. The highway was still a nightmare vision of the twentieth century, a four-lane representing (as Mencken has it) "the American lust for the hideous, the delight in ugliness for its own sake." After an hour, I gave up, turned onto Interstate 95, and got swept south toward Boston.

More statistics: if you poured all the sand, gravel, and cement in American interstates into a nine-foot-thick, ten-foot-high wall, it would circle the world fifty times. I went down the interstate miles — driving, driving. Each mile took up twenty-five acres or the equivalent of forty thousand loaves of bread. So I've heard.

Tractor-trailer rigs (using two-thirds more fuel per cargo-ton than a locomotive) blasted me all the way to Boston. Then, to the west, fifty minutes from Haymarket Square, I found Massachusetts 16, a quiet road out of Wellesley, that ran down through stands of maple, birch, and pine, down along brooks, across fens, down miles of stone walls covered with lichens.

Many New England stone fences built between 1700 and 1875 were laid by gangs of workers who piled stone at the rate of so much a rod. Edwin Way Teale says that in the latter years of the past century, before economic and social developments began obliterating some of the walls, there were a hundred thousand miles of stone fences in New England. Even today, for many of them, the only change has been the size of the lichens, those delicate rock-eating algae that can live nine hundred years.

At Holliston, I stopped and took a sandwich and bottle of Moxie (once advertised as "the only harmless nerve food known that can recover loss of manhood, imbecility and helplessness") into the old town burial ground and ate lunch while I walked and read the slanting slate tombstones. There were carved urns, hourglasses, and weeping willows; among the *mors vincit omnia* sentiments were some well-cut death's-heads and angels of redemption. Often it's hard to tell the difference because the death's-heads evolved into angels, the angels into cherubs, the cherubs into portraits of the deceased.

Near the south end of the cemetery, under a big ash, was Lieutenant Joseph Mellen's stone. The Minuteman died in 1787, the year of the Constitution, at the age of forty. Toward the bottom of the marker was a poem that appears on many colonial gravestones in numerous variations. Mellen's version:

> Behold and see as you pass by,
> As you are now so once was I;
> As I am now so you must be,
> Prepare for Death & follow me.

In other times, people came to burial grounds for contemplation. Next to the stone lay a crumpled sheet of rice paper. I opened it. There, in a half-completed wax rubbing of the old matrix on Mellen's stone, was a figure of death or redemption — make your choice.

While the grounds were appropriate for musing, for falling inward, the bright day wasn't, and I had no mind to take my darker self (that dogged soldier of the Indian wars) seriously. I picked up the rubbing and stuck it to a wall of Ghost Dancing and got moving — I didn't know where. "Our destination," Henry Miller says, "is never a place but rather a new way of looking at things."

Down state 115 southeast toward Taunton. I had to keep checking route markers for the northwest-bound traffic in order to stay on course. Rule of the blue road: the highway side to where you've been is better marked than the one to where you're going.

Perhaps inclined by days past, I found myself heading toward Narragansett Bay, an area in which I'd spent my Navy service during the sixties. The whole time, the shining waxen eyes of the old stone face, like Uncle Sam's on the recruiting posters, watched from every angle.

5

Fall River, Massachusetts, is chiefly memorable for me as the factory city I have never driven through without losing the way. Once there — predictably, inexplicably, and utterly — I am confounded by the knots of concrete. So, that day, entangled again, it was like old times. Maybe that's what set me up to expect Newport to be the same.

The island of Rhode Island is a misshapen boot in Narragansett Bay; just above the instep stands the old town center of Newport, and around the sole stepping into the Atlantic is the other Newport: that of the exclusive oceanside gilded estate "cottages," detached in space, attitude, and history. Old harborside Newport, however historic, was never quaint; it was much too rough and lusty for that. Nor was it ever a preserved relic like Wickford or picturesquely cute like Little Compton, other Rhode Island villages. In short, it was a *real* sea town.

I'd spent my share of Navy time in Newport down on Thames Street (also known as Bloody Alley), which had ever been the waterfront thoroughfare, although things had slipped and no longer was it the main business street. But in the seventeenth century only a madman or seer might have predicted that upstart New York City would have an avenue more important than the Alley.

Thames Street — a narrow, dark trench of a lane under hip roofs and gables and old doorways with fanlights — had seen the likes of Captain Kidd, Roger Williams, Benjamin Franklin, George Washington, Lafayette, Rochambeau, Kosciuszko, Baron Steuben, Count von Fersen (a lover of Marie Antoinette), Nathanael Greene, Gilbert Stuart, Stephen Decatur, Oliver Perry (Battle of Lake Erie), Matthew Perry (opening of Japan), Herman Melville, most of the Vanderbilts, Astors, Rockefellers, and Kennedys, and a thousand-thousand fishermen and sailors. Not bad for a street that began as a swamp.

Citizens of Newport hanged pirates at the north end of the Alley, buccaneers and merchantmen refitted ships at the Thames Street wharfs, and Englishmen impressed American seamen they found wandering "the Strand," as it was once called. The first cobblestones were bought with receipts levied on each slave imported from Africa (later, any Negro who owned a pig and sty could vote in a mock election for a black governor at the corner of Thames and Farewell streets). In one house nearby, a boy in his father's arms, upon seeing George Washington, said, "Why, father! General Washington is a man!" To which the general replied, "Yes, only a man."

After the British stole the town blind and devastated the area, following their three-year occupation during the Revolutionary War, new businesses grew up around Thames: sugar refining, rum distilling, malt brewing, the bottling of sperm whale oil. Sea captains' children, hoping for a pet monkey or a parrot from Brazil, came down to Thames Street to meet their fathers' ships; officers of the line walked between piled boxes of Turkish brass, Chinese porcelain, Persian carpets, Japanese lacquerware, Indian spices; and they caroused in clubs where they drank Newport Punch made of rum, lime juice, arrack, and loaf sugar.

Before the Civil War, summer colonists from Charleston, Mobile, Havana, and the Indies strolled the Strand, although few stayed after dusk. Fishermen pitched pennies and bet on impromptu dog fights and sold fish from wheelbarrows on Bannister's Wharf (Pero Bannister, a long-nosed oysterman, died suddenly and had to be buried in a makeshift coffin so shallow the undertaker was forced to cut a hole in the lid for Pero's nose).

When I saw Thames Street the first time in the sixties, it was still a dark little guttery thing filled with the odor of beer and fried food and dime-store perfume; the noise was music, shouts, laughter, gull screeches. The Navy remained its main order of business. At five o'clock on a summer evening, when the Alley really came to, you saw pressed white uniforms of the gobs, shining black oxfords, and faces wiped down with Old Spice;

but as the street emptied in the dark morning, the uniforms now smudged and rumpled and stinking of beer, there would be vomiting and sometimes fights. While the terms differed, to sailors and high society ("The Four Hundred") alike, Thames Street was "the asshole of Newport." Only when the cup races brought the regatta to town would the Four Hundred and the gentlemen from the War College come down to the Alley to play at the nautical life. Then the attitude was: SAILORS AND DOGS KEEP OUT.

Newport entrepreneurs neglected Thames because they believed that Broadway and the north-end highways should have the new commercial growth; and so, shopping centers saved the Alley from the twentieth century. From one war to the next, waterfront changes were small and slow, and the past, seamy and seedy and alive, continued. I came to like the street. It possessed something uncommon.

Now, nearly fifteen years since I'd last seen it, I walked into the lane where Washington Square — actually more an isosceles triangle — meets the old Long Wharf. The harborside of the street was gone. Where seventeenth- and eighteenth-century buildings had stood were parking lots and a mall. My expectation sank as if flushed down a scupper. Most of the city-side of the street (now called America's Cup Avenue) had been modernized into shops of concrete and glass that sold polymer plastic scrimshaw, driftwood lamps, lighted whelk shells, garish seascapes, marijuana-leaf beltbuckles.

The seamen's taverns had yielded to places with olde-style signs: SPIRITS AND VICTUALS. GROG HAPPY HOUR. Navy outfitters were now women's shoeshops, tattoo parlors perfume boutiques. Where jacktars had walked with the sway the sea teaches, now coeds from the Seven Sisters waggled their precious butts atop Pappagallos, and permanent-press matrons, safe in tummy-control Spandex, their triceps swinging in the wind, lugged purses the size of seabags.

I stopped for a beer. The bartender brought a Narragansett. I asked what had happened to Thames Street. "Redevelopment for urban blight."

The bar was crowded. America's Cup Avenue was clearly a money-maker. A man, young, said, "They trashed the place to save it. The American plan."

"How did it happen?"

"Navy cut back. Businessmen wanted tourists who'll spend more than sailors."

"But the history."

"American history is parking lots."

The room was full of girls with orchid-colored lips, signed trousers, and disco pumps; hands full of high-technology cigarettes and sugary, Day-

Glo drinks; faces agog with the fallal and frippery of the new Thames Street. They jabbered with twenty-one-year-old men of all ages.

I was glum and sour and critical of everything. The talk washed over me. One Touch & Glow girl had her arm wrenched behind her wiggling it about; I thought she was winding herself up, but she was just scratching her back. "Jesus!" she said. "I'm buying clothes like they were going out of style." A man with a voice hollow like the drip of water in an empty pan complained, "She's not so pretty — anyway, vanity's only skin deep." A squatty girl, working hard for that elusive leggy look, said, "He's so trite. Nobody talks like that."

I remembered an old fisherman I'd met in a tavern where a parking lot was now. He'd lost a thumb to a kink in a line, but he believed he'd had a good life. Around his neck hung a small scrimshaw, showing a crude yet detailed image of the Holy Virgin, carved from the knuckle of his thumb. "Your own bone," he had said, "she's the best luck."

And I remembered another conversation I sat in on across the street. A third-class gunner's mate told a seaman apprentice about peeling off the bandages and swiving a Haitian whore five days after his circumcision. He wasn't lying. The day we pulled out of Port-au-Prince, I saw the infection.

Somewhere between that vile past and the vacuous present, somewhere between history and trends, there must have been other possibilities for Thames Street that the burghers of Newport missed.

There was no point staying on; what I'd come for was gone, replaced by things available all over the United States.

The Newport-Jamestown ferry was extinct too, superseded by a two-mile bridge. I said to the tollkeeper, "Damn expensive bridge — the toll, that is."

"We got a joke here. It's high because it's high. Get it? They built it so aircraft carriers at Quonset Point could sail under. As soon as the paint dried, the Navy pulled its birdfarms out of Narragansett Bay."

"What's the bridge here for anyway?"

"Opens Newport up to New York City traffic. Lotta new businesses to support here now."

They might just as well have opened the old harbor town to the Four Horsemen of the Apocalypse. I went on toward Quonset Point, the homeport of the ship I had been assigned to. The U.S.S. *Lake Champlain*, a World War II flattop, once held the trans-Atlantic speed record, and it pulled out of the sea America's first spaceman, Alan Shepard. I'd heard the carrier had been sold for scrap, but I wanted to see the ships that had taken her berth — *if* I could get permission to go on the pier.

As things turned out, I didn't need to worry about permission. On the west side of the base, where Seabees invented the Quonset hut, was a carnival. The new Navy, I thought. I drove down the long road to the air station and wondered what excuse might get me in — ironic after all the time I'd spent years ago thinking up reasons to get out.

But the gates were open, sentry boxes unmanned, the ten-foot chain-link fence torn and leaning. Still, I expected base security any minute. One of the messhalls had a name on it like a restaurant. The new volunteer Navy.

At the end of the road, a mile in, the big pier was empty. Nothing but rusting stanchions and bollards, and weeds along the railroad tracks. The whole bay stood open and vacant. The *Champ*, the *Essex*, the *Wasp* used to fill the sky with gray masses of hull, gun, and antennas. The great carriers were gone, and also tugs, tenders, big naval cranes, helicopters, jets; the shouts and hubbub and confusion of sailors and machines and aircraft, all gone.

On the shore a man was stacking lobster traps. Lobster traps? "What the hell's happened here?" I shouted over to him, but it didn't carry. I walked out on the pier where a lone tern watched. Once there was a gull for every sailor. Lobster traps! I was mad at seeing my service come to this. I had lived and died walking off and on this pier and many times had dreamed of the day I'd come back as a civilian, free of the tyranny of the boatswain's pipe and his curses, free of working in a one-hundred-twenty-five-degree steel box. I felt cheated.

Where the hell was the diesel oil of yesteryear? Where the drawn faces when we left, the cockahoop faces when we returned, the sailors kissing girls and lugging seabags, mahogany statues, brass platters, straw hats, and black velvet paintings of bulls and naked native women; trucks honking, the sailors on duty cursing down from the deck and offering services to the women, the sea wind snapping the flag from the jackstaff, the last smoke blowing grit on us from the tall stacks? And now lobster pots! Christ. I knew you couldn't go home again, but nobody had said anything about not getting back to your old Navy base.

A horn blared. A man with a bulgy, bulbous head shouted, "Got official business out here, mac?" That was more like it. He was a Rhode Island Port Authority watchman with all the command bearing of a dirty rag, but he was better than nothing. Writing my license number down on his clipboard, he did his best to be properly official. "What's your name, mac?" That was much more like it.

"I was stationed here on the *Champ*, CVS–thirty-nine. She was a sub hunter."

"What's your name?"

"Drexel."

"What's your first name?"

"That's it. Drexel. Drexel Twitty. I can't believe it's all gone."

"Never saw it before the Navy turned it over to us. Okay, sailor, take your look-see and get your butt out of here by dark." He drove off, and that was my triumphal return to Quonset Point Naval Air Station.

In the evening I went down along the Pettaquamscutt River to find a restaurant on the sound at Narragansett Pier called The Sunnyside; it was the kind of eatery that people start talking about by saying, "I know a great little place . . ." We used to eat cherrystones on the halfshell, clam chowder, jonnycakes and sausage, and drink Ballantine Ale.

After what I'd been seeing, I didn't expect it to be there, and it wasn't. Instead, condominiums and tennis courts. So I had supper at the Green Inn, a huge green-shingled, Victorian-era hotel just down from what was left of The Towers, a last-century casino bridging Ocean Road. I ate little-necks on the halfshell and drank Ballantine Ale (once the most distinctive American brew until Falstaff bought the company and modernized the brewing process). Outside the window, in the last light, I could see the Atlantic horizon bent into a soft parabola by the old glass.

Plastic scrimshaw, carnival rides, condos. That was what history had come to. Then, like a night-blooming cereus, a thought opened: maybe the whole point of going to sea was to make room one day for lobster pots and roller coasters. To melt warships into Ferris wheels, that had to be progress. Maybe all I'd been cheated of was a preconceived notion of what the future looks like.

After dinner, I parked for the night on a jetty hooking into the sound and walked up the shingled beach. Breakers tumbled the round stones back and forth, ringing out of them curious metallic measures. For three hundred years warships had sailed the bay. Now dodge-em cars replaced gun tubs.

But it was all a fiction of progress. There were more warheads now than when I went to sea. Changes, yes, but movement away from the machinery of war, no. On another shingled beach in another century, Matthew Arnold spoke of ignorant armies clashing by night. Present situation report: as they say in Selma, ain't nothin' changed.

6

An Englishman once had a good laugh when I asked how far it was to Chichester, a name I hadn't come close to pronouncing properly. I tried three other ways and still didn't get it right. He was in stitches. "Oh, you Yanks just slay me."

"Okay, pal," I said. "Tell me the body of water Seattle is on. That ought to be easy — it's only five letters." I started to spell it.

"I can spell it, mate. P-u-g-e-t. And I'll pronounce it for you too. PUG-it." I laughed and he tried, "Poo-GET." More laughter made him desperate, so he tried a little French, the last resort of the English: "Pooh-ZHAY."

"Nope. It's PEW-jit. You Limeys just kill me."

"Look," he said, "all you have to do to pronounce Chichester is soften the vowels and swallow more than you say."

The English must do well in Rhode Island, what with all the softening and swallowing necessary to pronounce the descriptive Algonquian place names: Chepiwanoxet, Annaquatucket, Usquepaugh, Woonasquatucket, Nannaquaket, Quonochontaug, Quanatumpic (if you like the letter *q*, you'll love Little Rhody of the big names). Someone once said that if Niagara Falls were in Rhode Island, the English settlers would have pronounced it "Niffuls."

There are other names here, thank heavens, just as distinctive but still pronounceable. Take, for example, the meandering county roads that most states would identify by numbers or letters: Willie Woodhead Road, Widow Sweets Road, Hog House Hill Road, Molasses Hazard Road, Biscuit City Road, Boom Bridge Road, Yawgoog Road, Poppasquash Road. Or little Elder Ballon Meetinghouse Road, a lane you can drive faster than spell.

The night before, the sea and sky had been the same color — black — with only liquid spangles of reflected light distinguishing one from the other. When I woke, they were again the same color, but now like melted sapphire. Just off the jetty, a lobster boat rolled and bubbled as the skipper lowered his traps single-handedly.

I started down the coast. If "down" means southward, and you think of the Atlantic seaboard striking a longitudinal line, you'll be disoriented in Rhode Island and Connecticut as you follow the ocean. The coastline runs almost due east and west. Hence the name Westerly, Rhode Island, a town just off the Atlantic and west of everything in the state.

It was here, so I read, during the Dorr Rebellion in 1842, that General John B. Stedman was charged with maintaining martial law in the town. At one point, when he thought an attack imminent, he told his troops, "Boys, when you see the enemy, fire and then run. And as I am a little lame, I'll run now."

When I crossed the Pawcatuck River into Pawcatuck, Connecticut, just up the old Post Road from Wequetequock, I realized I was heading straight into New York City. I had two choices: drive far inland to bypass it or take the New London–Orient Point ferry to Long Island and cut through the bottom edge of the Apple. I headed toward New London, through Mystic, where they used to build the clipper ships.

Indians called New London "Nameaug." White settlers called it by a tribal name, "Pequot," and their descendants renamed it "New London," believing as they did that the little village on the deep-water harbor would become one day the greatest city of the East coast. They even changed the Monhegin River to the "Thames." And so went the native American names.

In New London, the only thing that smacked of old London was the old-world street system — nowhere a true square or rectangular block between Shaw's Cove and Winthrop's Cove. Even Benedict Arnold's 1781 torching of the town didn't help straighten the lanes. A policeman on foot motioned me to the curb for driving the wrong direction on a one-way street. I was only four blocks from the ferry slip, but it took a complex of turns to get through the labyrinth.

The ferry, an old oily tub holding a few cars, bucketed down the deep river that had seen Indian canoes, Revolutionary War privateers, whaling ships, Coast Guard rum-chasers, and three generations of submarines. At the railing, I tried to watch both sides of the river: the west bank with grassy homes and an old lighthouse and on the east bank the Groton shipyards.

An engineer for Singer Company (once only makers of sewing machines, but now also manufacturers of undersea warfare "systems") stood next to me. His face was a whorl of lines like fingerprint. I asked where they built the submarines, and he pointed to a dagger of a shadow. "That black thing is the *Ohio*. She's the first Trident. The orange bull on blocks is the *Michigan*."

"How can anything that big move under water?"

"They're longer than the Washington Monument. The *Ohio* will carry twenty-four missiles, each one with a dozen warheads: two hundred eighty-eight atomic explosions. One hell of a bitch with twelve sisters coming along behind at a billion dollars each." He offered a Chiclet. "They used to name battleships after states because they were the dreadnaughts of the sea, but there's your dreadnaughts of the next war."

"What next war?"

"You think war is finished? Whatever peace we'll know will come because of things like those devils. Let me tell you about my uncle who collected handguns and worked up at Colt in Hartford. He had an eighteen-seventy Colt revolver called 'The Peacemaker' because it was so deadly. Those Tridents are the new Peacemakers, but they call them 'deterrents' now."

"By that logic the greatest peacemaker would be a doomsday machine."

"Remember one thing — *Kremlin* is the Russian word for 'fortress.' If those uncivilized maniacs in the Fortress ever come to their senses, then maybe we can make some changes. It's not real fashionable now to believe in military power, but it will be again, and when that happens, people will love those exploding cigars. I've seen both sides — I was in the hooligan Navy."

"What's the hooligan Navy?"

"Where hooligans did the dirty work. I was on Red Beach in 'forty-four. I can still hear the blue whispers coming at us. A little streak of blue smoke and a hiss and you were gone. I was so scared I wished I was dead."

All the time we had been talking, a father on the other side of me entertained his baby with the blink of his LED watch; the baby, in a knitted cap that said PAULIE, burbled at the red numbers and reached a clumsy half-fist toward it. Paulie didn't know, but across the way, the General Dynamics Electric Boat Company was putting his world together for him.

I said to the engineer, "Isn't this ferry some kind of old Navy craft?"

"An LSM they brought out of the Pacific after the war and put a new superstructure on. She's been making this crossing since nineteen forty-eight, but she's in her last month. They got a new, specially designed boat just about ready."

When John Steinbeck began his 1960 tour of the United States that he describes in *Travels With Charley*, he crossed Long Island Sound on this very boat and worried about the nuclear submarines of an earlier day. Yet a couple of decades later, that great flash of light still had not shown mankind the way out. Watching the shipyards disappear from view, the engineer said, "Maybe it's a crazy way to be sane, but men are most reasonable when they're scared."

"Ever seen a cornered animal?"

"We're not animals."

We crossed the east end of the sound over a strip of water known as "The Race" and passed close by a small, brushy island topped with a smokestack.

"Talk of animals," he said, "there's what worries me — Plum Island. The Dangerous Animal Disease Laboratory."

"What do they consider a dangerous animal?"

"It's diseases that're dangerous, not animals. But I couldn't say for sure what they study there. Glanders, tularemia, plague — I'm not certain. I don't even know if the Pentagon has a role in the research. But give me an atomic warhead any day to disease warfare. The time's coming, though, when we'll fight with germs. Economics will force it because it's more efficient to kill with bugs than steel. Compared to a drum of cholera, a Trident's a thing of beauty."

"Myself, I've always preferred an earache to a toothache."

7

IF you want to hear distortions and misconceptions laced with plenty of dogmatic opinion, you have a choice of three places — excluding domed governmental edifices and buildings with steeples — bars, sport arenas, and gas stations (barbershops have lost position because of electronics: you can't hear over the hair dryers). As filling stations cease to be garages and community centers, as they become nothing but expensive nozzles, they too are losing ground. But, in the past, an American traveler depended on the local grease pit boys to tell him (a) the best route to wherever; (b) the best place to eat, although librarians give better recommendations; and (c) what the townsfolk thought about whatsoever. Now, it already may be too late for a doctoral candidate to study the ways that Americans' views of each other have been shaped while waiting for the tank to fill.

Orient Point, Long Island, was a few houses and a collapsed four-story inn built in 1810, so I went to Greenport for gas. At an old-style station, the owner himself came out and pumped the no-lead and actually wiped the windshield. I happened to refer to him as a New Yorker.

"Don't call me a New Yorker. This is Long Island."

"I meant the state, not the city."

"Manhattan's a hundred miles from here. We're closer to Boston than the city. Long Island hangs under Connecticut. Look at the houses here, the old ones. They're New England–style because the people that built them came from Connecticut. Towns out here look like Connecticut. I don't give a damn if the city's turned half the island into a suburb — we should rightfully be Connecticut Yankees. Or we should be the seventh New England state. This island's bigger than Rhode Island any way you measure it. The whole business gets my dander up. We used to berth part of the New England whaling fleet here, and that was a pure Yankee business. They called this part of the island 'the flukes' because Long Island even looks like a whale. But you go down to the wharf now and you'll see city boats and a big windjammer that sells rides to people from Mamaroneck and Scarsdale."

He got himself so exercised he overfilled the tank, but he didn't pipe down. "If the East River had've been ten miles wide, we'da been all right." He jerked the nozzle out and clanked it into the pump. "We needed a bay and we got a bastard river no wider than a stream of piss."

Thus chastised, I went down a pleasant little road numbered 25, down the north fluke, through neat vegetable truck farms with their typical story-and-a-half houses, past estuaries and swans, to Riverhead. I followed a pickup with four bloodied sharks laid out in the bed; it looked like a tin of evil sardines packed in ketchup.

The side road ended, and I got pulled onto an expressway as if I were part of a train. I buckled the seatbelt, popped in a piece of bubblegum, put on my twelve-o'clock-high sunglasses, and got ready for *the* city. You'd have thought I was going to run the Gaza Strip. But it was Islip, Babylon, Amityville, Merrick, Oceanside. The Belt Roadway showed the backsides of suburbs and miles of carpet sample, unclaimed freight, factory outlet, and furniture warehouse stores — half of them gone under, the others with windows blocked by giant prices. Things raced past like the jumpy images of a nickelodeon: abandoned and stripped cars on the shoulders, two hitchhiking females that nobody could stop to pick up, a billboard EAT SAUSAGE AND BE HAPPY, low-flying jumbos into Kennedy International, the racetrack at Ozone Park, bulldozed piles of dirt to fill the marsh at Jamaica Bay, long and straight Flatbush Avenue, Sheepshead Bay, Coney Island, the World Trade Center like stumps in the yellow velvet sky. Then a windingly protracted ascent up the Verrazano-Narrows Bridge (the Silver Gate of the East coast) with its world's longest center span, and below the bay where the *Great Eastern*, the *Monitor*, the *Bonhomme Richard*, and the *Half Moon* sailed.

The low sun turned the Upper Bay orange. Freighters rode at anchor or headed to the Atlantic, and to the north, in the distance, a little glint of coppery green that was the Statue of Liberty. I slowed to gawk and got a horn; the driver passed in a gaseous cloud and held aloft a middle digit opinion.

The lanes descended and shot me across Staten Island; just before it was too late, I pulled out of the oppression of traffic and drove down Richmond Avenue to find the bridge across the Arthur Kill into Perth Amboy, the city (if you follow your nose) that gets to you before you get to it. I don't know how I lost my way on a thoroughfare as big as Richmond, but I did. I could smell Perth Amboy, but I couldn't find it. Instead, I found Great Kills, Eltingville, Huguenot Park, Princess Bay, and Tottenville. I asked directions from a nervous teenager who was either tuning his engine or stealing someone's distributor.

Just as darkness was complete, I reached New Jersey and decided to take U.S. 9 to get through the congestion and into the Pine Barrens, the last great natural interruption in the Boston-to-Washington megalopolis. John McPhee's book on the Pines had convinced me that anyone wanting to see it should do so immediately, what with subdividing realtors, industrial parks, reservoirs, and supersonic jet ports.

Forty minutes later I was already in Lakewood, midway down the state. I stopped for the night, still surprised I'd begun the day in Rhode Island. I had forgotten to think in the compressed distances of the Northeast.

8

IT isn't widely known in America that the descendants of Jolly Roger pirates put an end to dirigible flight. So I heard at breakfast in a diner. Actually, it was a full restaurant, but it had started as a diner. It was done up in red drapes and coachman lanterns, and at the door a concrete Cupid stood in a dry fountain surrounded by a polymer privet hedge. The eggs had been fried in Vitalis, and the potatoes carried a crisp woody flavor. I felt fine anyway.

The waitress, with a grudge of a face and a golden chain cutting into a puffy ankle, complained her way around. Everyone seemed to like her although she had no good tidings for anybody.

"You get enough sleep last night?" she asked me.

"I don't know. I drove after dark. Almost missed New Jersey."

"Missed Jersey? So what's to miss?"

"New Jersey's to miss."

"Nobody comes to Jersey to *see* Jersey."

"I did. I'm going into the middle of New Jersey to see it."

"Middle? What's this middle? You got the shore and you got Philly. Middle? There is no middle. Fort Dix is the middle."

"The Pine Barrens. Twenty kinds of orchids growing in there, they say. Bug-eating plants too."

She rolled her eyes. "You're on the dirty side now. Ask any trucker. You want orchids, go to a florist."

A man next to me wore a shirt that repeatedly said, ORO! Around and around, the words looped his paunch, his droop of shoulders, his yellowed armpits; among the ORO!'s were golden things: coins, watches, medallions, coronets.

"Let me tell you about the Pines," he said. "Maybe you heard of the *Hindenburg* — the zeppelin — but I'll let you in on the true story of what really happened. I've lived here all my life, and I know what happened even if the government said they didn't know."

The gist was this: a storm forced the *Hindenburg* into a holding pattern (that was a fact I could check out). The airship, only a few hundred feet off the ground, circled central New Jersey for two hours. Lakehurst, where it was trying to land, is on the edge of the Pines, and everyone knows Pineys don't tolerate anyone poking into their woods. They figured the zeppelin was a government ship looking for their stills where they turn blueberries into whiskey, so they shot at the thing and opened leaks in the fabric. By the time the *Hindenburg* started to tie up, there was enough free hydrogen to blow the ship to kingdom come, which it did.

"The official explanation was St. Elmo's fire," he said. "Static electricity. St. Elmo never in his life set fire to any aircraft. People can believe it was anti-Nazi sabotage if they want, but I'm telling the truth. It was potshots by the Pineys, and it was nothing new. They're descendants of pirates and smugglers who ran into the woods to hide. Mixed in with a few Tories and Hessians."

When I paid the waitress, she filled with motherly counsel. "Look. You're a nice boy. Go to the shore. Go to Atlantic City. But for godsakes don't go to no middle. The Pineys breed like flies in there. Live like animals."

I'd heard those words across the country. It was almost an axiom that anyone who lived off a main highway was an animal that bred like a fly. An hour later, the June heat coming on, I was on New Jersey 70, heading for the middle. I stopped at Lakehurst Naval Air Station to look at the dirigible hangars, those thousand-foot-long, twenty-story buildings, where the Pineys allegedly did in the blimp. Another era of flight ended here too: Lakehurst was the last place the Navy trained carrier pigeons.

The road became a succession of gentle dips through the sandy woods; my head bounced as if my neck were a loose coil of wire. Miles of bouncy, bouncy. I was having fun in the middle. County road 563 cut through the center of the six hundred fifty thousand acres (equal to Grand Canyon National Park) of pine barrens. There were pitch pines and oaks and white cedars. Although the trees tended toward the spindly, the land was by no means barren in the sense of unproductive. Cranberry bogs and fields of high-bush blueberries opened the woods in places.

The sky was cloudless, not in the usual way, but rather bleached by glare to the color a pair of facing mirrors make between them — neither blue nor gray but rather an absence of color. Trees, shrubs, the day, all drooped dead still in the humid heat, and wherever the Pineys were, they weren't on the road.

Somewhere south of Jenkins, population forty five (five was more believable), I gave in to the heat and pulled up under the trees by a small bridge. A stream, about half the width of the highway, moved through with a good current. I took it to be the Wading River. Bog iron (cannonballs fired at Valley Forge were made here) and tannins had turned the transparent water the color of cherry cola. This "cedar water," as it is called, sea captains once carried on long voyages because it remained sweet longer than other waters. Even today, it is remarkably free of pollutants since all streams that flow through the Pines have their source here. I walked up a track into the woods, dead ferns and pine needles absorbing my steps. A silence as if civilization had disappeared. While the quiet was real, the isolation was an illusion: downtown Philadelphia lay forty miles west. What's more, McPhee says that on a clear evening you can see a light in the Pines from the Empire State Building.

I came to the stream again, took off my clothes, and went in. There was no shock in the water, only cooling relief. I let the current pull me downstream toward the Atlantic, then I paddled back up, and floated off again. A black terrapin, trimmed in red, surfaced, saw me float by, blinked, and went under. I climbed out and let the heat dry me as I ate.

McPhee reports that, in the twenties, a Philadelphia newspaper gave away lots in the Pines as premiums with new subscriptions, and that during the Depression movie houses passed out deeds to small tracts as door prizes, and that realty agents offered lots here for five dollars. McPhee writes:

> When prospective buyers actually came to see the land, promoters tied pears and apples to the limbs of pine trees and stationed fishermen in small boats in Pine Barrens lakes with dead pickerel on the ends of their lines and instructions to pull the fish out of the water every ten minutes.

But no one cared for the giveaways, and, even now, although the margins of the Pines were shrinking from commercial encroachments, the heart of Burlington County — the middle of the pinelands — still belonged to the quiet and Pineys. Whenever that last foot of concrete is poured to complete the Boston-Washington megalopolis, it's likely to be in the Pine Barrens.

I went on south, through Weekstown, past a wooden sign nailed clumsily to a tree: ALWAYS IN OUR MEMORIES — PETE. I came to the southern limits of the woods at Egg Harbor City, a landlocked town fifteen miles from Great Egg Harbor. The plan years ago to dig a canal from town to the Great Egg Harbor River and thereby link with the sea did not work out. It wasn't the first time so-called progress had got lost in the Pines.

IN the afternoon, when I was down along Delaware Bay and trying to find how Othello, New Jersey, got its name, I came across a story of the past, the future, the present.

As the pine belt disappeared, the state took on a Southern cast below Millville, an old glass-making town on the Maurice River flowing through the exposed silica deposits of lower Jersey. Near here, the first Mason jar was made. Outside Bridgeton, the Southern aspect showed plain: big fields of soybeans, corn, cabbage, strawberries, and fallow fields of dusty brown, and slopes of peach and apple orchards. Black men worked patch farms, and with cane poles they fished muddy creeks of the lowlands where egrets stepped meticulously through the tidal marsh.

I drove up and down. The map wasn't getting me to Othello and neither were the county roads. I came to Greenwich (pronounced GREEN-witch), population one thousand, a village built along a broad single lane called "Ye Greate Street" (*Ye* correctly pronounced as "the"), which ran from a rotting boat landing on the Cohansey River northwest for two miles, most of the way lined with old homes and buildings. In the seventeenth century, "greate street" meant "main street," but now, "great" in the sense of "grand" was also accurate. Of the nearly hundred homes and buildings along the three-century-old thoroughfare, about ninety percent were built before 1880 and more than a quarter dated from the eighteenth century. Even the Sunoco station was in a 1760 house. Although the old structures appeared sound, only a few had been restored.

Greenwich was a Williamsburg with a difference: it wasn't dug out of the ground and rebuilt. There was another difference too: it didn't have that unnaturally genteel, sanitized look of the Virginia village that turns it into a museum. Surely, the first Williamsburg must have been a knockabout frontier town, a place of skullduggery and war, where the laundry got hung out and dogs pissed in the muddy lanes, where the scent of dung and wet horses was strong. To resurrect that town and playact the past is a good thing for Williamsburg. But it wasn't the way of Greenwich. Hidden in the tall marsh grass of the coastal lowland, the whilom seaport that once rivaled Philadelphia was remarkable.

I stopped at Arnold's grocery, post office, and filling station (two pumps under a Southern-style canopy). Here the citizens considered it, built in 1860, a newer building. As I sorted through the cooler for a bottle of pop, the clerk eyed me suspiciously. In the tone that means, "Move along, buster," she said, "Can we help you with something?"

"Maybe you could. I'm looking for Othello."

"Won't find it in the cooler."

As I waited at the counter to pay for the soda, I noticed a frail codger outside writing down my license number. No wonder history had left the town be.

When I ordered a double-dip cone of chocolate and blueberry, the woman's expression changed, but I was at the door before she said in an accent almost Southern, "You'll find Othello straight down Greate Street a couple of miles. It's not marked, but you can ask at The Griffin, the antique shop."

From the door of the post office, the codger eyed me. "X-six-P–six-thirty-nine," I called out, and he ducked inside as if my words were stones.

Greate Street, under big sycamores, was a road of clapboard or Flemish-bond brick structures, several in the flattened, elongated rowhouse style, with a few ornamented, wooden Victorian homes for variety. Through colonial windows I could see Windsor chairs and ancestral portraits. Some of the paintings were of men who, three days before the Christmas of 1774, dressed like Indians and savaged a shipment of tea bound for Philadelphia but temporarily hidden by the East India Company in a Greenwich cellar. Today the descendants boast about being one of five colonial towns to burn British tea.

In front of The Griffin, I found the owner talking with her nephew. I told her I was looking for Othello, and she said, "You're standing in it."

"Isn't this Greenwich?"

"To some people."

"How did it get named Othello?"

"How does anything get named? Who knows the truth?"

"Where could I find the truth?"

"I really don't have the time," she grumbled, "but come in the shop. I'm about to close. You'll have to read fast." She handed me a big book printed in the last century. I learned nothing.

Barbara Rizzo, who shared the old building, said, "Why don't you ask Roberts Roemer? He knows about Greenwich. A dapper gent too unless you get him talking about A.C.E. Then he might lose his Southern hospitality."

"What's A.C.E.?"

"Ask him. He'll give you a balanced view. He's big enough to fight it. You ask us, we might get mad. He's out at Cohansey View Farm."

So I went out to the farm, a pleasant spread of land overlooking the winding river just a couple of miles above where it enters Delaware Bay. At the back of the fine old house, Roemer was painting a patio chair. He was Vice-President of Corporate Development for Wheaton Industries, a

Millville manufacturer making glass containers primarily for the phar-maceutical and cosmetics industries, although the wire-bail canning jars had become popular in boutiques.

Roemer once wanted to become an architect, but a high school principal talked him out of it. After serving as a cryptographic technician in the Second World War, he went off to Middlebury College, where he graduated with a degree in fine arts and additional coursework in differential equa-tions and calculus. But his deepest interest remained architecture.

I asked about Othello. "The tales I've heard," he said, "I wouldn't put much credence in. Othello is what they call 'Head of Greenwich' now. I'll tell you who to ask, though. If the old historian can't give a good answer, forget it." Roemer wrote out the name and address. "I'll call first and tell him you're a teacher — otherwise he might not talk to you."

"This isn't why I came, but what's A.C.E.?"

He frowned. "Look, when you get back, I'll tell you over a gin and tonic. Dinner if you're hungry."

10

THE door of the old house of the man who could explain how Othello got its name opened a few inches. "What is it?"

"I'm the one asking about Othello."

The door opened wider. It was the man who had written down my license number. "Why do you want to know? What's up your sleeve?"

To hell with these suspicions. I wasn't that curious. In truth, it was only the inertia of the first question pulling me along. "It's not important," I said. "To be honest, I'm finding whatever the answer is not worth the asking."

The man, thin and a little bent, said, "All right, come in then." The yellow shades were drawn, a dark portrait hung above the mantel, and on a table lay Walpole's *Diary* and on the sofa, Aubrey's *Brief Lives*. I sat in a deep, velvet chair tattered about the edges as if chewed on by mice.

"Before I tell you anything," he said crossly, "I want you to understand that if you go confabulating around our county, you leave my name out of it. And there's another thing — before I talk, I want to hear *you* talk. Let's see if you wear the colors. What are you doing here?"

"Driving around the country and looking into things."

"Traveling alone?"

"People, places, things, ideas — if you call that alone."

"*Homo viator?*" He was testing me.

"*Homo spectans.*"

He sneered. "Thoreau traveled extensively in Concord."

"And Socrates learned nothing from fields and trees."

The scowling almost twisted to a smile. "I take your point. You might be wearing the colors. All right, here's how Othello got the name. Ignore other versions. In Cumberland County we have a settlement of people called 'tri-bloods,' people that trace their history — or legend — back to a Moorish — Algerian, specifically — princess who came ashore after a ship-wreck in the first years of the nation. The Indians took her in, and, from the subsequent mixing of blood — later with a small infusion from the Negro — there developed a group composed of three races. The 'Delaware Moors,' they're called. A similar branch is the Carolina Yellowhammers.

"In the thirties and forties, governmental bureaucrats — especially in Delaware — they had a time trying to classify tri-bloods because the people considered themselves neither white, red, nor black. Usually they ended up in their own category, one so small as to be forgotten. To this hour, the people remain what you might describe as aloof, and they maintain themselves as independently as they can. Clannish, even secretive. But they always have been landowners and farmers. Never slaves. Still, they are — to use the phrase — 'men of color' and consequently suspect, es-pecially in border states, despite their features usually being more Indian than Negroid. Aquiline nose, straight hair, high cheekbones."

"I haven't seen any blacks in Greenwich."

"That may be. They live just up the road at Springtown, one of the first stops on the Underground Railroad. The name comes from a place a Negro could 'spring' for his freedom. A springboard. But I'm talking now about Negroes, not the Moors. People get it confused."

"So how does Othello fit in?"

"The upper end of Greate Street was always Presbyterian. The lower end, down on the Cohansey, was Quaker. The Friends Meetinghouse is still there. Both communities recognized an unspoken caste system and lived apart from 'men of color.' After some years of going two miles to pick up their mail, people at this end of the street applied for their own post office under the rubric 'Head of Greenwich.' Fearing confusion, the Postal Department rejected the name. The people met to consider another. At that time, we had a Shakespearian reading society here that performed in the Presbyterian church. One woman who fancied herself an actress, perhaps provoked over some snub, suggested with deliberate irony they call the town Othello. Realize that Negroes live *up* the road and Moors *down* the road but neither group lives in town. The whites agreed, all the while unaware that Othello, the Moor of Venice, is, as the play says, 'a great black ram tupping a white ewe.' "

"That's a pretty complex insult."

"It never carried because the residents didn't know the source. And today, even though interest in the old name is coming back, people consider the place part of proud and historic Greenwich."

"What about Greenwich? Where did that name come from?"

"Settlers from Connecticut, the Greenwich there — Quakers and Presbyterians — were persuaded to come here around sixteen eighty by William Penn's agent, Gabriel Thomas. Many of them wanted to escape the rigid theocracy of New England. Thomas told them of the deep soil here and the good fishing, the abundant shellfish and timber, the milder climate. When the Presbyterians arrived at the Othello end of the street, they set up a free school — something almost unheard of then. They taught a classical learning rather than the more practical education of the Quakers. They considered reading and writing adjuncts of civilized life, and Greenwich became an Anglo-Saxon island of civilized culture in the wilderness — which it still is in a different way. Italians have replaced Indians."

He watched for a response. "The Quakers contributed too," he said. "Their policy was always to purchase land from the Indians. They never purloined real estate, perhaps because establishing title is very important in Quaker thinking. A Friend always tries to pass to his heirs more land than he began with. So they established a strong base of landowners interested in law and order. They never had trouble with Indians. A peaceable moderation, you see. They established stability and wealth too. One Connecticut Friend carried down so much silver goods on his horses, his wife had to walk the whole way. The Quaker ideal is still here in this county for you to see — property bought in sixteen ninety even now feeds the descendants. Preservation is their watchword. Thee must never, *never* touch the principal."

The old Jerseyman got up. At the door, he looked again at my license plate. "The ancient Incas," he said, "when they traveled the great mountain empire, were required to wear their own distinct costume so they could be recognized. What do we have now? A license plate? Ideas are a man's costume, his colors."

I started to say something, but he waved it off and put his arm on my shoulder. He said, "Descartes believed traveling is like conversing with men of other centuries. Have your miles brought you to agree with the old phrasemaker?"

"I agree."

"And on your peregrinations, my pilgrim friend, have you met a man from the future yet?"

"I'd have to think it over. Look back."

"Look *back* for a man of the future? The logic of a teacher. The future is not usually memory projected forward, but I take your point. As a historian, I'm an optimist, and when I look ahead, I see back. I see man crawling out of the ooze again."

"A peculiar optimism."

"I speak to tell you — the pendulum is swinging toward the extinction of man. Do you wear those colors?"

"Don't know what your reference is."

"Another answer of a teacher. Here's an answer — I've seen our county come a far piece in my time. I'll not be alive when Greenwich becomes solidly obscured by industry, but you will, and you'll be younger than I am now when this nook of the bay is an industrial wasteland. There are all kinds of reasons why there will be industrial development here, the greatest of which is that to make change is the most human creation. And there are other reasons, reasons such as a corporate body having no soul. We've reached the point where we'll either take care of ourselves or extinction will be our inheritance."

He stopped and stared at me. "Your expression says you don't understand, but Bob Roemer can tell you the story of how we made Rome howl."

"Is this about that thing called A.C.E.?"

"This is about the limited capacity of men to understand because they measure time in terms of themselves. This is about men who won't see causes and therefore can't predict effects. This is about men who fail to realize that geographical refuge is central to our history. It's about men who exterminate the species of the earth at the rate of one every day."

He gave my shoulder another shake. "You see no worry in me because I know the natural amenities will finally be preserved for a single reason and for a single reason alone — the force of nature demands it. Its sway is greater than ours. We will have our time of destruction nevertheless. But, in a nutshell, that's why I'm an optimist." He released my shoulder. "And for one other reason."

"Which is?"

"Accidents, discovery, even enlightenment. Any projection must allow for man to change his history, a power second only to that of nature. A projection must allow for free will because only it does not despise or distrust or fear the unknown even if it knows the future is not a better place but only a different one. Any prognosis must consider that men can

change their angles of vision and therefore change the future." He stopped
to catch his wind. "And if you reject all that, then say I believe, as did
Tertullian, because it is absurd."

11

At the foot of the road in front of Roberts Roemer's home, just where
Maple makes a T-intersection with Greate Street, James Josiah Ewing built
a house in 1834. He placed it deliberately in the way of Maple to keep the
road from being extended to Delaware Bay and dividing his property. At
the time, people believed it was self-serving to force a more circuitous
route, but now some townsmen considered the Ewing house a preserver
of the integrity of Greate Street and, maybe, Greenwich as well. A man's
response to the house was a litmus test to see what colors he wore.

From Roemer's home, built in 1830 by a Quaker schoolmaster, we could
see egrets down on the tidal flats of the Cohansey as they nippered up
little crabs swarming the brown mud. From high marsh grasses between
skews of river came whistles of bobwhite and from the north a scent of
strawberry fields. Roemer handed me a gin and tonic and told the story
of A.C.E., the Atlantic City Electric Company.

The substance: A.C.E., using a straw company called Overland Realty
and working through local agents, started buying land around Greenwich
in 1966. In three years, they had most of the property fronting the bay.
Although the sellers did not know what the land would be used for, they
"covenanted" with Overland never to vote against any proposed zoning
change. Ignoring that a no-vote covenant constitutes an illegal disenfran-
chisement, A.C.E. bought the silence of nearly a fifth of the township.

Ninety-two residents, mostly farmers, sold forty-five hundred acres (about
twenty percent of the township) to Overland for two and a quarter million
dollars. Some of them sold blindly because Seabrook Frozen Foods, which
once purchased most of the local produce, had closed. Labor costs had
become prohibitive and the future of the asparagus fields looked bad for
a crop, subject to blight, that has to be harvested by hand. A.C.E. seemed
to offer salvation to the vegetable growers. Other residents, in or near
retirement, needed the quick capital. But a few people refused to sell,
refused even after fires of unknown origin began destroying abandoned
outbuildings on unsold land. Teenage vandalism, the word was.

Once Overland owned most of the property, they mortgaged it to Prudential Insurance (one of whose board of directors also sat on the Overland board) for four and one-half million dollars and dissolved the straw company. By then things were becoming clear. Unexplained telephone lines New Jersey Bell was running into empty marsh made sense, and construction of a nuclear generating station only fifteen miles northwest near Salem soon would provide cheap power for new industry.

"Other than the finagling," I said, "I don't see the cause for alarm."

"The alarm is that industry reaching to the perimeter of Greenwich threatens the survival of a town older than Philadelphia. Greenwich and Salem are the first permanent English-speaking settlements on Delaware Bay. Because of the high degree of preservation here, this village is as significant as Jamestown. It's unique. If it's destroyed, it cannot, in any way, ever be replaced. So when word leaked out that there were plans for tank farms three miles away at Bayside which would receive oil from ships anchored off Cape May and other plans to run oil north by railroad on the old Caviar line through our township, some of us got worried. Bayside's in our township."

"The Caviar line?"

"Bayside's just fishing shacks now, but it used to be a thriving place called 'Caviar' because of the sturgeon fishing. The trackbed down to the bay still exists. We also began hearing about plans for industry to come in, and we learned that another nuclear plant would be built down here. Suddenly, people were visualizing trailers next to a seventeen-thirty-seven house, a hamburger franchise where the British tea was burned. We visualized the end. Things came to a crisis when the township committee, as it was then, rewrote the zoning ordinance so that A.C.E. got the land packaged up as they wanted it. Goodbye to Greenwich. In spite of the township's own paid consultants and the county soil conservationist both advising against heavy industrial development, they rezoned anyway. This is marshland — a tidal zone."

Roemer joined with a hundred twenty other citizens to form the Greenwich Emergency Committee for the purpose of filing suit against the three-member township committee to prevent heedless destruction of a village that, undisturbed for most of three centuries, had sat literally at the end of the road. The Emergency Committee worked to elect a new township committee, to arouse residents who hadn't wanted the bother, to find new and compatible ways to produce income from the land.

"The struggle was to show that a certain amount of open area is absolutely necessary, not just to the atmosphere of the village, but to its health and survival. All of us have seen a continuing reduction in the size of the historic area. Houses being torn down or moved. The Greenwich

22. Roberts Roemer in Greenwich, New Jersey

post office was moved to an 'olde tyme' tourist village near Atlantic City. We had to show that one good historic structure can be worth the revenue equal to a one-hundred-thousand-dollar payroll. We wanted to prevent historic land from becoming a commodity."

The governor came to open the state bicentennial celebration, but the visit, in spite of the official recognition of Greenwich's historical significance, came to nothing. Finally, the committee took its case to the state superior court in Atlantic City. It lost and lacked the ten thousand dollars to appeal.

But by then, things no longer looked so grim. Changes in and outside Greenwich diminished the necessity of pursuing the case. The Emergency group had succeeded in changing the composition of the township committee, and the new committee rewrote the zoning ordinance after finding thirty-three errors in it. While the new ordinance prohibited oil storage and nuclear generating stations along the bay, it did set aside an area north of Greenwich near Springtown for commercial development and another to the west for light industry.

What's more, the group succeeded in having much of the village placed on the National Register of Historic Sites so that any proposed change in use would be reviewed by the Department of the Interior.

"Even the State of New Jersey," Roemer said, "now recognizes a historic district extending from the Cohansey to Othello. But they rejected our attempt to put an architectural review board into the new zoning ordinance. And other changes, mostly in Washington, have helped — the Wetlands Act protects the tidal zone, the Farmlands Assessment Act gives us a share of income from tillable acreage. There have been subtle changes too, like the Farmers and Merchants Bank people building their new facility in a Flemish-bond style rather than Howard Johnson contemporary. Individuals who privately refurbish homes help also."

And, of all things, soybeans helped preserve Greenwich. Because they can be planted, cultivated, and harvested by machine, soybeans have given value again to the area as cropland. For the vegetable growers, young members of the Seabrook family opened a new cannery near Bridgeton.

"We've had time to organize and make changes because the demand for power in the seventies didn't increase as much as A.C.E. predicted it would. Technical problems at the Salem nuclear plant gave us time too. Now, if you ask me, both regulations and time are on our side — on the side of history. It's easier to keep a developer under a quiet but continuous pressure to act with corporate responsibility. But for us, it was an awakening at the brink.

"The problem of what we're doing lies in deciding what's the benefit of history and what's the burden. We're not trying to hold back the future, but we do believe what *has happened* in Greenwich is at least as important as what *could happen* here. The future should grow from the past, not obliterate it."

When Roemer brought a second round of tonics, he said, "The evidence of history, whether it's archives or architecture, is rare and worth preserving. It's relevant, it's useful. Here, it also happens to be beautiful. Maybe I've been influenced by the old Quakers who believed it was a moral question always to consider what you're leaving behind. Why not? It's not a bad measure of a man — what he leaves behind."

12

JUDGE William Hancock, wealthy and influential, had no luck at all in his last year. In 1734 at Hancock's Bridge, a few miles northwest of Greenwich, he built a grand house that he later had to flee from when militiamen took over south Jersey. On the night of March 20, 1778, as Tories regained the area, the Loyalist judge elected to slip back; he didn't know that nearly a hundred revolutionists were bivouacked in his house. They captured him. Hancock probably would have been safe in the hands of his enemies had two hundred green-coated Loyalists not decided to retake the place that same night. They surprised the patriots in their sleep and bayoneted them even as the men begged for quarter. In the dark mayhem, Hancock's confederates killed him too. The house still stands, a monument to the judge's ill timing.

Salem, a colonial town to the west, was abundant with old buildings and homes that would be museums most anywhere else in the country, but here they were just more declining houses, even though many stood when the men of Salem sent beef to Valley Forge to help save Washington's troops from starvation. The town is the birthplace of Zadock Street, a restless fellow who left New Jersey in 1803 to make his way into the new western territory. As he went, he and his sons founded towns in Ohio, Indiana, and Iowa, and named them all Salem; in Ohio, his Salem sprouted North Salem, West Salem, South Salem, Lower Salem, and Salem Center. Americans can be thankful that Zadock Street was not born in Freidberger or Quonochontaug.

Under a milky industrial sky turning saffron in the afternoon sun, I crossed the Delaware River estuary south of Wilmington. The bridge was only twenty-four bird miles from Greenwich. A chance of history and geography had allowed the village to survive, but, with the spread of industry along the river, it seemed like a miracle.

Delaware, the first state historically (the Delaware convention ratified the Constitution first) and the next to last in size, has only twelve miles of interstate, excluding the business routes of Wilmington. Thinking I had come to a land of blue highways, I turned onto Delaware 9 to follow the bay down the south shore. And I *did* find the route a pleasant unraveling of macadam through six-foot marsh grass and cultivated fields being pecked over by sea birds. There were few houses and fewer villages. Although I couldn't see the bay, I could smell it and see evidence of it in an old steel lighthouse implausibly at the edge of a cornfield near Leipsic. But east of Dover, 9 came to an end. The Delaware blue roads run east and west, and the longitudinal highways are multilanes.

I stopped at Dover for the night. I roamed around, trying for some conversation, but the evening turned blustery and people took to their houses and I to Ghost Dancing. From the rubbing, the two-hundred-year-old eyes of Lieutenant Mellen's tombstone watched all. Whitman: "I have no mockings or arguments, I witness and wait."

13

ON the village green in Dover, citizens successfully buried the ghost of Chief Justice Sam Chew in broad daylight. Around 1745, the judge's shade developed a nocturnal penchant for meditating on the common and beckoning to passersby. His honor's whangdoodle began to keep the streets empty after dark and tavernkeepers complained. So residents dug a symbolic grave on the green, and, in full sunshine, tolled bells as clergymen spoke the restless soul to its peace.

Out of Dover, I took the road toward Delaware Bay: out past the Delaware Fried Chicken stand, across the Muderkill River, and into Sussex County, an area once known to English settlers as the Whorekill, a name they took from the Dutch who called Lewes Creek the Hoerekill ("whore's stream") after Dutch sailors, one theory goes, consorted with Indian women there. Governmental officials now argue that the Dutch name was actually Hoornkill, after Hoorn, a village in Holland, but surely the American past isn't always quite so proper as we hear it.

South of Rehoboth Beach, I stopped to eat breakfast on the shore. Even though the sky was clear, the windy night still showed in the high surf. At my back rose two silo-like concrete observation towers, relics from the Second World War. At the top of each were narrow openings like sinister eyes. A battering of starlings flew in and out of the slits, the shrill bird cries resonating weirdly in the hollow stacks. The towers were historical curiosities, monuments to man's worst war, one that never reached this beach; yet nothing identified them. To the young, they could be only mysteries. Had they come from the more remote and safer history of the Revolutionary or Civil wars, they would have been commemorated. Just when is history anyway?

I walked along the estuary. A horseshoe crab the diameter of a basketball lay at surf's edge. In spring the crabs, seemingly awakened from some lost Devonian deep, come up to the shallows of Delaware Bay to reproduce. The horseshoe crab does not look much like either a horse*shoe* or a crab, neither of which it is; its other common name, king crab, is also misleading. While the Alaskan king crab (truly a crab) is one of the culinary gifts of the sea, this Atlantic creature, this hoof of an arthropod, no longer even feeds chickens. But a generation ago, barefoot boys waded the bay and felt with their feet for horseshoe crabs and tried to stay clear of the lash of the spiky telsons, with which Indians once tipped fish spears; Delaware crabbers broke up the animals for chicken and pig feed, or they dried them in the sun for grinding into fertilizer. Today, horseshoe crabs again breed unmolested except for the old enemies of the sea bottom.

I drove on south. Near Ocean City, Maryland, the shore became a six-lane strip of motels and condominiums tied together by powerlines. The playground of Baltimore and Washington. Hoping to find the backwaters again, I turned toward the lower end of the Eastern Shore of Chesapeake Bay and came to Crisfield, "the crab capital of the world," where Main Street was wide because the railroad to the piers used to run down it. At its end, at the pier, near where fishermen once loaded bay oysters and crabs on trains, I found the Captain's Galley, a place of piled and bleached oyster shells.

In the small bar, a sign opposite the Hav-A-Hank and Ajax Unbreakable Comb boards announced the next meeting of the Maryland Oysterman's Association at the firehall. The watermen, as they call themselves, sat over beer and told stories in a quick speech that was part Southern and part Cockney London. All their long *i* sounds came out as "oy," but *oyster* came out as "arster."

A man with white curls like combers said, "Tommy, oy heard on the CB you hung up the phone on your mother-in-law."

"Oy did not," Tommy said. "You crazy? She's not danglin' a fuse at neither end for no reason. Besoydes, oy think too much of the gal to hang up on her. All oy did was pull the phone out of the wall."

An oysterman, whose crusty hands looked like the bottomside of a boat too long in the water, told about delivering blocks of ice in a dump truck on a scorching July day years ago: "We had a toyre blow. Toyme we got it fixed, the oyce had melted royght down. So oy says, 'Ain't but one thing to do now, boys. Let's go swimmin'.' Oy did the backstroke in the dump truck, and Tommy found an arster on the bottom and ate him."

"Man in for lunch the other day," a waterman said. "He wasn't no Amurcan, so he asks me — think he was a Dutchman — he asks me, 'An arster, sir, now what is that?' 'An arster,' oy answers him, 'an arster's between a fish and a muskrat. That's what your arster is.' "

Someone started a round of stories about a fellow called Weed whose insobriety and slow wit were legend. The one with the curls said, "Oy saw him last week roydin' his boyk down the hoyghway, troyin' to carry a forty-foot extension ladder, but he kept tippin' over."

"That's nothin' new."

"Yes it is. He didn't have the ladder closed up. Says oy to him, 'Weed, better put a red flag on that ladder.' Says he to me, 'Don't matter, Frank. She's on the ground most of the toyme.' "

I bought lunch in the next room, where light from the bay wavered on the walls. Softshell crabs were in season, and I did in four of them. The waitress, Diane Hinman, said, "Some think it's like eating spiders."

"Good. Keeps the competition down. Where do your crabs come from?"

She pointed out the window. "There."

The dock for the passenger boats to the islands was next to the Galley, so I asked her about the schedules. "Going to Tangier or Smith?" she said.

"Tangier, I guess. I've never heard of Smith."

"Everybody goes to Tangier. Why don't you go out to Smith Island? You could visit my aunt in Ewell. She's lived there since before they had electricity. She burned oil lamps in her house until a few years ago. 'Miz Alice,' they call her. But there aren't any hotels. You'd have to overnight in somebody's home."

She called and made arrangements. I got my duffel from the truck and went back to the pier to wait. A boxy man said, "Is it to Smith or Tangier?"

"Smith."

"Ah. The Methodist island. Different world out there. Ninety-eight percent of them earn a living off the water. Water, water, water. They follow the water. Marine biologists without degrees to the last man." He came up close. "Think I'm going to tell you something. You mayn't be returning."

"Why not?"

"The food."

"Is it spoiled?"

"Spoiled? That'll be you. They cook like every day's Thanksgiving."

The man was Bob Goldsmith, a contractor in Crisfield. He asked, "Have you seen the sights of Crisfield yet?"

"What should I see?"

"Get in," he said.

"But my boat."

"Not for an hour yet." He bounced us down Main in his pickup. "Train used to come in three times a day to haul out the catch — crabs and arsters. Forty-six shucking houses then, and forty are gone. The tracks are three feet under the tar. Our catch used to be so big, they built this whole end of town on arster shells. Stick a shovel in and see for yourself."

"Tell me something I've always wondered. Why hasn't the bay filled up with shells?"

"Can't say. Truth is, problem's the other way round. Not enough shells in the bay, so now the state dumps half the opened shells back in the shallows so the spat got beds to fasten onto." He turned off Main and slowed. "Would you like to die rich?"

"With a choice, I'd rather live rich."

"Here's how then. Invent a machine to shuck arsters and shell crabs." He pulled up and pointed. "There's the sight of sights in Crisfield."

"Where?"

"Right there. The pyramid. An exact scale model of the Great Pyramid of Cheops in Cairo, Egypt. Orientated exactly the same. On the twenty-first of December, the tip of the shadow falls at the same compass point just like in Egypt — except for a small difference caused by latitude."

The Great Pyramid of Crisfield was six feet three inches high — not as tall as an NBA guard. Goldsmith and his sons had designed and built the poured concrete monument to commemorate the national bicentennial; inside they had placed photographs, Nanticoke arrowheads, phonograph records, and other items.

"When they open it in twenty seventy-six, it just might contain the last 'forty-seven Mercury outboard motor on earth."

"I'd think a big concrete oystershell would make an appropriate time capsule here," I said. "Hollow inside and the way they clamp shut so tight."

Goldsmith was floored. "A reglar arster's ugly, but a six-foot arster?"

We drove back to the pier. He motioned toward Janes Island, a piece of marsh grass rising just a little above high tide. "I've found over five thousand arrowheads and spear points out there," he said. "That's almost more rock than there is island. Nanticokes used to hunt it, but they lived on the mainland. The islands take a beating. Janes doesn't look like much, but that little ground fed a lot of Indians for a couple thousand years."

The Smith Island boat, the *Captain Jason*, had tied up. Aboard were the two crewmen, three women, and a sack of groceries ordered by an islander. Clarence Tyler was at the helm, and Glenn Marshall, wearing a hat that said CAPTAIN, stood beside him. He had studied computer programming in St. Louis, before deciding what he really wanted was a working boat on Chesapeake Bay. He returned, found a partner in Tyler, and the two men bought the boat in 1977. They had made the twice-daily, eleven-mile run across Tangier Sound every day of the year since, except the month the bay froze over; then ice had piled up forty feet high, and people drove cars on the sound.

"A good job this one is," he said. "It's no bosses on the water, excepting one — weather. No bosses is better than money."

After fifty minutes, we headed up an inlet with two marshy islands on each side and pulled in to the pier at Ewell, the main village of Smith

Island; the boat would remain overnight at Tylerton on the southern end of the cluster of islands that comprise Smith. Marshall gave directions to Miz Alice's. "Look for a little skipjack on the weathervane. 'Scud In,' her place is."

I put my duffel over my shoulder and took off down the dirt lanes, under the steeple, toward the west side of the village, to "Scud In," a three-story red-shingled house overlooking an intricate network of coves and guts in a marsh that stretched so far I couldn't see the bay. Scrawled on the front door was BACK DOOR! That's where I went.

14

ALICE Venable Middleton was one of those octogenarians who make age look like something you don't want to miss. She stood in her kitchen and watched through the window as I stepped around her garden of kale, collard, and corn.

"Come in and close the door on that wind. I'm Alice. You're here about our place. Well, *Gallia est omnis divisa in partes tres*. And so is Smith Island. We really should say 'islands.' How's your Caesar?"

"A few years behind me, but I remember the three parts of Gaul."

"I taught school here more years than the bottom's got oysters. Retired eighteen years now. You passed my grammar school coming out."

"I think I passed everything — your school, the grocery, the church."

"The historical marker at the church — did you see it?"

"I read it."

"I wrote it. They limit you to forty-two words on the official state markers. Not much, but it's all cast in bronze. I like that. Runs in the family. My father was an ironmaster — a skilled blacksmith. Worked with the watermen all his life. Repaired sailing ships. Oh, but it was an art in his hammer." She swung her arm to show me. "Like this. Tap, tap, tap, atap, BANG! When they packed me off to the academy in Baltimore, I wanted to study something in the mechanical field — like ironworking, a strong and lasting craft. When my grandmother heard about that, she went hobble-dee-hoy. Wouldn't have a granddaughter in *that* work! Today, I could have been the oldest living woman blacksmith on the bay. Miz Smithy of Smith Island. So much for that."

Alice Middleton was born in Somerset County on the Eastern Shore but in 1915 moved to the six-by-four-mile island. Her husband and elder daughter died some years ago and her younger daughter lived in Princess Anne on the Shore, so now Miz Alice was alone with a cat named Jersey Red and a small nameless stray that attacked anything that moved.

"We've had electricity on the island for only the last twenty-nine years. Phones for less than that. We've been a rustic tribe." She paused. "Tea or a jigger of wine?"

"A jigger, if it's all the same to you."

"Pull a glass from the cupboard — don't get a chipped one." She put a small pot of water on to heat, and we sat at her kitchen table, and she talked. After ten minutes when the water still had not come to a boil, she said, "See if we have a frog in the pot."

I looked. "No frog but a million bubbles."

"So we've answered that question." She moved yesterday's *Baltimore Sun* out of the way and pushed forward a cup in her favorite pattern — Copper Lustre Tea Leaf — to have it ready for the pouring. "Now, here's about John Smith, the Pocahontas John Smith. First white man to visit our island. Named after him. He was out looking for harbors and salt for the Jamestown colony in sixteen oh eight. In his log he mentions the island and says the waters teemed so with fish that when he dipped a ship's skillet overboard it filled with several species. Got stung by a ray for his dipping, but he liked the bay islands. He thought heaven and earth had never agreed better in framing a place for man. He said it best in four words, 'The land is kind.' Somewhere in America they should cast those words in bronze. Cast them big. THE LAND, MY FRIENDS, IS KIND. But for years this was a dark and bloody ground during the fighting between the watermen of Maryland and Virginia. The Oyster Wars. They couldn't agree on who had the right to which oystering rocks. Killed each other over an inch. Then the oysters began dying out in the lower end of the bay — a parasite called MSX did it — and that's when the warring stopped. People said MSX was the hand of God."

"A Methodist island, I hear."

"To the last inch. In nineteen thirty-eight, a fire took the church. People knelt in the road and prayed up one side and down the other. Our houses stand close because we've got no terra firma to waste. That's why our roads are narrow. The fire was about to take the town. Then, while people were still on their knees, the wind shifted and only the church burned. The hand of God, they said."

I poured tea and my wine, and all the while Miz Alice explained.

"A teacher should carry a theme — a refrain to sing ideas from. Mine was what they call 'ecology' now. I taught children *first* the system of things. Later we went to grammar and sums. Always time for that. I wanted to show them there's only one place they can get an education — in the school of thought. Learning rules is useful but it isn't education. Education is thinking, and thinking is looking for yourself and seeing what's there, not what you got told was there. Then you put what you see together. It's more than difficult to get kids today to look for themselves. They want their visions to be televisions. 'Eyeballs!' I said to them. Once your own eyeballs start working, then you can see what's around, you can see history isn't a thing of the past. You can see the land is kind. But it's hard to make our people here nature lovers when they see so much of her in the raw. We have an attitude on this island that God will take care of it all — oystering, crabbing, water, the geese. 'I'll get as many crabs today as getting can get,' that's the way we talk. 'Then I'll get more tomorrow.' Now we've caught the bottom and haven't bothered much to put it back. Fished out the babies for years. But, as I hope to fly, a man's deeds count. Everything counts. We live in dependence, not independently. But don't tell an islander that, or he'll knock your talk into a cocked hat. Don't tell us 'No man is an island.' " She sipped her tea. "Let's not get too worked up. If people could say only what they'd bet their lives on, the place would go mute. No telling what we'd hear then."

"It seems as if there are still lots of oysters."

"They don't *teem* in here anymore. Why, the front yards of our houses are made from oyster shells. Throw down a bucket of shells, a bucket of dirt, and presto-chango, a yard! Don't need a growing hand here. We're at sea level plus four feet — maybe it's five feet now because of the oyster shells. But you don't appreciate what I'm saying until I tell this sentence — from my own house for better than half a century, I've seen three hurricanes and never a drop of water inside. Never a storm in *this* kitchen." She stopped. "But what were we talking about? Surely, it was never the tide. My tea is bewitched."

"Chesapeake oysters."

"A flavor that leaves you hanging between heaven and earth. That's where our big houses came from."

"Heaven?"

"Oysters. Oystering money. As for crabs, no one ate crabs here in the earliest days. Indians didn't eat crabs. You don't find crab shells in their kitchen middens, and I think I can tell you why. People only took to eating crabs when the oyster rocks started giving out. They knew the blue crab is the buzzard of the deeps — scavenges the bottom. Want to catch a crab? Load your pot or trotline with a pickled eel. Pickled and sour as rot. That's a crab's menu. Give his life to eat it. But now, some people prefer a baked pailer to a fresh oyster."

"What's a pailer?"

"Peeler. Here, they say 'pailer,' and 'dredging' is 'drudgin'.' The pailer is a metamorphosis, but watermen don't call it that. In all things except a ship's works, they use the simplest words. But when it comes to boats, you better know your bugeye from your batteau. The pailer splits his shell like a spider so he can grow. 'Softshell crab,' restaurants call them. Crabbing begins in early spring when the jimmies start walking up the bay to look for the sooks — the females. Mating season. Sometimes you catch a 'doubler' — a mister and missus arm in arm. You can go potting or trotlining or scraping eelgrass. Scrape and pot for crabs in summer, drudge for oysters in winter. You can tong for oysters too."

She took a yardstick and broom, crossed them like scissors to show how hand tongs work. "They look like twenty-foot rakes linked at the center, but it takes the back of Quasimodo to nipper up oysters. Now they have patent tongs, power machines that scoop up the bottom. Ten times as many tongers as drudgers today. Don't ask me what the machines do to the culch — the beds. Couldn't say. But I know nothing lasts long when you turn the machinery on." She stopped again. "Am I a reactionary?"

"I don't know."

"Not so sure myself anymore." She got up from the table. "I'm going to show you a book I wrote and then something else if I can find it."

The book was a pamphlet: *Maryland's Right, Tight Isle.* "That's my coinage and accurate it is. The book's our only history of the island. But remember half of *history* is *story.* It's the best we know. But to truly understand our right, tight little isle, you should read the life of Joshua Thomas, the Parson of the Islands. A 'powerful exhorter,' they say he was. Made the whole east bay into Methodists. He came from Potato Neck to the islands during the War of Eighteen Twelve or thereabouts. Arrived in his log canoe, *The Methodist.* Once he asked the mother of a crying child that was interrupting his sermon, 'Madam, won't you kindly give the babe a tater?' A sweet potato to quiet it. Maybe it works. Wouldn't for me. Sweet stops right in my throat. Have to eat a dill pickle to chase down sugar."

She went off to hunt the something else. I'd read much of her pamphlet when I heard a call from very far away. She was at the top of the steep stairs on the third floor.

"Can't find it," she said. "Can't find a Nanticoke spearpoint as long as my palm. Picked it off the beach one day just as if it had been a clamshell. A piece of craft it is. Brought to mind my father's work. So much for that."

In my hand she laid earrings and a necklace made from colonial-era pottery shards she had found on the beach. "Jewelry should have meaning.

Can you make out the numeral 'four' here? Is it four gallons? Four quarts? I don't know, but we have four of something."

She motioned me to the high window where, to the west, we could see across the entanglings of guts and coves and marsh grass, the far gray line of water scumbled by dusk.

"Chesapeake," she said grandly. "Not so many waters in the world as fertile as that one. Two hundred miles long. An inland sea. A drowned river at the bottom that runs miles into the Atlantic. In ten thousand years, the bay will be ocean when the Eastern Shore goes to sea. Straight across, that's where the Potomac comes into Chesapeake, and it's as wide as the upper bay."

In the salt marsh, during the Revolutionary War, watermen used the maze of coves as cover to launch sudden raids on passing British ships. "Our baymen took such a liking to the work, they kept at it for another half-century after the war. When they gave up pirating, they began hunting ducks and geese with cannons mounted in sneak-boats. A single blast could bring down a hundred birds. More than one game warden has been put to the bottom of those guts. We've known our lawlessness."

The steeple on the west shore marked Rhodes Point. "They first called it Rogue's Point. Pirates. As the town became decent, they changed the name. Kept the sound but not the sense. Renamed it after Cecil Rhodes — as in Rhodes Scholars and Rhodesia. It's all watermen now, but I hear they want to attract the yachting mob. Pirates to yachtsmen, there's history."

From the attic window, Miz Alice once had watched big schooners out of Baltimore sail seaward and also many of the two thousand Chesapeake oystering boats beat along the bay: skipjacks, bugeyes, pungies, sloops, now all extinct but for the skipjack. "Just before the edge of dark, the light would turn the working sails gold as angels' wings. It was a glory."

The low rises on the island, the hummocks, islanders called "hammocks." A square of pines grew from one hummock where the Teackle mansion had stood. "Closed up for years. Full of antiques. The Tylers just walked away from it. Don't know why. A marsh fire swept it up fifteen years ago. A deal of lost history, and I couldn't tell you if the fire was by hook or crook."

She was silent to let me take in the great spread of flatness. Then she said, "It was from this window that my husband saw me walking across the ice after being marooned all night in the *Island Belle* when the sound froze over. Caught on the island boat coming home from the Eastern Shore. What a night that was! The Chesapeake, the boat, and us. Nothing lost, not even the *Belle*. When the water opened, they just motored her away."

Miz Alice pointed out an island to the north. "In a couple hundred years, that one will be gone. I've seen them go. Holland's Island washed down to nothing. People moved their houses by boat to Crisfield — carried them across the water. About nineteen ten." She wiggled a thumb toward Tylerton to the south. "Third village of the island. They have their own opinionation down there, and make no mistake about it. But the families on the island are related, and I can prove it. All English and Cornish. It's a special concern to me because of my younger daughter. She's one of two islanders to contract multiple sclerosis. Two out of only seven hundred fifty people. I want to see something done about the genetic connections of the disease, and this may be just the place for research."

She motioned to the network of waterways. "They go every direction you can point, but they never stop going to the sea. A thousand directions inside a grand direction. Going forward by going sideways — like the crab. That's how they get the feeling of the territory. Narrow at the head, wider at the shore. A picture of a life lived well, I deem."

At the east window she showed me Point Comfort Island, an uninhabited place heavy with small pines and only a hundred yards across the narrow inlet from the Ewell pier. "Our people won't live on it. Too far from things. Besides, it's an island."

"What's Smith?"

"Land surrounded by water. Like Australia."

We went downstairs. Miz Alice pulled out a big bony thing with a vague, skull-like appearance. "Oysterman drudged it from the bay. Brought up a whole passel of bones. In nineteen fifty-nine my students packed two orange crates of the bones off to the Smithsonian. Here's what they said." She handed me a letter thanking her and identifying the bones as the spine of an extinct species of whale. "Whale vertebra! Look closely." She stood the massive bone on end. "Eyes here, mouth, nose. Don't you see a monster skull?"

"I lean toward a vertebra."

"Ye gods and little fishes! Life is stranger than that!" She looked out the front door. "What do you think of our right, tight isle?"

"I like it."

"So you say. I'll give you a hiking tour tomorrow over to Rogue's Point."

Miz Alice phoned a friend, the wife of a tonger, to secure a room for me. I walked down to the harbor and ate dinner at Ruke's Grocery, an old shingled place with a broken cash register drawer standing full and open. Beach flotsam hung about the room: embossed bottles turned iridescent with age, antique running lights, a worn dip net, broken crockery, an eroded block and tackle. The watermen drank coffee topped with melted cheese and lounged about in the sweetness of fresh produce and frying crab cakes. Five boys, all looking alike although only two were brothers, pitched pennies over the floor that rose and dropped like a wooden sea.

I rambled around the village in the cool night, then, at eight, went to the home of Mrs. Bernice Guy, who showed me my room, a small thing with a sagging bed and oval photographs of women from the time of Chester A. Arthur.

She said, "Our island's a nice place, but people visit once and not again. One time, though, in your bed Henry Cabot Lodge slept."

The next morning, Miz Alice and I tramped the dusty road over the guts, through the tall waterbush, toward Rogue's Point. She named the trees, few as they were: loblolly pine, gum, pin oak, red cedar, poplar, even a pomegranate and fig. The larger trees were ones that could survive when the taproot grew long enough to reach salt water. She pointed out the sights too: a house where six boys and six girls were reared to adulthood, a heron pecking and swallowing.

As we walked, a speeding, unmuffled car forced us to the edge. "Wherever Hoss is going, he'll soon be there," she said. "When I came to the island, we all had working feet. Courting was nothing but strolling unless you wanted to go sing in church. We traipsed the lanes at night. Cows would snort at you from shadows and scare the lantern out of your hand. Cattle slept anywhere they pleased because there's not enough high ground for pasturage, but we never had to cut lawns. Footmen we were then."

The car whipped past the other way. "Swoosh, yourself," she said. "Here we can never be more than a mile or so from any place we can reach by feet, and yet our people aren't walkers any longer. They keep two cars — one on the island, another at Crisfield. As for kids, they know one thing to do — drive from Ewell to Rhodes Point and back. Up and down, slow or fast, it matters not. They know every inch of the way but can't distinguish an egret from a crane."

The salt marsh was a place of beauty, yet along much of the road lay junk: mattresses, rusted barrels, appliances, a drive shaft, tires, a sofa. At one gut full of cans, Miz Alice said, "I've yet to see a bean can sprout. Won't be long for that gut now." She shook her head. "The grave's for people when they've seen enough, but how can you see enough when you're twenty? I read in the *Sun* that kids feel disconnected. How can that be? Connections lying over the land like stardust. They live in the Land of Nod."

We came to a high piling of rusting automobiles, where a teenager was stripping wheels from a smoldering pickup. "He's found a drowned man with a pocketful of money," she said. "We're a dead end here when it comes to merchandise. There aren't any repair shops on the island, so whatever gets shipped out here stays. We're at the end of the assembly line, and there it is. Not enough space to hide from our junk. You'd think living beside trash we'd do something about it, but all we do is get used to it. We think it's the way of things."

"Is the cause poverty?"

"We have no poor except those that choose to be — those that would be poor as gar broth anywhere, the ones who work only so they can quit. No, the cause is education. Not enough of the proper kind at the right time."

She told about the organization of the island: no mayor, no jail, no local taxes, no water bill unless you counted the annual twenty dollars for maintenance of the artesian wells. The water, delicious and cold, has its source in the Blue Ridge Mountains. "A natural underground 'pipeline' from Virginia to us. I think it was our good water that finally got us to build a sewage system to replace septic tanks. In the nick of time."

We came to Rhodes Point, a single street of watery yards hung with fishing nets and stacked with chicken-wire crab pots. Everywhere lay oyster shells, their pearly interiors gleaming like bits of a broken necklace. We weaved in and out of the yards, and Miz Alice commented on more sights: a birdbath supported by three plastic sea horses ("Properly belongs on a wedding cake"), a peculiar house with a chimney above the front door ("Do you enter through the fireplace?"), and, overlooking the bay, an old house with a new picture window on the second floor ("Wouldn't catch me up there in a nor'wester unless you chloroformed me"). When we came to a front yard with a stone obelisk in memory of Job A. Evans, who drowned in Tangier Sound, I asked why it wasn't in the cemetery.

"It's not rightly a grave. Never found the man. Chesapeake keeps her dead. But the islanders do sometimes dig graves in their yards because land is at such a premium."

Yet, next to the old Methodist church, a big wooden building not at all of a size commensurate with the tiny fishing village, was a burial ground of watermen's tombstones carved with bugeyes and skipjacks.

Miz Alice stopped at a fresh grave. "Fifteen years old. Sitting in his car one night, made a little sound, and fell over dead with dope. Went to his funeral. The young find their drugs, even out here."

At one empty home, a large telescope house built by Captain Hoffman, we looked in the broken windows. "Never did get my curiosity cured," she said. "Some people sit around and wait for the world to poke them. Right here in this old curiosity shop of a world, they say, 'Poke me, world.'

23. Alice Venable Middleton on Smith Island, Maryland

Well, you have to keep the challenges coming on. Make them up if necessary."

At the end of the street, which was also the end of dry ground, the island became a tangle of water and weed, neither solid nor liquid but a treacherous in-between running most of the way to Tylerton. On the bay side of Rhodes Point stood crab houses and pounds with shedding floats where peelers were held until they molted. "Once the crab peels, you have to pull him out directly or the water will start him to hardening again. That is, if another doesn't eat him first, soft morsel that he is for a few hours."

Tied up at the pier was the *Island Belle*, an old skinny wooden boat of quaint lines. Miz Alice said, "Listen to this sentence: the *Island Belle* — she's a gas boat — she changed our social pattern. Some people wouldn't agree, but it's the truth. She made her first crossing the month I arrived sixty-three years ago. She's never been underwater, and that's something here."

"How was it she changed the island?"

"Before the *Belle*, people got to the Eastern Shore once a year — at

Christmas. She brought passage. Regular comings and goings. We got outside and the outside got in. She ended our isolation. Carried mail and medicine, the sick and dying. Brought news, food, gas, firewood. Even ideas, I deem. There aren't many places in the country that can point to one thing and say, 'Right there, *that's* the thing which changed us. *That's* what made us the way we are now.' "

"It's hard to imagine."

"Imagine what America would look like without the car, then you'll know what this island would be like without the *Belle*. Now, of course, teenagers ride to high school in Crisfield on the bus boat. I'm not even sure we're an island anymore, unless you spell it capital I-hyphen-l-a-n-d. Catch the difference?"

She looked down a narrow cove. "Land sakes! Tide's coming in. Let's hoof it back. I'll be getting tired around the knees soon."

The walk to Ewell was quieter and slower. Miz Alice asked how I came to be in Maryland. I told her and used Whitman's phrase about "gathering the minds of men."

She said, "When olden-day travelers went about, they might carry something called an *Album Amicorum* to gather the signatures and sentiments of learned men they visited along the way. Is that what you're doing?"

"I've thought of the trek more as just the bear going over the mountain to see what he could see."

At "Scud In" I stopped to get my duffel so I could catch the afternoon boat to Crisfield. "I have a question for you," I said. "Tell me what's the hardest thing about living on a small, marshy island in Chesapeake Bay."

"I know that and it didn't take sixty-three years to figure it out. Here it is, wrapped up like a parcel. Listen to my sentence. Having the gumption to live different *and* the sense to let everybody else live different. That's the hardest thing, hands down."

15

THE telescope house may not be indigenous to the Eastern Shore, but there were more of them here than anywhere else. The name derived from the linking of three houses, each successively larger, so that the two smallest ones look as if they could slide, telescope fashion, into the largest house. The design came about for economic reasons: a young family built a small two-room home; as the family and income grew, they added a "wing" of usually four rooms and later another addition of six rooms. Along the back roads north of Crisfield were many of them, most with standing-seam metal roofs.

On a peninsula between the Choptank and Tred Avon rivers, I came to Oxford, a seventeenth-century village of brick sidewalks and nineteenth-century houses. Only a few small streets branched off the main trunk, Robert Morris Street, a way of aesthetically cohesive homes and yards fenced by the Oxford picket — a slat with a design at the top that looks like an ace of clubs with a hole shot in it. The pickets were popular, even though painting the holes could take all spring.

At the bottom of Morris Street, across from the Tred Avon ferry slip, sat the Robert Morris Inn, the 1710 portion of which, built by a shipwright, was once the home of Robert Morris — Senior and Junior — a family of fortune and misfortune. The father died when wadding from a cannon fired in his honor struck him in the arm. The son, one of the wealthiest men in eighteenth-century America and a financier of the Revolution, was sentenced to three years in a Philadelphia debtor's prison after a spell of reverses, one of which was the failure of the new government to repay his loan to the Continental Army.

Like some of the homes on Morris Street, the inn had fallen into disrepair by the 1940s after Oxford, a commercial port of entry the equal to Annapolis in the early years, lost its trade and, later, most of its fishing fleet. But, in the last decade or so, people from Baltimore, Washington, and Philadelphia began recognizing the calm and beauty of the little harbor town, and the new bay bridges across the Chesapeake near Annapolis made the Eastern Shore easily accessible. Newcomers moved in and started renovating the old homes. Now, in the boatyards rode motor-sailers and sloops and cabin cruisers; in the inn, mail-order-catalog yachtsmen and wives leafed through picture books of Eastern Shore hunting decoys and referred to the old houses as "architectural statements." That was the new old Oxford. But between the inn and the harbor lay an old old Oxford: a tight cluster of worn houses of the blacks who had spent their lives here.

I took the Tred Avon ferry, at three centuries the oldest operating cable-free ferry in the United States, to Bellevue and drove out the double-fingered peninsula toward Tilghman Island. On the way was St. Michaels, "the town that fooled the British" by inventing the blackout. During the War of 1812, word reached the citizens that a night bombardment was imminent. Residents doused all lights except candles in second-story windows and lanterns they hung in treetops. British gunners misread the lights, miscalculated trajectories, and overshot the town. The trick preserved numerous colonial buildings, including one home where a stray cannonball fell through the roof and bounced down the stairway past the startled lady of the house.

By dusk, I was on Tilghman Island, an island only by virtue of a streamlet called Knapps Narrows. I parked near the wharf where much of the last sail-powered fishing fleet in America tied up. Against the clouding sky, I could make out the tall masts and long bowsprits of the skipjacks, ships that hoist twelve hundred feet of sail to pull port and starboard dredges over the oyster rocks. Some people believed the skipjacks were the last of an era while others held they were, once again, the future.

A storm came on, and I ran for Ghost Dancing. Inside, I listened to the rain beat out a hard, steely number on the roof; not yet ready for sleep, I lay on the bunk to watch the electric night.

Black Elk loved thunderstorms because in their "swift fire" he heard the Great Voices. For me, I heard more the Heyokas, those beings of lightning, those dancing human clowns who do things foolishly backwards. In his time on the blue road, the immaterialist Black Elk often heard voices from the clouds; in my season on the blue highways, the voices I heard were those of men — men who knew about stumbling not from observation as gods know it, but rather from having stumbled. For that reason, their words carried a force cloud voices could not match.

If clouds gave Black Elk his visions, they merely made me wet. But, like any man of ordinary cut, I sometimes heard *human* voices that showed the power not of visions but of revision, the power to see again and revise.

Lightning, flickering in the Ghost, flashed the rubbed image of the ancient stone face of redemption or death on the Minuteman's marker into a spectral reflection. Whitman:

> *Can each see signs of the best by a look in the lookingglass?*
> *Is there nothing greater or more?*
> *Does all sit there with you?*

Something opened. Call it the Lookingglass Syndrome.

Like a crazed enemy running amuck, ego, that excessive looking inward, had had its way in the Indian wars and now the old life with the Cherokee was lost. But what had not been lost was the chance, as Black Elk says, "to make over." A man cannot remake ego because it is able to grow only in size like a simple cell. A locked form unable to change its structure, it is ever only what it is. Not so an angle of vision — as the old Jerseyman had called it — *that* a man could make over. To remake is his potential, his hope.

A human being is not a waxen rubbing, a lifeless imprint taken from some great stony face. Rather he is a Minuteman or a dog soldier at liberty to use the inclinations of the past as he sees fit. He is free to perceive the matrix, and, within his limits, change from it. By seeing both the futility in trying to relive the old life and the danger in trying to obliterate it, man can gain the capacity to make anew. His very form depends not on repetition but upon variation from old patterns. In response to stress, biological survival requires genetic change; it necessitates a turning away from doomed replication. And what of history? Was it different?

Etymology: *educate*, from the Latin *educare*, "lead out."

Ten

WESTWARD

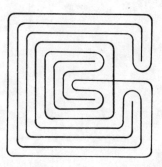

NOBODY was sure about the figures around here. According to one waterman, of the hundreds of skipjacks once dredging oysters from Chesapeake Bay, about a dozen remained at Tilghman Island and perhaps an equal number at Deal Island; another man thought there might be as many as forty on the entire bay. Two men said skipjacks were doomed, but another held that expensive fuel would bring them back. He believed the old ships, with refinements, would become the new ships and that the diesel boats replacing the skipjacks were the temporary ones.

Even though no new skipjacks had been built since 1956, the aging fleet still survived by virtue of a Maryland law, designed to prevent overharvesting, that allows dredging under motor power only on Mondays and Tuesdays. One other thing made for the survival of that single-masted, double-sailed boat of low and majestic lines. People here, now that the bugeyes are gone, consider the skipjack the very symbol of the Eastern Shore. It is to them what the beanpot is to a Bostonian.

I went north, crossed Chesapeake Bay, and stopped at the city market down among the eighteenth-century streets of Annapolis to eat a dozen fresh clams at Hannon's stone counter; for the road I bought a cut of smoked chub, a quart of slaw, and six bottles of Black Horse Ale. I took Maryland 2 over the hills along the bay, turned west at Prince Frederick, crossed the wide Patuxent River, on through Burnt Store and Allen's Fresh, across the even wider Potomac. I came into Virginia on state 218, an old route now almost forgotten. The towns, typically, were a general store and a few dispersed houses around a crossroads: Osso, Goby, Passapatanzy.

In Fredericksburg (home of George Washington's brother-in-law, Colonel Fielding Lewis, a cannon manufacturer whom the Episcopalians buried in an honored position under the steps of Saint George's Church — *salve lucrum!*), I stopped at a U-pump gas station — one of those places where you push your credit card through a slot to the on-duty commandant of the fuel islands. I asked for the air hose. "Ain't got no air," he said. I might as well have gone to a fireplug for service. The age of self-serve.

I suffered a reflex of nostalgia: back in the age of inner tubes, Vernon's

Service actually sold gasoline *and* service. Vern wore a little black plastic clip-on bowtie and stub-billed cap that gave him the look of a smudged motorcycle cop; with a faded red wiping rag hanging from his hip pocket, Vern over the years made an oily trail between the pumps and grease pit. He washed windshields with real sponges that he ran through a little wringer kept by the ethyl pump; I think his wife laundered them twice a week. But the men's restroom wasn't any cleaner than now, and there wasn't a hot water faucet then either; but you didn't need a key to get in, and his mother wouldn't let him install quarter machines vending latex health aids.

There were only two posted rules at Vernon's (one an old gas station apothegm): WE AIM TO PLEASE, YOU AIM TOO PLEASE. The other, NO TOOLS LOANED, was necessary because people liked Vern and actually asked to borrow his tools. Tools: Vern had no diagnostic equipment other than a good ear and eye, and he could correct a surprising assortment of problems with a screwdriver and adjustable wrench.

Even then, Vern was an anachronism. We boys who collected at his station didn't call him that, of course. We called him, as I remember, "an old fart." Vern, in his antique ways, believed that anyone who got behind a steering wheel could rightly be expected to operate the car rather than just steer it; that's why you were issued an *Operator's* Permit. He believed the more work a driver did, the less the car had to do; the less it had to do, the simpler and more reliable and cheaper to repair it would be. He cursed the increasing complexity of automobile mechanics. But, as I say, he was a man of the old ways. He even believed in narrow tires (cheaper and less friction), spoked wheels (less weight), and the streamlined "Airflow" designs of Chrysler Corporation cars of the mid-thirties — designs Chrysler almost immediately gave up on before proceeding to build the biggest finned hogs of all. We boys of the fifties loved their brontosaurean bulk.

Another of Vernon's themes we laughed at was his advocacy of the comparable economy and safety of three-wheels (he drove a motorcycle with a sidecar) for city driving. He would say to us, "Two wheels ain't enough, and four's too many. So where does that leave you, boys?" "Three wheels!" we'd shout back, mocking him. "No sir, it leaves money in your jeans."

So much for antiquity.

I went down to Civil War Spotsylvania for the night. The heavy fighting for control of the important crossroads in front of the Spotsylvania County Courthouse occurred in fields and woods a couple of miles away, and now the intersection linked the bluest of back roads, a crossing of so little economic, logistic, and strategic importance as to make the conflict between Lee and Grant appear imbecilic. The big battlefield outside town is today a national historic site marking the series of battles that began at a place called "the Wilderness."

Atop one hill, with forest behind and open land in front, at a little bend in the breastworks, troops fought what may have been the longest and most savage hand-to-hand combat of the war: the Battle of Bloody Angle. The fighting here in the wet spring of 1864 was so close that cannoneers, standing ankle deep in mud, fired at point-blank range; soldiers, slogging it out in a smoky rainstorm, fought muzzle to muzzle, stabbing with bayonets, thrusting swords between logs of the parapet, clubbing each other into the mire from dawn to midnight, and trampling fallen men out of sight into the muck. The intense rifle fire cut in half oak trees two feet in diameter. One soldier, Horace Porter, wrote: "We had not only shot down an army, but also a forest."

On that single day of May 12, nearly thirteen thousand men died fighting over one square mile of ground abandoned by both sides several days later. Yet, had anyone been paying attention, the battle could have shown the futility of trench warfare, a lesson that would have to be learned again at even higher cost in the First World War.

At that "bivouac of the dead," as one monument had it, I ate the smoked chub. Across the grassy meadow stood a shaft commemorating the Ohio contingent; among the carved names: Gashem Arnold, Elam Dye, Lewis Wolf, Enos Swinehart.

Three children raced from under the oaks out over the grass to reenact the battle with guttural gunshots from their boyish throats. They argued briefly about who would be who: one chose the Americans, one the Germans, one the Irish. The small cries of the boys, and the bugs chirring out the last of spring, and the warmth of the evening sun almost turned Bloody Angle to an idyllic meadow. But its history was the difference. Even though Titans and Tridents and MX's have not made "the red business," as Whitman called it, a thing of the past, they have eliminated future battlefield parks where boys can play at war — unless scientists find means to hang monuments in the sky.

2

CAPTAIN Jack Jouett probably didn't have a chance against the fame of Paul Revere, yet Jouett's deed was comparable: on June 4, 1781, Captain

Jack rode his bay mare, Sallie, forty miles from Cuckoo Tavern to Charlottesville to warn Thomas Jefferson, Patrick Henry, and that nest of sedition, the Virginia General Assembly, that Bloody Tarleton's Green Dragons were coming. Jouett rode without stopping, while the British raiders stopped three times — once to burn a wagontrain — and thereby lost both the rebels' capture and a chance at dramatic incident. A good thing for American history. And for Henry Wadsworth Longfellow. Jouett is a devilish name to rhyme.

When I saw Cuckoo, Virginia, it was a historical marker and a few houses at an intersection. I went up U.S. 33 until the rumple of hills became a long, bluish wall across the western sky. On the other side of Stanardsville in the Blue Ridge Mountains, I stopped in a glen and hiked along Swift Run, a fine rill of whirligigs and shiners, until I found a cool place for lunch. Summer was a few days away, but the heat wasn't.

Water striders and riffle bugs cut angles and arcs on smooth backwaters of the stream that reflected cirrus clouds crossing the ridges. They would make West Virginia before I did. I was sitting at the bottom of the eastern side of the Appalachians; when I came out of the mountains again, I would be in the Middle West. Sixteen dollars in my pocket. The journey was ending.

In a season on the blue roads, what had I accomplished? I hadn't sailed the Atlantic in a washtub, or crossed the Gobi by goat cart, or bicycled to Cape Horn. In my own country, I had gone out, had met, had shared. I had stood as witness.

I took a taste of Swift Run, went back to the highway, and followed it up Massanutten Mountain. Again the going was winding and slow. Near sunset, I reached West Virginia and drove on to Franklin, a main-street hamlet sharing a valley with a small river as the Appalachian towns do. Above the South Fork, above a hayfield, and under the mountains, I pulled in for the night.

After a small meal in the Ghost, I marked on a map the wandering circle of my journey. From the heartland out and around. A blue circle gone beyond itself. "Everything the Power of the World does is done in a circle," Black Elk says. "Even the seasons form a great circle in their changing, and always come back again to where they were. The life of a man is a circle from childhood to childhood, and so it is in everything where power moves."

Then I saw a design. There on the map, crudely, was the labyrinth of migration the old Hopis once cut in their desert stone. For me, the migration had been to places and moments of glimpsed clarity. Splendid gifts all.

THE state seal of West Virginia is not a used tire hanging on a fencepost any more than the state flag is a tattered cloth used as an automobile gas tank cap. But well it could be. Heaped in yards, sliding down hills, hanging from trees and signs were old tires. It seemed as if West Virginia sat at the bottom of a mountain where Americans came annually to throw away their two hundred million used tires.

Along highway 33 lay hardscrabble farms, as the thirties called them, of rocky fields, dwindly crops, houses partly painted in two or three colors, trumpet vine crawling iron bedstead trellises, and jimson weed taking warped five-rail fences (kiss the middle rail to cure chapped lips). In the few places large and level enough for true fields, men were putting up hay by hand.

The road, a thing to wrench an eel's spine, went at the mountains in all the ways: up, down, around, over, through, under, between. I've heard — who knows the truth? — that if you rolled West Virginia out like a flapjack, it would be as large as Texas. Where possible in the mountainous interruptions, towns opened briefly: Judy Gap, Mouth of Seneca, Elkins.

At Buckhannon, I drove southwest on state 4. Beautiful country despite hills clobbered with broken appliances and automobile fragments, which children turned into Jungle gyms. Should you ever go looking for some of the six hundred million tons of ferrous scrap rusting away in America, start with West Virginia.

Then Sutton, hidden in the slant of mountains at the heart of the state, a town that began in 1805 when John O'Brien took up residence in a hollow sycamore along the Elk River. Now Sutton was an old place of grizzled and maimed men who could have been the last survivors of the Union Army: one missing a right hand, one the left, another with a patched eye, one minus a nose, one an ear; as for limps and bent spines, I couldn't count them all. And the teeth! Broken, rotted, snaggled, bucked, splintered. An orthodontist's paradise. But that wasn't what struck me about Sutton. What struck me was the similarity in the faces, as though a man's father were his brother and his uncle his first cousin. A town of more kin than kith. Sutton, I think, may be the place where those people you see waiting in bus stations for the 1:30 A.M. express are going.

In the frayed, cluttery hamlet everything — people, streets, buildings — seemed to be nearing an end. In one old survivor, Elliott's Fountain (CIGARS CANDY SUNDRIES around the window, Ex-Lax thermometer by the tall door,

YOUR WATE AND FATE scale there also, and inside a ceramic tile floor in the pattern of a diamond-back rattler), I drank a Hamilton-Beach chocolate milkshake, the kind served alongside the stainless steel mixing cup.

The owner, Hugh Elliott, laid out a 1910 photograph of the drugstore when you could buy a freshly concocted purge or balm, or a fountain Bromo-Seltzer, or a dulcimer; although the pharmaceuticals were gone, you could still get a Bromo or a dulcimer (next to the Texas Instruments 1025 Memory Calculator). The photograph showed one other change: what had been a spacious room of several bent-steel chairs and tables was now top to bottom with merchandise. What had been a place of community was now a stuffed retail outlet. Across the nation, that change was the history of the soda fountain pharmacy.

A crisp little lavender-and-lace lady, wearing her expansion-band wristwatch almost to the elbow to keep it in place, sipped a cherry phosphate and pointed out in the photograph the table where her husband — dead these twenty years — had proposed to her. She said, "You won't find me at the grave. Always feel closer to him in here with a phosphate."

When I drove out of Sutton, clouds moved in and the heavy sky sagged with drizzle. It was part of the sixty inches of yearly rainfall here. I fought it a few miles, then gave up and stopped in the old railroad town of Gassaway at the Elk Lunch, formerly the Farmers and Merchants Bank. Handpainted vertically down the worn Doric granite columns: LUNCH BEER. I had one of each.

Next to me a man, whose stomach started at his neck and stopped below his groin, said, "Ain't from around here, I see."

"How's that?"

"Wiped that beer bottle off fore you swigged on it."

As I ate my hamburger, the fellow explained the best means of taking a catfish. During the long explanation rivaling Izaak Walton's for detail, the man periodically formed a funnel with his index finger and thumb and poured salt into his bottle of Falls City. "Used to could taste the beer in our country," he said. The angling method was this: first "bait" a catfish hole with alfalfa and pork fat for three weeks; then, the night before a rain, put a nine-lived Eveready in a sealed Mason jar and lower it into the water to hang just in front of the baited hook.

"And it works well?" I asked.

"It works sometimes."

When I left, the day had turned to mist, and a red grit came off the highway and glazed the windshield. Like looking through a great bloodshot eye. State 4 followed the Elk River, an occluded green thickness that might have been split pea purée. The Elk provided a narrow bench, the only level land, and on it people had built homes, although the river lay between them and the road and necessitated hundreds of little handmade bridges — many of them suspension footbridges, the emblem of Appalachia. From rock ledges broken open by the highway cut, where seeps dripped, hung five-gallon galvanized buckets to collect the spring water.

Again came the feeling I'd had all morning, that somehow I'd made a turn in time rather than in space and driven into the thirties. The only things that showed a later decade were the pickup trucks: clean and new, unlike the rattling, broken automobiles.

West Virginia 36, a quirk of a road, went into even more remote land, the highway so narrow my right tires repeatedly dropped off the pavement. Towns: Valleyfork, Wallback, and Left Hand (a school, church, post office, and large hole once the Exxon station). On west lay the Pennzoil country of small valleys barbed with rusting derricks, the great flywheels turning slowly, inexorably like the mills of God that grind exceeding fine.

I hunched over the steering wheel as if to peer under the clouds, to see beyond. I couldn't shake the sense I was driving in another era. Maybe it was the place or maybe a slow turning in the mind about how a man cannot entirely disconnect from the past. To try to is the American impulse, but to look at the steady continuance of the past is to watch time get emptied of its bluster because time bears down less on the continuum than on the components. To be only a nub in the eternal temporary is still to have a chance to see, a chance to pry at the mystery. What is the blue road anyway but an opportunity to poke at the unseen and a hoping the unseen will poke back?

At Spencer, I turned west onto U.S. 33. The Appalachians flattened themselves to hills, and barnsides again gave the Midwest imperative: CHEW MAIL POUCH. With what was left of day, I crossed the Ohio River into old Gallipolis, a town of a dozen pronunciations, a gazebo-on-the-square town settled by eighteenth-century Frenchmen. Although a priest once placed a curse on Gallipolis — I don't know why — residents today claim it's the loveliest French village on the Ohio.

4

"INQUIRE Locally," the road should have been marked. Of the thirteen thousand miles of highway I'd driven in the last months, Ohio 218 through

Gallia County set a standard to measure bad road by with pavement so rough I looked forward to sections where the blacktop was gone completely. Along the shoulders lay stripped cars, presumably from drivers who had given up. Yet the sunny county was a fine piece of washed grasses, gleams in hounds' eyes, constructions of spiders, rocks broken and rounded — all those things and fully more.

At Ironton I took the river road down a stretch of power lines, rail lines, water lines, and telephone lines (the birds sleep across the water on the wooded Kentucky bluffs, they say). The old riverbank towns — Franklin Furnace, New Boston, Portsmouth, Friendship, Manchester, Utopia — now found the Ohio more a menace than a means of livelihood, and they had shifted northward to string out along the highway like kinks in a hawser. I had no mind for stopping. God's speed, people once wished the traveler.

At Cincinnati, I looped the city fast on the interstate and came to Indiana 56, where corn, tobacco, and blue-sailor grew to the knee, and also wild carrot, fleabane, golden Alexander. Apples were coming into a high green, butterflies stitched across the road, and all the way the whip of mowers filled Ghost Dancing sweetly with the waft of cut grass. Each town had its feed and grain store, each farm its grain bin and corncrib. Rolling, rolling, the land, the road, the truck.

I dropped south to New Harmony, Indiana, twelve miles downstream from Grayville, Illinois, where I'd spent that first grim night. New Harmony in June piles up with the sprinkle from golden rain trees, here called "gate trees." The town is known for two experiments in social engineering, both of which failed. Yet those failures put in motion currents that changed the course of what came after: the abolition of slavery, equal opportunity for women, progressive education, emancipation from poverty. The futuristic village was once even the headquarters for the U.S. Geologic Survey.

Rappites from Pennsylvania created the town of Harmonie out of bosky Wabash River bottomland in 1814. They grew wheat, vegetables, grapes, apples, and hops; they produced wine, woolens, tinware, shoes, and whiskey. The Rappite Golden Rose trademark, like the Shaker name, became an assurance of quality. A decade later, however, as the struggle of primitive life eased, members began finding more time for reflection; to blunt a growing discontent, the leader, George Rapp, sold the village to Robert Owen and moved the colony back to Pennsylvania, where the people could again start from scratch and live the peace of full occupation. Seventy-five years later, their Shaker-like refusal to have any truck with the future brought about their disappearance.

Owen, the British industrialist, utopian, and egalitarian, who worked to create a society free of ignorance and selfishness by eliminating the "causes of contest among individuals" (his basic tenet was "circumstances form character"), renamed the town New Harmony and built a cooperative community that developed into a center for creative social and scientific thought in antebellum America. Yet, before the first settler died, egotism and greed did the experiment in. New Harmony survived, but only as a monument to idealism and innovation.

Not far from a burial ground of unmarked graves that the old Harmonists share with a millennium of Indians, the mystical Rappites in 1820 planted a circular privet-hedge labyrinth, "symbolic" (a sign said) "of the Harmonist concept of the devious and difficult approach to a state of true harmony." After the Rappites, the hedges disappeared, but a generation ago, citizens replanted the maze, its contours strikingly like the Hopi map of emergence. I walked through it to stretch from the long highway. Even though I avoided the shortcut holes broken in the hedges, I still went down the rungs and curves without a single wrong turn. The "right" way was worn so deeply in the earth as to be unmistakable. But without the errors, wrong turns, and blind alleys, without the doubling back and misdirection and fumbling and chance discoveries, there was not one bit of joy in walking the labyrinth. And worse: knowing the way made traveling it perfectly meaningless.

Before I crossed the Wabash (Algonquian for "white shining"), I filled the gas tank — enough for the last leg. From the station I could see the blue highway curving golden into the western afternoon. I'd make Columbia by nightfall.

The circle almost complete, the truck ran the road like the old horse that knows the way. If the circle had come full turn, I hadn't. I can't say, over the miles, that I had learned what I had wanted to know because I hadn't known what I wanted to know. But I *did* learn what I didn't know I wanted to know.

The highway before, under, behind. Through the Green-River-ordinance-enforced towns. Past barnlot windmills that said AERMOTOR CHICAGO. On and on. The Mississippi River. Then the oak risings of Missouri.

The pump attendant, looking at my license plate when he had filled the tank, asked, "Where you coming from, Show Me?"

"Where I've been."

"Where else?" he said.

Lines from a
Navajo Wind Chant

Then he was told:
Remember what you have seen,
because everything forgotten
returns to the circling winds.

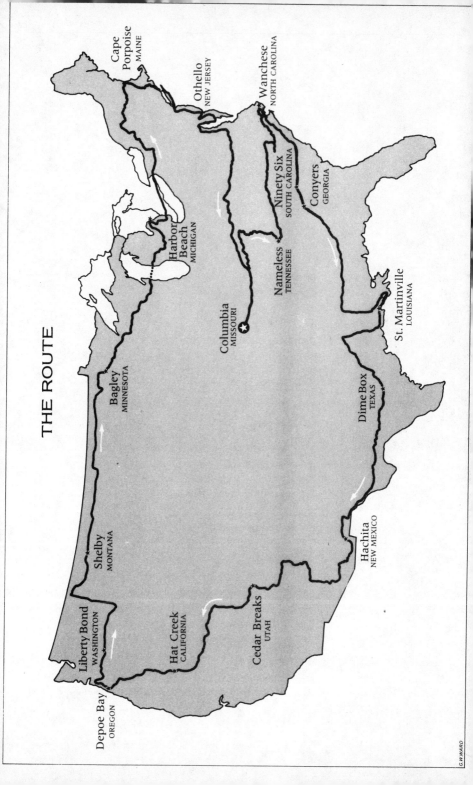

THE ROUTE

Cape Porpoise MAINE

Othello NEW JERSEY

Wanchese NORTH CAROLINA

Ninety Six SOUTH CAROLINA

Conyers GEORGIA

Harbor Beach MICHIGAN

Nameless TENNESSEE

Columbia MISSOURI

St. Martinville LOUISIANA

Bagley MINNESOTA

Dime Box TEXAS

Shelby MONTANA

Hachita NEW MEXICO

Liberty Bond WASHINGTON

Hat Creek CALIFORNIA

Cedar Breaks UTAH

Depoe Bay OREGON

G.W. WARD

Index of Towns and Cities

*Indicates place of encounter or extended comment.

Acknowledgments

Not only, but principally, my heart thanks to these people: Jack LaZebnik, playwright, whose eye and tooth for language is here everywhere; Edwin S. Miller, a careful reader and early believer; the late John Neihardt (Flaming Rainbow), who offered his students at the University of Missouri a high piece of the old light; the Stephens College library and its librarians; Paul and Doris Milberger, Ken and Lyn Steele, Larry Deck and Nancy Rimsek, all of whom gave table and shelter; Peter Davison and Natalie Greenberg, editors of fine vision, and their assistant at the Atlantic Monthly Press, Jennifer Reed; and Peggy Freudenthal of Little, Brown; and very much also to Lezlie, who helped the journey begin, and to Linda, who helped bring it home.